"WHATEVER GOD WANTS"

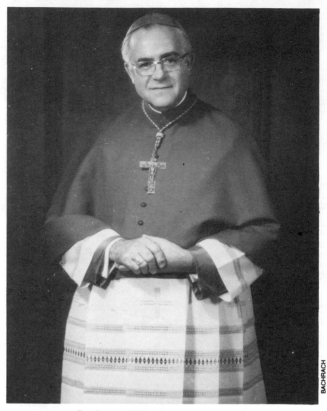

BACHRACH

October 6, 1915—September 17, 1983

"Whatever God Wants"—these were
the final words of the late Archbishop of Boston,
Humberto Cardinal Medeiros, spoken as he entered
the operating room at St. Elizabeth's Hospital
in Brighton, Massachusetts.
The Cardinal lived these words
throughout his life
and taught this lesson through his pastoral mission.

"*Whatever God Wants*"

PASTORALS AND ADDRESSES
BY
HIS EMINENCE
HUMBERTO CARDINAL MEDEIROS

Compiled and Indexed by Daughters of St. Paul

ADVENIAT REGNUM TUUM

ST. PAUL EDITIONS

ISBN 0-8198-8208-9 c
      0-8198-8209-7 p

CONTENTS

STEWARDS OF THIS HERITAGE

PASTORAL REFLECTIONS
ON CONSCIENCE

MAGISTERIAL TEACHING ON LIFE ISSUES

APPENDIX

Christ Our Victory

Pastoral Letter
for Pentecost, 1974

Preface

Dearly beloved in Christ:

1. With faith in the Holy Spirit of love, I come to you through this Pastoral Letter as a believer in the inspired word of God entrusted to the Church founded by Our Lord Jesus Christ, to be handed down through the centuries until the end of time for the salvation of the world. I come to you as your bishop and as your father in Christ who is at the same time your brother in the community of believers which is the holy Catholic Church. My relationship to you entails many grave responsibilities, but it is also the source of countless spiritual blessings and joys for me. As your bishop I am your teacher: I am a witness to the Faith entrusted to the Church to be the light that shines in the darkness of this world in order to draw to Christ and to the Father all the children of Adam scattered on the face of the earth (cf. Acts (26:17-18).[1]

2. It is with a joyful heart that I repeat to you in the Holy Spirit the Good News that Jesus Christ is risen from the dead, that He died in order to free us from bondage to Satan, sin and death, so that we might live as free children of the Father, ever struggling against the enemy within and without, but certain of final victory in Christ Our Lord (cf. 1 Cor. 15:20-26).

3. We believe, dearly beloved, that in and through Christ we overcome sin and death, that the Passion and Resurrection of Jesus spell the defeat of Satan and the victory over the evils he seeks to inflict upon the human race (cf. Heb. 2:14-15). Christ is truly our victory. For this reason we praise the Son of God, made man, whose sacrifice has made us free to serve the living God and one another in faith, hope and love. Since we believe that Christ is our victory, we should accept also in faith the way He traced for us which leads to our own victory in Him and through Him. St. Paul sums it up beautifully: "Since you have been brought back to true life with Christ, you must look for the things that are in heaven, where Christ is sitting at God's right hand. Let your thoughts be on heavenly things, not on the things that are on the earth, because you have died, and now the life you have is hidden with Christ in God. But when Christ is revealed—and he is your life—

you too will be revealed in all your glory with him" (Col. 3:1-4).

4. We do not want to be cheated of our glory with Christ. We want to win eternal victory through Him and with Him. But if we are to win the battle, it is important for us to know our enemies, to know their strengths and their weaknesses as well as our own. Accordingly, in this Pastoral Letter, I want to comment on one of these enemies, the common enemy of God and men, Satan, the Adversary, the Prince of this world (Jn. 12.31). But more than that, I fervently wish that you focus your prayerful attention especially on Christ's victory over him, and on out own victory in Christ and through Christ.

5. More than two years have passed since I first resolved to talk with you on the very important topic of our spiritual combat in these days, days characterized by such painful trial for many and by defeat for not a few. I have prayed, I have consulted, I have listened. Impelled by my pastoral responsibility as well as by my realization of the doctrinal and moral confusion of the times, and inspired by the words of Pope John XXIII and the Fathers of the Second Vatican Council, I have now decided to give very special witness to my faith in Christ's victory over the powers of evil and to my hope of our final victory in Him and through Him.

I.

The Spiritual Combat

6. When Pope John XXIII announced on January 25, 1959, the celebration of an Ecumenical Council, he said that it was for him a happy spectacle to see the grace of Christ in men produce such abundant fruit everywhere. But he continued:

"On the other hand, it is a sad spectacle when confronted with the abuse and compromise of the liberty of man, who, not knowing the open heavens and refusing faith in Christ, the Son of God, redeemer of the world and founder of the Holy Church, turns his search entirely to the pursuit of so-called earthly goods, under the inspiration of him whom the Gospel calls the Prince of Darkness and whom Jesus Himself in His last discourse after the Supper called the Prince of this world. This Prince of Darkness organizes the contradiction of and the battle against truth and welfare, the nefarious position which accentuates the division between those called by the genius of St. Augustine the two cities, and he keeps ever active the effort to confuse so as to deceive, if possible, also the elect and bring them to ruin."[2]

7. Pope John was quite concerned with the excessive attention given by modern man to technical and material progress, which in itself, he said, is morally indif-

This is his thought upon it, de-
on the same occasion:

his—we speak of this progress—
it distracts from the search for higher
, weakens the energies of the spirit,
s to a relaxation of the structure of
discipline and of the good ancient order,
with serious prejudice to that which constituted the strength of the Church and her
children against the errors which in reality,
in the course of the history of Christianity,
have always led to fatal and sad divisions,
to spiritual and moral decadence and to
the ruin of nations."[3]

8. With these and other considerations
in mind, Pope John resolved to convoke
the Second Vatican Council. At its very
outset, the bishops of the Catholic world,
under the Holy Father's guidance,
issued a declaration of intent in which
they proclaimed that renewal in Christ
was essential if the world were to accept
the light of the Son of God and be saved
from ruin. Here is what they said in
October of 1962, soon after the opening
of the first session of the Council:

"We wish to convey to all men and to all
nations the message of salvation, love and
peace which Jesus Christ, Son of the living
God, brought to the world and entrusted
to the Church.... Under the guidance of
the Holy Spirit, we intend in this meeting
to seek the most effective ways of renewing ourselves and of becoming increas-

ingly more faithful witnesses of the of Christ.... Faithful, therefore, to th date of Christ, who offered Him holocaust 'in order that he might p to himself the Church in all her g but that she might be holy and wi blemish' (Eph. 5:27), we shall devote o selves with all our energies, with all our thoughts toward renewing ourselves and the faithful entrusted to us, that the image of Jesus Christ, which shines in our hearts 'to give enlightenment concerning the knowledge of the glory of God' (2 Cor. 4:6), may appear to all people."[4]

9. The Holy Father and the bishops publicly affirm that a spiritual combat is being waged, with the eternal welfare of mankind at stake. The enemy of God and man does not sleep. He organizes the forces against Christ and His holy Church. He promotes confusion so as to deceive, divide and conquer. The man of faith knows that from the beginning the work of Satan has been to seduce and effect spiritual ruin. At this moment in history, many signs indicate that the Prince of Darkness is busier than ever with his nefarious work precisely because Christ, the Light of the World, is so clearly active in the renewal of His Church.

10. We must bear in mind, however, the realistic and balanced view taught by

the Gospel parable of the wheat and the weeds: "The kingdom of heaven may be compared to a man who sowed good seed in his field. While everybody was asleep his enemy came, sowed darnel among the wheat, and made off. When the new wheat sprouted and ripened, the darnel appeared as well. The owner's servants went to him and said, 'Sir, was it not good seed that you sowed in your field? If so, where does the darnel come from?' 'Some enemy has done this,' he answered." The owner proceeds to urge his servants to allow both the wheat and the weeds to grow together until the harvest lest the wheat be uprooted; at harvest time the weeds would be burned and the wheat stored in his barn (cf. Mt. 13:24-30).

11. The message is clear: we must not be surprised at goodness and evil in the Church; we must carefully discern between the two; we must be alert to the source of evil; while we continue to do battle with it now, we must wait until the end of time for its ultimate elimination.

12. As Christians, it is our privilege to believe confidently in the providence of the Father, in the victory of Christ over the powers of evil, and in the power of the Spirit to strengthen us in the combat. The call of baptism invites us to enter courageously into the ascetical struggle

wherein we stand for Christ and His message and resist the devil and his deceits. But while we enjoy many victories even now in our daily lives, it is only at the end of time that the ultimate victory will be experienced.

13. Because of these profound Christian realities, sometimes misunderstood and even gravely distorted, it is my duty to clarify somewhat for you the Church's understanding of one adversary we face as we try to live the Christian life, and to remind you of the powerful resources we have in Christ to combat him. It is certainly true that much of the confusion and disorder we experience today can be traced to our own human condition, but we must also realize that the devil seizes on our weakness to seduce us and increase our turmoil and confusion. As St. Paul puts it, "For it is not against human enemies that we have to struggle, but against the Sovereignties and the Powers who originate the darkness in this world, the spiritual army of evil in the heavens" (Eph. 6:12).

14. In our day there is much misunderstanding about the devil and the demonic. Some seem to deny or ignore this fact. Some see the demonic influences as controlling all the events of today. Some become so fascinated with the occult and the

preternatural realm that they become victimized by its hypnotic grasp. The Christian must be realistic, indeed, about the snares of the devil. However, he must have calm confidence in Christ's power working through the Church to overcome the evil one. He must share the Church's confidence of victory over the Prince of Darkness and all the forces of evil.

II.
The Christian Challenge in the Bible

15. It is important for us to realize, my dear brothers and sisters, that the opening pages of Sacred Scripture proclaim that the entire world was fashioned by the hand of God and is, therefore, good (Gn. 1:1-31). From the first chapter of the Bible to its last book, the world is affirmed as an essential part of God's plan of salvation (Rev. 21·1-22, 5).

16. Yet the Scriptures also make it clear that the goodness of God in His creative love has met with opposition from the very beginning of man's history (Gn. 3:1-19). All of Scripture can be seen as describing an extraordinary drama in which God, wishing to respect the freedom of men and women, woos, chides

and even reprimands His people as He expresses His desire to save them. It is the drama of redemption wherein God offers "again and again His covenant to man."[5]

17. At the same time, the Scriptures point out that God's redemptive plan is consistently opposed by a power of evil that is real, strong and destructive. This adversary, although unable to achieve ultimate victory, has actual power to deceive man and even to encourage evil in the world through man's active cooperation. One of the most explicit descriptions of this reality is presented in the Scriptural account of man's fall.

18. Under the guise of a serpent, Satan is depicted in the book of Genesis seducing the first human couple, thereby extending to the earth the battle already underway between the forces of good and evil.[6] The temptation is expressed as a conversation setting in motion a spirit of criticism and inducing "a frame of mind in which the woman will call in question the law laid down for her and the authority imposing it."[7] From insinuated doubt Satan is described as moving on to categorical denial of the truth, revealing a distinctive characteristic of demonic temptation, the lie. Under satanic influence, then, the first sin is committed

(Gn. 3:6-7), and evil enters into the life of man in the world. The Bible makes it clear that the effects of Adam's sin, the "original sin," were disastrous, not just for him but for the whole human race. As the Council of Trent affirmed, the original sin led to immediate loss of holiness and justice, a fall both in body and soul, and the penalty of death.[8]

19. Theologians seek to explain this primordial fall in various ways, but one truth is central: in origin man was good, but his seduction by the tempter and his fall from grace have had ongoing moral impact for all generations. Man was wounded in his struggle for God and against Satan.

20. The sacred author of the Genesis account goes on to show how sin led to further sin: envy to fratricide (Gn. 4), lust to the enslavement of women (Gn. 6), pride and greed to confusion, strife and the disintegration of the human family (Gn. 11). This gradual escalation of sin increased the influence of evil in the world and eventually led to more explicit divine intervention, as in the Flood.

21. But with Abraham, the marvelous yet mysterious redemptive plan of God begins to unfold more clearly. The faith of Abraham is heralded as reversing the trend of sin and contributing to his own

salvation and that of his posterity (cf. Heb. 11:8-19). Later, God made even more explicit His salvific intervention in the world through the dramatic liberation of His people, under Moses, from slavery in Egypt (Ex. 14) and the eventual entrance into the Promised Land under Joshua (Jos. 11). In subsequent times, the prophets consistently reminded the people of their Sinai covenant with God and of their commitment to resist sin. Frequently they were rejected, but they persevered in their efforts to enlighten and inspire God's people.

22. In the Wisdom literature of the Old Testament, the sacred authors reflected on the continuing presence of evil among God's people and expressed hope in the ultimate defeat of all the enemies of the Lord (cf. the Psalms *passim*). One particularly profound attempt to deal with the perduring presence of evil is preserved in the Book of Job, which offers a dramatic story describing man's spiritual combat with unexplained evil. The sacred author portrays Satan, the Adversary (the meaning of his name in Hebrew), receiving permission from God to inflict suffering and trials on his innocent servant, Job, in order to test his fidelity and his love under the harshest of circumstances. Although severely shaken and led to rue the day of

his birth, Job remains steadfast in his faith. The essential purpose of the Book of Job is to impart moral teaching: it offers an inspired reflection on the mystery of evil by telling a story about an afflicted and innocent man. It acknowledges the presence and the power of an Adversary, subject to God but at work against God. Its message is one of encouragement and hope since the innocent Job prevails over Satan with the assistance of God's power and grace.

23. Dearly beloved, it is in the New Testament that the victory of God over the powers of evil is most explicitly revealed. Jesus Christ is presented as the conqueror of man's tempter, who is the sower of deceit and confusion. When the evangelists describe the devil's temptation of Christ in the wilderness (Mk. 4:1-11; Mt. 1:12-13; Lk. 4:1-13), an event which they place at the beginning of His public ministry, it is as though they wanted to narrate in early biblical language how Jesus struggled with Satan for the soul of man.[9] Remember how the Hebrew people, while still a fledgling nation making their way through the Sinai desert, endured severe temptation through hunger (Ex. 16:2-3) and thirst (Ex. 15:24), through the temptation to reject God's way of doing things (Ex. 14:12) and the temptation to idolatry (Ex. 32:1). Because of the

effects of the original fall of the first Adam,
they failed in fidelity and God had to
come to their rescue.

24. Jesus, the new Adam, faced the same
desert temptations and won a signal victory which was to be lived out in His
public ministry and sealed in His triumph
over suffering and death. Christ resisted
and rejected every allurement of the
tempter, especially his outrageous demand that Christ fall down and adore
him. At the outset, therefore, the devil
was thwarted in his plan to seduce Christ,
a plan which St. Irenaeus a century and
a half later described in this way: "But
the devil, because he is an apostate angel,
can only do this much (which he revealed
in the beginning): seduce and distract
the mind of man to transgress the commandments of God and gradually blind
the hearts of those who try to serve Him,
and make them forget the true God and
adore him instead, as if he were God." [10]

25. In a striking way, Christ demonstrated
His power over the Evil One through
exorcisms. Even though there are those
who maintain that many of the Gospel
descriptions of possessed people reveal
symptoms which might be explained
today in terms of physical or emotional
causes, still the consistency with which
Christ cured, as well as the abrupt and
definitive change in the people them-

selves, indicate realities that go beyond medical explanation.

26. In His ministry generally, Christ repeatedly broke the power of Satan through His forgiving repentant sinners. For example, He led the promiscuous woman in Samaria to repentance, and through her conversion many in the town came to believe in Him (Jn. 4). He rescued an adulterous woman from harsh condemnation, yet urged her to sin no more (Jn. 8:3-11). He ate with tax collectors and sinners in order to help them experience conversion (Mt. 9:10-13; Lk. 19:1-19). Even when He was in conflict with the civil and religious authorities, He stood for truth while resisting violence (Lk. 22,51).

27. In Christ's struggle with Satan, however, our attention should be focused primarily on the inner mind and heart of Jesus who embraced the human condition to share the lot of every man, while remaining perfectly obedient to the Father's will (Phil. 2:5-8). It was in the hour of His Passion that the climactic combat was waged with the powers of darkness. Christ Himself recognized this dimension in His last discourse to His apostles: "I shall not talk with you any longer, because the prince of this world is on his way. He has no power over me, but the world must be brought to know that I

love the Father and that I am doing exactly what the Father told me" (Jn. 14:30-31). At the same time Christ predicted His own triumph: "Now the prince of the world is to be overthrown. And when I am lifted up from the earth, I shall draw all men to myself" (Jn. 12:31). By the words "lifted up," He intimated not only the type of death He would suffer, but that this death of His, uplifted on the cross, would become the rallying point by which to draw all men to Himself, and be also the cause of His victory over Satan and of His glorification by the Father. The Epistle to the Hebrews clearly affirms that Christ by His death destroyed the power of the devil: "Since all the children share the same blood and flesh, he too shared equally in it, so that by his death he could take away all the power of the devil, who had power over death, and set free all those who had been held in slavery all their lives by the fear of death" (Heb. 2:14-15).

III.

The Church Witness to Christ's Victory

28. The unanimous acceptance of this teaching of Scripture by the Fathers

of the Church is well represented by St. Augustine, who said, "In this redemption the blood of Christ was given as the price for us, as it were, by the acceptance of which the devil was not enriched but enmeshed, so that we might be freed from his bonds." [11]

29. This teaching of Sacred Scripture and the Fathers is echoed in several of the documents of the Second Vatican Council. For example, the Decree on the Mission Activity of the Church states that God "intervened in human history in a way both new and final by sending His Son, clothed in our flesh, in order that through Him He might snatch men from the power of darkness and Satan and reconcile the world to Himself in Him" (n. 3). In the Constitution on the Church in the Modern World, the Council Fathers declare: "The Lord Himself came to free and strengthen man, renewing him inwardly and casting out that 'prince of this world' (Jn. 12:31) who held him in bondage of sin" (n. 13). The Constitution on the Sacred Liturgy affirms that it was this very message the Apostles were sent to proclaim: "Just as Christ was sent by the Father, so also He sent the Apostles, filled with the Holy Spirit. This He did, that, by preaching the gospel to every creature, they might proclaim that the Son of God, by His death and resurrection

had freed us from the power of Satan and from death, and brought us into the kingdom of His Father" (n. 6).

30. Christ, then, has triumphed over the powers of darkness and liberated us from their control. This is the cause of our strength and the reason for our standing firm, for His victory is the pledge of our own — in fact it is our own. This is exactly what St. Paul told the Colossians: "You will have in you the strength, based on his own glorious power, never to give in, but to bear anything joyfully, thanking the Father who has made it possible for you to join the saints and with them to inherit the light. Because that is what he has done: He has taken us out of the power of darkness and created a place for us in the kingdom of the Son that he loves, and in him we gain our freedom, the forgiveness of our sins" (Col. 1:11-13).

31. Perhaps one of the most beautiful expressions of the Church's sense of triumph and joy in Christ's victory is to be found in the Book of Revelation as St. John, reflecting on the effects of Christ's sacrificial death, sees in a vision the heavenly reception given to Christ, the Lamb that was slain:

"The Lion of the tribe of Judah, the Root of David, has triumphed, and he will open the scroll and the seven seals of it. Then I saw, standing between the throne with its

four animals and the circle of the elders;
a Lamb that seemed to have been sacrificed.... The Lamb came forward to take
the scroll from the right hand of the One
sitting on the throne, and when he took it,
the four animals prostrated themselves before him and with them the twenty-four
elders; each one of them was holding a
harp and had a golden bowl full of incense
made of the prayers of the saints. They
sang a new hymn:

'You are worthy to take the scroll and
break the seals of it, because you were
sacrificed and with your blood you
bought men for God of every race, language, people and nation and made
them a line of kings and priests, to
serve our God and to rule the world.'

"In my vision, I heard the sound of an
immense number of angels gathered round
the throne and the animals and the elders;
there were ten thousand times ten thousand of them shouting, 'The Lamb that
was sacrificed is worthy to be given
power, riches, wisdom, strength, honor,
glory and blessing!' Then I heard all the
living things in creation—everything that
lives in the air, and on the ground, and
under the ground, and in the sea, crying,

'To the one who is sitting on the
throne and to the Lamb, be all praise,
honor, glory and power forever and
ever'" (Rev. 5:4-14).

32. It is in this glorious vision that we,
the Church of the living God, must find
our strength and confidence in the face

of the powers of darkness. The Book of Revelation proclaims the triumph of Christ and confidently looks to the coming of a new heaven and a new earth (Rev. 21:1ff.). But *Revelation* also contains the prediction that in the meantime our struggle is by no means over: Christians must continue to carry on in the face of persecution and evil and suffering (Rev. 6:9-11), manifesting all the while loyalty and trust and faith in God and in the Lamb that was slain.

33. The evangelists recognize that all disciples of Christ must participate in His struggle in order to share in His victory. The call to discipleship is gentle and gradual (Jn. 1:35-51), but the cost is great. The person who really wants to follow Christ must be willing to fix his eyes on the Lord without turning back (Lk. 14:28-33). The disciple must be willing to embrace the cross, prefer Christ to family and friends, even to his own health and life (Lk. 14:25-27). It is God's grace that makes possible what seems, and is, impossible to man alone (Lk. 1:37). The apostles themselves were subjected to temptation. St. John states that Judas Iscariot was influenced directly by the devil (Jn. 13:2); St. Luke reports Jesus revealing that Satan was behind Peter's denial, that he wanted to sift the apostles "like wheat," but that Jesus had prayed for Peter that his faith should not

fail and that he should eventually strengthen his brothers (Lk. 22:31-32).

34. The first generation Christians faced the disheartening fact of the uneven response of people to the call to discipleship. This experience led them under the Holy Spirit to remember the parable of the sower which the Lord had shared with them. So they interpreted faintheartedness or apostasy as due less to the inefficacy of the word of God and more to the condition of the hearts of the hearers. They concluded that "the devil was at work carrying away the word from their hearts in case they should believe and be saved" (Lk. 8:12). St. Luke recorded that St. Peter saw Satan's influence in Ananias's deception of the early Christian community (Acts 5:1-5), and St. Paul attributed to Satan's interference his inability to fulfill his desire to visit the community he had established in Thessalonica (1 Thes. 2:17-18).

35. Recently our Holy Father, Pope Paul VI, in an address to a General Audience, November 15, 1972, turned his attention to the very topic of this Pastoral Letter. He asserted:

"This matter of the Devil and of the influence he can exert on individuals as well as communities, entire societies or events is a very important chapter of Catholic doctrine which should be studied again, al-

though it is given little attention today."
He also reminded the audience that "evil
is not merely an absence of something but
an active force, a living spiritual being
that is perverted and that perverts others.
It is a terrible reality, mysterious and frightening…. The Devil is the number one enemy, the pre-eminent tempter. So we know
that this dark, disturbing being exists and
that he is still at work with his treacher-
ous cunning; he is the hidden enemy who
sows errors and misfortunes in human
history." [12]

IV.

The Christian Response
to the Challenge

36. It has not been my principal intention
to write a theological treatise on Satan,
but simply to remind you, as your concerned and loving Shepherd, of his sinister
influence in our lives. Neither the Bible,
nor the Church as our teacher and guide,
focuses our attention primarily on the
activity of the devil. Rather, both proclaim
the centrality of Christ's victory over
Satan and summon us to share in it. Yet we
are admonished to be aware constantly of
the power of our adversary and to embrace
accordingly an asceticism in life which
acknowledges realistically the dimensions

of the struggle against him. We are cautioned that we distort it if, at the other extreme, we exaggerate his influence and lose sight of the good news of Christ's definitive victory and of our own in Him and through Him.

BAPTISMAL COMMITMENT

37. It is useful for us to remember that the Church has always presented the Sacrament of Baptism as the call of the Christian to renounce Satan and his subtle deceits, and, at the same time, to profess confidently Jesus Christ as his Lord and God. The Church also exhorts us each year to enter into a Lenten observance which serves to renew and strengthen this baptismal consecration. By prayer, fasting and works of charity we are encouraged to turn more toward God and His grace. We are urged to control and overcome those tendencies within us that yearn for immediate gratification and lead to enslavement even by the devil. Our acceptance of the Christian life does involve warfare and combat, and in this battle we cannot be pacifists. "If anyone wants to be a follower of mine, let him renounce himself and take up his cross and follow me" (Mk. 8:34). [13]

38. The first epistle of St. Peter is frequently cited as a type of early baptismal instruction. In this letter, the first Pope

gives thanks to God the Father for the
rebirth in grace experienced in Christ
Jesus, and sees the Spirit revealing the
meaning of Christ's life for the new
Christian. He then shares with all of us the
exhortations that flow from an awareness
of what this new life implies: filial obedience, a journey toward holiness, fraternal
charity (1 Pt. 1:1-22).

39. It is the journey toward holiness
that St. Peter treats at greater length. The
new Christians now belong to a family committed to being a priestly people by
reason of the consecrated offering of their
lives to God. This involves the elimination
of malice, deceit, pretense, envy, slander
and the control of carnal desires which
war against the soul. It presupposes an
ever closer relationship with Jesus Christ
(ch. 2:1-11). St. Peter recognizes that each
Christian is expected to make his spiritual
journey within his particular walk in life.
Accordingly he offers specific suggestions
to free citizen and slave, to wife and
husband, to ordained priest and lay person. He is especially conscious that suffering is the lot of every man and he urges
the Christian to embrace the suffering
which derives from the following of a right
conscience and from living in union with
Christ (chs. 3-5).[14]

40. While presenting the positive call
to holiness, St. Peter is nevertheless

realistic about the strength and the cleverness of the Adversary: "Be sober; be on the alert. Your adversary the devil prowls about like a roaring lion, looking for someone to devour. Take your stand against him, firm in the faith, knowing that the same sufferings are being undergone by your brotherhood throughout the world. And the God of all grace, who has called you to his eternal glory, will himself, after you have suffered a little while, perfect, establish, strengthen you. To him be the empire throughout the eternal ages! Amen" (1 Pt. 5:8-9).[15]

41. Faithful to the Old Testament tradition, Peter speaks of the devil as our enemy and adversary, symbolized this time not as a serpent but as a roaring, hungry lion. His advice is that we must stand up to this adversary with faith as the source of our strength and victory in Christ.

42. St. Paul gives the same advice to the Ephesians, telling them to be "strong in the Lord" as he warns them that their fight is not against human enemies but against the Powers who lurk in the darkness in this world. Our best weapons in this contest are the armor provided by God.

"Finally, grow strong in the Lord," he writes, "with the strength of his power.

Put God's armor on so as to be able to resist
the devil's tactics. For it is not against
human enemies that we have to struggle,
but against the Sovereignties and the
Powers who originate the darkness in this
world, the spiritual army of evil in the
heavens. That is why you must rely on
God's armor, or you will not be able to
put up any resistance when the worst
happens, or have enough resources to
hold your ground. So stand your ground,
with truth buckled round your waist, and
integrity for a breastplate, wearing for
shoes on your feet the eagerness to spread
the gospel of peace, and always carrying
the shield of faith so that you can use it to
put out the burning arrows of the evil one.
And then you must accept salvation from
God to be your helmet and receive the
word of God from the Spirit to use as a
sword" (Eph. 6:10-17).

43. It is clear then that both St. Peter
and St. Paul urged their contemporaries
to be strong and full of faith in their
response to the Christian challenge. Like
them, St. Augustine also identified faith
in Jesus Christ as the crucial element in
the struggle. Citing in his text St. Paul's
letter to the Galatians (5:6), he writes:
"'For in Christ Jesus neither circumcision
is of any avail, nor uncircumcision...but
faith which works through charity.'
This is the very faith which separates
God's faithful from the unclean demons,
since even these, as the apostle James

says, 'believe and tremble' (2:19), though
they do not perform good works. Therefore, they do not have that faith by which
the just man lives, namely a faith which so
works through charity that God rewards
it with eternal life in accordance with its
works."[16]

EUCHARISTIC LIFE

44. Dearly beloved in Christ, the collective wisdom of the Church Fathers
leads us to recognize that our participation in Christ's struggle and victory is experienced in a particular way through the
sacramental life of the Church. We have
seen already some of the implications of
our baptism. We must also become ever
more conscious of the centrality of the
Holy Sacrifice of the Mass in our life.
Let me assure you that it was not an
arbitrary decision of the Church to affirm participation in Sunday Mass as a
serious responsibility for all.

45. An indication of the Church's great
concern here can be seen in the fact that
the Second Vatican Council in its very
first Constitution addressed itself to the
subject of the Liturgy. It considered in a
special way the celebration of the Eucharist, which it called "the outstanding
means whereby the faithful may express
in their lives, and manifest to others, the

mystery of Christ and the real nature of the true Church" (n. 2). From the first Pentecost, as the Council Fathers noted, "the church has never failed to come together to celebrate the Paschal Mystery: reading those things 'which are in the Scriptures concerning him' (Lk. 24:27), celebrating the Eucharist in which 'the victory and triumph of his death are again made present,'[17] and at the same time giving thanks 'to God for his unspeakable gift' (2 Cor. 9:15) in Christ Jesus."[18]

46. This is the same advice St. Ignatius of Antioch gave to the Ephesians in his letter to them at the very beginning of the second century: "Take heed, then, to come together quite often for giving thanks to God and for His glory. For when you come together frequently as one, the powers of Satan are destroyed, and his pernicious activity is ruined by the unity of your faith."[19]

47. I sincerely urge all who are in a responsible teaching capacity or guiding role in the Church, to bring others to a better understanding of the depth of the mystery we celebrate at Mass. Let us never be impatient with the human complaint that the Mass is not meaningful, but rather let us hear that complaint as a cry for guidance to appreciate the essential richness of the Church's most treasured gift.

CONTINUING CONVERSION

48. As we enter the spiritual journey with seriousness of purpose, the Fathers of the Church remind us most clearly of the constant and abiding need for conversion. Thus St. John Chrysostom in his Baptismal Instructions urges his people to preserve their innocence by a life of virtue and steady effort to avoid sin. He writes:

"Each day, then, let us be eager and careful to keep this bright robe of ours without spot or wrinkle. Even in things that are considered to be trifles, let us keep close watch, so that we may also be able to escape the serious sins. If we shall begin to scorn some sins as insignificant, little by little as we walk the way of life we will come to falls which are disastrous. Hence, I urge you to carry in your mind at all times the memory of your contract and to flee the disgrace of all those things you have put behind you — I mean the devil's pomps and all the other snares of the wicked one; I urge you to keep whole and entire your contract with Christ, so that you may be untouched by the tricks of the devil, while you continue to reap the benefit of these spiritual banquets and to be strengthened by the nourishment they give." [20]

49. It is significant that one of the most respected psychiatrists in America today has recently called for a reaffirmation of the concept of sin and of personal responsibility in wrongdoing. He regrets that although "sin" remains a fact of the human

condition, the concept and the term have almost disappeared from modern usage. "There is 'sin,'" he says, "which cannot be subsumed under verbal artifacts such as 'crime,' 'disease,' 'delinquency,' 'deviancy.' There *is* immorality; there *is* wrongdoing." [21]

50. We who are Christ's Body (1 Cor. 12:27) must do more than recognize the reality of sin in our lives. We must repent all sinful acts and control all inclinations that undermine the life begun at Baptism and nourished through the Eucharist. In the early stages of the spiritual journey we will be tempted to deny or gloss over our sinfulness. This must be resisted in faith. Only an honest and humble confession of the ways in which sin can pervade a person's life will open the way to adult conversion to the Lord. Listen to the consoling words of St. Ambrose: "But the Lord who has taken away your sin and pardoned your faults, is powerful to safeguard and defend you against the wiles of the devil, your adversary, that the enemy, whose practice it is to generate wrongdoing, may not creep up on you. But the one who commits himself to God does not fear the devil. For if God is for us, who is against us?" [22]

51. The more we progress on the Christian path, the more we sense the subtle

sinfulness that separates us from closer union with the Lord. This, too, should lead us to sacramental confession. The recent reform of the rite for this sacrament of reconciliation should result in a deeper and more meaningful sacramental encounter with Christ. We are also encouraged today to recognize the social dimensions of our sins and to express our repentance through communal services as a preparation for the personal sacramental confession of our sins. Hopefully this approach will enable many who have neglected confession to rediscover the special saving and healing presence of Christ to be found in the sincere acknowledgment of sin to Him in the Church. This must, of course, be always accompanied by genuine sorrow and a firm purpose of amendment. Our repentance of sin will then undercut the power of Satan and release the power of the Holy Spirit.

PRAYER

52. The committed Christian, in imitation of Christ Himself, always has searched for deeper discernment of the ways of God in prayer. It is in this spiritual activity that a person comes before God as he really is. In sustained prayer, sham and pre-

tense cannot survive; in continuing prayer, the truth becomes clearer and more real; in faithful prayer, the power of Satan is undermined. Recall the time when the disciples brought to Christ an epileptic demoniac they had been unable to heal. He rebuked them roundly for their lack of faith: "You faithless generation, ...how much longer must I put up with you? Bring him to me." The boy's father asked Christ to help. Jesus responded, "Everything is possible for anyone who has faith." He then ordered the evil spirit out of the boy. Later the disciples asked Him privately, "Why were we unable to cast it out?" "This is the kind," He answered, "that can only be driven out by prayer" (Mk. 9:14-29).

53. Prayer is central to the spiritual journey that begins with the first moments of genuine conversion and leads on to holiness of life. St. Augustine says, "It is by true piety that men of God cast out the hostile power of the air which opposes godliness;...and they overcome all the temptations of the adversary by praying, not to him, but to their own God against him. For the devil cannot conquer or subdue any but those who are in league with sin; and therefore he is conquered in the name of Him who assumed humanity and that without sin." [23]

54. This need for prayer is stressed by St. John of the Cross, one of the great-

est writers on the spiritual life. In his *Spiritual Canticle* he reflects on the power of the devil and on the need for prayer: "There is no human power that can be compared with the power of the devil, and therefore the divine power alone can overcome him, and the divine light alone can penetrate his devices. No soul, therefore, can overcome his might without prayer, or detect his illusions without humility and mortification."[24]

V.

Some Contemporary Aspects of the Spiritual Combat

55. It seems to me that this advice of St. John of the Cross is especially appropriate now, in that 1974 has been declared an official year of preparation for the Jubilee Year 1975. The theme of the Holy Year is Renewal and Reconciliation, as our Holy Father, Pope Paul VI, declared when he first announced it in an Address on May 9, 1973:

"It is necessary to stress the essential concept of the Holy Year, and that is the interior renewal of man: of the thoughtful man, who in his thinking has lost the certainty of truth; of the working man, who in his work has realized that he is so extroverted that he no longer is sufficiently in touch with his inner self; of the man enjoying life, who so amuses himself and has so many exciting ways to gain pleasurable experiences that he soon feels bored and disillusioned. Man must be renewed from within. This is what the Gospel calls conversion, penance and a change of heart. It is the process of self-rebirth.

"Now the Holy Year is oriented precisely to this personal interior renewal, which under certain aspects is also exterior. It is at the same time an easy and an extraordinary therapy which should bring spiritual well-being to every conscience and indirectly, at least to some extent, to the attitude of society. This is the general idea of the next Holy Year, which is also centered on another special theme oriented to practical living: reconciliation....

"We need above all to re-establish a genuine, vital and happy relationship with God, to be reconciled with Him in humility and love, so that from this first basic harmony the whole world of our experience may express a need and acquire a virtue of reconciliation, in charity and justice with men whom we immediately recognize by the new name of brothers. Moreover, reconciliation takes place in other vast and very real areas: in the ecclesial community itself, in society and political life, in ecumenism, in the sphere of peace, and so forth."[25]

56. Since this first announcement, the Holy Father has returned many times to

the themes of renewal and reconciliation in his addresses, seeking to intensify and expand our appreciation of the goals he has set for the Holy Year. In a special way, he has emphasized the need for asceticism and a return to penitential practices. "We trust that the value of penitential practices will be rediscovered as a sign and way of grace, as a commitment for the inner renewal which receives its full efficacy in the Sacrament of Penance, to be used and administered according to the Church's provisions, for renewed progress by individuals and communities along the pathway of salvation."[26]

57. Another path to the goal, according to Pope Paul, is "real, religious, doctrinal and sacramental contact with Christ," which should hold "first place for re-animating our Christian life with the grace of the Holy Spirit," and a "passion for truth in the inward composition and outward profession of our Faith. Without orthodoxy, without the light of God's word, tested by the charism of the Church's magisterium, we will have no renewal, but will lose our way in the byways of recurring doubts, personal hypotheses and inner torment."[27]

58. For my own part, I would like to reinforce in your minds what we should be striving for during this year of preparation in advance of the Jubilee Year. "We are

seeking to accomplish a transformation and renewal which will make it easier for us to be what we ought to be when the Holy Year itself comes upon us. Changing the human spirit is never easy; reforming ourselves, even in ways we know we should, runs against the grain; becoming the people we ought to be to project into life our own best values is a slow and sometimes painful process. Without this year of preparation, we will find ourselves in 1975, as the Holy Year begins, floundering about trying to find ways that will change us for the better, but not really knowing where to begin. In this way, the Holy Year itself will be passing by and the rededication and renewal expected of it will be in evidence in only the most minimal way." [28]

59. Yet inner renewal of the individual is not the only goal toward which we should be striving. We must also reach for the goal of reconciliation among men at all levels of society, a truly challenging task today, but one from which we cannot shrink. We must try to eliminate all the barriers that divide men. We must seek to root out the "injustice a man suffers because of the color of his skin; the injustice he suffers because he is poor and unprotected; the injustice, which is his because he is old and ill." [29] It is in these areas and in many others like them, that

we must seek to make our mark as true Christians who have a genuine sense of the common brotherhood of man, upon whom God our common Father looks with unfailing providence and abiding love.

60. In our efforts at renewal and reconciliation we are sure to confront our common adversary. Let us ask the Holy Spirit for wisdom to detect his ruses, and for power to defeat him in his struggle for the minds and hearts of men. There is a great need for Christians to face squarely the spiritual challenges of the moment. There is so much good emerging, but evil always attempts to impede authentic redemption. In addition, therefore, to drawing general attention to the realities which I consider of paramount importance today, I would like to make some special pleas.

61. To all Christians, I urge careful discernment. May we grow in our ability to distinguish the ways of God from the ways of the Evil One. We cannot be naive about the powers of evil. First and always we must go to God in humble faith, relying on His victory in Christ Jesus.

62. To those who are disposed to deny or ignore the reality of Satan, I recommend a deep reflection on the consistent teaching of our Judaeo-Christian tradition

and, indeed, on the testimony of experience. As Father Karl Rahner has said, "The teaching of Scripture and revelation about the devil appears to be a presupposition of human experience which is incorporated, critically corrected, into the doctrine of the victory of the grace of God in Christ and of the liberation of man from all 'principalities and powers.'"[30] The devil, he goes on to say, is not to be regarded as a "mere mythological personification of evil in the world; the existence of the devil cannot be denied."[31]

63. To those who, on the other hand, tend to exaggerate the presence and the power of the devil and who interpret practically all of the turmoil around us as evidence of the demonic, I recommend and counsel a sounder understanding of the ways of God toward men. Biblical fundamentalism can lead to an increase of irrational fear and an unwarranted recourse to rites of exorcism or deliverance.

64. I wish to commend those who are deeply involved in the continuing reform of social structures and the alleviation of social ills. I applaud their generous efforts. I also want to urge them to recognize the dimensions and the depth of the struggle. It is not merely a social or a political contest. Rather, the common enemy of all who champion the cause of true reform is

the Adversary depicted in the Scriptures as seeking the soul of man.

65. To the young particularly, I address a special word. In so many ways they manifest a genuine concern for the relevant and the authentic, a dissatisfaction with the materialism of this technological age, a quest for the transcendent. It is reassuring to see so much good potential here; but it is also a source of anxiety to see some of it wasted on ill-conceived pursuits, especially if these involve an unwholesome fascination with the occult and pseudo-mystic. Dabbling in this area can often be harmful; at best it is frivolous.

66. I am also concerned with those who pay heed too easily to the Pied Pipers who pass through with preparations as elaborate as their claims, who tickle the ears of their listeners[32] for a while but have nothing of substance to offer that will endure for a lifetime and an eternity beyond. I urge all to find again the true source of union with God in His only Son, our Lord Jesus Christ, and in what He has given to us in His Mystical Body, the Church. Let us hear again the unremitting summons of the Church to an awareness of God's enduring love, to a lively sense of sin and the consoling presence of grace and hope of forgiveness, to integrity of life and fidelity to vocation. Let us hear

and heed the call of Christ who said, "I am the Way, the Truth and the Life. No one can come to the Father except through me" (Jn. 14,6). I am certain that in our loving loyalty to Jesus rests the hope for true freedom for all mankind and for lasting peace among the nations.

VI.
Concluding Remarks

67. Dearly beloved in Christ, I believe there is no more fitting way for me to close this Pastoral Letter than to ask you to focus your attention on the liturgy of the Easter Vigil, the culmination of Lent and Holy Week. This calls to mind one of the most ancient practices of the Church, the custom of baptizing those who have received instruction in the Faith during the weeks of Lent. Baptism signifies many things, but it has a special relationship to the Paschal Mysteries. As St. Paul tells us, "You have been taught that when we were baptized in Christ Jesus we were baptized in his death; in other words when we were baptized we went into the tomb with him and joined him in death, so that as Christ was raised from the dead by the Father's glory, we too might live a new life. If in

union with Christ we have imitated his death, we shall also imitate him in his resurrection" (Rom. 6:3-5). These words explain the ancient association of the Sacrament of Christian initiation with Holy Week and the prominence it has even to this day within the Easter Vigil Liturgy, where the two elements I have stressed in this Pastoral find graphic dramatization, namely in the threefold renunciation of the devil and the threefold proclamation of our Faith.

68. The celebrant invites the congregation to renew their baptismal promises as he presents the questions asked of the candidate for Baptism since earliest times: "Do you reject Satan?" "I do." "And all his works?" "I do." "And all his empty promises?" "I do." Having thus renewed the promises of our baptism, let us heed the admonition of St. Ambrose, "Be mindful of your words, and never let the chain of your pledges slip from your memory."[33]

69. Now this rejection of Satan and his works implies attachment to Jesus Christ, "a transfer from one master to another,"[34] a determination to identify oneself completely with Jesus Christ, who lives now in us as we live in Him (cf. Gal. 2:19). As a sign, then, of this new attachment to Christ, the celebrant asks for a threefold proclamation of Faith:

"Do you believe in God, the Father Almighty, creator of heaven and earth?" "I do."

"Do you believe in Jesus Christ, His only Son, our Lord, who was born of the Virgin Mary, was crucified, died and was buried, rose from the dead and is now seated at the right hand of the Father?" "I do."

"Do you believe in the Holy Spirit, the Holy Catholic Church, the Communion of saints, the forgiveness of sins, the resurrection of the body, and life everlasting?" "I do."

In this public way, we profess the Faith that is God's gift to us in Baptism, the Faith which is the illumination of our lives, the light which enables us to see in the darkness, the very light of Christ Himself, symbolized in the Vigil Service by the Paschal Candle. From this Candle are lighted one by one the candles of all the congregation, who together give light to every corner of the Church. Now we understand what St. John meant when he said that Christ is the "true light that enlightens all men" (Jn. 1:9).

70. Dearly beloved, we believe that in Christ we have our victory and that without Him we can do nothing (Jn. 15:5). Joyfully and confidently we come close to Him in prayer, in good works, but especially in the Sacrament of Penance and in the celebration of the Holy Sacrifice of the Mass. We come to Him in the company

of all the saints in heaven and on earth because we believe in the Communion of Saints. At the head of these is Mary, the Mother of God and the Mother of the Church, and with her Saint Joseph, the Patron of the Universal Church. Of all the valiant defenders of God and man against the wicked snares of Satan, Michael the Archangel stands pre-eminent, as the Scriptures reveal (Rev. 12:7f.). Let us then pray with confidence to the Immaculate Virgin Mary who through her Son crushed the head of the ancient serpent. Let us pray to Saint Joseph, her most chaste spouse, and invoke devoutly the powerful assistance of the Captain of the Heavenly Hosts, St. Michael. With these holy intercessors before the throne of God, we shall overcome through Christ, and we shall obtain for the world the light and the peace it yearns to have but cannot find without Him.

NOTES

[1] All quotations from Sacred Scripture are from *The Jerusalem Bible* unless otherwise noted.

[2] Pope John XXIII, address given in the Basilica of St. Paul-Outside-the-Walls, January 25, 1959: Cf. *Council Daybook, Vatican II, Sessions 1 and 2*, ed. Floyd Anderson (Washington, D.C., 1965), p. 2.

[3]*Ibid.*

[4]Message to the World. Cf. *Council Daybook*, p. 45.

[5]Cf. Eucharistic Prayer IV.

[6]For Scriptural passages which refer to the fall of the rebel angels and their punishment, see 2 Pt. 2:4 and Jude 6. For Old Testament identification of the serpent of Genesis with the devil, see Wis. 2:22: "It was the devil's envy that brought death into the world."

[7]Nicolas Corte, *Who is the Devil?*, tr. D.K. Pryce (New York, 1958), p. 25.

[8]Council of Trent, Session 5, 1 (*Denz.* 788). Cf. Session 6,1 (*Denz.* 793).

[9]Cf. Jacques Dupont, "The Origins of the Narrative of Jesus' Temptations," *Theology Digest*, vol. 15 (1967), pp. 230-235.

[10]St. Irenaeus, *Adversus Haereses*, 5, 24, 30 (PG 7, 1188).

[11]St. Augustine, *On the Trinity*, 13, 15, 19 (PL 42, 1029).

[12]Pope Paul VI, "Confronting the Devil's Power," Address to a General Audience, November 15, 1972, *The Pope Speaks*, vol. 17, 4, pp. 315-319.

[13]Cf. my Lenten Message 1974.

[14]Cf. Joseph A. Fitzmyer, S.J., "The First Epistle of Peter," *The Jerome Biblical Commentary*, edd. Raymond E. Brown, S.S., et al., (Englewood Cliffs, N.J., 1968), pp. 362-364.

[15]Translation from the Greek by Francis Aloysius Spencer, O.P., edd. Charles J. Callan, O.P., and John A. McHugh, O.P. (New York, 1948).

[16]St. Augustine, *Grace and Free Will*, 7, 18 (PL 44, 892).

[17]Council of Trent, Session 13, 5 (*Denz.* 878).

[18]Second Vatican Council, Constitution on the Sacred Liturgy, 6.

[19]St. Ignatius of Antioch, *Epistle to the Ephesians*, 13 (PG 5, 656).

[20]St. John Chrysostom, *Baptismal Instructions*, 4, 32, tr. Paul W. Harkins (Westminister, Md., 1963), p. 78.

[21]Karl Menninger, *Whatever Became of Sin?*, (New York, 1973), p. 46 (italics are the author's).

[22]St. Ambrose, *On the Sacraments*, 5, 4, 30 (PL 16, 474).

[23]St. Augustine, *The City of God*, 10, 22, tr. Marcus Dods (New York, 1950), pp. 326-327.

[24]St. John of the Cross, *The Spiritual Canticle*, 3, 12, tr. David Lewis, second ed. rev. (London, 1891), p. 193.

[25]Pope Paul VI, Address to a General Audience, May 9, 1973, *The Pope Speaks*, vol. 18, 1, pp. 6-7.

[26]Pope Paul VI, Letter to Cardinal Maximilian de Furstenburg, May 31, 1973, *The Pope Speaks*, vol. 13, 2, p. 180.

Cardinal Furstenburg is the chairman of the Holy Year Central Committee. See also the beautiful pastoral letter on Penance recently issued by Bishop Bernard J. Flanagan of Worcester.

[27] Pope Paul VI, Address to a General Audience, July 4, 1973, *The Pope Speaks,* vol. 18, 2, p. 129.

[28] Cf. my address to the combined meeting of the Kiwanis, Lions and Rotary Clubs of Cambridge, Massachusetts, on February 21, 1974, *The Pilot,* March 1, 1974, p. 14.

[29] *Ibid.*

[30] Karl Rahner, S.J. "The Devil," *Sacramentum Mundi, An Encyclopedia of Theology,* edd. K. Rahner et al., (New York 1968), vol. 2, p. 73. Cf. Vatican Council II, Constitution on the Church in the Modern World, 13.

[31] *Ibid.*

[32] Cf. 2 Tm. 4:3; 2 Pt. 2:1; 1 Jn. 4:1-3.

[33] St. Ambrose, *On the Sacraments,* 1, 2, 5 (PL 16, 437).

[34] A.-M. Roguet, O.P., *Christ Acts Through the Sacraments,* (Collegeville, Minn., 1960), p. 50.

Growing Together in Holiness

Lent, 1976

Introduction

Putting on Christ
The Baptismal Robe

My dear brothers and sisters in Christ:

On all sides, the cadence of contemporary life urges change. Yet on the most profound level, there must be constant, unchanging characteristics in the Christian life. And Lent is the liturgical reminder of this spiritual truth.

No matter in what form, Christian holiness has always been wrapped in and enveloped by the Paschal Mystery — the Mystery of the Death and Resurrection of the living Lord. As the history of Christian holiness attests, our advance into the appropriation of this Mystery is not a process which is completed once-and-for-all at a particular date. We continually need to grow in insight as to how the brilliance of Christ's redeeming activity should be reflected in our own lives — and, through us, to our world. This demands time for

prayer, reflection, penance, and contemplation. From at least the fourth century
onwards,[1] the Church has called upon
all Christians to cultivate this graced
perspective especially during the holy
season of Lent.

For this reason, Lent is not an anach-
ronistic routine — something that can be
indifferently dismissed. A reflection upon
our own spiritual life-stories indicates how
easily we develop eyes of clay — a certain
opaqueness to the dimensions of divine
love operating in our world and in our lives.
Many times, God and His redemptive ways
grow dim and distant. And because such
spiritual dullness is "not removed until
[men] turn to the Lord" (2 Cor. 3:17), we
are all obliged — especially in times of
confusion and agitation such as ours — to
pray for God's gift of the knowledge of the
Truth who is Christ.

It would be impossible, in a pastoral
letter such as this, to construct a complete
and connected discourse on the many
aspects of Christian conversion. It would
be awkward. Rather, simplicity is my aim.
With a heart which deeply feels the agitation of my brothers and sisters in Christ,
I prayerfully hope to point out directions
and areas for deepening our faith-response
amid the confusions of today.

Again, the tradition and evolution of
Lent assist us in this effort. From the very

outset, this holy season has been intimately connected with the rite of Christian
initiation (as our Easter Vigil so well attests to and synthesizes). Thus, for example,
the weeks preceding Easter were at one
time exclusively dedicated to explaining
and discerning the dynamic personal implications of Baptism: what God's personal
and gentle love for us means; what it means
to die to self and live in Christ. Consequently it is no wonder that in the present-
day Rite of Baptism — as in earliest times —
we should find a simple, concrete, yet
stunning symbol which in so many respects
gathers the various strands of the mystery
of Christian holiness together to express
its meaning: the bestowal of the baptismal robe.

Because we are so accustomed to what
is complicated, the very simplicity of the
gesture often hides the treasury of spiritual
truths which the bestowal of this white
garment is meant to convey. In a way, it is
a visible summary of St. Paul's teaching
on Baptism. The Apostle himself saw in
this imagery much more than a metaphor.
It was a tangible expression of the mystical
fact that through Baptism Christ envelops
the redeemed like a garment. "Baptized
into union with him, you have all put on
Christ as a garment" (Gal. 3:27).

The expansive energy of this simple
symbol, drawn from everyday life, can be

seen in the Apostle's further teaching regarding Baptism. Since one's outer garment is man's most visible projection to the world, St. Paul saw our "clothing in Christ" as an expression of the new identity which transforms the whole person and is to be projected to those around us — an identity which he describes in Galatians 2:20: "I have been crucified with Christ: the life I now live is not my life, but the life which Christ lives in me; and my present bodily life is lived by faith in the Son of God who loved me and gave himself up for me." We are inwardly transformed by Christ to live His life.

The close physical contact between man and his garments may have led the Apostle to select this precise symbol to express the intimacy of the mystical union between Christians and Christ — an intimacy which calls the Christian to undergo exactly what Christ underwent in His death and resurrection; for the Christian, death to sin and the attainment of a new life. In the very act of enveloping us like a garment, Christ draws us to Himself and gently initiates us into an imitation of His earthly pilgrimage.

Our "clinging to Christ," which is so beautifully expressed in this imagery, calls to mind a correlative conception which is not absent from the Apostle's thought. The dynamic relation to Christ begotten in

5

Baptism requires the ongoing moral development of the Christian. We must grow into the enveloping Christ (Eph. 2:10). Again, the common experience of clothing helps us to understand his meaning. So often, adjustments and refinements in the clothes are required. But now, they are required from us. We must grow to "fit" into Christ and His redemptive scheme. And St. Paul leaves us no doubt that these adjustments will be painful because they touch the inner core of our being.

Reflecting upon his own spiritual pilgrimage, St. Paul, as well as the authors of the entire New Testament, knew that a continual communion of immolation with our Lord was the key to Christian holiness: "With Christ, I am nailed to the cross" (Gal. 2:19). The death to our sin-infected humanity reinforces our contact with the Savior. By dying to self, the "precious blood of the undefiled Lamb" (1 Pt. 1:19) flows over us and allows us to participate personally in Christ's redeeming mystery.

I must remind you, my dear brothers and sisters in Christ, that St. Paul is not a preacher of pessimism or a disciple of despair but a preacher of hope and a disciple of life. Such painful and long-sustained dying to self would be impossible, were it not for the fact that through

it we achieve a new type of existence: "You
have been taught that when we were baptized in Christ Jesus we were baptized in
his death; in other words, when we were
baptized we went into the tomb with him
and joined him in death, so that as Christ
was raised from the dead by the Father's
glory, we too might have a new life" (Rom.
6:3-4). This new life—a sharing in Christ's
resurrection—gives us the "spirit of wisdom," bringing us "to the full knowledge of him." The eyes of our mind are so
enlightened that we understand "what hope
his call holds for us," what "rich glories
he has promised us as his inheritance" and
"how infinitely great is his power and
love" for us (Eph. 1:17-21). In short, we
receive the gift of inner peace—"a peace
which the world cannot give" (Jn. 14:27).

The central difficulty for Christians in
any age, however, is to accept dying as
a way of living. There can be no doubt that
St. Paul, with the entire New Testament,
is saying that our personal faith is not
to be founded on hearsay about this mystery, but that it is to be grounded in our
personal experience of this truth only after
we have received it through hearing (cf.
Rom. 10:17). Thus we can say with a full
heart, "Father, my Father" (Rom. 8:15).
Precisely because the risen life that Jesus
offers comes only out of death, the Good
News contains an invitation to die, in

order that we may experience the fullness of being alive.

Perhaps the most basic experience of death to self comes in the acknowledgment of our own inadequacy. Our biographies often parallel St. Paul's experience: "I cannot understand my own behavior. I fail to carry out the things I want to do, and I find myself doing the very things I hate" (Rom. 7:15). But pride often prevents us from admitting this radical weakness and, unlike Paul, we hesitate to ask that God's Spirit transform our fragility.

The invitation to die also contains an invitation to embrace another type of interior mortification. It is the type of mortification suggested by the Fourth Gospel where Jesus promises that the Spirit of truth will come to lead His followers to "the complete truth" (Jn. 16:13). In the mind of the Lord, it is evident that this "complete truth" involves a new kind of self-awareness whereby the Christian readily recognizes in the concrete circumstance of his life and in the current of the time how the message of the cross is to be appropriated. It is to this precise point that the remainder of this letter will be dedicated.

The Fathers of Vatican II noted that "in a particularly appropriate way...holiness shines out in the practice of the counsels, customarily called 'evangelical.'"[2] Traditionally, these have been understood as poverty, chastity and obedience. While we generally associate these counsels with religious life, there is *in an analogous but profound sense* a way in which we are all called to embrace these counsels in today's world. And it is through them that we can better understand and experience the truth of dying as the way to achieve the fullness of the Christian life.

I.

Obedience

Quite simply, beloved in Christ, history seems to have worn out the Christian ideal of obedience. The dynamic of contemporary life is rooted in the cry for freedom. It almost permeates every facet of modern man's existence. Modern men and women want freedom from hunger, freedom from poverty, and freedom from every form of oppression, whether this be political, economic or even what they believe to be nothing more than ritualistically sustained values. Since the man of today's world has often been scarred by the promised panaceas of the past (especially in the political and social arenas), there is abroad an ingrained skepticism which leads many people to question all absolutes. The same skepticism frequently spills over into the spiritual and moral sphere of life.

It is often overlooked that Catholic spiritual tradition has always revered freedom. In the prologue to his treatise on man and the moral life, St. Thomas Aquinas states that freedom is the indispensable condition of all religion and morality. It is the first truth about man: man, he says, "is made in the image of God; and by image here is meant that man is intelligent, free in his power of choice, and *of himself the master of himself...the active source of what he does.*"[3] But Catholic spiritual tradition, while reverencing freedom, has also issued a warning: if this truth is debased, it becomes our most destructive and embittering illusion.

Because of the strange spiritual amnesia which affects the human race, the wisdom of this warning has been forgotten. Freedom has become destructive. One merely needs to think of the hundreds of thousands of abortions justified in the name of freedom. In the name of religious freedom, a spiritual illusion has been fostered. Making man "the measure of all things," this belief has canonized the idea that we are *free to search out God in our own way.* Sadly, so often this is not the way of our Lord Jesus Christ. It is not God's way.

Precisely because we are enveloped by Christ through Baptism, and inwardly transformed by Him, His interior attitudes must become ours. We must appropriate the spiritual dispositions of His humanity. Now, the New Testament leaves no doubt concerning the role obedience played in His life. The first moment of His human will was an act of obedience: "...and this is what he said, on coming into the world... 'God, here I am! I am coming to obey your will'" (Heb. 10:5-7). The first word of Christ that is known to us declares His submission to the Father's will: "Did you not know that I must be busy with my Father's affairs?" (Lk. 2:49) Christ defined His mission and life on earth in terms of obedience: "...I have come from heaven, not to do my own will, but to do the will of the one who sent me" (Jn. 6:38). And the declaration, "Father...let your will be done, not mine" (Lk. 22:42) began the redemptive action that crowned His life.

Out of this renunciation of His self-will, the Son's love became inscribed in human history. And in reflecting upon the nature of Christ's obedience, the paradoxical nature of Christian obedience appears: it leads to true freedom. The Son's obedience grew from a deep and affectionate love—as can be seen from the intimacy with which He addressed

God as Father. There is not a hint of fear or constraint in the New Testament's portrayal of Jesus.

Nor was His human nature mutilated or impoverished because of His obedience. On the contrary, His total self-renunciation, surrender and self-emptying led to total freedom. The Gospel records His freedom from anxiety (Mt. 6:25). Every stage of His earthly pilgrimage indicates that He was free from autonomous self-assertion (Mt. 11:29). His entire life enfleshed the fullness of freedom—the ability to give Himself completely to others in love.

The remarkable expression of the Epistle to the Hebrews (5:8): "Son though he was, he *learned obedience from the things that he suffered,*" indicates how agonizing and difficult that path of perfect obedience was even for Christ. And the Apostle Paul—who boldly proclaims that the Gospel is a call to freedom (Gal. 5:1) —warns us that the shadows of sin can blur our perception of the ideal of Christian freedom. Man must continually struggle within himself to overcome the perennial temptations against true freedom—autonomous individualism, selfish withdrawal and narcissistic pursuits (Gal. 5:13). They can be conquered by love *(ibid.).* But in order that the redemptive pattern of freedom through obedience be realized in our lives, this love requires direction (Rom. 5:17f.).

It is in this broad context that today's tension between authority and obedience in the Church should be interpreted. Since the Church is a living communion bound together by the mystical motion of the Holy Spirit, any resolution to today's confusion must be resolved in the context of love. Certainly, this leaves little room for a crude authoritarianism which annihilates individual responsibility and crushes human dignity. On the other hand, the inflated individualism which bitterly resists or irresponsibly ignores the directive guidance of authority does not appreciate the gifted nature of authority. *Authority is a grace for the People of God:* "God is the one who has given us the qualifications to be the administrators of the new covenant, which is not a covenant of written letters but of the Spirit" (2 Cor. 3:6).

While the full profile of the delicate equilibrium between freedom and authority may never emerge into complete clarity for many, still our growth together in holiness demands that all the faithful cultivate a listening love in this essential aspect of the spiritual life. Bishops and priests must be aware of and listen to the charismatic dimensions of God's grace operating in the People of God, His Church.

As the Fathers of Vatican II remind us, our task is "not indeed to extinguish the Spirit, but to test all things and hold fast to that which is good."[4] It is under the impetus of this listening love that the laity comes to understand the profound spiritual and faith dimension of the Council's doctrine that "bishops, teaching in communion with the Roman Pontiff, are to be respected by all as witnesses to divine and Catholic truth. In matters of faith and morals, the bishops speak in the name of Christ and the faithful are to accept their teaching and adhere to it with a religious assent of the soul."[5]

It is the same listening love, born of a living and coherent faith — itself the fruit of the Holy Spirit — that readily disposes and gently compels the whole Church on the pilgrimage to show "this religious submission of will and mind... in a special way to the authentic teaching authority of the Roman Pontiff, even when he is not speaking *ex cathedra*. That is, it must be shown in such a way that his supreme magisterium is acknowledged with reverence, the judgments made by him are sincerely adhered to, according to his manifest mind and will."[6] All are led, under grace, to embrace such teachings in a spirit of free obedience, which to be free must be true and to be true must be free with the freedom of the love infused into us by "the Holy Spirit who is given to us" (Rom. 5:5). In the "obedience of faith" the whole Church advances into the ever greater freedom of the children of God.

Since the patterns of redemption remain constant, there is another scriptural theme that sheds some light on the difficult and delicate spiritual struggle to become "free in obedience": that of friendship. Throughout the scriptures the love between God and men is described as a friendship: God spoke of "Abraham, my friend" (Is. 41:8), "the Lord used to speak to Moses face to face, as a man speaks to his friend" (Ex. 33:11), and Christ told His disciples that they were not His servants but His friends (Jn. 15:13-15). Since the overwhelming weight of psychology indicates that there can be no truly human community without friends, perhaps the Fathers of Vatican II have provided us with an intuition as to how we should view authority in the Church by their understanding of the bishop as a "friend."

There is a deep sense in which the bishop in the Church can rightly be looked upon as our friend. God's only call to holiness remains: "Follow me. Leave everything which is not me (pride, selfishness, envy, etc.) behind." So often, however, we find this call confusing. The smoke of self-centeredness clouds the path God wishes us to follow. We need friends to support us, direct us, and guide us. God in His goodness has provided us with such "friends" in the persons whom He has graced with the charism of authority —a gift given to the bishops that they might be "authentic teachers" and guides "endowed with the authority of Christ who preach to the people committed to them the faith they must believe and put into practice. By the light of the Holy Spirit, they make that faith clear, bringing forth from the treasury of revelation new things and old (Mt. 13:52), making faith bear fruit and vigilantly warding off any errors which threaten their flock (cf. 2 Tm. 4:1-4)."[7]

II.

Poverty

The whole Christian life is enveloped in the eternal call to "put on Christ." But, once again, the paradox of Christian truth appears. The language is deceiving. In the last analysis, this experience must be one of deep inwardness. It only takes place in the depths of the spirit where God calls, gives life and forgives. And man, moved by the inner impulses of the Spirit, replies in the secret of his heart by being converted each day to choose God. Sadly, though, there are so many Christians for whom this call is not much more than a variety of external experiences. To recall the symbol of the baptismal robe, they forget that they must grow to "fit" into Christ and His redemptive scheme. Christ cannot be tailored to "fit" into our molds.

Even though a man is buried with Christ in Baptism and his life is nourished by the Eucharist, yet he is not "another Christ" unless he opens his whole being to Him. Moreover, the Lord Himself indicated that the radical transformation He requires would be viewed with apprehension and skepticism by many. The seed He had come to sow, He prophesied, would indeed be implanted in a multitude of His followers, but it would come to full fruition in so few (Mt. 13:4-9).

Because sin had shifted God's order, Christ calls for a reappraisal of all our values and attitudes toward life. This is the global message of the Sermon on the Mount. The characteristics He treasures truly appear to be in disharmony with the rhythm of our modern, success-oriented society. Simplicity of life, for example, is a direct contradiction to the mindless consumerism our world encourages. In our quest for self-sufficiency, the Christian qualities of meekness and mercy are often presented as something negative—the absence of strength, vigor, and of leadership. Nor does Christ call blessed those who lead a prosperous life, but rather the poor who are not attached to earthly goods and who thus are better able to appreciate the spiritual riches of the kingdom of heaven. It is in the context of our See City's racial problems that we lament the ugly violation of one of Christ's great counsels—His call that all His followers become "peacemakers": men and women dedicated to the reconciliation even of enraged enemies.

Yet Christ's convulsing challenge must not lead us to consternation. Rather, it should lead us to participate more deeply in His Mystery. It is an invitation to share in the spiritual strength wherein true joy, compassion, and inner peace can be found. As the Man of Peace, He can give others perfect peace with God and with men. As the gentle Savior who will not bruise even a reed (Is. 42:3) and who cares for the sick and afflicted, He can envelop our lives with a sensitive and indefatigable tenderness. No one doubts that these virtues need to become alive in our world. And finally by handing over our existence to Him, the paradox and puzzle which we often become to ourselves—the fusions of hopes and fears, of the desires and disappointments which lead to anguish, alienation, frustration and tears—are resolved in the joy of our spirit's marriage to Christ.

Since the New Testament does not admit of romantic interpretation, it would be wrong to dismiss the Beatitudes as mere idyllic expectations. God's Word is never empty (Is. 55:11). It has the power to make all things new (Rv. 21:1-7)—especially men and women. Although it is impossible to provide detailed blueprints for each unique individual's pilgrimage to God, we do know that such an ascent to the Father through Christ, this reorientation of our values, must begin with a psychic crucifixion. We must acknowledge our own inadequacy and dependence upon God and His love.

The Lord's bewildering command in Matthew 5:48: "You must therefore be perfect as your heavenly Father is perfect" has to be interpreted in this light. By proposing this unaccommodating and superhuman ideal, He wishes to liberate man from any bonds of self-sufficiency. It is a challenge directed against man's chronic ailment of pride. When in prayer we lay bare the true and naked face of the soul—where there can be no rationalizations and no self-defense—who of us is not forced to admit that we have easily become entrenched in our virtue? Who of us can claim to be free from willfulness, intellectual arrogance, and the desire to celebrate our own ego—mistaking our desires for God's will?

Only as man is liberated from the roots of his egoism is he able to fulfill the ethic of a child of God. By becoming "poor in spirit"; by recognizing our helplessness and thus cultivating a deeper reliance upon God, the seemingly irreconcilable — Christ's ideals and man's nature — are joined together. The Christian life acquires beauty.

Such a spiritual striving — the quest to become "poor in spirit" — is energized by prayer and the contemplation of the nature of God's personal love for us. Whatever else prayer may do, it generates redemptive insight regarding our relationship with God. It also awakens in us the desire to explore the endless recesses of God's love. In this process, we gradually learn to appreciate how this spontaneous gift of the Father has initiated us into the very life of God (1 Jn. 3:26). As His love invades us and assumes more and more control over our faculties, we learn that this love is selfless in its human manifestation! "Love is always patient and kind; it is never jealous; love is never boastful or conceited; it is never rude or selfish; it does not take offense, and is not resentful. Love takes no pleasure in other peoples' sins but delights in the truth; it is always ready to excuse, to trust, to hope and to endure whatever comes" (1 Cor. 13:4-7).

This odyssey into inwardness is not, however, without external fruit. To one who is striving to become "poor in spirit," the piercing presence of God's love leads

him to show to all the Father's children
the tenderness which characterizes truly
divine charity. It slowly softens the heart
and assimilates it into the heart of Christ,
full of pity. Only this and this alone forms
an adequate basis for understanding and
appreciating the Church's strivings in
today's social arena.

It was this love springing from Christ's
heart which led Him to console His brothers, to feed them, to feel their evils and
sorrows, and eventually to self-sacrifice
for them, to achieve a kingdom of justice for
them. The Christian must continually strive
to do the same Many of our ecclesial
activities provide us with this opportunity.
The recent collection for the victims of
the earthquake in Guatemala, for example,
was not merely another "second collection." Rather, it was a personal invitation
to all of us to enflesh the true catholicity of
Christ's love—a love which embraces all
of suffering humanity: "...insofar as you did
this to one of the least of these brothers of
mine, you did it to me" (Mt. 25:40). Our
annual Stewardship Appeal which supports
so many apostolates for rich and poor alike
also inserts the Church in Boston into the
same mystery of Christ's love. In a similar
manner, the Church's Campaign for Human Development, the continual activity
to affirm and achieve the rights of man,
its strivings in the field of international

justice, and all its good works, are not mere excursions into political theory. They are a finite (and often painful) attempt to concretize in the Church's life the goal of Christ for all men—a sharing of His kingdom of justice and peace.

I am not unaware that emotional and cultural cataracts often blind men— especially in many areas of social concern. Their vision simply focuses on the accidents of existence—the glitter of affluence, the gleam of a good reputation, or the color of a man's skin. But can a Christian, striving to be open to the Lord's love, remain blind to the light that Christ's word—whose authoritative interpreters are the bishops—offers them? Can a Christian, in good conscience, blaspheme Christ's image which the Lord revealed to be in all men, by word (such as "nigger," "whitie," "spic," "chink," etc.) and by action (like the repulsive acts of racial violence, here and elsewhere)? As recorded in the media these provide an adequate, even if oftentimes distorted, commentary. Is this an attempt to assimilate our hearts into the heart of Christ? I think not.

Can a person whose heart is trying to be full of Christ's pity casually become a disinterested spectator at the atrocity of abortion: an act whereby God's image is clinically and antiseptically blasphemed by destruction of the absolutely helpless? I think not. I will go further by stating that the detached compassion which claims that this is a "political problem" or a "matter of the individual's conscience" is likewise incompatible with our growth together in holiness.

III.

Chastity

Chastity was once a strong word, a serious word. But the word has almost disappeared—along with the notion. At best, it has been mutilated to mean joylessness, unfreedom, guilt, or the depreciation of human love. The effective neutralization (if not annihilation) of the concept of chastity in the twentieth century, moreover, indicates a shift in our value-systems. Ultimately, its absence from the current discussions within society regarding sexuality gives us a clue as to why our modern culture is seriously lacking in its ability to give a vital, personal, and vibrant meaning to sex.

There can be no doubt that the moral nakedness of the new "sexual gospel," while seemingly sincere, has nevertheless catapulted our civilization into the dark caverns of hedonistic confusion. In the name of psycho-sexual health it was promised that the new sexual freedom would promote a new and richer dimension of personal fulfillment. But this unbounded optimism has ultimately led to the "sexploitation" of the lower end of Washington Street and the leprosy of pornography peeping out of corner newsstands. The accelerating pace of sex corruption continues under the guise of sexual freedom. And the Christian community must not add to society's mad mathematic in this area.

In utter seriousness, the Christian must constantly recall the fact that he has been "clothed in Christ." In the light and strength of His unspoiled innocence, we are called to walk. We give visible witness to our spiritual compatibility with the innocent Christ by leading "the kind of life which the Lord expects of you, a life acceptable to him in all its aspects; showing the results in all the good actions you do.... You will have in you the strength, based on his own glorious power, never to give in..." (Col. 1:10-11). The inescapable conclusion of this supernatural logic thus compelled St. Paul again and again explicitly to catalogue chastity among the principal signs of true conversion to Christ (2 Cor. 3:16f.; Gal. 5:23; 1 Tm. 2:2, 3:4, etc.).

Nor did his sacred horror of sins of the flesh proceed from a psycho-sexual disorientation. There is another, more profound reason — to which the astigmatism of our age often remains blind. The Christian's body itself forms a temple in which the Spirit of God dwells (1 Cor. 3:16f.; 1 Cor. 6:16f.). Because God is the Holy One, the holiness which is intrinsic to His nature must be reproduced insofar as possible in the life of the individual Christian. Every part and aspect of existence must be offered to God the Father in the sacrifice of Christ. Just as uncleanliness was utterly incompatible with the perfection and sanctity of the sanctuary in the Old Dispensation, St. Paul sees a similar "sacrilegious" dimension to bodily impurities. They simply defile what God has made holy.

The redemptive transformation of man by Christ has raised human love and sexuality into the realm of Mystery. The love of the Lord must be the light to illuminate what in our day has become the shadowy area of sex. From this faith-filled perspective, we see countless lived-parables of God's grace associated with human sexuality. The faithful and self-giving love of married Christians, for example, becomes a sign to the Christian community of God's loving faithfulness towards us. On the other hand, the celibate and the virgin — by their striking and mysterious consecration to Christ — remind the Church that every Christian belongs to Christ as an offering to the Father. Examples could be multiplied.

The delicacy with which Sacred Scripture draws its teaching about sexuality is, indeed, a thing of beauty—as is the reality it describes. But it has become misshapen when translated into the modern idiom, e.g., the justification of homosexual relations, "living together," etc. Nor has the Christian community remained unaffected by this atmosphere. The recent public reaction of many within the Christian community against the Congregation for the Doctrine of the Faith's *Declaration on Certain Questions Concerning Sexual Ethics* (which reaffirms the traditional teaching of the magisterium and reflects the moral sense of the faithful) provides us with a concrete illustration of this statement. One wonders why?

There seems to be the unconscious trend to see tradition as being superseded by the insights of psychology. While far from dismissing the positive insights of this science, I believe that it must be made clear that the purpose of Christianity is not to canonize the newly discovered attitudes towards psycho-sexual health. Nor is Gospel truth to be viewed as nothing more than an adjunct to modern psychology. It is something deeper and wider, and more mysterious. And Jesus, in saying, "I am the Way, the Truth and the Life" is revealing that "only in the mystery of the Incarnate Word does the mystery of man take on new light"[8] and that only in Him will the puzzle man has become to himself be solved.

It can happen that within the Christian community our greatest strength can become our greatest source of temptation. Somehow our hearts can be led to place their complete trust in the infallibility and inerrancy of our personal intuitions of uncritical compassion. Because we "feel compassion" towards our brothers and sisters who find themselves in difficult situations, we are led to mutilate those parts of the Church's teaching which tend to prevent us from making an immediate response—on our own terms and suited to our personal conception of salvation. An example of this would be those who hold out private "solutions" to divorced Catholics which they maintain cannot be preached publicly. This is wrong.

Whenever our own feelings of compassion become our supreme moral guide, there is a tendency to maintain a cool diffidence toward Church teaching and to reduce unreasonable people's responsibility. But, echoing the insight of Pope Paul VI, I would remind those entrusted with the care of souls that "to diminish in no way the saving teaching of Christ constitutes an eminent form of charity for souls."[9]

Furthermore, God's "word of righteousness" which was manifest in Christ (Heb. 5:11-14) is the same word which is being manifest under the Spirit in and through the teaching office of the Church. Indeed, Christ instituted His Church as "the pillar and bulwark of truth" (1 Tm. 3:15). This is integral to Catholic tradition. While this may seem tasteless and indigestible to many, one cannot overlook and ignore this truth without spiritual ruin. In the precise context which we are discussing (i.e., the intuitions of compassion vs. the teaching authority of the Church) the "I's" inner dynamism can be deceptive. It ignites the flame of ego-excitement. It also leads one to forget that, as St. Paul points out, the Spirit distributes ecclesiastical graces to the members of the Church according to the needs of the entire Body. The mission allotted to me, seen from this viewpoint, is not up to me. It is predetermined by the Spirit. Quite simply, the individual cannot take it upon himself to proclaim new solutions which are not in harmony with the Church's teaching, since the authentic teachers, in our tradition, are the bishops in communion with one another under their head, the Roman Pontiff.

On a more personal and pastoral level, my heart has always felt the sufferings of my people who are wrestling with their weaknesses in this area. This type of struggle is too intimate and personalized to allow broad and generalized descriptions. Such would be indelicate. But their spiritual pain is and has been obvious. Because by divine will I am one with my people as their Bishop, their sufferings are intimately my own. And I know that the memories of failure often lead to discouragement and despondency.

The Christian message, the "good news," is, however, one of hope—a hope which can fill even these private abysses of discouragement. But in the Christian life, knowledge is not enough. Redemptive truth must permeate our whole being. And in our very struggle to be chaste, we actually experience our radical spiritual poverty. Our very discouragement is a call to abandon ourselves to God's power and goodness: "Gladly therefore will I glory in my infirmities, for when I am weak then I am strong" (2 Cor. 12:10). It is part of the process of learning to die to self. And herein lies our hope. In the mystery of God's grace, the experience of my inward poverty (and my acknowledgment of it) can be a means of opening my soul to God's healing grace. And God's grace is never wanting.

In a paradoxical phrase, St. Augustine was fond of stating that "even sin serves" to illustrate the truth that good can spring

from evil, just as the greatest good, the
salvation of all mankind, came from the
greatest evil, the putting to death of the
God-man. In this context, those who have
succumbed to weaknesses of the flesh can
find comfort. One should not concentrate
on the memories of failure. Rather, reflecting upon our spiritual biographies, can
we not discern how through the sacrament
of reconciliation we encountered the Lord
and learned that He lives, that He loves
us, and that He forgives us? And because
God's healing love endures, cannot we,
even in the darkest moments of failure,
find true Christian hope? It is not in deny-
ing sin in us that we find healing, but in
humbly confessing it in truth that we find
forgiveness and peace.

On Holy Saturday evening, at the
Easter Vigil, the priest prays:

Almighty, ever-living God,
only hope of the world,
by the preaching of the prophets
you proclaimed the mysteries we are
celebrating tonight.
Help us to be your faithful people,
for it is by your inspiration alone
that we can grow in goodness.

The foregoing pages have been written
in the spirit of this prayer. As your brother
in the Lord, who has been invited by Christ
to be the spiritual shepherd of this Archdiocese, I have tried to offer directives and

guidelines as to how we as a faith-filled people can grow together in holiness. I ask you to meditate upon these truths.

No one knows more than I do how words can never capture the spiritual dynamics of the Christian life. Words are so inadequate. But I do know prayers can transform these dead and static words into miracles of grace. That is why throughout the composition of this letter, I have offered my prayers on your behalf for this intention.

Please pray for me.

NOTES

1. Herman Schmidt, S.J., *Introductio in Liturgiam Occidentalem* (Rome, 1960), p. 509.

2. *Dogmatic Constitution on the Church*, no. 38.

3. St. Thomas Aquinas, *Summa Theologica*, I-II, q. 1, a. 1 (Introduction).

4. *Dogmatic Constitution, op. cit.*, no. 12.

5. *Ibid.*, no. 25.

6. *Ibid.*, no. 25.

7. *Ibid.*, no. 25.

8. *Pastoral Constitution on the Church in the Modern World*, no. 22.

9. Pope Paul VI, Encyclical *Of Human Life*, 299.

The Holy Eucharist
and the Hunger
for Understanding

Homily at the Liturgy for Military Personnel, 41st Eucharistic Congress, Friday, August 6, 1976.

St. Thomas Aquinas, the Angelic Doctor, concisely expresses the striking thought that the Holy Eucharist produces in each one of us the same effect as the Incarnation produced with respect to mankind in general: "Just as by coming visibly into the world He conferred upon the world the life of grace,…so also coming sacramentally into man He causes the life of grace, as John says: *He who eats me will live because of me*" *(Sum. Theol.*, III, q. 79, a. 1).

It is a striking thought. For immediately it reduces the whole vast work of the redemption of the human race to the terms of your redemption and my redemption. It underscores the abiding personal concern of Jesus Christ for you and for me. It brings to a focus His understanding of each one of us.

The gift of Jesus Christ in the Holy Eucharist is the gift of Himself—the Second Person of the Blessed Trinity-made-man, body and blood, soul and divinity. What this total giving of self really means is so difficult for us to comprehend. For His is a divine action, comparable in profundity to the innermost relations of the Blessed Trinity. In the thought-provoking words of one distinguished modern theologian: "As God gives His entire nature in the eternal generation of the Word and the spiration of the Holy Spirit, as God willed to give Himself in person in the Incarnation of the Word, so Jesus has wished to give Himself in person in the Eucharist.... When our Lord was about to deprive us of His sensible presence, He wished to leave Himself to us in person under the Eucharistic veils. Loving us as He did, He could not bend down any lower toward us, toward the lowliest, the poorest and most wretched. There was no way by which He could unite Himself or give Himself more completely to each of us" (R. Garrigou-Lagrange, *Our Savior and His Love for Us*, pp. 262-263).

Should it surprise us, therefore, that in the Holy Eucharist, each one of us in the particular circumstances in which we find ourselves, in joy or in sorrow, in success or in failure—each one of us will find the answer to our hunger for understanding—yours and mine? For is not the Holy Eucharist, as Pope Paul VI says, "the sacrament of the permanency of Christ, who now lives in the eternal glory of the Father, in our time, in our history, and in our earthly pilgrimage"? (Pope Paul VI, cf. *Faith: Response to the Dialogue of God*, ed. Daughters of Saint

Paul, p. 58) And is not the Holy Eucharist, as the same Pontiff says, "Christ for each of us, clothed precisely by the species of bread, to let Himself be known as accommodating and ready to satisfy our hunger, to make Himself wanted, and to be approached, received, and to be assimilated with Himself"? (Pope Paul VI, cf. *ibid.*, pp. 58-59)

Jesus Christ, present in the Holy Eucharist, is the same Person who once was born in a stable in Bethlehem, who worked in a carpenter shop in Nazareth, who trudged through country fields and city streets in Palestine, who preached on the slope of a hill in Galilee and from the prow of a boat on the Lake of Genesareth, who sweated blood amid the agony of Gethsemane and died the death of crucifixion on Mount Calvary. He is the Incarnate Son of God, truly human in nature as He is truly divine in nature. It is precisely because He is like unto us in all things save sin (cf. Heb. 4:15) that He knows and cares and understands.

Read the Gospel pages. Study the life of Jesus Christ upon earth. Did He ever show unconcern for the troubled and the suffering? Did He ever refuse to listen? Did He ever answer brusquely or impatiently or offensively? Did He ever deny the plea of someone in need? Did He ever berate a timid soul? Was He ever harsh or unkind? Did He ever bear a grudge? Was there ever any bitterness in His speech or vindictiveness in His acts? Did He ever show, by what He said or by what He did, that He lacked sympathy and compassion and kindness and considerateness and understanding?

Though hard on Himself (remember the cold of Bethlehem, the hunger of the desert, the agony of Gethsemane, the ignominy of Golgotha)—though hard on Himself, was He not always mild and gentle toward others? Was there ever any penitent sinner whom He refused to pardon? When some ridiculed His teaching and termed Him an imposter and called Him a blasphemer and shouted for His death and nailed Him to a cross, did He ever answer in anger; did He ever harbor revenge? "Father, forgive them for they know not what they do" (Lk. 23:34).

He taught His followers to love their enemies and to do good to those who hated them; He told them not to judge or condemn, but always to forgive: He bade them to feed the hungry and to give drink to the thirsty and to welcome the stranger and to clothe the naked and to come to the sick and to visit the imprisoned. Could He not command these things because He Himself, by what He thought and said and did, was a Model whom they could follow?

Understanding? Did you ever reflect upon the parable of the prodigal son, and upon the parable of the shepherd who left the ninety-nine sheep to go out in search of the one that had strayed away?

Understanding? The centurion came to Jesus Christ with the plea: "My servant is ill" (Mt. 8:6). The lepers stood afar off and begged that they be made clean. The poor blind beggar of Jericho kept crying out: "Jesus, Son of David, have pity on me" (Lk. 18:38). And because in the goodness and generosity and tenderness of His heart He understood, Jesus Christ healed them all.

Understanding? Do you remember how one of the rulers of the synagogue, named Jairus, fell down at the feet of Jesus Christ and "besought him much: 'My daughter is at the point of death' " (Mt. 5:23)? And because Jesus Christ understood a father's grief, He went down to his home, and took his daughter by the hand and raised her from the dead.

Understanding? Do you remember how sympathetically Jesus Christ listened to Mary of Bethany: "Lord, if you had been here, my brother would not have died" (Jn. 11:32)? He Himself wept at the tomb of His friend, Lazarus. And because Jesus Christ understood the sorrow of Martha and Mary, He brought their brother back to life.

Understanding? Do you remember how pitifully the widow at Naim was weeping, as her only son was being carried to the grave? And because Jesus Christ understood the heartsickness of that poor mother, He not only commanded the boy: "Young man, I say to you, arise" (Lk. 7:14), but with delicate gentleness and infinite thoughtfulness, He took the boy by the hand "and he gave him to his mother" (Lk. 7:15).

The sick and the diseased and the crippled and the maimed and the troubled and the halt flocked to Him—because they knew that He understood. Little children ran after Him, so that He might throw His arms about them and bless them—because they knew that He understood. His Mother, Mary, pointed out to Him the embarrassment at the wedding feast when the wine supply had failed—because she knew that He understood. The woman troubled for twelve years with an issue of blood pushed her way through the jostling crowd, that she might touch the hem of His garment—because she knew that He understood.

He always understood.

But it was not only the sorrows and burdens of men and women and children that Jesus Christ understood. He understood their joys as well. That is why He loved to visit with Martha and Mary and Lazarus in Bethany. That is why He shared in the happiness of the newly married couple at Cana. That is why He honored the publican Zacchaeus in Jericho by entering into his house in order to dine with him.

Jesus Christ loved people. He had a reverent sense of the dignity of all persons because He understood that every human being is an image of God, and so valuable in His sight that He would shed the last drop of His precious blood on Calvary to redeem him. He appreciated the strengths and the weaknesses of every individual—and so He dealt with every individual on a personal basis.

He drew to the faith the Samaritan woman at the well of Sichar, promising her: "The water that I will give...shall become...a fountain of water, springing up into life everlasting" (Jn. 4:14).

He rescued the woman taken in adultery, granted her forgiveness because of her repentant love, and then set her free: "Go, and sin no more" (Jn. 8:11).

He looked with such compassion upon Peter after his denial that the apostle went out and wept bitterly—the strong, manly, gruff, impetuous fisherman.

He called Judas—"friend"—and taught the whole world the lesson that it is never too late to try to save a human soul.

It is this same Jesus Christ, dearly beloved brothers and sisters, who is present in the Holy Eucharist. "Jesus Christ is the same yesterday and today and forever" (Heb. 13:8). True, He is present in His glorified body (cf. B. Van Acken, *The Holy Eucharist*, pp. 62-63), but it is still the Second Person of the Blessed Trinity made man, body and blood, soul and divinity, who remains with us under the appearances of bread and wine. There is only one Jesus Christ.

Today, men and women and children all over the world hunger for understanding. I hear them plead: "I want to be appreciated as a human person." "I want to be treated as the work of God's creative hand." "I want to be esteemed as a child of God." "I need to be wanted, to be loved." "I need someone who will defend me from injustice and protect me from hatred." "I need someone who will not become angry at my failures nor vindictive because of my sins." "I need someone who is concerned with me as an individual." "I need someone to whom I can speak, and in whom I can trust."

The starving millions, the indigent, the destitute, the beggared, cry out to Jesus Christ in the Holy Eucharist: "Do You understand my poverty?" He points to a manger and a stable, and He reminds them: "Foxes have holes, and birds of the air have nests; but the Son of man has nowhere to lay his head" (Mt. 8:20).

The forgotten and the abandoned; the shut-ins in apartments whom no one ever visits; the men and women on the fringe of society in chronic hospitals and public institutions; the elderly who live only on memories—all these cry out to Jesus Christ in the Holy Eucharist: "Do You understand my loneliness?" He points to an olive garden where no one could watch even one hour with Him, where His desolation was so overpowering that He pleaded with His Father that the chalice be taken from Him, and where moments later His closest followers fled from Him in terror, while one of His chosen friends planted upon His lips a kiss of betrayal.

The harrassed and the deprived and the disadvantaged and the cheated and the vic-timized and the persecuted cry out to Jesus

Christ in the Holy Eucharist: "Do You understand the injustice that I must bear and the
hatred that I must face, the misinterpretations
of my motives and the misconstruing of my
words?" He points to the Sanhedrin where false
witnesses testified against Him, to the court of
Herod where He was made a fool of, and to the
judgment seat of Pilate where He was scourged.
And He reminds them how His sublimest
teachings were ridiculed and the miraculous
works by which He alleviated suffering and
need were ascribed to the devil.

"Do You understand my suffering and pain
and anguish?" cry out the sick and the diseased
and the crippled and the infirmed. Jesus points
to a hill of skulls under a blackened sky: tattered
flesh, thorn-wounded forehead, nail-pierced
hands, blood-spattered body, and a gaping hole
in His side opened by a soldier's spear.

Understand? Why, understanding is only
a facet of love, my brothers and sisters, and
"Greater love has no man than this, that a man
lay down his life for his friends" (Jn. 15:13).

Understand? His invitation in the Holy
Eucharist is as open and as pressing today as it
was 2,000 years ago. He says again and again to
each one of us, "It is I; do not be afraid" (Mt.
14:27). "Come to me, all you who labor and
are heavily burdened, and I will refresh you"
(Mt. 11:28).

Understand? Why do you think that He
instituted the Holy Eucharist? Why do you
think that He gave us this sacrament in such a

personal way? Was it not "that He might unite Himself with individuals in communion and become one body with them..., that He might become man in each man, by taking the human nature of each into union with His own"? (M. Scheeben, *The Mysteries of Christianity*, p. 486)

And is it possible for our human minds to conceive of any action more understanding than this?

There is another aspect of the subject, "The Eucharist: and the Hunger for Understanding," that calls for our reflection this afternoon.

It is an astounding thought, and yet it is true, that when Jesus Christ abides in us in the Holy Eucharist, in some mysterious and miraculous way, we are transformed into Him. This is no new doctrine; this is no exaggerated concept. It is to be found in the writings of many of the great Fathers and Doctors of the Church, and has been taught constantly by the magisterium of the Church over the centuries. With scholarly insight, an outstanding modern theologian has discussed several Patristic passages on this point. Treating of St. John Chrysostom, for example, and his comments upon the words of St. Paul ("Is not the bread we break a sharing in the body of Christ?"), Taymans d'Eypernon describes how this Father of the Church pointed out "that St. Paul was not satisfied with his explanation of the union between Christ and the Christian until he had affirmed that in Holy Communion the Christian *becomes* the Body of

Christ.... Why, asks St. John Chrysostom, does St. Paul use the word *communicatio* and not *participatio?* The reason is that he wished to express a more intimate degree of union. Even when he uses the word *communicatio*, which supposes a distinction of persons between him who communicates and him who receives the communication, St. Paul is at pains to attenuate this distinction, adding immediately, 'We are all one bread, one body'; as if he were to say, 'Why speak of communication or communion? We are the same body.'

"For what is the bread we eat? It is the Body of Christ. And those who communicate become the Body of Christ; not several bodies but *one* Body. Just as bread is compounded of many grains in such a way that their union obliterates their individual differences, so too with us; we are united one with the other, all united in Christ because all are nourished by the same Body.

"With even greater vigor of expression, St. Chrysostom thus describes our transformation in Christ: 'We are the Body which we receive.'

"Finally, we have the words of St. Leo the Great: 'Participation in the Body and Blood of Christ changes us into that which we eat'" (Taymans d'Eypernon, *The Blessed Trinity and the Sacraments*, pp. 136-137).

Dearly beloved, because of our union with Christ in the Holy Eucharist we must let Christ live in us. "For me to live is Christ" (Phil. 1:21).

Our attitudes and our actions, the things that we think and say and do, must be conformed to Him, because He lives in us. It is not enough to imitate Christ. Rather, we must let Christ live and act in us, in such wise that we can one day say with St. Paul: "It is no longer I who live, but Christ who lives in me" (Gal. 2:20).

In concrete, practical terms of day-to-day living this means that we must feed the hungry and give drink to the thirsty and visit the lonely and console the sorrowing and counsel the doubting—because this is what He did. "He went about doing good" (Acts 10:38). In a word, we must love—with patience and kindness, without jealousy or boastfulness, without arrogance or rudeness, without stubbornness or irritableness or resentfulness (cf. 1 Cor. 13). We must never cease trying to satiate the great hunger of modern man for understanding. We must be alive to modern man's yearning to be appreciated as a human person, to be treated as the work of God's creative hand, to be esteemed as a child of God, to be wanted and to be loved, to be defended from injustice and protected from hatred, to be accepted in spite of his failures and transgressions. Like Jesus Christ we must give ourselves to modern man as persons to whom he can speak and in whom he can trust. And all of this, precisely because in the Holy Eucharist we become one Body with Jesus Christ, who assimilates us to Himself.

How desperate is the need today that we love and understand one another—and ourselves too—in the context of our becoming one Body with the Eucharistic Christ! Thomas Merton's memorable statement is no exaggeration. He wrote, "The whole problem of our time is the problem of love: how are we going to recover the ability to love ourselves and to love one another? The reason why we hate one another and fear one another is that we secretly or openly hate and fear our own selves. And we hate ourselves because the depths of our being are a chaos of frustration and spiritual misery. Lonely and helpless, we cannot be at peace with others because we are not at peace with ourselves, and we cannot be at peace with ourselves because we are not at peace with God" (T. Merton, *The Living Bread*, pp. xii-xiii).

It is important to make clear, however, that this living of Christ in our day-to-day lives because we have become His Body in the Holy Eucharist; this sympathetic response by us, united with the Eucharistic Christ, to the hunger of modern man for understanding—all of this implies an ecclesial dimension too. The Second Vatican Council urges bishops to exert themselves constantly "to have the faithful know and live the paschal mystery more deeply through the Eucharist, and thus become a firmly knit body in the solidarity of Christ's love" (*Christus Dominus,* no. 15).

It is substantially the same thought that Thomas Merton expresses in this way: "We must always remember that we are not sanctified as isolated units but as members of a living organism, the Church: we are sanctified as 'members one of another.' The growth of each individual person in Christlike virtue contributes all the more to the Christlikeness of the whole Church.... It is therefore not only a question of individuals *imitating* the divine Redeemer and thus perfecting their own lives, but above all, of Christ living more and more perfectly in His Church by virtue of the fact that His Spirit takes fuller and deeper possession of all its individual members, uniting them more perfectly to one another and to Himself.... We will never appreciate the Real Presence fully until we see the intimate connection which exists between the Mystery of the Eucharist and the Mystery of the Church, two sacred realities which completely interpenetrate to form a single whole.... Communion is not a flight from life, not an evasion of reality, but the full acceptance of the responsibilities of our membership in Christ and the total commitment of ourselves to the lives and aims of the Mystical Body of Christ" (T. Merton, *op. cit.*, pp. 80-81, 133, 86-87).

My dear brothers and sisters in Christ, to summarize and to conclude: the Holy Eucharist is the living answer to mankind's hunger for understanding. And this, chiefly for two reasons. First, present in the Holy Eucharist is the loving, compassionate, consoling, sympathetic, encouraging, understanding Christ. And secondly, through our oneness with Jesus Christ in the Holy Eucharist—through our becoming

Him because He assimilates us to Himself—our brothers and sisters in our day must find in us also the living answer to their hunger for understanding.

Somewhere I once happened upon the text of an old and unidentified manuscript that seems especially pertinent to our reflections this afternoon on "The Eucharist and the Hunger for Understanding." The title of the manuscript is "This Is My Friend."

> "Let me tell you how I made His acquaintance.
>> I had heard much of Him, but took no heed.
>> He sent daily gifts and presents, but I never thanked Him.
>> He often seemed to want my friendship, but I remained cold.
>> I was homeless and wretched and starving and in peril every hour; and He offered me shelter and comfort and food and safety; but I was ungrateful still.
> At last He crossed my path and with tears in His eyes
>> He besought me saying, Come and abide with me.
> Let me tell you how He treats me now.
>> He supplies all my wants.
>> He gives me more than I dare ask.
>> He anticipates my every need.
>> He begs me to ask for more.

He never reminds me of my past ingratitude.

He never rebukes me for my past failures.

Let me tell you further what I think of Him.

He is as good as He is great.

His love is as ardent as it is true.

He is as lavish with His promises as He is faithful in keeping them.

He is as jealous of my love as He is deserving of it.

I am in all things His debtor, but He bids me call Him Friend" (cf. R. H. Benson, *The Friendship of Christ*, p. ix).

It is this Friend, the Eucharistic Christ, who answers the hunger of mankind for understanding. Truly, "he who comes to me shall not hunger" (Jn. 6:35). It is the Eucharistic Christ who "has satisfied the empty soul, and has filled the hungry soul with good things" (Ps. 106:9).

Pastoral Letter
on the Holy Eucharist

October 1, 1977

My dear brother priests, revered religious, beloved brothers and sisters in Christ:

1. One day in September of 1621, in the city of Rome, an old man of seventy-nine years of age lay dying. Preparations were being made in the sickroom, so that he might receive Holy Viaticum. The dying man was a priest, a member of the Jesuit Congregation. One of the most brilliant theologians of his century and, indeed, of the entire history of the Church, he was also a famous professor, an eloquent preacher, a distinguished writer, an illustrious diplomat, and a master of the spiritual life. Archbishop and Cardinal, he would one day be canonized a saint and proclaimed a Doctor of the Church.

2. When all the preparations had been completed and the dying man was ready for Holy Viaticum, despite his extreme weakness he slowly rose from his bed. Totteringly he sank to his knees. And then in simple faith and burning love, with profound humility and heartfelt gratitude, with awesome reverence Robert

Bellarmine received for the last time the Eucharistic Body and Blood of Jesus Christ.

3. O my dear brother priests, religious and people! The attitude of St. Robert Bellarmine toward the Holy Eucharist must be ours too: faith, love, humility, gratitude, reverence! Indeed every day of our lives should find a deepening of these virtues in our souls!

4. It is the faith of the Church that the Holy Eucharist is the real Body and Blood, soul and divinity of Jesus Christ. So often have we taught this truth and talked about it and preached about it and heard about it that the stupendous wonder of it may unfortunately have begun to wear off. God's gifts to us are so lavishly bestowed that they surpass the mind's ability to comprehend them. Yet no one of His gifts can even begin to be compared with the Holy Eucharist—for in the Holy Eucharist God gives us Himself. Our response to Him must be: faith, love, humility, gratitude, reverence.

5. The Holy Eucharist is the marvel of the Incarnation extended to our day and to our locality! The Holy Eucharist is the Food from God, given to us in the loving intimacy of the Last Supper, that we might be transformed into Him whom we consume! The Holy Eucharist is Calvary's awesome Sacrifice made sacramentally present in our midst, as if the gap of twenty centuries suddenly disappeared! In the light of these wonders our attitude must be: faith, love, humility, gratitude, reverence!

6. The Holy Eucharist! What a breath-taking manifestation and ever-continuing proof of God's infinite love for us! Pope Leo XIII did not hesitate to say of the Holy Eucharist, "To know with an entire faith what is the excellence of the most Holy Eucharist is in truth to know what that work is which, in the might of His mercy, God-made-Man carried out on behalf of the human race" *(Mirae caritatis)*.

7. Do not the words of our Divine Savior provide for each one of us a subject for endless meditation? "I am the bread of life" (Jn. 6:48). "If any man shall eat of this bread, he shall live forever; and the bread which I will give is my flesh, for the life of the world" (Jn. 6:52). "Unless you eat the flesh of the Son of Man and drink his blood, you shall not have life in you" (Jn. 6:54).

8. For the purpose of our present meditation we may look upon the Holy Eucharist from three points of view. First, Jesus Christ becomes sacramentally present on the altar through the changing of bread and wine into His Body and Blood. That is the Holy Sacrifice of the Mass. Secondly, Jesus Christ present in the Eucharist actually becomes our Food when we receive His Body and Blood under the sacramental species. That is Holy Communion. Thirdly, Jesus Christ present in the Eucharist remains with us in our tabernacles for our devotion and worship. That is the Blessed Sacrament reserved—the abiding Presence.

And toward each aspect of the same Holy Eucharist our attitude must be: faith, love, humility, gratitude, reverence!

9. What should the Holy Eucharist mean in our lives? Pope Leo XIII called the Holy Eucharist "the chief means whereby men are engrafted on the divine nature" *(Mirae caritatis)*. The Second Vatican Council declared, "Through the ministry of priests, the spiritual sacrifice of the faithful is made perfect in union with the sacrifice of Christ, the sole Mediator" *(Presbyterorum ordinis)*. The Eucharistic Sacrifice "is the font and apex of the whole Christian life..." *(Lumen gentium)*. "The renewal in the Eucharist of the covenant between the Lord and man draws the faithful into the compelling love of Christ and sets them afire" *(Sacrosanctum concilium)*. "The most Blessed Eucharist contains the Church's entire spiritual wealth, that is, Christ Himself, our Passover and living bread" *(Presbyterorum ordinis)*. And Pope Paul VI has written, "Anyone, therefore, who approaches this august Sacrament with special devotion, and endeavors to return generous love for Christ's own infinite love, experiences and fully understands, not without great spiritual joy and profit, how...great is the value of converse with Christ, for there is nothing more consoling on earth, nothing more efficacious for advancing along the road of holiness" *(Mysterium fidei)*.

10. Is it any wonder that the attitude expected of us who are priests, without whom there is no Eucharist, should be our attitude of faith, love, humility, gratitude, reverence?

11. As you know, dearly beloved in Christ, our Holy Father, Pope Paul VI, recently authorized the bishops of the United States to allow the faithful the option of receiving Holy Communion in the hand, along with the centuries-old practice of receiving on the tongue. The bishop of each diocese is to make his own decision as to whether permission for the exercise of this option is to be granted to his people. After prayerful reflection and considerable consultation, I have decided to grant and implement this permission in the Archdiocese of Boston.

12. Before the restored option of receiving Holy Communion in the hand begins to be used—this option will start on the Feast of Christ the King on November 20—there must be a special catechesis in every parish church and public chapel in the Archdiocese. I cannot adequately stress the importance of this catechesis. It is my hope that it will assure the most careful handling of the Holy Eucharist on the part of all Eucharistic ministers and the most reverent reception of Holy Communion by the faithful. The Holy See has warned that "it is a matter of great concern to the Church that the Eucharist be celebrated and shared with the greatest of dignity and fruitfulness" *(Memoriale Domini).*

13. It is likewise my hope that there will be a resurgence of devotion to the Holy Eucharist within this Archdiocese, reflected in an increase in Mass attendance, a more fervent reception of Holy Communion, and a renewal of such practices as Exposition of the Blessed Sacrament, Benediction of the Blessed Sacrament, and the Forty Hours Devotion. The request for the option from the Holy See and the granting of it had these pastoral aims in view.

14. Moreover, this catechesis will concern itself not only with the proper method of receiving Holy Communion in the hand, but also with the Eucharistic Mystery Itself—the Mass, Holy Communion, the abiding Presence. It must explain the teaching of the Church, exactly according to the Church's mind. It must stress the requirements for worthy and fruitful reception of Holy Communion. It must make clear beyond any doubt that the faithful are free to receive Holy Communion either on the tongue or in the hand—the option is theirs alone. There must be no attempt to persuasion or pressure to induce anyone to adopt or reject the new way of receiving Holy Communion. Under no circumstances is any one of the faithful ever to be refused Holy Communion merely because he/she wishes to receive the Sacrament on the tongue or in the hand. Nor is anyone to be placed in an embarrassing situation because he/she seeks Communion on the tongue or in the hand. Moreover, no one of the

faithful is to be prevented from receiving Holy Communion while kneeling, nor is any attempt to be made to compel the recipient to stand. A proper reverence before receiving the Holy Eucharist is highly recommended.

15. The catechesis should stress the need for faith, love, humility, gratitude and reverence toward the Holy Eucharist. It must make clear that what the faithful are receiving, either on the tongue or in the hand, is not mere bread, not even some sacred object—but rather a Divine Person, Jesus Christ, God and man, through the reception of His Body and Blood. Obviously every precaution must be taken to guard against the danger of disrespect or irreverence or casualness toward the Holy Eucharist. Thus, hosts that crumble easily should not be used. And for the same reason the faithful must be instructed to consume the Sacred Species immediately before returning to their place, making sure that all fragments, no matter how small, are likewise consumed. Children must be given the attention which their age requires.

16. It goes without saying that along with the whole Church, I expect every priest in the Archdiocese to prepare carefully this catechesis, in order that the faithful will understand ever more profoundly the need for faith, love, humility, gratitude and reverence toward the Holy Eucharist.

17. I beg you to join with me in prayer for a renewal of fervor toward the Holy Eucharist in all its aspects, in our Archdiocese and through-

out the country. I make my own the stirring words of Pope Pius XII in his monumental encyclical on the Sacred Liturgy: "The Divine Redeemer is ever repeating His pressing invitation: 'Abide in me.' By the sacrament of the Eucharist, Christ remains in us and we in Him. And just as Christ, remaining in us, lives and works, so should we remain in Christ and live and work through Him" *(Mediator Dei)*.

On Preparing
for the Holy Eucharist

Feast of the Holy Rosary—1980

My beloved brother priests,
My dear brothers and sisters in Christ:

As I reflect once again on the Lord's Last Supper to prepare with Him for this conversation with you, I search in the Gospel for a deeper insight into the heart and mind of Jesus on that most crucial occasion in His life—and in ours. Of course I find it impossible to reach the depths of His infinite wisdom and love, but with all of you I am fascinated by the beauty of the Word of Life and meditate upon it—ever more prayerfully—to draw inspiration for life and for our ministry of charity.

I humbly ask you to pray with me as we listen to Jesus, as we talk with Him together, as He reveals the depths of His love to us at the Last Supper, so that our hearts may burn within us as He speaks, and we may vow to please Him, especially in the Sacrament of His love as the Church celebrates it.

I am always deeply impressed by the exquisite care and concerned preoccupation of Jesus and His disciples to find a suitable place to make worthy preparations for the celebration of the solemn Passover Supper. It was a Jewish meal with a most profound religious significance for the people of Israel. For Jesus and His own, the Last Supper was the most significant of all the Passovers ever celebrated!

First of all the disciples were eager to know where Jesus wished them to prepare for the Supper. "Where do you want us to prepare for it?" He Himself was to choose the place. It was not left to them, much less to chance. It was He also who sent them into the city to a place selected by Him. They did not send themselves or even draw lots for the privilege. He gave them signs to lead them to the room of His choice. "Listen," He said, "as you go into the city you will meet a man carrying a pitcher of water. Follow him into the house he enters and tell the owner of the house, 'The Master has this to say to you: where is the dining room in which I can eat the Passover with my disciples?' The man will show you a large upper room furnished with couches. Make the preparations there." They set off and found everything as He had told them, and prepared the Passover (Lk. 22:9-12). As you can see, nothing was left to mere chance, nothing was casual. The event about to take place involved God and man in their deepest and most sublime relationship: love and worship!

When all the preparations were made, Jesus gathered the Apostles together in the Upper Room and said to them, "I have longed to eat this Passover with you before I suffer: because, I tell you, I shall not eat it again until it is fulfilled in the kingdom of God" (Lk. 22:15).

Jesus had longed for this hour. He had longed to do what He was about to do—at the very time of His betrayal by one of His own— and only a few hours before His death on the cross! He had a promise of life and love to keep, a promise He had made in the synagogue at Capernaum to the people He had come to save from their sins:

> "Do not work for food that cannot last,
> but work for food that endures to eternal life
> the kind of food the Son of Man is offering you,
> for in him the Father, God himself, has set his seal" (Jn. 6:27).

. . . .

> "I am the bread of life.
> He who comes to me will never be hungry;
> he who believes in me will never thirst."

. . . .

> "I am the bread of life.
> Your fathers ate the manna in the desert and they are dead;
> but this is the bread that comes down from heaven,

so that a man may eat it and not die.
I am the living bread which has come down
    from heaven.
Anyone who eats this bread will live for-
    ever;
And the bread that I shall give
is my flesh, for the life of the world."

. . . .

"For my flesh is real food
and my blood is real drink.
He who eats my flesh and drinks my blood
lives in me,
And I live in him.
As I, who am sent by the living Father
myself draw life from the Father,
so whoever eats me will draw life from me.
This is the bread come down from heaven;
not like the bread our ancestors ate:
they are dead,
but anyone who eats this bread will live
    forever" (Jn. 6:26-58).

This promise—to give His flesh and blood
as food and drink for everlasting life to all who
believe in Him—was pressing for fulfillment
within the Sacred Heart of Jesus as He spoke to
His disciples at the Last Supper. In ways of love
beyond understanding, He kept revealing to
them the mystery of His union with them and of
their living union with the Father through Him
—a union to be perfected by eating His flesh

and drinking His blood which was to be poured
out for the forgiveness of sins:

> "As the Father has loved me,
> so have I loved you.
> Remain in my love..." (Jn. 15:9).

. . . .

> "This is my commandment:
> love one another
> as I have loved you.
> A man can have no greater love
> than to lay down his life for his friends.
> You are my friends,
> if you do what I command you"
>   (Jn. 15:12-14).

. . . .

> "Father, may they be one in us,
> as you are in me and I am in you,
> so that the world may believe it was you
>   who sent me.
> I have given them the glory you gave me,
> that they may be one as we are one.
> With me in them and you in me,
> may they be so completely one
> that the world will realize that it was you
>   who sent me
> and that I have loved them as much as you
>   loved me" (Jn. 17:21-23).

Longing to give Himself to us so that we
could become one with Him—and through Him
one with the Father in the Holy Spirit and

thereby have life everlasting—Jesus took bread at the Last Supper, and "when he had given thanks, broke it and gave it to (the disciples), saying, 'This is my body which will be given for you; do this as a memorial of me.' He did the same with the cup after supper, and said, 'This cup is the new covenant in my blood which will be poured out for you'" (Lk. 22:19-20).

The following day, Friday afternoon, His body was given for us and His blood was poured out on the cross for us—for the forgiveness of our sins—so that we could be reconciled through Him with the Father—and live!

We, the forgiven, the redeemed, the living because of His loving death, we who follow Him and constitute His Church, have from the beginning gathered together to celebrate His Last Passover Supper in the way and for the purpose He willed it: "Do this in memory of me." St. Paul tells us that "Until the Lord comes, therefore, every time you eat this bread and drink this cup, you are proclaiming his death, and so anyone who eats the bread and drinks the cup of the Lord unworthily will be behaving unworthily towards the Body and Blood of the Lord.

"Everyone is to recollect himself before eating this bread and drinking this cup; because a person who eats and drinks without recognizing the Body is eating and drinking his own condemnation" (1 Cor. 11:26-29).

We, His Church, most recently at the Second Vatican Council, professed our faith in the reality of the Lord's Supper. In its dogmatic *Constitution on the Sacred Liturgy,* no. 47, the Council reaffirms the constant faith of the Church:

"that at the Last Supper
on the night He was betrayed,
our Savior instituted the eucharistic
    sacrifice
of His Body and Blood.
This He did in order to perpetuate
the sacrifice of the cross throughout the
    ages
until He should come again,
and as to entrust to His beloved Spouse,
the Church,
a memorial of His death and resurrection:
a sacrament of love,
a sign of unity,
a bond of charity,
a paschal banquet in which Christ is
    consumed,
the mind is filled with grace,
and a pledge of future glory is given to us."

The ineffable mystery of God's love for us as revealed in Jesus through the power of the Holy Spirit is the heart of the sublime mystery of the most Holy Eucharist, the divine invention of the New Covenant which enables the Victim of our reconciliation, Jesus Christ Himself, to abide with us sacramentally throughout the ages, everywhere on the face of the earth, to call us and bring us together in faith, to sustain us with hope in His promise, and to bind us together in Him through love. His Presence among us through the power of the Sacrament is the fruit of that longing of His most Sacred Heart to eat the Last Passover with His disciples. It is the last gift of His love for us, it is the gift of His life—His very Self. Through the power of the mystery—of the Sacrament—He is the gift, ever present in His Church and in the world to reconcile it to the Father.

What word is there to describe aptly the Eucharistic gift? I am certain that the best of dictionary writers cannot come up with the word or words to describe fittingly this sublime mystery. But one thing we know it is. The Church says it is holy and sacred, and this of course it is to the highest conceivable degree, since the Son of God-made-man is present "body, soul and divinity" in It.

Longing as Jesus did to give Himself completely to us at the Last Supper out of love for the Father and for us, is it any wonder that He chose the place so carefully and ordered the disciples to prepare it so reverently? Is there anything so holy, so sacred, so deserving of our reverent and careful attention as Jesus in the Supreme Act of His Love for the Father and for us, His brothers and sisters, whom He came to rescue from everlasting death by His Sacrifice on the Cross?

This was and is His supreme act of religion!
He gave Himself up because it was the
    Father's holy will!
He and the Father are one!
Their love for each other is equal and
    eternal!
This is the infinite love that makes the
    Eucharist
and fills the Heart of Jesus present in It!
It is ever active in the Church,
building it up for the glory of the Father
and the salvation and peace of the world!
Is there anything more holy,
more sacred,
more deserving of respect and reverence—
of love?

Pope John Paul II, transmitting to the
present generation the constant faith of the
Church, teaches us that the Holy Eucharist is

holy and sacred, because in It are the
continued presence and action of Christ,
"the Holy One" of God; "anointed with the
Holy Spirit," "consecrated by the Father"
to lay down His life of His own accord and
to take it up again, and the High Priest of
the New Covenant.

The sacredness of the Mass, therefore, is
not a "sacrilization," that is to say, something man adds to Christ's action in the
Upper Room, for the Holy Thursday supper was a sacred rite, a primary and

constitutive liturgy, through which Christ, by pledging to give His life for us, Himself celebrated sacramentally the mystery of His passion and resurrection, the heart of every Mass.

Our Masses, being derived from this liturgy, possess themselves a complete liturgical form, which, in spite of its variation in line with the families of rites, remains substantially the same. The sacred character of the Mass is a sacredness instituted by Christ. The words and actions of every priest, answered by the conscious, active participation of the whole eucharistic assembly, echo the words and actions of Holy Thursday (*On the Mystery and Worship of the Eucharist,* no. 8).

Because the Eucharist is God's most precious gift to His Church, to His priestly and holy people, it is reasonable to expect that the Church prepare to celebrate it with the utmost reverence and love—her faith reveals to her the ineffable Reality of the Presence of Christ, the Son of God, in her midst—*Emmanuel!*

Learning from Jesus in the Eucharist the supreme lesson of total giving, of self-sacrifice out of love for God and for us, the Church has endeavored through the centuries to respond to this divine love by going out to all peoples in all forms of service for the love of God and for the sake of the Kingdom. From the Eucharist the Church learns constantly as from no other source how to live in the service of love. In every way the Eucharist is indeed the source and summit of the life of the Church (*Decree on the Ministry and Life of Priests,* no. 5).

Hence, those to whom the Lord has entrusted the ministry of shepherding and governing His people on their earthly pilgrimage, have, as Pope John Paul II says, "the strict duty to specify everything which concerns participation in it and its celebration. We should therefore act according to the principles laid down by the last Council which, in the Constitution on the Sacred Liturgy, defined authorizations and obligations of individual Bishops in their dioceses and of episcopal conferences, given the fact that both act in collegial unity with the Apostolic See" (*On the Mystery and Worship of the Eucharist,* no. 12).

Because the Eucharist is the common possession of the Church and the Sacrament of her unity, it is not the private possession of any one individual member of it; consequently, no part of it—not even a word—is ever to be changed by anyone, except by the Holy See alone or by its authority. What is given to us to unite us must never be used to divide us. This would be against the manifest will of the Lord!

My beloved brother priests, upon us most especially rest the burden and the privilege of leading all our people to that proper and fruitful celebration of the Eucharist willed by Our Lord Jesus Christ for the glory of the Father and the peace of the world. I began this brief and prayerful conversation with you by looking into the Heart of Jesus at the Last Supper so that we might come to know Him better and to share more intimately with Him in the Holy Sacrifice of the Mass—His sacrifice made ours also by His loving will—the concrete expression of His longing in the Upper Room as He fulfilled His promise of life and love made at Capernaum.

> As for Jesus,
> The Will of the Father was and is His passion.
> It is forever His own will:
> "I do always the things that please my Father."
> As for us,
> It is His will we wish to accomplish.
> It is God we want to please.

We find His will for our union with Him and with one another through Him within His Church, made known to us by those to whom He has entrusted the shepherding of His people. The careful and reverent preparations for the celebration of the Eucharist—echoing the preparations He ordered for the Last Supper—are set up for the whole Church in the instructions issued by the Holy See. We are not at liberty to change any of these without injury to our unity. To do so is to be unfaithful to Jesus and to our people, creating external divisions which may end up in tragic separations—thus dividing the Body of Christ! The Eucharist is *ours*, not *mine!* It is the *Lord's* Supper with us, not *any* supper! *He* speaks! *He* gives! We gratefully accept. It is *our* Eucharist!

But all external preparations are of little or no avail, if the heart is not ready to receive the Lord. St. Paul warns that those who eat the Body of the Lord and drink His Blood unworthily do it to their condemnation. Hence, reflection, prayer, examination of conscience, confession of sins and reception of the Sacrament of Reconciliation when needed—or out of simple devotion—are the principal preparations for fruitful participation in the Eucharist. This preparation is almost sure to guarantee the deep and intelligent understanding, together with the loving and humble acceptance, of the instructions of the Church for the worthy celebration of the Eucharist—the loving worship of the Great God our Father, through Jesus Christ, our Lord, in the Holy Spirit.

Dearly beloved in Christ: the Instruction from the Holy See, *Inaestimabile Donum*, notes with great joy the many positive results of the liturgical reform in the Church, but it also manifests serious concern at the "varied and frequent abuses being reported from different parts of the Catholic world." After mentioning some of these abuses—and some of these are to be found in the Archdiocese of Boston, unfortunately—the Holy See's Instruction continues, "In these cases we are face to face with a real falsification of the Catholic Liturgy: 'One who offers worship to God on the Church's behalf in a way contrary to that which is laid down by the

Church with God-given authority and which is customary in the Church is guilty of falsification' (St. Thomas Aquinas, *Summa Theologiae*, 2-2, Q. 93, A. 1)."

Celebrating the Eucharist as I do all over this great and vast Archdiocese of Boston, I am happy to note the careful preparations for the Eucharist made almost everywhere. It is a great joy to be with our priests and people as they participate intelligently and devoutly in the Holy Sacrifice of the Mass. I am deeply grateful to our Archdiocesan Liturgical Commission, to our zealous priests, deacons, religious and laity who prepare so lovingly and so reverently for the Eucharistic Sacrifice. I know that the preparation of the heart has preceded the preparation of the altar and sanctuary. The one leads to the other. Faith leads the way. For the strength and beauty of your faith I thank the Father of all good gifts.

However, I do hear of abuses here and there within the Archdiocese of Boston. This pains me deeply as it must pain the Heart of Christ! With this in mind—and reflecting on what the Mystery of the Eucharist is in the life of the Church—I humbly join our Holy Father, Pope John Paul II, and beg God's forgiveness for myself, for you, my brother priests, and for all who in any way prepare and participate in the Holy Sacrifice of the Mass. In the words of the Holy Father, I beg the Lord for forgiveness

for everything which, for whatever reason, through whatever human weakness, impatience or negligence, and also through the at times partial, one-sided and erroneous applications of the directives of the Second Vatican Council, may have caused scandal and disturbance concerning the interpretation of the doctrine and the veneration due to this great Sacrament. And I pray the Lord Jesus that in the future we may avoid in our manner of dealing with this sacred Mystery anything which could weaken or disorient in any way the sense of reverence and love that exists in our faithful people.

May Christ Himself help us to follow the path of true renewal towards that fullness of life and Eucharistic worship whereby the Church is built up in that unity that she already possesses, and which she desires to bring to ever greater perfection for the glory of the living God and for the salvation of all mankind (*On the Mystery and Worship of the Eucharist*, no. 12).

My dear Fathers: I am sending you Pope John Paul II's Encyclical *On the Mystery and Worship of the Eucharist*, and the Instruction *Inaestimabile Donum* of the Sacred Congregation for the Sacraments and Divine Worship which followed it. Obviously both call for our prayerful meditation and study, if we are to be faithful to our duties as shepherds of God's people, leading them to "green pastures," to feed them with the bread of Truth and of Life for the greater unity of the Church and the success of the Gospel of Christ, according to the prayer and the will of Jesus, "May they be so completely one that the world will realize that it was you who sent me, and that I have loved them as much as you have loved me" (Jn. 17:23).

May the Queen of the Most Holy Rosary intercede for us as we join with her in prayer for the unity of the human family and for peace in the world through Christ in the Holy Eucharist.

With profound gratitude for your priestly zeal and cooperation, and with a hearty blessing, I am

Devotedly yours in Our Lord,
✠ Humberto Cardinal Medeiros
Archbishop of Boston

Mary Our Mother

—Given to the Mariological Society of America, Providence College, October 24, 1981.

I am profoundly grateful for the kind invitation extended to me by Fr. Morry, the Director of the New England Region of the Mariological Society of America, to deliver the Keynote Address at this meeting. I am delighted to be able to be with you on this occasion—an occasion which is an expression both of our interest in the theology of the Blessed Virgin Mary and of our love and veneration for her.

At the outset I want to congratulate the Mariological Society of America. During the more than three decades of its existence, its members have made a very valuable contribution to the solid and scientific development of the theology of Mary. You have my heartfelt admiration for your scholarly interest in Mariology, for your studies and writings which have done so much to promote a deeper understanding of an increase of devotion to Mary, the Mother of God and our Mother.

Your Regional meeting this year has special significance, for 1981 marks the 1550th Anniversary of the proclamation, at the Council of Ephesus, of Mary, Mother of God *(Theotokos)*. I suppose that all of us have read many times, with a tingling thrill in our souls, how, after the doctrine of the divine maternity had been defined by the Council, great throngs of the people of Ephesus, their hearts overflowing with joy, escorted the Council Fathers to their residences with boundless enthusiasm, singing songs of thanksgiving, carrying flaming torches and burning fragrant incense.

That was what we might call the pastoral reaction to the theological definition—indeed, the faith definition. And such is precisely the nature of my remarks this morning. My approach will be theological/pastoral, and my ultimate aim is to seek to foster an ever more fervent devotion to Mary, God's Mother and ours, through theological reflection upon who she is and what her function is in the divine plan of salvation. Specifically I would ask you to meditate with me on Mary's spiritual maternity of the human race and on Mary, the Mother of the Church. My particular point of view is the relationship that exists between Mary as the Mother of God and Mary as the Mother of mankind, between Mary as the Mother of God and Mary as the Mother of the Church.

Cornelius á Lapide (Cornelius Cornellisen van den Steen), the Flemish biblical exegete of the late 16th and early 17th centuries, in his celebrated commentary on Holy Scripture, has a strikingly beautiful passage on the Lord's last testament to His Mother and to St. John, as the dying Savior spoke from the cross on Calvary. I quote it now at some length, because it would be difficult to find another commentary on our Savior's words so tender and so touching. Cornelius á Lapide writes: "Christ pierced her heart with the wound both of love and sorrow, for He meant: 'Mother, I am, as thou seest, dying on the cross. I shall not be able to be with thee, to attend to thee, to provide for thee, and assist thee as I have hitherto done. I assign to thee, in my place, John to be thy son: a man in the place of God, a disciple for a master, an adopted son instead of thine own by nature; in order that he, as a virgin, and most beloved by thee as the Virgin Mother of God, may bestow on thee all the solace, and all the devotion, which both thy dignity and thy advancing age demand, and which the zeal and love of John promises and assures to thee....'"

Cornelius á Lapide then comments on the words of our Savior to St. John. *"Behold thy mother!* And the mother also of thy fellow-Apostles. Accordingly all the faithful, as Saint Bernard teaches, should betake themselves to her with full confidence and love. She is the Eve of the faithful, the mother of all living, to whom the wise and saints of every age betake themselves" *(The Great Commentary of Cornelius á Lapide*, trans. by T. W. Mossman, St. John's Gospel, ch. 19).

Universally today (and for many, many centuries), theologians and the faithful in general see in St. John at the foot of the cross the representative of the entire human race. All of us are Mary's spiritual children, for she was given to us by God as our Mother.

When the dying Christ spoke to St. John as the representative of all mankind, Mary's spiritual maternity over the human race was divinely reaffirmed. What I mean is that Mary's spiritual motherhood does not rest solely on this biblical passage. The doctrine that Mary is the Mother of the entire human race has very deep theological roots, going back to the Incarnation itself. And so, the words of our Divine Savior on Calvary, spoken to the Blessed Virgin and to St. John, do not constitute Mary as the Mother of the human race. Rather, they are a sign or manifestation of Mary's spiritual motherhood over all mankind, which flows from the association of Mary in mankind's redemption by her Son, Jesus Christ, the Second Person of the Blessed Trinity made man.

The Second Vatican Council teaches us that Mary "is a mother to us in the order of grace" (*Lumen gentium*, no. 61). Further, "this maternity of Mary in the order of grace began with the consent which she gave in faith at the Annunciation and which she sustained without wavering beneath the cross. This maternity will last without interruption until the eternal fulfillment of all the elect" (*ibid.*, no. 62).

We know from the words of our Divine Lord to Nicodemus that the way in which we are initiated into the supernatural life is the way of spiritual birth. "Unless one is born of water and the Spirit he cannot enter the kingdom of God" (Jn. 3:5). Only if a person is reborn into the supernatural life can he become a sharer in the divine nature and ultimately attain eternal life. The sanctifying grace which is the principle of the supernatural life has been won for mankind through the sufferings and death of Jesus Christ. By His merits we are granted supernatural life, which then grows and matures and develops until the complete flourishing of that life in the Beatific Vision. The words of St. Paul are verified in us: "If any one is in Christ, he is a new creation" (2 Cor. 5:17).

How is Mary our spiritual Mother? Since the essence of motherhood involves the transmission of life to a new being through the process of generation, Mary is our spiritual Mother because she had a share in our spiritual rebirth through her association with her Divine Son Jesus Christ in the redemption. Mary is not our Mother in a merely symbolic sense. She is not our Mother merely because she is an intercessor with God in our behalf. But she is our Mother because of her cooperation in the work of our redemption—that is, in the work by which we are enabled to be born to the supernatural life. In the words of Pope Pius XI: "She, by the very fact that she brought forth the Redeemer of the human race, is also in a

manner the most tender Mother of us all, whom
Christ our Lord deigned to have as His brothers" (Encyclical, *Lux veritatis*). Thus, Mary's
spiritual motherhood of the human race is
linked essentially to Mary's physical motherhood of the Redeemer.

Pope St. Pius X, in his Encyclical *Ad diem
illum*, was very explicit on this point. "For is not
Mary the Mother of Christ? She is therefore our
Mother also.... The Virgin conceived the Eternal Son not only that He might be made man by
taking His human nature from her, but also that
by means of the nature assumed from her He
might be the Savior of men.... Consequently,
Mary, bearing in her womb the Savior, may be
said to have borne also those whose life was
contained in the life of the Savior. All of us,
therefore, who are united with Christ and are,
as the Apostle says, 'Members of His body,
made from His flesh and His bones,' have come
forth from the womb of Mary as a body united to
its head. Hence, in a spiritual and mystical
sense, we are called children of Mary, and she is
the Mother of us all."

Theologians are not in complete agreement
as to when in the history of theology Mary's
spiritual motherhood of the human race was first
written about in explicit terms. This is neither
the time nor the place to enter into a discussion
of this point. Whatever may be said as to when
theologians and spiritual writers first began
explicitly to call Mary the Mother of the human
race, one cannot overlook the many indications

and adumbrations of this doctrine, going back almost to the very dawn of Christianity. Let me refer expressly to only one author, Origen († 254), the Alexandrian biblical exegete and theologian. In the preface to his commentary on the Gospel of St. John, Origen points out that the dying Christ declared to Mary that John was her son. He did not merely say: "Behold, this one is also thy son." And so, keeping in mind that Jesus was Mary's only Son, we must interpret Christ's words as being equivalent to this: "Behold John is the Jesus Whom you have borne." But how is this possible? Origen explains: "Whoever is perfect no longer lives himself, but Christ lives in him. Since Christ lives in him, it is said to Mary of him: 'Behold thy Son, Christ.'" In other words, it is the fact that John and every other person in the state of grace are one with Christ—it is that fact that Jesus implied in His words to Mary on Calvary, and that constitutes the foundation of the spiritual maternity of Mary.

Perhaps this is an interpretation of our Divine Savior's words to His Mother on Calvary, to which we have not given much reflection. Ordinarily we look upon St. John on Calvary as representing the human race—which, of course, is true. But a more profound interpretation of Christ's words is that offered by Origen—in a sense, John is Christ, because, through the sanctifying grace in his soul he is in some way identified with Christ. Consequently, it is precisely insofar as Mary is the Mother of

Him Who was born to redeem mankind and
thus to bestow sanctifying grace in the souls
of human beings, that she is John's spiritual
Mother and our spiritual Mother. For by sanctifying grace we are born to the supernatural life,
and, by becoming sharers in the divine nature,
in some way we become identified with Christ
Himself. Hence the Second Vatican Council can
say that Mary "is a mother to us in the order of
grace" (*Lumen gentium*, no. 61), and can further
specify that "this maternity of Mary in the order
of grace began with the consent which she gave
in faith at the Annunciation and which she
sustained without wavering beneath the cross"
(*ibid.*, no. 62).

Much attention has been given in recent
years to the title "Mary, Mother of the Church."
As all of us know, our Holy Father, Pope Paul VI
—whom I love to call Paul the Great—at the
close of the third session of the Second Vatican
Council, solemnly proclaimed Mary to be the
Mother of the Church.

Mary is, of course, as we have seen, the
spiritual Mother of the entire human race. But
she is, in a special way, Mother of the Church
founded by her Divine Son, Jesus Christ.

On November 21, 1964, Pope Paul VI
delivered an inspiring address, concluding the
third session of the Second Vatican Council. (I
was blessed to be there and to hear it.) It was an
address in which our Holy Father expressed
profound thanks to God for the blessings which
He had bestowed upon the Council, and espe-

cially upon its third session. (For the English
translation of the address of Pope Paul VI
concluding the third session of the Second
Vatican Council, cf. *Catholic Mind,* January,
1965, pp. 56-64). The Pope spoke of the admiration in his heart for the participants in the
Council, "gathered together in one place, in one
sentiment, with one prayer, one faith, one
charity on their lips and in their hearts." He
described the Council as an "incomparable
assembly entirely intent on proclaiming the
glory of the Father, the Son and the Holy
Spirit." And then in a passage of rare lyrical
beauty our Holy Father went on: "This is an
assembly of men free like none other from self-
interest, and engaged in giving witness to divine
truths; men as we are, weak and fallible, but
convinced of being able to pronounce truths
that admit neither contradiction nor termina-
tion; men who are sons of our own times and our
own earth, yet above time and above earth, in
order to take upon our shoulders the burdens of
our brothers and to lead them to spiritual
salvation. This we do with a love greater than
these same hearts that house it, with a strained
effort that might seem foolhardy, but which is
full of serene trust in its search for the meaning
of human life and history to give it value,
greatness, beauty, union in Christ, only in
Christ our Lord!"

Going back over the work of the third
session of the Council, the Pope emphasized
especially the importance of the Constitution on

the Nature of the Church, *Lumen gentium* (which he was then promulgating), declaring that "from now on we can enjoy greater understanding of divine thought relative to the Mystical Body of Christ...." The purpose of all the work and all the study of the Council with respect to the Church "has been to provide a fair treatment of every part, every function and every aim of the Mystical Body."

The Pope laid particular stress on *Lumen gentium* "as a completion of the First Vatican Ecumenical Council." "It would seem to us," he declared, "that the best commentary is that through this promulgation nothing in traditional doctrine is really changed. What Christ wants, we also want. That which was, remains. What the Church has taught for centuries, we likewise teach. The only difference is that what was simply lived previously is now declared expressly; what was uncertain has been clarified; what was meditated on, discussed and in part disagreed with, now reaches a serene formulation."

I have dwelt at some length upon this address of our Holy Father, because, in my view, it is only in this setting of the Church as the Mystical Body of Christ, restated by Pope Paul VI in this address, that we can truly appreciate the significance of the magnificent papal declaration that occurred toward the end of the address. It would seem that our Holy Father's words worked up to this declaration as a climax. The Pope spoke of Mary, "the holy

Virgin," as "the protectress of the present Council, the witness of our toil, our most kindly adviser." He recalled that in the previous year a solemn act of homage had been paid to her in the gathering in the Liberian Basilica "round the image venerated with the glorious title of *'Salus Populi Romani.'*" He explained the homage of the Council, in the present year, to be "much more precious and significant." He declared the "crown and summit" of *Lumen gentium* to be "a whole chapter dedicated to our Lady"—the first time "that an Ecumenical Council presents such a vast synthesis of the Catholic doctrine regarding the place which the Blessed Mary occupies in the mystery of Christ and of the Church."

The reality of the Church, as Pope Paul VI pointed out, does not consist only in its hierarchical structure, in its liturgy, in its Sacraments, in its juridical ordinances. Rather, "the intimate, the primary source of its sanctifying effectiveness is to be sought in its mystic union with Christ—a union which we cannot conceive as separate from her who is the Mother of the Word Incarnate, and whom Jesus Christ Himself wanted closely united to Himself for our salvation."

Having established the context of the Church, the Mystical Body of Christ, as the *situs* for the proper perspective of Mary's role and Mary's function, the Pope then went on to state specifically and expressly that "the loving contemplation of the marvels worked by God in

His Holy Mother must find its proper perspective *in the vision of the Church.* And knowledge of the true Catholic doctrine on Mary will always be *a key to the exact understanding of the mystery of Christ and of the Church."* (Emphasis added.)

And now, in this "most solemn and appropriate moment" the Pope, in response to those Council Fathers who were "pressing for an explicit declaration, at this Council, of the motherly role of the Virgin among the Christian people," consecrated a title in honor of Mary "which is particularly dear to us because it sums up in an admirable synthesis the privileged position recognized by the Council for the Virgin in the Holy Church."

Then came the climatic moment with the solemn proclamation from the lips of the Sovereign Pontiff. "Therefore, for the glory of the Virgin Mary and for our own consolation, we proclaim the Most Blessed Mary Mother of the Church...."

The desire that Mary formally be declared "Mother of the Church" was not something new in the heart of Pope Paul VI. He had given expression to this desire at the end of the second session of the Council. Referring to the difference of views within the Council (On October 29, 1963, a vote had been taken as to whether the schema on Mary should be included in *Lumen gentium* or should be issued as a separate document: 1,114 Fathers voted in favor of the insertion; 1,074 Fathers voted in

favor of a separate document)—referring to the
difference of views within the Council, Pope
Paul VI stated: "We hope that this Council will
give the very best solution to our problem about
the schema of the Blessed Virgin Mary, so that
the Assembly in unanimous consent and with
greatest devotion will acknowledge the eminent
place proper to the Mother of God in the Holy
Church—in that Church which is the principal
matter of this Council. We say that, after Christ,
her place is the most prominent in the Church,
yet closest to us; so that we may honor her with
the name 'Mother of the Church,' to her glory
and our benefit" (cf. *Marian Studies,* XXXI, 69).

What is the theological justification for this
title "Mary, Mother of the Church"?

The Pope finds its justification "in the very
dignity of the Mother of the Word Incarnate."
The Pope's explanation proceeds in this way.
The basis for Mary's special relationship with
Christ and for her role in the economy of
salvation brought about by Christ is her divine
maternity. The fact that Mary is the Mother of
Christ Who is God, undergirds the whole
structure of all her relationships with Christ and
with His providential plan for the salvation of
the human race.

In the same way it is the divine maternity
which "also constitutes the principal basis for
the relations between Mary and the Church."
Why is this so? Precisely because she is the
Mother of Him Who, "from the time of His
Incarnation in her virginal womb, joined to

Himself as head His Mystical Body which is the Church." Thus, Mary is not only the spiritual Mother of each individual who is born into the supernatural life by sanctifying grace; but she is, in a special way, the Mother of all the faithful who —from a communitarian point of view—make up the Mystical Body of Christ which is the Church.

The Pope went on to a pastoral exhortation urging devotion to Mary, and insisting on the close links between Mary and all mankind. Indeed, "in her, the entire Church, in its incomparable variety of life and of work, attains the most authentic form of the perfect imitation of Christ." Yet it must never be forgotten that "Mary, the humble handmaid of the Lord, exists only in relation to God and to Christ, our sole Mediator and Redeemer." So, too, "devotion to Mary, far from being an end in itself, is instead a means essentially ordained to orient souls to Christ and thus unite them with the Father in the love of the Holy Spirit."

In summary, the core of the Pope's teaching on the theological justification for proclaiming Mary to be the Mother of the Church is this: Just as the maternity of Mary constitutes the basis for her special relationship to the physical Christ, so also it constitutes the basis for her special relationship to the mystical Christ, which is the Church.

Permit me to make two parenthetical remarks to you, who, as theologians, are particularly interested in the area of Mariology. First:

It seems to me that there has not yet been
sufficient attention given to a very significant
assertion of Pope Paul VI in the address which
we have been considering. Let me suggest
serious study and deep exploration of the Pope's
statement: "...knowledge of the true Catholic
doctrine on Mary will always be a key to the
exact understanding of the mystery of Christ
and of the Church." Time and again the Virgin
Mary has been studied from the point of view of
the mystery of Christ and of the Church, since it
is through the mystery of Christ and of the
Church that we can better understand Mary.
But what are the implications to be drawn from
the Pope's statement that the way to understand
better the mystery of Christ and of the Church
is precisely through an understanding of Catholic doctrine on Mary? Surely here is a field for
scholarly and pastoral theological exploration.

My second parenthetical remark has to do
with the ecumenical dimension of the title
"Mary, Mother of the Church." It is the well-
known non-Catholic theologian, Professor John
Macquarrie, who has stated that the best clue to
the interpretation of Mary's place in the New
Testament teaching is afforded by the title
"Mother of the Church." And the same theologian has further declared that it is his belief that
this title "more than any other, provides an
interpretation of Mary's place, on which Roman
Catholics, Orthodox, Anglicans and Protestants
could agree" (quoted in *Marian Studies*, XXIII,

57). Need I emphasize the opportunity given here for dialogue and discussion?

Subsequent to his proclamation at the end of the third session of the Second Vatican Council, on several later occasions during his pontificate, Pope Paul VI spoke of Mary as the Mother of the Church. For instance, in his Apostolic Exhortation *Signum magnum,* issued on May 13, 1967, our Holy Father referred to his previous proclamation of Mary as Mother of the Church, and then went on to explain, in a more pastoral and hortatory way, why it is that Mary is the Mother of the Church. "Mary is the Mother of the Church—not only because she is the Mother of Jesus Christ and His closest associate in 'the new economy...when the Son of God takes on human nature from her in order to free men from sin by the mysteries of His flesh,' but also because she 'shines as the model of virtues for the whole community of the elect.' No human mother can limit her task solely to the procreation of new human beings; she must also undertake the task of nourishing them and educating them. So it is with the Blessed Virgin Mary. She participated in her Son's sacrifice for our redemption in such intimate fashion that He designated her the Mother not only of John the Apostle but also—it seems legitimate to say this—of the human race, which he somehow represented. Now in heaven she carries on her motherly role, helping to nourish and foster the divine life in the souls of redeemed men. This truth is a most consoling one, and God in His wisdom had made it an integral part of the mystery of human salvation. Hence all Christians must hold to it in faith" (TPS, vol. 12, no. 3, p. 280).

In his famous "Credo of the People of God," issued on June 30, 1968, Pope Paul VI summarized Catholic teaching on Mary. Here again he specifically referred to Mary as Mother of the Church. "We believe that the Blessed Mother of God, the New Eve, Mother of the Church, continues, in Heaven, her maternal role with regard to Christ's members, cooperating with the birth and growth of divine life in the souls of the redeemed" (TPS, vol. 13, no. 3, p. 278).

It seems to me to be clear that there can be no genuine understanding of what Mary as the Mother of the Church means and what the theological justification of this title really is, apart from an understanding of the Pauline concept of the intimate union that exists between the Head and the members of Christ's Mystical Body—which is the Church.

In studying and reflecting upon the words of Pope Paul VI proclaiming and explaining Mary to be the Mother of the Church, one cannot but go back to the magnificent encyclical of Pope Pius XII, *Mystici corporis.* In that encyclical our Holy Father at first hints at the relationship between Mary and the Church ("Within her virginal womb Christ our Lord already bore the exalted title of Head of the Church"), and then goes on to state specifically: "Thus she who corporally was the Mother of our

Head, through the added title of pain and glory became spiritually the mother of all His members" (For the English translation of the encyclical, cf. *Encyclical Letter on the Mystical Body of Christ.*)

Perhaps we might digress here for a moment to point out how concisely Pope Pius XII in the encyclical *Mystici corporis* sums up the many phases of the relationship between Mary and the entire human race. It was "in the name of the whole human race," he says, that Mary "gave her consent for a 'spiritual marriage between the Son of God and human nature.'"

Furthermore, in giving birth to Jesus Christ, Mary "brought Him forth as source of all supernatural life...." Surely it would seem to follow that since He is the Source and Author of the supernatural life of grace, she is our Mother and precisely because she is the Mother of the Source and Author of our supernatural life.

What a rich font for meditation is to be found in the thought of Pope Pius XII—not only that Mary, united with her Son, offered Him on Golgotha to the Eternal Father for all the children of Adam (in some way, therefore, a Co-Redemptrix), but even that "her mother's rights and her mother's love were included in the holocaust." In other words, in some mysterious way—precisely because of her intimate relationship with her Son—she not only offered Him on Golgotha, but she was also, in some sense, a victim with Him on Golgotha. And in virtue of this role the influence of her victimhood continues to be felt in the members of the Mystical Body—precisely because of "her mother's care and ardent love." Listen to the words of Pope Pius XII: "Bearing with courage and confidence the tremendous burden of her sorrows and desolation, truly the Queen of Martyrs, she more than all the faithful 'filled up those things that are wanting of the suffering of Christ…for His body, which is the Church'; and she continued to show for the Mystical Body of Christ…the same mother's care and ardent love with which she clasped the Infant Jesus to her warm and nourishing breast."

It was only natural that, once Mary was proclaimed Mother of the Church by papal decree (though, of course, for centuries the Church had taught this truth, at least in an implicit way), this title should become the object of ever-increasing investigation and study. I urge you, as theologians concerned especially with the theology of Mary, to continue that investigation and that study.

The limitations of time forbid any lengthy elaboration on my part on this occasion. But I do want to call your attention to the fact that several important insights have emerged in the past few years.

I find extremely interesting and thought-provoking, for example, the concept, found in the Homily of Pope John Paul II delivered at Ephesus on November 30, 1979, wherein he explains that in the very Incarnation the Church itself began to exist after the manner of a seed, because present there were the Redeemer and the first of the redeemed. And hence Mary is truly the Mother of the Church. In the words of our Holy Father: "In saying her *'Let it be done'* Mary not only becomes the Mother of the historical Christ; her action also makes her the Mother of the whole Christ, the 'Mother of the Church.' St. Anselm remarks that 'from the moment of her *Let it be done* Mary began to carry us all in her womb.' That is why, says St. Leo the Great, 'the birth of the Head is also the birth of the body.' St. Ephraem, too, has a beautiful phrase describing this point: Mary, he says, is 'the soil in which the Church was sown.' And at that point of time, from the moment when the Virgin became the Mother of the Word Incarnate, the Church also began to exist—secretly, after the manner of a seed—in her essence as the Mystical Body. For there are present here the Redeemer and the first of the redeemed" (TPS, vol. 25, no. 1, p. 30).

I have endeavored in these reflections today to open up some avenues of thought with respect to Mary the spiritual Mother of the entire human race and Mary the Mother of the Church. And to what should all of this lead in our everyday lives, from a pastoral viewpoint?

It seems to me that Mary's essential role in the work of your salvation and mine, by reason of her intimate association with the redeeming Christ, should prompt us to recognize the importance of her function in the distribution also of sanctifying grace. This is a function that did not come to an end either with Christ's death on Calvary or with Mary's Assumption into heaven. It is not entirely true to say that Mary was our Mother, or that Mary was the Mother of the Church. Rather, she *is* our Mother; she *is* the Mother of the Church. It is our loving and tender and compassionate and understanding Mother whom we must honor, and in whom we must confide, and in whom we must place our trust. It is to our Mother that we must turn, now and at the hour of our death. And with absolute confidence—for never was it known that anyone who fled to her protection, implored her help or sought her intercession, was left unaided.

Mary is the Mother of all mankind, and Mary is, in a special way, the Mother of the Church. Each one of us here, each in a different way—and indeed every member of the Church —has a God-given mission to fulfill. But the goal of all is a common goal: "to maintain this dynamic link between the mystery of redemption and each human being" as Pope John Paul II explained in his first encyclical *Redemptor hominis*. Let us close with the words of Pope John Paul II, for they are indeed significant. "If we are conscious of this task," declared our Holy Father, "we shall better understand, I think, what it means for the Church to be mother, but also what it means for the Church at all times, but especially today, to be herself in need of a mother.... Mary is the Mother of the Church because, due to the ineffable choice the eternal Father made of her and to the extraordinary action in her of the Spirit of Love, she gave human life to the Son of God 'for whom and through whom all things exist and from whom the entire people of God have received grace and the dignity of election. Her own Son expressly willed to extend the scope of her motherhood—and to do so in a way that would be clear to every heart and soul—when from the cross, He gave to her as a son the disciple whom He especially loved. The Holy Spirit indicated to her that after the Ascension of our Lord she should remain in the upper room and wait with the Apostles until Pentecost, the day on which the Church had her visible birth and came forth, as it were, from the darkness into the light. Since then, all generations of disciples and of all who confess and love Christ have spiritually taken her to themselves as their Mother, as John the Apostle had done. Thus, from the very beginning, that is, from the moment of the Annunciation, she has been an integral part of the history of salvation and the mission of the Church" (TPS, vol. 24, no. 2, pp. 144-145).

Let us, then, strike the keynote of this meeting with the simple but fervent plea: "Mary, Mother of God and our Mother—Mary, Mother of the Church, pray for us."

---

1. Available from any of the addresses at the end of this book.

Renewal
of Marian Piety

May, 1971

My dear brothers and sisters:

The month of May prompts us to direct
our thoughts to the Virgin Mother of God.
Although it is not a liturgical season like
Christmas or Easter, still by provident
design and ancient custom it belongs to
the devotional life of the Church. As one
Maytime hymn expresses it: "To the fairest
of creatures be the fairest of seasons, sweet
May." May spreads out its glorious beauty
in bright green fields and bursting lilacs;
its soft air freshens our city streets. Little
wonder that lovers of our Lady have so
readily reserved this month to honor the
Mother of God.

Mary, "the Mother of Jesus" (Mk. 6:8)
does not figure largely in New Testament
writings. The event primarily proclaimed
in the Scriptures is the death and resurrection of her Son. St. Paul was among the
earliest to reflect upon her part in God's

mysterious plan of salvation: "But when the time had fully come, God sent forth His Son born of a woman, born under the law" (Gal. 4:4). For Christianity is at once the unity of the Spirit and the Word made flesh. In the person of Jesus, this unity is a permanent gift of God's grace—a unity between heaven and earth, liberty and law, body and spirit. Mary, the handmaid of the Lord, welcomed and received this incarnate Word both in her flesh and in her heart. Through her personal assent she became by faith the Virgin Mother of God and the first redeemed among men.

Among the early Fathers, St. Ambrose was the first to express another dimension of Mary's intimate relationship with Christ when he spoke of her as "Maria Typus Ecclesiae"—Mary, the Model of the Church. The Church is not a place, but a happening; it is an event by which union in Christ is constantly taking place among men. Mary who stood at the decisive moment in saving history, accepting by her personal act God's saving Son, thus becomes the supreme instance of that continuing event which is the Church. What the Church is and does is seen in its most complete purity in Mary's total acceptance of God's grace for herself and for all mankind.

Recent theologians have elaborated still further on the ecclesial character of Mary's mission in the Church. They see her calling us as clerics and laity to the common apostolate of her Son. Her "fiat" to God stands in protest against extreme divisions of clericalism and laicism, of institution and people, of action and prayer. Her openness to God claimed her whole person, her innermost being, in a loving assent to the Spirit. It was intensely personal and charismatic, and in this respect, Mary reproaches that clericalism which is simply institutional, official and authoritarian. But likewise her silent submission to legally prescribed practices of her day, her self-effacement in her Son's public life, her standing beneath the cross, and her unpretentious presence at Pentecost equally repudiate that laicism that would deny that the Spirit ever needs to become incarnate and that resents each and every appeal to obedience, humility, and sacrifice for others. Such division was harmoniously reconciled in Mary's total assent to God, and she continues to resolve our present differences through her abiding intercession for the Church.

The Fathers of Vatican II likewise sought a balance between an exaggerated Mariology which exposes itself to theological criticism, on the one hand, and a false irenism which sacrifices truth and suggests little love for the Blessed Mother of God. Much of the press coverage at the time of the Council gave a false impression that the Fathers were actually divided among themselves as for or against our Lady. A study of the Constitution on the Church, however, shows that the Fathers agreed that Marian beliefs and practices should be grounded in the central mystery of Christ and His Church, and not appear as an independent outgrowth or addition to our faith. They knew the pastoral value that such an approach would have upon our faith and upon the orientation of our devotional life. Consequently, while they insisted upon the unique mediation of Christ and the direct union of all the faithful with the saving Lord (Lumen Gentium, 60), at the same time they spoke of our Lady as: "Mary, the Model of the Church." Pope Paul VI addressed the Council in these words: "We wish above all that this fact be shown in full light: that Mary, humble servant of the Lord, is completely oriented and related to God and to Jesus Christ, our only Mediator and Savior" (L'Osservatore Romano, November 22, 1964).

Authentic piety, and, above all, Marian piety must always lead to Christ who is the source and goal of our spiritual life. Thus, Mary's powerful assistance waits for us at the heart of God's unfolding mystery of man's redemption within the Church.

As the Model of the Church, Mary, now radiant in glory, stands before us as a promise and pledge of the Church in its final perfection. "In the bodily and spiritual glory which she possesses in heaven, the Mother of Jesus continues in this present world as the image and first flowering of the Church as she is to be perfected in the world to come. Likewise, Mary shines forth on earth, until the day of the Lord shall come as a sign of sure hope and solace for the pilgrim people of God" (Lumen Gentium, 68).

This ecclesial image of Mary explains her maternal role as "our mother in the order of grace." As a loving mother, she conceived, brought forth, and nourished Christ. "She presented Him to the Father in the temple, and was united with Him in suffering as He died on the cross. In an utterly singular way she cooperated by her obedience, faith, hope and burning charity in the Savior's work" (Lumen Gentium, 61). By her total dedication to God's plan, Mary has become the Mother of us all. This privileged position of hers arises neither from divine necessity nor from any merit of ours.

It arises from God's unfathomable love. It depends totally upon Him and derives all its power from Him. As Jesus Himself reminds us, "My mother and my brothers are those who hear the word of God and put it into practice" (Lk. 8:21).

The Church's devotions to Mary have periodically taken on various local and cultural forms. The rosary, the Angelus, scapulars and litanies are dear to all of us. Marian shrines and May devotions ever serve to suggest the many titles of our Lady whom we hail as "Refuge of sinners," "Comforter of the afflicted," and "Cause of our joy." What is important for us to bear in mind in these and other devotions, as the Council Fathers warned, are the dangers of passing emotion and empty sentimentality. Genuine devotion to Mary is necessarily rooted in faith and moves to a clear understanding of her role in Christ's Church, and culminates in a filial love that seeks to imitate her virtues (Lumen Gentium, 67).

Our traditional May devotions to our Lady appear to have originated spontaneously with chanting processions of children through the streets to the various Marian shrines of Rome. Many of our parishes preserve this annual May procession and decorate our Lady's altar with flowers and hymns of praise. The rosary of our Lady has also been a popular and almost universal devotion in the Church. It is recited faithfully by all ages and in all walks of life; in our city churches and at our suburban shrines, on retreats, in hospitals, and at vigils for our beloved dead. The rosary gradually developed with the Church's understanding of Christ's incarnation, passion and resurrection, along with popular Marian piety and a desire to give the unlettered faithful a closer participation in the Church's liturgy. The rosary was even called the "poor man's breviary," its fifteen decades substituting for the one hundred fifty psalms (chanted in Latin by clerics) and divided into antiphons to Mary, each of which recalled her many mysteries in Christ. The rosary is both vocal and mental prayer, a summary of our Christian faith, a compendium of our liturgical life.

On two recent occasions, the Catholic Church has witnessed Mary solemnly urging us to pray her rosary. At Lourdes and Fatima especially, she revealed herself to peasant children and, through countless miracles and processions, she still appeals to us to pray with her the joyful, sorrowful and glorious mysteries of our life in Christ. The Church has acknowledged these apparitions as authentic and has consecrated these Marian shrines to remind us of our Lady's plea for penance and prayer. We would not be "thinking with the Church" if we allowed ourselves out of pride or indifference to disregard these messages from God.

Every Pope since then has dedicated a special encyclical letter extolling the intercessary role of Mary and advocating the daily recitation of her rosary. And what they preached, they daily practiced. Pope John XXIII religiously said all fifteen decades of the rosary every day. Pope Paul VI has told us to value highly "the pious practices and exercises directed to the Blessed Virgin and approved over the centuries by the teaching authority of the Church."

In the Litany of Loretto, the Queen of the Most Holy Rosary is also honored as Queen of Peace. During the month of May, with our nation still fighting a war, we might do well to ponder and to pray with Mary for "the things that are really for our peace." Let each one of us examine this question personally. There are limits to what political and social programs can accomplish. Our problems go much deeper than war, injustice, and poverty. These major problems and others—like drug addiction and sexual exploitation—are rooted in man's basic predicament of prejudice, violence, ignorance and ambition. The cause of this predicament is not political, but theological, and the judgment of God upon every sinful man cannot be wished away. Any political or social dream that would do away with violence and oppression, without reconciling each man to God, is doomed to failure. We do not wish to retard in any way the pursuit of social justice in our land, but neither can we neglect each man's personal debt to God and to his brothers in Christ. Mary teaches us just how great is our debt and how vast are our brothers' needs. Her rosary invites us into all the mysteries of life, and awakens in us a heart more like hers than our own—a heart open to God's will and to the mission of Christ's Church among men.

We have tried so many other things, and still there is no peace. Perhaps in our anxiety for solutions we have forgotten the most powerful force of all. The power of God and God's ability to change us from within—as He did for Mary—and to enable us "to walk in the newness of Christ's life." The kingdom His Son came to establish on earth and which the Church continues to maintain among men is the kingdom of men's hearts. It is a kingdom which cannot be invaded, unless each man freely surrenders it, as Mary did, with trust. And her trust in God was not given in vain.

As individuals and as a nation we have little time for God and even less confidence in prayer. We search for beauty, but not the good. We have almost lost our sense of what is sacred. Let us during this month, so dear to Mary, open our hearts in prayer for peace. Let us approach Mary, so dear to her Son, through the rosary and make this month a real beginning of that "peace which the world cannot give."

The Rosary

Feast of the Holy Rosary
October 7, 1979

Dearly beloved in Christ:

When Pope John Paul II spoke so feelingly of the Rosary before thousands of the faithful gathered in St. Peter's Square, and disclosed to them that the Rosary was his favorite prayer, he was reaffirming once again for the whole Church to hear the oft-repeated teaching of many of his predecessors in the See of Peter. "So wonderfully simple," our Holy Father declared of Mary's beads, "yet so wonderfully profound" (*L'Osservatore Romano*, English Edition, November 9, 1978).

Yes, wonderfully simple! For centuries men and women of every economic and social condition and intellectual attainment have found in the Rosary a source of intimate spiritual union with Jesus through Mary. With her as a tender Mother and patient teacher, they have found the secrets of the merciful Heart of Christ. They have found how easy for them—and how effective—is the way of Mary's Rosary to the profound mystery of the salvation we have in Christ Jesus. Indeed, did not our Blessed Mother herself commend the Rosary to Bernadette at Lourdes and to Lucy at Fatima as a means to achieve inner peace and even peace among men in the whole world?

Joyce Kilmer speaks of it beautifully:

"There is one harp that any hand can play,
And from its strings what harmonies arise!
There is one song that any mouth can say,
A song that lingers when all singing dies—
When on their beads our Mother's children
    pray,
Immortal music charms the grateful skies."
            (Joyce Kilmer: *The Rosary*)

The Holy Father says that the Rosary is wonderfully profound. Brilliant minds have seen in the Rosary a compendium of the truths of our Christian faith.

The eminent theologian, Romano Guardini, has described the Rosary as a "perfect blending of progressing contemplation with recurring prayer theme" *(Prayer in Practice,* Image Books Ed., 1963, p. 95).

The great master of the spiritual life, Abbot Marmion, wrote of the Rosary: "Each mystery of the life of Christ contains a secret virtue for those who meditate on it with faith and love. In the mysteries of the Rosary...Christ is not only a Model for us but a living source of sanctity" (cf.

M. M. Philipon, *The Spiritual Doctrine of Dom Marmion*, Sands & Co., London and Glasgow, 1957, p. 215).

The contemporary theologian, Louis Bouyer, declared of the Rosary: "It is probably the most generally fruitful development achieved by the inventive genius of medieval piety in the West, lending itself equally well to satisfying the elementary piety of unlettered people...and to bringing the most meditative souls to the summits of the life of prayer" ("The Rosary," *Our Sunday Visitor*, October 2, 1966, p. 3).

Aptly has our Holy Father described his favorite prayer, the Rosary: "so wonderfully simple, yet so wonderfully profound."

Pope John Paul II has also characterized the Rosary as being, in a sense, "a prayer commentary on the final chapter of the Constitution *Lumen gentium*, the chapter which deals with the wonderful presence of the Mother of God in the Mystery of Christ and the Church" *(L'Osservatore Romano*, English edition, November 9, 1978).

In proclaiming the faith of the Catholic Church, the Fathers of the Second Vatican Council express the belief that "Mary has by grace been exalted above all angels and men to a place second only to her Son, as the most holy Mother of God who was involved in the mysteries of Christ" *(Lumen gentium*, no. 66). The Council teaches that while surpassing all men and angels in dignity because of the gift of grace received from God, Mary is still of the "race of Adam...and is at the same time united to all those who are to be saved; indeed, 'she is clearly the Mother of the members of Christ...since she has by her charity joined in bringing about the birth of believers in the Church, who are members of its head.' Wherefore she is hailed as preeminent and as a wholly unique member of the Church and as its type and outstanding model in faith and charity. The Catholic Church taught by the Holy Spirit, honors her with filial affection and devotion as a most beloved Mother" *(Lumen gentium,* no. 53).

Far from diminishing devotion and devotions and practices of piety to our Lady, as some have unwisely suggested, the Fathers of the Council admonish "all the sons of the Church that the cult, especially the liturgical cult, of the Blessed Virgin, be generously fostered and that the practices and exercises of devotion towards her, recommended by the teaching authority of the Church in the course of the centuries be highly esteemed, and that those decrees which were given in the early days regarding the cult of the images of Christ, the Blessed Virgin and the saints, be religiously observed" *(Lumen gentium,* no. 67).

Any downplaying of the place of Mary in our faith and of her Rosary in our devotional life, dearly beloved brothers and sisters in Christ, is not the work of the Second Vatican Council but the foolish or even wicked scheming of the enemies of the Mother of Christ and of His

Church. Because we are faithful to the teachings of the Church and of the Council, and because we want to grow in our understanding of the mysteries of our salvation so that we may the better promote the advancement of the Kingdom of Christ, we humbly ask His Immaculate Mother to lead us ever so briefly together through the mysteries of our Redemption with the eyes of faith fixed on the teachings of the Vatican Council.

We contemplate the mysteries of our salvation, of God's infinite love for us as revealed in Christ Jesus Our Lord, together with Mary His Mother, who was an integral part of God's loving plan from beginning to end, and without whom it would not have taken place. Seeing all of this through the eyes of the Woman of Faith, we not only come closer to Jesus her Son but we also come closer to her, and come to understand better her inspired song of joy and thanksgiving for what God in His mercy has chosen to do for her and for mankind through her unique sharing in the mystery of our Redemption. After going through all the beads of the Rosary with Mary, we should have a deeper faith-insight into her incomparable outpouring of humble, joyful thanks to God: "My soul proclaims the greatness of the Lord, and my spirit exults in God my savior, because he has looked upon his lowly handmaid. Yes, from this day forward all generations will call me blessed, for the Almighty has done great things for me" (Lk. 1:46-48). From our deeper faith we should have a deeper trust and brighter hope to shed light on the path of our pilgrimage together, strengthened by the one love which is poured forth into our hearts by the Holy Spirit who is given to us (cf. Rom. 5:5).

I. *The Joyful Mysteries*

1. *The Archangel Gabriel announces to Mary* that God has chosen her to be the Mother of His Divine Son. The Second Person of the Blessed Trinity is to take on human flesh and to be born into our world. Yet in God's divine design the final decision is to be hers. "The Father of mercies willed that the consent of the predestined mother should precede the Incarnation, so that just as a woman contributed to death, so also a woman should contribute to life" (*Lumen gentium,* no. 56).

We stand in admiration of Mary's humble acceptance of God's Will. "Behold, I am the handmaid of the Lord; let it be done to me according to your word" (Lk. 1:38). And at that instant the Second Person of the Blessed Trinity assumes human nature. The Word is made flesh. God becomes man. The Creator becomes a creature. The Omnipotent stoops infinitely low, in order to raise our human nature infinitely high. Human beings are made sharers in the divine nature. "By His Incarnation the Son of God united Himself in some fashion with every man" (*Gaudium et spes,* no. 22). God's

Divine Son becomes our Brother; and so, Mary becomes our Mother.

2. *Mary visits her cousin Elizabeth.* Mary's presence brings Elizabeth closer to God. Does not our devotion to Mary do the same? In no way impeding the union of the faithful with Christ, does not devotion to Mary rather "foster this union"? (cf. *Lumen gentium,* no. 60)

As Mary brings Jesus Christ into the home of Elizabeth, may she likewise bring Him into our families. For "the family has received from God its mission to be the first and vital cell of society" *(Apostolicam actuositatem,* no. 11). And "the Christian family, which springs from marriage as a reflection of the loving covenant uniting Christ with the Church, and as a participation in that covenant, will manifest to all men the Savior's living presence in the world..." *(Gaudium et spes,* no. 48).

We pray to Mary to obtain for us the grace to imitate that charity which prompted her to hasten to the assistance of someone in need. We believe that "the greatest commandment in the law is to love God with one's whole heart and one's neighbor as oneself. Christ made this commandment of love of neighbor His own, and enriched it with a new meaning" *(Apostolicam actuositatem,* no. 8). Indeed, is it not "the love of God and of neighbor which points out the true disciple of Christ"? *(Lumen gentium,* no. 41)

3. *Jesus Christ is born* amid the piercing winds of an open stable in the little town of Bethlehem. Could there be any more powerful

incentive to disengage our hearts from the love of earthly things in imitation of the poverty of the Infinite God? Are not the poor in spirit blessed, for theirs is the Kingdom of heaven? (cf. Mt. 5:3)

Does not the birth of the Infant God in a rude stable teach us the inestimable value of eternal riches, and the transitory character of the things of time? Are not all of us pilgrims, and is not ours a pilgrim Church having upon this earth no lasting dwelling place? "The Church on earth, while journeying in a foreign land away from her Lord, regards herself as an exile. Hence she seeks and experiences those things which are above, where Christ is seated at the right hand of God, where the life of the Church is hidden with Christ in God until she appears in glory with her Spouse" (*Lumen gentium*, no. 6).

Dare we refuse to see the Infant of Bethlehem in the poor and the needy and the destitute of our day? Just as Jesus Christ was sent by the Father to bring good news to the poor, does not the Church encompass "with love all those who are afflicted with human weakness," recognizing "in the poor and the suffering the likeness of her poor and suffering Founder"? (*Lumen gentium*, no. 8) And as for the poor themselves, is it not true "that in a special way they are united with the suffering Christ for the salvation of the world"? (*Lumen gentium*, no. 41)

4. In fulfillment of the requirements of the Mosaic Law, forty days after the birth of Jesus, *Mary presents her Child in the temple*. For all of us this is an unforgettable lesson—that we "can always find a wondrous model of such docility in the Blessed Virgin Mary" *(Presbyterorum ordinis,* no. 18). There was never a moment in the life of Mary when, deep down in her heart, she was not convinced that "obedience is the hallmark of the servant of Christ" *(Ad gentes,* no. 24)—and never was there a more perfect servant of the Lord than she. "Rightly the holy Fathers see her as used by God not merely in a passive way, but as cooperating in the work of human salvation through free faith and obedience. For, as St. Irenaeus says, she 'being obedient, became the cause of salvation for herself and for the whole human race.' Hence in their preaching not a few of the early Fathers gladly assert with him: 'The knot of Eve's disobedience was untied by Mary's obedience'" *(Lumen gentium,* no. 56).

Simeon's life ambition is fulfilled: the tenacious and persistent craving to see, before his death, Christ the Lord. "Lord, now lettest Thou Thy servant depart in peace" (Lk. 2:29). With the deep conviction of faith, ours is the absolute certainty that if we are tenacious and persistent in our fidelity to God, He will bestow upon us the reward of seeing Him and of being united with Him in an eternal home "whose blessedness will answer and surpass all the longings for peace which spring up in the human heart" (*Gaudium et spes*, no. 39).

5. *Mary finds Jesus teaching in the temple* in Jerusalem after having lost Him for three days. The heart-rending anxiety, the haunting fear, the frantic search come to an end.

We, too, are always to diligently and unintermittingly seek Christ, never resting save in finding Him. For He is "the goal of human history, the focal point of the longings of history and of civilization, the center of the human race, the joy of every heart and the answer to all its yearnings" (*Gaudium et spes*, no. 45). He is "the light of the world, from Whom we go forth, through Whom we live, and toward Whom our journey leads us" (*Lumen gentium*, no. 3).

There is so much turbulence and turmoil all around us, so much confusion and doubt that it is indescribably reassuring for us to realize that "beneath all changes there are many realities which do not change, and which have their ultimate foundation in Christ, Who is the same yesterday and today, yes and forever" (*Gaudium et spes*, no. 10).

II. *The Sorrowful Mysteries*

1. *Jesus Christ suffers agony* in the Garden of Gethsemane. Stumbling amid the darkness, He falls upon His knees against a huge rock in an olive grove. Flat upon the ground, He cries out in distress: "Father, if Thou art

willing, remove this cup from Me. Nevertheless, not My will but Thine be done" (Lk. 22:42).

Physical suffering, such as no one had ever endured before or since, would befall Him later. Now it is the bitter chalice of mental suffering, the sense of abandonment and desolation and loneliness that He must drink.

How pathetic the abandonment, how bleak the loneliness, how stark the desolation of the tender Heart of Jesus when there is no one to watch even one hour with Him! "My soul is very sorrowful, even to death" (Mt. 26:38). The Precious Blood oozes from the pores of His Body as He foresees, not only the humiliation and the ridicule, not only the torture and the torment, not only the scourging and the crowning and the crucifixion, but also the seeming uselessness of all His suffering in so many lives—for many there would be who would deliberately reject Him, spurn His graces, disdain His appeals! Indeed, down through the centuries men would never cease, through seemingly endless forms of evil and immorality, to "crucify again for themselves the Son of God, and make Him a mockery" (Heb. 6:6). Losing the sense of sin, they would pervert the very concept of freedom—offending the Infinite God and obstructing their own fulfillment. For man's "freedom has been damaged by sin" (*Gaudium et spes,* no. 17) and "sin has diminished man, blocking his path to fulfillment" (*Gaudivm et spes,* no. 13).

2. *Jesus is scourged.* Ironically, at the precise moment when the judicial sentence is handed down that "no cause" can be found in Him, the Roman governor surrenders Him for the scourging. "I will therefore chastise Him and release Him" (Lk. 23:16). Then, they tie Him to a pillar and flay Him with thong-tipped whips so relentlessly that His whole body becomes one raw, gaping wound of tattered flesh and gushing blood.

From the day of Adam down to this very hour, human beings have sinned. "Although he was made by God in a state of holiness, from the very dawn of history man abused his liberty, at the urging of personified evil.... Often refusing to acknowledge God as his beginning, man has disrupted also his proper relationship to his own ultimate goal" *(Gaudium et spes,* no. 13).

But our God is a God of mercy. "Freely creating us out of His surpassing and merciful kindness, and graciously calling us moreover to communicate in life and glory with Himself, He has generously poured out His divine goodness and does not cease to do so" *(Ad gentes,* no. 2).

But God's forgiveness, dearly beloved in Christ, is not granted without sorrow for sin on our part. And while it is true that our regret for having sinned must extend to the social consequences of sin, most important of all is it to impress upon our minds and our hearts "the fact that the real essence of the virtue of penance is hatred for sin as an offense against God" *(Sacrosanctum concilium,* no. 109).

3. *A crown of thorns is forced down upon the forehead of Jesus.* If He is a King, as He claimed to be, He must needs have a crown. And so, the Roman soldiers make a crown, press it down on His head, drape His scarred shoulders with a scarlet rag, kneel before Him in mockery, and hail Him as a King.

Of course, King He is! And Kingdom has He established—His Church! "The mystery of the Holy Church is manifest in her very foundation, for the Lord Jesus inaugurated her by preaching the good news, that is, the coming of God's Kingdom, which, for centuries, has been promised in the Scriptures" *(Lumen gentium,* no. 5).

In the midst of all the distractions and struggles of life, we may sometimes tend to overlook the nature of God's Kingdom and the essential purpose for which Jesus Christ founded that Kingdom. "While helping the world and receiving many benefits from it, the Church has a single intention: that God's Kingdom may come, and that the salvation of the whole human race may come to pass" *(Gaudium et spes,* no. 45).

Each of us—priest, religious, lay person—has a role to play in the advancing of the Kingdom of Christ. It is not priests alone nor religious alone who must become involved in the mission of the Church, Christ's Kingdom on earth. "The lay apostolate is a participation in the saving mission of the Church itself. Through their Baptism and Confirmation all are commis-

sioned to that apostolate by the Lord Himself"
(*Lumen gentium*, no. 33).

"Thy Kingdom come." To this goal each
one must pledge himself or herself. And let me
urge you, my brothers and sisters, never to lose
sight of the fact that "the Lord Himself renews
His invitation to all the laity to come closer to
Him every day, and, recognizing that what is
His is also their own, to associate themselves
with Him in His saving mission" (*Apostolicam
actuositatem*, no. 33).

4. *Jesus carries His Cross to Calvary.*
Down over the steps from Pilate's balcony the
Lord Jesus is pushed, and then rough wooden
beams in the form of a cross are cruelly loaded
upon His wounded shoulders. Through Jerusalem's narrow and winding streets the Way of the
Cross proceeds. Jesus stumbles and falls. Suddenly He catches sight of His Mother, and halts
in the street to embrace her. She will follow
Him to Calvary, stand at the foot of the cross,
and finally receive His bruised and blood-
stained Body after His death. But now the death
march continues. Fearing that His strength may
vanish before He reaches Golgotha, the soldiers
force a Cyrenean to help Him to carry His cross.
Then a compassionate woman runs forward and
tenderly wipes His face with a soothing towel. A
moment later He halts again, to utter a word of
consolation to the women of Jerusalem. Finally
the mob arrives at Calvary. The Victim is
stripped of His garments, and then nailed to His
deathbed!

No human life can escape suffering. To carry the cross is the lot of each and every one of us. Daily the human race is wending its way toward Calvary. Without God no one of us can bear up under the burden of the cross. "When a divine substructure and the hope of life eternal are wanting, man's dignity is most grievously lacerated.... The riddles of life and death, of guilt and of grief go unsolved, with the frequent result that men succumb to despair" *(Gaudium et spes*, no. 21).

The Church too "must walk the same road which Christ walked: a road of poverty and obedience, of service and self-sacrifice to the death, from which death He came forth a victor by His Resurrection. For thus did all the Apostles walk in hope. On behalf of Christ's body, which is the Church, they supplied what was wanting to the sufferings of Christ by their own many trials and sufferings" *(Ad gentes,* no. 5).

The Way of the Cross indelibly imprints upon our minds and hearts this tremendous truth: that "by suffering for us He not only provided us with an example for our imitation; He blazed a trail, and if we follow it, life and death are made holy and take on a new meaning" *(Gaudium et spes*, no. 22).

5. *Jesus dies on the Cross.* Now it is over! Into the hands of the Father, the Son of God commends His spirit. The Sacrifice of Calvary has been accomplished.

And yet, in an awesome and mysterious way that only Divine Intelligence could devise and only Divine Power could bring to pass, Calvary's Sacrifice continues. "At the Last Supper, on the night when He was betrayed, our Savior instituted the Eucharistic Sacrifice of His Body and Blood. He did this in order to perpetuate the Sacrifice of the cross throughout the centuries until He should come again, and so to entrust to His beloved spouse, the Church, a memorial of His death and resurrection: a Sacrament of love, a sign of unity, a bond of charity, a paschal banquet in which Christ is consumed, the mind is filled with grace, and a pledge of future glory is given to us" *(Sacrosanctum concilium,* no. 47).

From the rising of the sun to its going down, from East to West there is constantly being offered the Holy Sacrifice of the Mass. And each time, as Calvary's Sacrifice is being reenacted on an altar, the work of our Redemption is being carried on (cf. *Lumen gentium,* no. 3).

It is in the Holy Eucharist that the Covenant between God and man is renewed. It is through the Holy Eucharist that we are drawn into the compelling love of Jesus Christ. And it is through the Holy Eucharist that the sanctification of men in Christ and the glorification of God are most powerfully achieved (cf. *Sacrosanctum concilium,* no. 10). In very truth "the most blessed Eucharist contains the Church's

entire spiritual wealth, that is, Christ Himself,
our Passover and living bread" *(Presbyterorum
ordinis*, no. 5).

III. *The Glorious Mysteries*

1. *Jesus Christ rises from the dead.* Our
Divine Savior had promised that He would
conquer death, that if the temple of His Body
were destroyed, within three days He would
build it up again. Now on Easter Sunday, that
mysterious promise is stupendously fulfilled.
Truly the Resurrection is the climactic point of
Christ's entire mission.

St. Paul tells us very clearly that if Christ
be not risen from the dead, our faith is vain. The
Resurrection is not incontrovertible proof of the
truth that Christ's claim to be the Son of God
must be accepted.

The Resurrection of Christ is also a pledge
of our own resurrection from the dead. The
glorious triumph of Christ over death has merited for us the victory of eternal life. The
Resurrection teaches beyond all doubt that for
those who are faithful to God, eternal joys will
follow temporal sufferings.

It is by overcoming death through His own
death and Resurrection that the Son of God not
only redeemed man, but transformed him into a
new creation. Thus, "we who have been made
like unto Him, who have died with Him and
been raised up with Him, are taken up into the

mysteries of His life, until we reign together with Him" *(Lumen gentium,* no. 7). It is a basic tenet of our faith that "God has called man and still calls him, so that with his entire being he might be joined to Him in an endless sharing of a divine life beyond all corruption. Christ won His victory when He rose to life..." *(Gaudium et spes,* no. 18).

2. Forty days after His Resurrection, *Jesus ascends into heaven.* He Who had been sent by the Father to redeem mankind now triumphantly returns to be enthroned in glory at the right hand of the Father.

Many wonders had been wrought by God among the people of the Old Testament. Yet all these were but "a prelude to the work of Christ the Lord Who is redeeming mankind and giving perfect glory to God. He achieved His task principally by the paschal mystery of His blessed passion, resurrection from the dead, and glorious ascension, wherby 'dying, He destroyed our death, and rising, He restored our life'" *(Sacrosanctum concilium,* no. 5).

As little children we were taught the most fundamental and most important truth of all life—that God made us to know Him, to love Him and to serve Him in this world, and to be happy with Him forever in heaven. God is our origin. God is our goal. Heaven is our destiny. Union with God is our eternal reward. God made us for Himself, and our hearts are restless till they rest in Him. From the very dawn of creation a loving and compassionate God "cease-lessly kept the human race in His care, in order to give eternal life to those who perseveringly do good in search of salvation" (*Dei Verbum*, no. 30).

3. On Pentecost Sunday the *Holy Spirit descends upon Mary and the Apostles*, gathered together in the Cenacle. Holy Scripture relates the sound from heaven, the violent wind, the tongues of fire, the speaking in foreign languages. Timid, fearful men are transformed into courageous preachers of the Good News. "Men of Israel," Peter preaches, "hear these words: Jesus of Nazareth, a man attested to you by God with mighty works and wonders and signs, which God did through Him in your midst...this Jesus, delivered up according to the definite plan and foreknowledge of God, you crucified and killed by the hands of lawless men. But God raised Him up.... Let all the house of Israel therefore know assuredly that God has made Him both Lord and Christ, this Jesus whom you crucified" (Acts 2:22-36).

In our times there must be, through a reawakening of devotion to the Holy Spirit, an increased appreciation of the fact that "wherever they live, all Christians are bound to show forth, by the example of their lives and by the witness of their speech, that new man which they put on at Baptism, and that power of the Holy Spirit by Whom they were strengthened at Confirmation" (*Ad gentes*, no. 11).

The people of our day especially are in critical need of the help of the Holy Spirit for firmness in holding fast to their faith and for courage in professing it. Skepticism and doubt concerning even the most fundamental matters of faith surround us on every side. Relativism and situationism about truths of morality are in the very air we breathe. Desperately we need the light and the strength that only the Holy Spirit can bestow. "Reborn as sons of God, they (the faithful) must confess before men the faith which they have received from God through the Church" *(Lumen gentium,* no. 11).

Does not Jesus Christ Himself admonish us: "Everyone who acknowledges Me before men, I will also acknowledge before My Father Who is in heaven. But whoever denies Me before men, I also will deny before My Father Who is in heaven" (Mt. 10:32).

4. After her life on earth has come to an end, *Mary is assumed into heaven.* While the revealed truth that Mary's body never suffered corruption but that she was taken up, body and soul, into heaven, is not explicitly found in Sacred Scripture, nevertheless it has been universally held throughout the Church for centuries, and was infallibly defined by Pope Pius XII in 1950. Mary's life of intimate union with God was eternally rewarded in this unique way so that now she is the only human person dwelling in heaven—a precursor of all who will ultimately have body and soul reunited in heaven. "In the bodily and spiritual glory which she possesses in heaven, the Mother of Jesus continues in this present world as the image and

first flowering of the Church as she is to be perfected in the world to come" *(Lumen gentium,* no. 68).

Mary is our intercessor with God because she is God's Mother and our Mother too. "Taken up to heaven, she did not lay aside this saving role, but by her manifold acts of intercession continues to win for us gifts of eternal salvation. By her maternal charity, Mary cares for the brethren of her Son who still journey on earth, surrounded by dangers and difficulties, until they are led to their happy fatherland" *(Lumen gentium,* no. 62).

There have always been some, of course, who are reluctant to pay honor to Mary, because Christ alone is our Mediator. But "the maternal duty of Mary toward men in no way obscures or diminishes this unique mediation of Christ, but rather shows its power. For all the saving influences of the Blessed Virgin on men originate, not from some inner necessity, but from the divine pleasure. They flow forth from the superabundance of the merits of Christ, rest on His mediation, depend entirely on it, and draw all their power from it" *(Lumen gentium,* no. 60).

5. *Mary is crowned Queen of Heaven.* She is indeed "exalted in heaven above all the saints and angels" *(Lumen gentium,* no. 69).

Mary had a unique role to play in the Redemption of mankind effected by Jesus Christ her Son. From the earliest days of the Church, Christians have believed that Mary cooperated in our salvation. She gave birth to the Redeemer. She reared the Redeemer. She spiritually shared with the Redeemer His death on the cross. Even more. She was closely associated with the Redeemer in His victory over sin, as Eve was associated with Adam in man's fall from grace. Truly she is Co-Redemptrix—not indeed in any sense derogating from Christ's unique salvific role, but rather in some way, together with her Son Jesus Christ and subordinately to Him, satisfying divine justice by her sufferings, and meriting for us grace and salvation. And so, properly understood, the terms "Mediatrix" and "Co-Redemptrix" can appropriately be applied to her (cf. *Lumen gentium*, no. 62).

Hence, the Second Vatican Council can say of the Blessed Virgin Mary that "led by the Holy Spirit she devoted herself entirely to the mystery of man's redemption" *(Presbyterorum ordinis*, no. 18). "This union of the Mother with the Son in the work of salvation was manifested from the time of Christ's virginal conception up to His death" *(Lumen gentium*, no. 57). "In an utterly singular way she cooperated by her obedience, faith, hope and burning charity in the Savior's work of restoring supernatural life to souls" *(Lumen gentium*, no. 61).

Dearly beloved in Christ: The mysteries of the Rosary are clearly the mysteries of our salvation. Mary our Mother has led us through them into a deeper faith in their power to renew us for peace, in the hope they generate in us in the promises of Christ her Son and in His love.

As the Rosary—"so wonderfully simple, yet so wonderfully profound"—is the favorite prayer of our Holy Father, so too may it be our favorite prayer. And through it may the longing of the Fathers of the Second Vatican Council be realized. "Let the entire body of the faithful pour forth persevering prayer to the Mother of God and Mother of men. Let them implore that she who aided the beginnings of the Church by her prayers may now, exalted as she is in heaven above all the saints and angels, intercede with her Son in the fellowship of all the saints. May she do so until all the people of the human family...are happily gathered together in peace and harmony into the one People of God, for the glory of the Most Holy and Undivided Trinity" (*Lumen gentium*, no. 69).

"Come, Follow Me"

Pastoral Letter to all youth...
Feast of Our Lady of the Rosary
October 7, 1977

Come, Live in Christ Jesus

1. My beloved young brothers and sisters in Christ: Recently our Holy Father, Pope Paul VI, delivered a most inspiring address by video-tape to a gigantic youth rally held in a huge stadium in one of our American cities. In his pastoral message, he both urged and invited all young people to "live in Christ Jesus." "This will be your greatest contribution to society," Pope Paul declared, "the most complete measure of your personal fulfillment, your most effective service to humanity, your most lasting impact on the world." [1]

2. I cannot read these words without being deeply moved, for they contain a message which is of the greatest importance to all of us. But this is especially true for Bishops because we are deeply interested in the young people entrusted to our care.

COME, LET US HAVE A TALK

3. It is, therefore, in a spirit of genuine and loving concern that I write to you, the youth of the Archdiocese of Boston. I would rather speak with each one of you personally and individually, but that, of course, is physically impossible, for there are more than two million Catholics in the Archdiocese of Boston. And so, since I am unable to speak to each one of you as I would wish, I am addressing this letter to you.

4. As I write, I do not intend to speak down to you, nor speak at you; rather I would like to speak with you, very simply and from my heart, as your shepherd, as your father, as your brother in the Lord Jesus Christ.

5. Let me begin by telling you very sincerely how important I think you are. I am not speaking this way simply to flatter you; I speak from the perspective of faith. There is no way that I could emphasize sufficiently the importance of the years between your childhood and your adulthood, not only in terms of physical, psychological and social development, but especially in terms of spiritual growth. It is particularly during these years that your capacity for a deeper personal relationship with Christ blossoms. Once you are capable of such a personal relationship with Christ and as you mature in it, your activity is increasingly the responsible fruit of Christ's life in you.[2]

6. Now, to be very frank with you, there are some things about youth's relationship to the Church and her teachings that distress and concern me. Perhaps nothing concerns me more with regard to that relationship than this: Why is the Church—a Church which is both the Pilgrim People of God and the Mystical Body of Christ, Jesus Christ in our very midst—apparently failing to reach some of our young people? I am sure that in your hearts you are aware of the identification of Christ with His Church. Are we, the Bishops of the Church, reflecting Christ, the Head of this Church, as He should be reflected?

COME AND UNDERSTAND

7. Sometimes I wonder whether some persons, including many young people, have an accurate understanding of the Church. Do they consider her as a community of the perfect or near-perfect, rather than a community of followers of Christ on their pilgrim way? We have all heard complaints recently about the alleged inability of the Church to adapt and to be effective in modern society. Perhaps we forget that the Church must be accepted as Christ founded her, a Church made up of the good and bad, yet constantly striving to become more holy and to lead all men and women to their eternal destiny.

Jesus Is Calling You

THE LORD CALLS TO YOU

8. For a long time now, the gentle, trusting, yet firm and pressing invitation of the Lord Jesus Christ has been calling out to young people: "Come, follow Me" (Mt. 19:21). Over the centuries many have understood these words of our Divine Lord as having been addressed especially to those upon whom God has bestowed a special vocation to the priesthood or to the religious life. While this is indeed true, nonetheless the fact is that our Lord Jesus Christ is calling us all to follow Him. He is calling you, the youth of our Archdiocese and the youth of our land, calling each and every one of you to come and follow Him.

THE LORD IS IN YOU

9. No one alert to life around us will deny that we live in difficult times, times of stress and strain, of tension and upheaval, times of confrontation. How does this troubled society look upon you? I think the answer is: in various ways. Some persons read and accept only the sensational newspaper accounts of bewildered youth. Delinquency, crime, drugs, alcohol, the abuse of sex, all paint a rather negative picture of youth. Some go to the other extreme, thrusting undue responsibility and pressure upon young people by soliciting their views on almost every

topic under the sun. Still others display a rather patronizing, condescending attitude toward you, and see you simply as "lovable, crazy, mixed-up kids."

10. You have been described in diverse ways: alienated, rebellious, iconoclastic, immature, escapist, committed, authentic, concerned. Whatever tag or tags may fit, what all must admit is that many of you are wrapped in uncertainty and confusion—an uncertainty and confusion caused in large measure, perhaps, by the contradictory values of many of your elders. And all must admit, too, that young people in general are searching for fundamental answers, and that you and your peers sorely need and deserve love, affection and respect as unique individuals, as creatures and children of our loving Father.

And how do I look upon you? I see in you the Lord Jesus Christ!

THE LORD HAS REDEEMED YOU

11. We hear so much today about the dignity and worth of the human person that we are apt to consider these terms simply as clichés. I beg of you, do not fall into that mistake. The fact is, you have been created in the image and likeness of God; you have been redeemed by the Precious Blood of Jesus Christ Who is the Son of God.

12. Moreover, when you received Baptism you received a new life. You became a sharer in the divine nature. The Blessed Trinity began to dwell within you. And, as the grace of God increased in your souls through prayer, the sacraments and good works, that supernatural life continued to grow and to develop but will reach its fullness and fruition only in the life to come. "Dignity," "worth," "sacredness"—these can only dimly express the marvel of this reality.

THE LORD IS YOUR BROTHER

13. A wonderful fact of Divine Revelation we must accept is this: Jesus Christ is your Brother and mine. He assumed human flesh at His Incarnation, becoming like us in all things except sin. He lived for us and He died for us. Then, rising from the dead, He returned to His Father in heaven where, without ceasing, He intercedes for us.

THE LORD IS YOUR GOD

14. If you want to know how valuable you are in God's sight, look at a Crucifix. That is the price Jesus Christ paid for you. And if you want to know how much He loved you, remember what He Himself once said, "There is no greater love than this: to lay down one's life for one's friends" (Jn. 15:13).

Hear His Voice

RESPOND TO HIS CALL

15. The words which Jesus Christ spoke while on earth were not only meant for the men and women and children of His day. "Come, follow Me" is His call to you, no less today than it was His call to the youth of Palestine two thousand years ago.

BE THE GOOD SOIL

16. What is your response to the Lord Jesus' "Come, follow Me"? Perhaps you may find it in the parable of the sower. Like the seed which falls on rocky ground, the call may have no chance to grow; it withers and dies within you. Like the seed that falls into the midst of thorns, perhaps the call will be choked out by the cares and concerns of your lives. Or, like the seed which falls on fertile soil, the call will grow and blossom forth into the fullness of life.

YOU NEED NOT BE ALONE

17. Some years ago a survey conducted among college students came to the significant conclusion that the strongest force driving young people today to search for God is a strange and deep sense of aloneness. Facing, interpreting and overcoming that aloneness constitute powerful elements in a contemporary spirituality of

the young.[3] It is only Jesus Christ Who really can assuage that loneliness. I can assure you that He understands and cares.

HE IS WALKING TOWARD YOU

18. You tell me that so often you feel lonely, unwanted, rejected. As you search relentlessly to fill up the void in your hearts, I suppose it is only natural that you look to things that satisfy your longing immediately. But soon you do learn that things cannot really appease your desires. It is Jesus Christ Himself Who in His own way is whispering to your souls: "These are not enough." In your at times frantic search to overcome loneliness and to find meaning in your lives, listen to the words of Pope Paul VI: "Perhaps you do not know it, but you are walking toward Him. And we can tell you, He is walking toward you."[4]

KNOWING ABOUT HIM
AND KNOWING HIM

19. But do you recognize Him? To what extent do you know Jesus Christ? As His follower, you are, of course, obliged to know *about* Him. That is why it is so essential for you to continue your formal religious education. But it is not enough simply to know *about* Christ. If you would answer His call, "Come, follow Me," you must know *Him* personally—His attitudes

and values, His reactions and points of view, His manner of thinking, His mind and His heart. And so, you come to understand the admonition of St. Paul when he insists, "Your attitude must be that of Christ" (Phil. 2:5), "Put on the Lord Jesus Christ" (Rom. 13:14).

HE UNDERSTANDS

20. To have the attitude of Christ Jesus, and to put on the Lord Jesus Christ, demand that you imitate Christ in your own lives. This demands making your own the virtues of Christ —His understanding, His thoughtfulness, His gentleness, His kindness, His compassion, His caring, and His love. Not only had He an understanding of the problems, the cares, the anxieties and the sorrows of those whom He met, but, in a sense, He made them His own. And He continues to do the same today. He accepts you and me as we are, and loves us as we are, not our mistakes and our failings— certainly not our sins—but ourselves in spite of our mistakes and our failings and our sins, if only we repent of them and strive unceasingly to heed His call, "Come, follow Me."

Need for Commitment

A SPECIAL CALLING

21. As you must have detected by now, I have been speaking with you about the general

vocation addressed to each one of you by our Lord Jesus Christ: "Come, follow Me." Over the centuries, the Church has been teaching— and this truth was strongly reaffirmed by the Second Vatican Council—that we are all called to be saints. Holiness is for all.

22. Personal sanctification is the desired goal of all who hear God's call. For some, this sanctification may come through a vocation to the married state, for others to a dedicated single state, and to still others, Almighty God addresses a singular invitation—the call to the priesthood or to consecrated lives as religious men and women. This is an invitation to a special share in service to Him and to His people.

A PERMANENT COMMITMENT

23. This is not the place to discuss in detail the theology of a vocation to the priesthood or to the religious life. But I do want to speak with you from my heart about commitment, for the man or woman who accepts this call must make a permanent celibate commitment to the Lord Jesus Christ. I am fully aware that there exists today a certain hesitancy to make such a permanent commitment. There are many reasons for such hesitancy.

24. Perhaps one reason for hesitancy is anxiety. Possibly some are afraid to make a life-long commitment. We find ourselves engulfed in an environment in which everything appears

to be constantly changing, and a great many of us are restless, uneasy and unsure. To pledge our lives until death in any state of life is difficult, and, in some cases, even looks forbidding.

25. Yet, the fact of ceaseless change in the world—something we experience daily—should, in itself, be an incentive to look to the things that last, to the promise of eternity. There the peace, happiness and security of union with God will never change, never end.

26. In the midst of all the insecurity, restlessness and turmoil of the world, I urge you to place unbounded and unfaltering trust in God. Recall the words of David the Psalmist: "You are my hope, O Lord; my trust, O God, from my youth" (Ps. 71:5), and "Happy the man who makes the Lord his trust" (Ps. 40:5).

A FAITHFUL GOD

27. Why, you might ask yourselves, should you make the Lord your trust? Because God is faithful. He is a God of power—all powerful in fact—Who can help you, a God of goodness Who wants to help you, and a God of fidelity Who will fulfill His covenant to help you. With such trust in a loving God, we are certain in faith that God will be with us each day of our lives, and this presence of God-in-us will give us the strength to do His will, since "for God all things are possible" (Mt. 19:26).

28. God's fidelity! Here is the source and basis of our hope. Here is the reason why you should have no fear to commit yourselves completely and permanently to the Lord Jesus Christ in the priesthood, or in the consecrated lives of religious men and women. In the words of St. Paul: "This great confidence in God is ours, through Christ" (2 Cor. 3:4).

A DIFFICULT COMMITMENT

29. Is such a commitment difficult? Of course it is. But do you think that God's grace will fail you? Has not the Lord Jesus promised that for those who accept His invitation in love and trust His yoke would be easy and His burden light? (cf. Mt. 11:28-30)

30. I have already noted that one reason why some of you may hesitate to make a permanent commitment to the Lord Jesus Christ in the priesthood, the sisterhood or brotherhood is anxiety. But there is a second reason, and if I am to be completely frank with you, I must not ignore it.

PERSEVERE

31. Unfortunately there are some—and this has happened more frequently in our day than previously—who have not persevered in their lifelong commitments. I need not point out to you that this failure of commitment occurs not only among priests and religious, but

among married persons as well. Personally, I am deeply disturbed, not only by the renunciation of the permanent commitments made at the time of the reception of the sacraments of Matrimony and Orders, but also by the confusion which the failure to persevere in these commitments causes. But, I plead with you, in these restless times, never lose heart. Do not close your ears to the invitation of Almighty God. Never lose confidence in Him, for God will always be faithful to those who persevere in His call.

CELIBACY: A VALUED GIFT

32. Perhaps a third reason for hesitancy in making a permanent commitment to the Lord is the demand for celibate living made of the priest and the consecrated religious man or woman. The Decree of the Second Vatican Council on the Training of Priests spoke to this concern. The document indicated that those who respond to God's call to "Come, follow Me" in a church vocation are asked to renounce marriage for the sake of the kingdom of heaven. They are to hold fast to the Lord with that undivided love which is profoundly in harmony with the New Covenant, for they bear witness to the resurrection in a future life. Vatican II further stated that those who accept the call should embrace the celibate state gratefully. Celibacy is far more than a simple demand of Church law, wise and sacred as this may be.

Rather it is a supernatural and valued gift of God which is given and received under the inspiration and with the assistance of the Holy Spirit. Coming from God, celibacy in no way inhibits interpersonal relationships; on the contrary, it frees the person for love. The charism of celibacy allows the individual to love deeply and warmly, yet without finding it necessary to move toward exclusivity and finalize the relationship in marriage. It is in the vocation of marriage that men and women naturally gravitate toward one exclusive relationship as the springboard of all the other loves in their lives.

POWERFUL WITNESS TO CHRIST

33. In speaking of the challenges of celibacy courageously and gratefully accepted by those who listen to the call of Christ to "Come, follow Me," we speak of something more than the mere virtue of chastity. Chastity is that respectful self-control that preserves one's capacity to see and to fulfill one's sexuality in a perspective of true Christian love (cf. 1 Cor. 7:25-35 and 13:1-13). In a final analysis, chastity lives for love and through love, as well as for self-respect and respect for other persons. Thus, everyone is called to the chastity proper to his or her state in life. And what an eloquent and powerful witness to Christ and to His Church we have in the millions of men and women of all ages who have committed themselves to lives of

chastity over the centuries—many of them willingly dying as martyrs in defense of their chastity.

34. But the chastity demanded of those who freely choose the celibate state is a chastity "for the sake of God's reign" (Mt. 19:12), and must be esteemed as an exceptional gift of grace. It is a very significant fact that Jesus Christ chose consecrated chastity as His way of life. Not only was this choice a symbol of His total dedication to the service of God and man, but it must be understood precisely in accordance with His mission as God-man to be the mediator between the Father and the human race. Even if the world does not always recognize it or appreciate it, consecrated chastity remains a powerful witness to Christ's love in the world.

The Need for Chastity

A LOVING RESPONSE

35. As part of our loving response to God Who calls us to love Him and one another, every one of us is to live a chaste or pure life in celibate love or marital love. While a select few are called within their Christian vocation to permanent celibate love, chastity must be at the root of both marital and celibate love.

36. The response to the Divine Call, made by those who have dedicated themselves to lives of consecrated chastity, should be truly a

response of love—total, inclusive, permanent—
and such a love can be an irresistible incentive
even to heroism in the service of God and
neighbor. Little wonder that the Second Vatican Council describes such chastity as a surpassing gift of grace, one which "liberates the
human heart in a unique way and causes it to
burn with greater love for God and all mankind."[5]

MARY OUR MODEL

37. I write these words to you because I
feel deeply that the world today sorely needs
the witness to the Lord Jesus Christ and to His
Kingdom that is given in a life of consecrated
chastity. I am fully aware that there are those
who ridicule or ignore this profoundly Christian
value. Again, I beg you to walk forward unafraid, answering the call of Christ, "Come,
follow Me." I plead with you to seek Mary's
intercession in your lives, for she is our human
model of purity.

The Christian Challenge

DISDAIN MEDIOCRITY:
SEEK EXCELLENCE

38. The same Lord Jesus Christ Who invites
you to "Come, follow Me" has warned that "He
who is not with Me is against Me" (Mt. 12:30).

Whatever form your vocation may take, whatever sacrifices may be demanded of you, Jesus Christ hurls a ringing challenge to each and every one of you: the challenge to disdain mediocrity and to strive for excellence. Saint Ignatius of Loyola, the founder of the Jesuits, penned these words in his youth: "To give and not to count the cost, to fight and not to heed the wounds, to labor and ask for no reward." This is the epitome of selflessness and sacrifice in the service of an ideal. And what ideal could be more noble, I ask you, than to follow Jesus Christ? Is He not the Model as well as the Master of us all?

39. To accept the challenge of His discipleship is not easy. It entails inconvenience, hardship, perseverance, even heroism. There were many among the early followers of Christ who were invited to follow Him, but some said: "This sort of talk is hard to endure! How can anyone take it seriously?" (Jn. 6:60) "From this time on, many of His disciples broke away and would not remain in His company any longer" (Jn. 6:66).

LIVE HIS LIFE

40. But never be misled into believing that the life to which you are called as a disciple is drab, monotonous, dull, routine. The fact is that such a life is Christ's own life. St. Paul said: "To me, 'life' means Christ" (Phil. 1:21). And so, one who accepts Christ's challenge to "Come, follow

Me" shares in, yes even lives, the life of Christ. Indeed His Spirit is alive in the world today. Evidence of His presence is all around us. Open your hearts to Him in prayer. Never be afraid to let people know that God lives in you and that you live in God.

TURN TO GOD

41. I sense that, more and more, you who are concerned with the conditions besetting modern society are beginning to realize that conversion of heart is an indispensable requisite for the solution of the problems that weigh so heavily upon our twentieth century world. Since you are eager to make the world a place in which justice, peace and love prevail, you must also be conscious of the presence of sin, of human failing in the world. Often refusing to acknowledge God as their source, men and women upset their relationship which should link them to their last end. It is only God who can change the hearts of men and women; it is only with the help of God's grace that the enemies of mankind can be conquered: ignorance, starvation, injustice, hatred, oppression, persecution, war. And it is only men and women permeated with the Divine Life who can accomplish God's designs in and for the world.[6]

GENUINE JOY

42. The Church longs for you, my young brothers and sisters, to be filled with eagerness and joy. She knows that it is only the man or woman without faith and without hope who is really sad. The Church knows that technological society having provided wide opportunities for seemingly endless pleasures has, in actual fact, caused boredom, depression, dejection and despair among the millions of young people your own age. And so, in urging you to follow Christ, the Church knows that the genuine Christian joy which will be yours is an authentic participation in the joy that fills the heart of Jesus Christ glorified.[7]

COME AND LEAD OTHERS TO CHRIST

43. Let me say a word about the apostolate of youth to youth. What an inexhaustible source of reflection Pope John XXIII offered us when he said: "Every believer in this world of ours must be a spark of light, a center of love, a vivifying leaven amidst his fellowmen. And he will be this all the more perfectly, the more closely he lives in communion with God in the intimacy of his own soul."[8]

44. No one who has seriously and sincerely answered the call of Christ to "Come, follow Me" can be indifferent to the thousands of our brothers and sisters who have not as yet heard that call, or, having heard it, are ignoring it. Do

you remember the Gospel account of how the first meeting of Jesus with Simon Peter came about? Andrew, Peter's brother, had spent the day with Jesus and had been fascinated by His words and His very presence. Unable to contain his enthusiasm, Andrew ran off to tell his brother: "We have found the Messiah!" (Jn. 1:41) And he led him to Jesus. How significant it is that Simon Peter, who later was to be designated the visible head of Christ's Church on earth, first met Jesus because his brother, in his zeal, brought him the Good News and led him to the Savior.

YOUTH TO YOUTH

45. It is especially to you, the youth of our day, that Jesus Christ and His Church look, to act as apostles in leading other young people to follow Christ. Could anything be clearer than the words of the Second Vatican Council? Speaking of young people, the Council declared: "Their heightened influence in society demands of them a proportionately active apostolate. Happily their natural qualities fit them for this activity. As they become more conscious of their own personality, they are impelled by a zest for life and abounding energies to assume their own responsibility, and they yearn to play their part in social and cultural life. If this zeal is imbued with the Spirit of Christ and is inspired by obedience to and love for the shepherds of the Church, it can

be expected to be very fruitful. They themselves ought to become the prime and direct apostles of youth, exercising their apostolate among themselves and through themselves...."[9]

"Come, Follow Me"

LIFE AND LIGHT

As your Bishop, your father and brother in the Lord Jesus Christ, I beg of you again to listen to His gracious yet pleading invitation: "Come, follow Me." For those who accept His call, He has pledged His life and light, His peace and happiness for all eternity. He has promised: "No follower of mine shall ever walk in darkness; no, he shall possess the light of life" (Jn. 8:12). It is my fervent prayer that your response will rise up from the depths of your heart, that it will be eager, enthusiastic, generous, vibrant, committed, faith-filled and love-motivated; that it will be, simply: "Teacher, wherever you go I will come after You" (Mt. 8:19).

NOTES

1. *Our Sunday Visitor,* March 20, 1977.

2. Cf. USCC Department of Education, *A Vision of Youth Ministry.*

3. Cf. J. Langford, "Power and the New Generation," *Spiritual Life,* Summer 1968.

4. Pope Paul VI, *L'Osservatore Romano,* July 27, 1972.

5. "Perfectae caritatis," paragraph no. 12.

6. Cf. NCCB Pastoral Letter, "Behold Your Mother: Woman of Faith."

7. Cf. Pope Paul VI, *Apostolic Exhortation on Christian Joy.*

8. Encyclical Letter *Peace on Earth,* April 11, 1963, paragraph no. 164.

9. *Decree on the Apostolate of the Laity,* paragraph no. 12.

Show Us the Way

Pastoral Letter to Youth
Easter, 1979

1. My dear young brothers and sisters in Christ: I am delighted to have the chance to talk with you again. I feel a special thrill in doing so during this season of Hope for peace in joy. As you may know, Easter is the feast of Hope. I think there is no time more fitting for me as your Archbishop and friend to share with you some of my personal thoughts and reflections, enlightened by our common faith and united in brotherly love. After all, you are very special to the Lord and to me. You are the young Church of our Archdiocese, and in the Heart of Christ I have a deep affection for you.

A Time for Sharing

2. Some of you know, and others may have heard, that during the past year I visited with many of you within the parishes and high schools of the Archdiocese. We talked candidly about our common hopes and dreams, our

struggles and disappointments, our joys and sorrows. As I went from city to suburb and talked with young people in Roxbury and Randolph, Winchester and Westwood, Mattapan and Brockton, I was impressed by the trust and confidence you had in me, their brother and father in Christ. I must confess that my visits were a source of joy and strength for me. I trust they were the same for them.

Show Us the Way

3. Following one of my visits, I received a letter from a young lady suggesting that if I should write to you again, my next letter might be entitled: "Show Us the Way." I was touched deeply. I felt and feel that her sensitive suggestion was an open and candid request coming from all of you. In response, I would like to try candidly and humbly to show you the Way. Let me begin by asking for your help in this beautiful task given to me by you and by the Lord Himself—help me to show you the Way. As I seek your help joyfully, I turn with confidence to Christ, for He is the Way. It was He who said to all of us, "I am the Way and the Truth and the Life" (Jn. 14:6).

The Challenges of My Youth

4. In writing to you, I am reminded of my own teenage years. I came to this country when

I was fifteen and one-half years of age. As an immigrant from the Azores, I experienced much of the confusion that you experience almost daily in your lives, even though the times were different. Moreover, I had to deal with other problems as well. I moved into a culture and an environment with which I was very unfamiliar, to say the least. I knew no English and had to adjust to rather new circumstances and surroundings. Each of these experiences of my youth, coupled with the ordinary pressures of daily living, was difficult and painful for me as a young man. Every day offered surprising and at times even bewildering challenges for me, just as each new day may challenge you.

The Signs of God's Love for Me

5. In looking back, I can recall with gratitude the many signs of God's love for me. My parish church, as a community of caring persons, was a vital force in my life. There I came to understand and love the Scriptures with greater appreciation, for they reminded me so beautifully of God's enabling presence in my life. There I also came to know the lives of the saints who inspired me with courage because of their love for God and neighbor. The sacraments, seen even then to be special moments of growth in the knowledge and love of Christ, strengthened me when things seemed to be and were difficult. And what can I say of my youthful joy in being able to participate in the Mass? It

was there that I could unite my struggle and suffering more intimately with Christ and draw great comfort and strength to grow in Him Who is the Way.

6. So many wonderful persons helped me along the way—my parents and family, priests, teachers, neighbors, friends. All in their own way and with their own gifts and talents, manifested God's love for me. And supporting all of this was the gift of Faith from our loving Father, which strengthened me as I, like you, lived through my adolescent and youthful years. As your Archbishop and friend, indeed as your brother and father in Christ, I welcome this opportunity of sharing my story with you (ever so briefly) and being present in love as your own personal story is lived and experienced during these days of your life and growth.

The Experience of Loneliness

7. I think I am old enough, and wise enough, to ask you to expand your vision and broaden your horizons. Many changes indeed have occurred in almost a half century since I came to America, but you still face challenges as did I. You may experience loneliness while being in the midst of many, even among friends! I realize that this feeling of loneliness can cause you to become discouraged and downhearted at times.

The Search for Belonging

8. This discouragement can and often does lead you to ask the question which youth of every era have asked, "How and where do I fit in?" It is natural to want to belong; no one enjoys feelings of loneliness. Each of us longs to be accepted and appreciated. Friendship is an important and necessary part of living and growing. People need one another, and you need the support and encouragement of your parents and families and friends just as surely as did I.

The Achievement of Inner Peace

9. I know that relationships within the family, school and neighborhood can present particular difficulties for you at this time in your life. It is not easy to set the balance between freedom and responsibility, dependency and "being one's own person." To be heard and to be understood are very important in growing up. As you probably realize, sometimes it is easier to speak than to listen, to expect to be understood than to understand. St. Francis of Assisi was able to achieve inner peace in following the Way which is Christ by praying for the gift to understand rather than to be understood. This inner peace can be found in prayer. It is in prayer as well that we can begin to accept the task of choosing a direction in this life. As free

people we must accept the privilege and the burden of making choices. The fulfillment of this responsibility requires thought and prayer, determination and work. It calls also for commitment and courage. Ultimately it demands a personal knowledge of Christ Who is the Way, and Who knows our strengths and talents, our weaknesses and needs.

Challenges and Pressures Facing Youth

10. It may be true, as some historians, sociologists and psychologists claim, that the youth of today face challenges and pressures unparalleled in human history. The young people I met last year shared some of their concerns with me. We discussed problems related to drugs, the abuse of alcohol, sexual promiscuity, stealing and peer pressure, and the attitudes which young people form about these current concerns. All of these attitudes and actions would seem to flow from the desire to escape the harsh and unpleasant realities of life, or they would flow from the hope of gaining a false sense of self-confidence, or from a deep longing just to be accepted.

11. We also discussed a dissatisfaction with society's competence to improve itself, a certain disillusionment with the Church, and a misunderstanding on the part of many, of the Church's true nature and mission. Finally, we

talked of young people who give in to bitterness
and hostility, oftentimes manifesting their frustrations in violence and destructive behavior.

12. It would be a mistake to think that no
other young people in history had ever been
challenged to respond creatively in their own
social and religious climates to the pressures of
growth such as these. The pages of Scripture,
the biographies of the saints, the stories of
young people in every age present a vivid
picture of youth like you who faced responsibly
the struggles and pains of living and growing. In
each instance they came to acknowledge and
appreciate God's presence in their lives.

Scriptural Models for Youth

13. For a few moments you and I can
reflect prayerfully and profitably for ourselves on
some of them. Right at the beginning of the Bible,
in the very first pages of the Book of Genesis, we
are reminded of God's love for His children.
God promised that, even in the midst of human
failure and sinfulness, He would not forget
those whom He loved. The fact is that because
He loved, He simply could not forget. And so
God was always with His people. In their exile,
in the midst of famine or plagues, God did not
abandon the Israelites. Sometimes His presence
was perceived as signified by a cloud. At other
times it was experienced in a gentle breeze. He
was recognized in a burning bush or a strong

wind. And oftentimes, He was present simply in the challenging or comforting words of a prophet. But one thing was clear. God remained faithful in His love for His people. He showed that He understood their confusion and bewilderment. He was there to answer their questions and dispel their fears.

The Prophet Isaiah

14. Isaiah, as a youthful prophet, recognized the presence of God in his life. He believed that the Spirit of the Lord was upon him. No matter where Isaiah traveled, no matter what sufferings or difficulties he experienced, he was convinced that God was with him. Isaiah acknowledged with gratitude the fidelity of the loving Father.

The Prophet Jeremiah

15. Jeremiah, while still in his teens, was renewed in spirit and filled with courage as he faced the challenges and responsibilities of life. He accepted the Word of the Lord. Jeremiah heard and trusted in God's promise to guide and strengthen him. He appreciated the presence of an intimate and loving God. This awareness was a comfort and strength to Jeremiah as he responded to God's call through the experiences of his life.

The Message of Jesus

16. And in the New Testament, even as He began His public ministry, Jesus reminded His listeners of God's love for each of them. He invited those who would follow Him to repent and believe the Good News. Jesus challenged them to acknowledge their need for God's love and forgiveness. He reminded them that they could not stand alone and could not walk alone. Unhesitatingly Jesus proclaimed, "Apart from me you can do nothing" (Jn. 15:5). Jesus urged His hearers to be converted to Him, to turn toward Him, listen to His words and observe His actions. He was the Way to the Father.

Jesus, Sign of the Father's Love

17. How did Jesus understand Himself and His mission? He stated unhesitatingly, "The Father and I are one" (Jn. 10:30). He reminded Philip, "Whoever has seen me has seen the Father" (Jn. 14:9). Knowing Himself to be the Son of God and equal to the Father as God, He also knew He was the Son of Mary, equal to us in all things but sin. In the Holy Spirit, Jesus accepted the responsibility of proclaiming to all mankind the Good News of His Father's love. Thus in His person He made visible to us the invisible life and love of His Father. By His life

among us Jesus enabled us to see, hear and experience God's presence in our midst.

Jesus, a Man of Prayer and Action

18. As Jesus fulfilled His ministry of caring for everyone, He turned to His Father in prayer. Often He showed the need of prayer and fasting for developing one's relationship with the Father. Frequently He went off by Himself to pray. In so doing, He praised the Father and thanked Him in the name of the human family for His love and concern, His care and compassion. In worship He lovingly submitted to His Father's holy will and lived in perfect harmony with it. That is why He could say, "I am not seeking my own will, but the will of him who sent me" (Jn. 5:30). Jesus' life and lifestyle, His words and deeds reflected perfectly His prayerful union with God the Father and proclaimed the Father's desire that those whose lives Jesus touched be also united with the Father. The ministry of Jesus, then, was one of calling others to union with God through conversion and reconciliation, through healing and renewal in Him.

19. There are so many wonderful examples in Scripture where Jesus manifested clearly His desire to strengthen and support people like you and me. He gave of Himself completely so that others might come to know the Father's

love and turn to Him with thanksgiving. Jesus understood the fears and anxieties, the loneliness and confusion, the pain and suffering of those whom He met along the way. He gently invited them to accept His love and cultivate the gift of Faith. That Faith entails a willingness to recognize Him as the most perfect sign of God's caring presence in us and among us. Peter was able to say to Him, "You are the Messiah, the Son of the living God" (Mt. 16:16). So also Jesus asks us to acknowledge that He is the anointed one sent by the Father to each one of us to lead us and to save us!

Faith in Christ as the Way

20. Faith involves our trusting in the love of Christ. It should inspire us to say to Jesus like St. Thomas, "My Lord and my God." Faith includes our learning from Christ and following His example. It is not surprising that He would say to us, "Learn from me, for I am gentle and humble of heart" (Mt. 11:29). Faith shows Him to us as the Way.

Mary of Magdala

21. Do you remember the Gospel account when Mary of Magdala met Jesus in the Garden after the Resurrection? There were several ways in which she could have addressed Jesus. Yet,

she chose to call Him Rabboni, "Teacher" (Jn.
20:16). She understood that He taught by word
and by deed. She accepted the fact that His
ministry was to teach. She realized that she
personally was invited to be His disciple, His
follower, and so are we. Each of us is called by
Jesus to accept Him as Teacher. He asks us to
come to Him, to listen to His words, to observe
His deeds, to accept His attitudes, to reflect His
values, to follow Him as the Way.

The Call To Become a Disciple

22. Jesus invites each of you to become His
disciple, His follower. You may be fourteen or
eighteen, weak or strong, smart or not so smart.
You may live in Ashby or Abington, Boston or
Burlington, Peabody or Plymouth. Wherever
you may live, He calls each of you as a very
special, a very unique person, even though He
knows you are not perfect. If He called only the
perfect, would He have anyone to call? He
realizes, better than you and I do, that you can
still grow, that you are not always as loyal as you
might be. He accepts us as persons, as we are,
in order to heal us and help us and make us
better. Jesus asks His disciple, His follower, to
accept Him also as a Person, and then, in Faith,
to accept His whole message as true and valuable, and to live in its light, the light of the Way,
His light.

23. Each new day with its new challenges
is a concrete invitation for you to accept His love

and teaching, to share His message of peace and joy, and to grow in His spirit of hope and confidence.

The Promise of Jesus

24. Jesus promised His disciples, as those whom He loved, that He would be with them all days. Just as He committed Himself to a permanency of relationship, so He asked that they too bind themselves to Him with a firm commitment to walk along His Way all the days of their lives. The relationship, then, was not intended by the Teacher to be temporary. It was to be a permanent relationship on both sides. So Jesus invites each of you as His disciple, His follower, to respond generously to His call for a never-ending relationship.

The Importance of Friendship

25. As young persons, you realize the importance of friendship in your lives. You have and must develop friendships. They are supportive and strengthening. Without friends each one of you would be the poorer. Indeed I can say that you would be lost and alone.

"It Was I Who Chose You"

26. As you cultivate a friendship, you know that give-and-take is necessary. A true friend-

ship depends on a mutual openness and trust, if it is to be nurtured and enriched. Jesus described the relationship He longed to develop with His disciples when He said, "I no longer speak of you as servants, for a servant does not know what his master is about. Instead, I call you friends, since I have made known to you all that I heard from my Father. It was not you who chose me, it was I who chose you to go forth and bear fruit. Your fruit must endure, so that all you ask the Father in my name he will give you. The command I give you is this, that you love one another" (Jn. 15:15).

"Come, Follow Me"

27. As Friend, then, Jesus invites those who are His disciples, His followers, to be open to His love, His concern, His teaching, His Way of Life. He reminds His disciples that if they are nurturing their friendship with Him, not only will they accept His teaching, but they will assimilate His values and share His message with others. As Teacher and Friend, He is truly the Way. In calling those to whom He extends the hand of friendship, He offers the invitation, "Follow me" (Mt. 9:9).

"I Will Not Leave You as Orphans"

28. As in centuries past, today Jesus continues to reach out as a friend to you personally.

That is why after rising from the dead on Easter
Sunday, He lives in our midst. He reminds you
that you need His ever-present love if you are to
mature in life. He invites you to consider the
depth of His love for you personally. You, as His
young brothers or sisters, are most precious to
Jesus. He reminds you that His love for you,
His friendship with you will never wane or
weaken. No matter what the situation of your
lives at any given moment may be, Jesus will be
present as Friend. When He said to all of us, "I
will not leave you as orphans" (Jn. 14:18), He
was speaking to you also as very special persons.
At the same time, He respects you as responsible individuals who can make choices. Each of
you has the ability to accept or reject His
friendship, to weaken or destroy the bond that
He established with you at Baptism. The response that you make to the call of Jesus for
friendship is never forced. It is and must be a
free response. Yet, it is necessary to respond
faithfully and lovingly if you are to grow as
disciples and friends of Jesus, if He is to be your
Way, freely chosen in love.

The Jesus of the Scriptures Speaks to Us

29. I believe that each of you, as a disciple
and friend of the risen Lord, can come to know
Him better and understand His concern for you
more fully by reflecting prayerfully upon certain

Scriptural events within which He meets very different persons and extends a hand of friendship to each of them. Then too, as you and I read the Scriptures, we can identify often with the thoughts and feelings, the questions and hopes of those whom Jesus meets. St. Paul reminds us that Scripture was written to support and encourage us as well as to enlighten and challenge us.

The Woman
Whom Jesus Forgave

30. Let us consider together the situation of the woman who was to be put to death by the angry crowd, which felt it was acting within the Law (cf. Jn. 8:3-11). Imagine the thoughts and feelings racing within her. She undoubtedly felt alone, helpless, confused and bewildered. There was nowhere to go and, seemingly, no one to help her. The crowd, on the other hand, was overwhelmingly bent on carrying out the Law, and perhaps going beyond the Law! Jesus, as Teacher and Friend, Healer and Redeemer, was in the crowd but not one of the crowd. By word and gesture He manifested clearly that the woman was not the only sinner among them or among us. While she stood guilty before the Law and before the crowd, God sought her out through the love of His Son. At the same time, Jesus reminded the would-be executioners of the importance of compassion and mercy. After

the crowd was dismissed, He forgave the woman and challenged her to sin no more, which in this case meant to begin a new life, to continue to be open to His love and mercy, His teaching and friendship.

Jesus Is Always Present with Compassion and Love

31. It is not surprising to hear that some young people today can identify with that woman's sense of being alone and helpless, confused and bewildered. Then, too, for whatever reason, and for many good reasons, some youth feel a sense of guilt. Guilt is not necessarily bad. In fact, it is not bad at all when it follows our choice of what is bad. If one has done wrong, one should feel guilty. Despair, however, is never justified. Tragically, some young folks turn to alcohol or drugs to quiet their feelings of guilt or of depression. In doing so, they do not help themselves. They fail to explore and cultivate all their rich possibilities. After all, Jesus is present to the young today just as He was to the woman in the Scriptures. He does not have to be seen in the flesh to be present. He invites the youth to be open to His presence and love. He reminds them that they should never give in to feelings of confusion and helplessness. Rather, they should turn to Him in prayer for help and guidance, for forgiveness and renewal. With healing He offers hope.

Zaccheus and Jesus Meet

32. Do you recall the Scriptural account of the meeting which took place between Zaccheus, the tax collector, and Jesus? (Lk. 19:1-6) Zaccheus had learned that Jesus was coming through the neighborhood and was anxious to catch a glimpse of Him as He passed by. Because he was small in stature, he did not hesitate even to climb a tree so that he might get a better view. As He walked along, Jesus caught sight of Zaccheus. There and then He extended a hand of friendship to the short man on the tree. He invited Zaccheus to come down and meet Him. Jesus then told Zaccheus that He wished to dine with him in his home. Imagine how Zaccheus must have felt as they spent that time together! There was no doubt that his life was changed, because as Jesus said to him, "Today salvation has come to this house, for this is what it means to be a son of Abraham. The Son of Man has come to search out and save what was lost" (Lk. 19:9-10). The vision of Zaccheus was expanded! His horizons were broadened! We can be sure that Zaccheus would never again be the same.

Jesus Wishes To Dine with Us

33. There are so many young people who can appreciate how Zaccheus must have felt as he climbed that tree because he was not able to

see from the ground like the rest of men. They, too, have known the feeling of being unpopular because they were different. They have known what it is to be laughed at and not taken seriously. Unfortunately, when they do not deal with such feelings properly they tend to become downhearted and discouraged. Yet, if they try like Zaccheus they will find that Jesus desires to be a Friend to each of them. He asks them to welcome Him into their lives. He wishes to dine with them and share His life and His love with them. To tell you the marvelous truth: each time they participate properly and fully in Mass, Jesus comes to them as Friend and Teacher. In addition to being their Way, He also becomes their nourishment for the Way.

The Faith of Peter

34. Another biblical scene that should be significant for many young folks is that of Peter jumping from the boat and walking on the water toward Jesus (Mt. 14:22-23). Feeling the wind and the waves, Peter became hesitant and began to sink. He screamed out to Jesus, "Lord, save me!" At that moment Jesus rebuked and assisted him at the same time. "How little Faith you have! Why did you falter?" Jesus asked. It was natural for Peter to doubt in his own ability to walk on water, to perform a task that was beyond human capability. However, he should have known that all things are possible for those who have Faith in Christ. Jesus chided Peter for

his lack of Faith. At the same instant, Jesus, the Friend and Teacher, extended the hand of compassion and brought the sinking Peter lovingly to Himself.

Jesus, Our Strength and Our Way

35. This Scriptural event could speak to many young people today. So many youth are struggling to be loyal friends and disciples of Jesus. Yet, they tend to doubt themselves, their God-given talents and abilities. They fail to recognize or cultivate the God-given power that is within them. While this may be normal for the present wounded human condition, we who believe in Jesus are certain of His healing help. Jesus is, and can be, our strength. Too often we get the impression from contemporary society that we can accomplish little, that we are unimportant or insignificant. Such an interpretation of the meaning and value of life does not come from Jesus. In your uniqueness each one of you has an unrepeatable contribution to make in the building up of His Kingdom of life, love, justice, peace and joy. You can achieve so much as you come to a deeper understanding and appreciation of the power of His love in your life. Please remember that you are never alone. Jesus, as Friend, is always at your side inviting you to continue walking with Him along the road of life filled with a spirit of confidence in self and trust in Jesus who is our strength and our Way.

36. You should turn to Jesus often in prayer, asking Him to help you to see yourselves as He sees you. So often in the Gospels He reminds those whom He loves that they should never be hesitant or afraid. You, my young brothers and sisters, have been renewed by the Spirit of the Lord and have no adequate reason to doubt your own value and potential. Listen to Jesus your Friend and learn from Jesus your Teacher.

Jesus, the Friend of Martha and Mary

37. Do you remember the time when Jesus was standing with Martha and Mary at the grave of Lazarus? (Jn. 11:1-41) They were so sad and downhearted. Their brother Lazarus, whom Jesus loved, had died. The sacred writer tells us that when Jesus stood there with Martha and Mary, He, too, wept. He identified with their grief. He understood their emptiness. He sympathized with their loneliness. But that was not enough for Him. Since He could do something about the situation—He alone could—He called Lazarus back to life! What a magnificent scene: Jesus, as Friend, responded to the grief of those whom He loved.

Jesus Understands Our Needs

38. On occasion, young people experience the pain of sadness and discouragement. They,

too, know the meaning of loneliness and emptiness. Sometimes they respond to these feelings
by destructive behavior. By word and deed they
express their anger and disappointment because
they believe that no one understands them or
cares about them. They should be encouraged
by the story of Martha and Mary. Jesus understands them better than they or any one of us
can appreciate. He, as Friend, desires to reach
out to them with sensitivity and compassion. He
wishes to remind them that His presence and
love should renew them and assist them to carry
on. Jesus asks that you take seriously the words
that He spoke long ago, "Come to me, all you
who are weary and find life burdensome, and I
will refresh you" (Mt. 11:28). He does not
promise that there will be no pain in your lives.
Pain is integral to growth and to life in the
world. But He does assure each of you that His
friendship and love are sufficient to enrich and
encourage you as you experience these uncom-
fortable moments.

39. The message of the world around you
and of the culture in which you live seems to be
that you should experience no pain, that pain
should be eradicated instantaneously by pleasure and drugs. Jesus, on the other hand, teaches
that pain has value and should be integrated
within the life of anyone who recognizes the
value of happiness itself and the presence of
love.

Turn to Jesus
as Friend and Teacher

40. I pray that you, my young brothers and sisters, will respond to the presence of Jesus as Friend and Teacher. I pray that you will appreciate the compassion and sensitivity that Jesus desires to show you. In doing so, you will turn to Him in those moments of sadness, loneliness and disappointment, and come to realize the emptiness of passing pleasure and the foolishness of the world's advice.

St. Paul, the Disciple of Christ

41. Listen to the words of the great Apostle, St. Paul, "In him who is the source of my strength I have strength for everything" (Phil. 4:13). Paul is a striking example of one who faced challenges and made difficult decisions all his life. The truth of Christ took deep root in Paul's being and Christ was ever present to him. He grew to appreciate ever more the depth of Christ's love for him. His faith in Christ, as his Way, supported and strengthened Paul. In his sharing of the Good News with others, Paul stressed that Jesus was like you and me in every way except sin; Jesus was misunderstood by many; He was scorned by others; Jesus was even rejected by those He came to save. Yet, sustained by the Father's love, He fulfilled His ministry of care with courage and conviction. By

word and deed, Jesus responded to the needs
and fears of those whom He met along the way.

42. The Epistle to the Hebrews explains
briefly to us why we should place all of our trust
and hope in Jesus, Who is our Way. "Since,
then, we have a great high priest who has
passed through the heavens, Jesus, the Son of
God, let us hold fast to our profession of faith.
For we do not have a high priest who is unable
to sympathize with our weakness, but one who
was tempted in every way that we are, yet never
sinned. So let us confidently approach the
throne of grace to receive mercy and favor and
to find help in time of need" (Heb. 4:14-16).

43. St. Paul points to our ultimate destiny
with Christ as the goal of all our strivings and
the fulfillment of all our hopes. He speaks about
the total happiness to which we ardently aspire
when he writes in his letter to the Philippians,
"As you well know, we have our citizenship in
heaven; it is from there that we eagerly await
the coming of our Savior, the Lord Jesus Christ.
He will give a new form to this lowly body of
ours and remake it according to the pattern of
his glorified body, by his power to subject
everything to himself" (Phil. 3:20-21).

Mary, Our Mother and Model

44. Finally, we could not leave the pages
of Scripture without a word about the Virgin
Mary who, early in her life, responded so

gratefully and so enthusiastically to the presence of God within her. She opened her heart to His light and love. Mary placed her faith in Him and trusted in His saving grace. She may have appeared a bit startled and even surprised when she was invited to become the mother of the Son of God. Yet, convinced of the fidelity of a loving Father, she accepted courageously the call to do the will of God. She welcomed the opportunity to participate in the mystery of His plan of salvation as it unfolded in her life. She was to share her Jesus with the human family. Let us look together with reverence and love into her soul as she reveals herself to us in her inspired song of praise to God for His goodness to her, "The Magnificat." Notice the attitudes which this song reflects. Mary is filled with gratitude. With humility, she acknowledges her value and dignity before God. She understands the importance and necessity of responding to Him in prayer. With conviction and courage she meets the challenge of her life without fear and anxiety.

45. Mary is such a brilliant and magnificent model for you, the young people of our day. Oh, how she truly accepted and followed the Way! And for Mary the Way brought her from the cradle of Bethlehem through the hills and valleys of Galilee and Judea to the cross of Calvary; from the empty tomb even to the lasting glory of heaven.

The Church, the Body of Christ

46. As I mentioned before, I was supported greatly by the life of Christ's Church in which I shared during my youth. Jesus brought me into it when I was baptized on the Feast of All Saints. As I grew up in the midst of a Catholic family, the Faith God gave me through the Church also grew. I was fortified by the teachings of the Church, guided by her laws and enriched by her sacraments. The Church, as you know, is empowered by God to continue the saving and healing work of Jesus. Jesus knew that as we face the challenges of life, we would need the guidance of the Church.

47. To do this effectively she must be engaged always in self-renewal in Him who is the Way. The Second Vatican Council was called by Pope John XXIII so that the Church might look at herself in the light of her faith and continue this task of renewing herself in the image of her Lord and Savior Jesus Christ. Please keep in mind that in a very real sense the Church is perfect, and needs no renewal because of Christ, her Head; because of the Holy Spirit, Who gives her life; and because of all the means of salvation with which she is endowed by the Redeemer. All these are holy and perfect. Yet, in another sense, also real, the Church is imperfect, because of failings, shortcomings and even sinfulness in her members who are wounded and in need of the healing of

our Lord and Savior Jesus Christ. Christ her
Hope and her Way forever calls her forth from
her weakness to the strength of His love, as the
Church, enlivened in that love, shares the Good
News with others. She endeavors through her
children—through all of us, that is—to be open
and responsive to Christ's message as well. The
Church strives to follow the same Way which
she proclaims to all.

The Church and You

48. Let the Church become important in
your lives, for the Church is entrusted with the
task of teaching each of you, as God's special
child, in Christ's name; guiding you to grow in
the climate of Christian moral living; and sanctifying you, as one called to mature in holiness,
when you meet Christ in the sacraments.

The Sacraments: Encounters with Christ

49. Please allow the sacraments to be graced
moments for you when you truly encounter
Christ. In a very special way during this period
of your lives, the sacraments of Reconciliation
and Eucharist are particularly vital for you, and
so it is encouraging for me to see such large
numbers of you opening your lives to Christ
through these sacraments. These signs and
sources of God's love are shared with you so that
you might be reconciled with God, with your-

selves, with one another, yes, with the universe around you; and that you might also be re-newed, enriched and encouraged, supported and strengthened, forgiven and forgiving. As you face the decisions and tensions of your lives, these blessed moments of intimacy with Christ are intended by the Lord to comfort you and, at the same time, to allow you to continue to walk in His Way as you grow in His Spirit. I hope you never underestimate nor fail to appreciate the significance of the sacraments in your lives, for they are God's vital gifts to you today and every day.

Youth as God's Gift

50. I mean it sincerely when I say that you, as young people, are God's invaluable gifts to the Church. As those whom He loves more than you can ever fully understand, you are called to enrich the life of the Church. Without you, those of us who are adults would be seriously poor, and so sad! Your vision and enthusiasm, your ideals and values, your searching and questioning are very important to us. Christ touches your lives so that you, with enthusiastic generosity, might touch ours. We must dialogue with you in honesty, listen to you with respect and hope, and learn from you with prudence, humility and joy. We hope that you, in turn, will listen to us with openness, and profit by our experience and wisdom as you learn how to live

and love His Way. The Lord asks us to share our experience with you, as we catch the spirit of your dreams. Try to remember that you, as God's unique sons and daughters, are gifts to the Church. I try never to forget this, and rejoice in it and have hope because of it.

Youth as Open to New Life

51. As your Archbishop and friend in the Lord, I pray that you will be open to the possibilities and the challenges of each new day. There is no room for boredom in your lives if you have faith in the Way. It leads to the greatest love. Please keep in mind that the extraordinary is hidden in the ordinary. Look around you with the eyes of Faith. See also the beauty, goodness and truth as these are found within you. This is not pride, but true humility because you are ultimately God's creation, the work of God's hands. I beg you to acknowledge the signs of God's love in the persons and events that surround you. I hope that you will evaluate critically those manifestations of evil that will be counter-productive in your lives as you are called to mature in age, wisdom and grace. As you avoid sin and all the occasions of sin which might keep you from following the Way, you will be enabled to cultivate the good and the true as you face with confidence the possibilities of each new day.

Youth as an Example of Growth

52. Remember that growth is integral to life. Realize that growth also involves change. Appreciate the fact that some tension will be involved in this change or transformation. Don't be surprised or discouraged if you feel this tension, or even some confusion, as you continue to grow as young sons and daughters of God. Be glad that each of you is offered so many opportunities to mature as a person who believes in God and as a self who is created by God. The outstanding young saints in the life of the Church should comfort and challenge you to advance and grow in the way of the Lord. Consider the lives of St. Francis of Assisi, St. Dominic Savio, St. Maria Goretti, and so many other young people who were inspired by God's love for them and accepted the invitation to follow His Way and mature in His love.

Heroes for Today

53. In an age when true heroes do not seem to surface, and when we tend to criticize weaknesses rather than acknowledge strengths in people, imitate the Christ-like qualities of those young persons whom you know, admire and respect. At the same time, learn about and emulate the wonderful qualities of Christian growth reflected in the lives of so many youthful saints who are a magnificent part of the heritage of the Church.

Youth as an
"On-the-way" Experience

54. My dear young friends, as I stated in the beginning of this letter, I think of you with reverent and joyful affection during this Easter season, as I do throughout the rest of the year, for I know how much God loves you. Each day, as I celebrate the Sacrifice of the Mass and look at the Cross, I realize how much Jesus loves you and how He has truly shown you the Way you should follow. I have tried to keep in mind what we talked about during my visits in our schools and parishes. I have attempted to share with you some thoughts about Christ, who is your Way and my Way. He is truly our Way, for it is in Him that we meet.

55. I never cease to thank God for His goodness in gifting the Church with your lives and talents, your restless devotion and tireless generosity. I thank you for the joy you give me and trust that I can be of some little help to you as you grow in Him Who is the Way. I understand and appreciate the challenges that are part and parcel of your lives. Some of them have been shared by young people of every age; others are caused or heightened by the society and culture in which we live. But I recognize as well the blessings and graces that are yours in abundance today.

Never Lose Hope in Him

56. I beg you never to lose hope as you continue to walk along the Way, His Way. Remember that you are still on the way and that you are not traveling alone. There are many others who follow that same way. There are so many who do care. We are pilgrims together. Just as Jesus said, "Follow Me," so He says to you, "I am with you all days." Open your hearts to Christ. Do not hesitate to turn to Him. Respond to His presence in Faith. Look to Him with hope. Cling to Him with love. Continue to dream and to search. Keep Him in your dreams and in your search. My thoughts and my prayers are with you. Pray for me that I, as your Archbishop and friend, may strive ever more faithfully to share God's love in word and deed with you, and thus continue to show you the Way.

"Come, Meet Me in My Church"

Christmas, 1982

The Church:
a Caring Community

My Dear Young Brothers and Sisters,

I am pleased to write to you once again because you are always in my mind and heart, especially during this Holy Christmas season. You are indeed always in my prayers. I have come to know how much God, our Father, loves you in Christ who was born to us in Bethlehem about two thousand years ago. I believe that God has created each of you uniquely in His image and likeness. In addition, with a love beyond all telling, through Jesus His Son, He has gifted you with His life in the wonderful Sacrament of Baptism and is inviting you each day to open your minds to His truth, your hearts to His love.

It is a great joy for me to speak of Jesus with you, Jesus who knows you and whom you know. It is indeed the privilege of my life as a priest and Bishop to ask you in His name, "Come, Meet Me in My Church."

Believe me when I say that you, young members of the Church founded by Jesus Christ, are most important to me. Would that I could talk with each of you personally—to listen to you, to look into your eyes, to learn from you, to encourage you, to support you, and to be encouraged by your youthful enthusiasm and strength. I am aware that you meet many challenges and difficulties in growing up in today's world—more so than I did, even though I had my share. I can well understand that some of you may become confused and even discouraged as you face those forces from inside of you, or from outside of you, that can weaken or even destroy you. I am living in the midst of them with you. This is our age. As someone has put it, "These may not be the best of times, nor the worst of times, but they are our times." It is for us to be in charge, with the help of the Lord, and by sticking together with Him.

Recently I met with many young people who attend Catholic and public high schools within the Archdiocese of Boston in order to prepare for this letter to you. During our conversations we discussed some of the pressures that many of you experience. The young men and women spoke frankly about the power of peer pressure; the difficulty of communication within the family; the availability of alcohol, drugs and illicit sexual activity; the feelings of loneliness, boredom, helplessness and guilt; their concern and anxiety regarding the future.

Even though quite concerned, the youth with whom I met were not downhearted or depressed. They were keenly aware of the presence of various pressures that must be dealt with responsibly in the lives of teenagers. They were serious about life today. But they spoke as well about those aspects of their lives and experiences that have been sources of strength and encouragement for them. I was deeply impressed by the sincerity and openness of these young men and women as we examined together the relationship between Faith and life. During our conversations they spoke honestly about the value of Faith in their lives and were eager to grow in their knowledge and love of Jesus Christ and His Church. This is the reason for the title of this letter which is a loving invitation from Jesus to you, "Come, Meet Me in My Church."

When I met with the young people, each of you was in my mind and heart, in my thoughts and prayers. Although I could not invite all of you to visit with me—it would be a physical impossibility—I welcome the opportunity of writing to you during this blessed Christmas season. I pray that you will be comforted and challenged as you read this pastoral and hopefully personal letter to you. I pray that as you catch the spirit of my conversation with your peers you will be encouraged and enriched. Since I am your priest and Bishop, and therefore love you, my sincerest hope is that you will be happy as you make your way in life—what we call in the Catholic Church "our pilgrimage of Faith together to our everlasting home in heaven."

I.

The Truth from Jesus

1. JESUS: OUR SAVIOR

During our conversations we discussed to some extent the meaning and importance of the mysteries of Jesus Christ and His Church in our lives. We recalled that Jesus, who is true God and true Man, was sent by God our Father to infuse His life and love into us, to give us His forgiveness and peace. The basic truth of our Faith which Jesus revealed to Nicodemus, the Pharisee who became His follower, is meant for you and for me also. Each of us should reflect prayerfully upon the personal significance of His living words:

> Yes, God so loved the world
> that he gave his only Son
> that whoever believes in him may not die
> but may have eternal life.
> God did not send the Son into the world
> to condemn the world,
> but that the world might be saved
> through him (Jn. 3:16-17).

Please notice that Jesus did not come among us to condemn us but that we might have forgiveness, peace, life and joy through Him. He is first and foremost and always our Savior. He is Jesus: the one who saves us from our sins (cf. Mt. 1:21). However, at the end of time He will also be our judge, for He shall come again in glory to judge both the living and the dead (Nicene Creed).

We discussed other teachings of Jesus that speak directly to the young person today. For example:

2. JESUS TEACHES THAT WE ARE VALUABLE

Jesus teaches that each of us is unique and valuable in God's eyes and that we are more important to Him than we will ever realize. In speaking to His disciples Jesus reminds us of our true value and assures us that God will never abandon us. Try to reflect slowly and peacefully with me on these marvelous and inspiring words of His:

Look at the birds in the sky.
They do not sow or reap,
they gather nothing into barns;
yet your heavenly Father feeds them.
Are you not more important than they?
Which of you
by worrying
can add a moment to his life-span?
As for clothes,
why be concerned?
Learn a lesson from the way
the wild flowers grow.

They do not work; they do not spin.
Yet I assure you,
not even Solomon in all his splendor
was arrayed like one of these.
If God can clothe in such splendor
the grass of the field,
which blooms today
and is thrown on the fire tomorrow,
will he not provide much more for you?
(Mt. 6:26-30)

In spite of appearances and cases you may bring up, God never fails to provide for our real needs. It is we who often fail to be just in our distribution of the good things He provides for the benefit of all. Our greed and laziness are sources of injustice and suffering for others. God's good earth somewhere does provide! Think about it!

Jesus is telling us constantly that God loves us and cares for us. We are more important to God than all other living things in creation for which He provides abundantly. Jesus teaches clearly that God does and will provide for us. He invites us to trust in God's faithful and caring presence—in His Divine Providence. He urges us not to be overly concerned and worried about our needs and wants. He stresses that such an attitude is foolish and fruitless. But Jesus does not tell us to do nothing about our real and legitimate needs. What He does teach is that we should not create unnecessary needs, nor should we perform sinful actions to satisfy our needs, whether real or imaginary.

If we are to be faithful friends and followers of Jesus, we must accept His teaching that honest work, prayer and trust in God's love will bring us true happiness and peace even if not material wealth. What we must be about is to work for justice in our hearts and among us so that God's goodness may reach everyone on the face of the earth. He provides! We must cooperate with Him in the just distribution of what He so generously provides, even at the cost of personal sacrifice. This is what love calls for.

3. JESUS TEACHES US TO USE OUR TALENTS RESPONSIBLY

Jesus teaches that we should use our talents and gifts responsibly as we apprecjate the gift of life. Let us listen together to Him addressing His disciples:

Jesus spoke this parable: "A man had a fig tree growing in his vineyard and he came out looking for fruit on it but he did not find any. He said to the vinedresser, 'Look here! For three years now I have come in search of fruit on this fig tree and I found none. Cut it down. Why should it clutter up the ground?' In answer, the man said, 'Sir, leave it another year, while I hoe around it and manure it; then perhaps it will bear fruit' " (Lk. 13:6-9).

If you pray over this parable, you will understand that Jesus is telling us to do all we can to develop what we have and are in ourselves so that we may be able to bear fruit. In other words, our responsibility as believers is

to please God by what we are and do and to be
of greater service to others as we learn to love
one another as Jesus loves us. We have the
privilege of making the loving concern of God
for all a reality in the lives of those we touch by
loving and serving them as God does and
commands us to do. This is one way we bring
about His justice in the world, meet Jesus in His
Church, and so build up His Kingdom of peace.

4. JESUS SHOWS US THAT
WE ARE DEPENDENT BUT RESPONSIBLE

Jesus teaches that we are totally dependent
upon God but are also made responsible by the
Father in His loving care for those in need. He
states clearly that we must never permit any
relationship to keep us from loving God, from
accepting his Holy Will or obeying His commandments. He reminds us that if we are to be
His friends and followers we must view service
on behalf of others as essential to our lives. Each
of us is called to respond generously to God's
love and to the needs of our brothers and
sisters.

Let us reflect prayerfully upon the words of
Jesus:

One of the scribes came up, and when he heard
them arguing he realized how skillfully Jesus
answered them. He decided to ask him, "Which is
the first of all the commandments?" Jesus replied:
"This is the first: 'Hear, O Israel! The Lord our
God is Lord alone! Therefore you shall love the

Lord your God with all your heart, with all your soul, with all your mind, and with all your strength.' This is the second, 'You shall love your neighbor as yourself.' There is no other commandment greater than these" (Mk. 12:28-30).

God is always first, but we are to love all others second, because of Him, since they are all created in His image and likeness and are destined to be happy with Him forever.

5. JESUS ASSURES US THAT HE WILL NEVER ABANDON US

Jesus assures us that He shall always be with us to comfort and challenge, encourage and enrich, support and strengthen us as we face the pains and pressures of life. Let us try to fathom the love in the Heart of Jesus as He speaks to each of us personally:

Come to me,
all you who are weary
and find life burdensome,
and I will refresh you.
Take my yoke upon your shoulders
and learn from me,
for I am gentle
and humble of heart.
Your souls will find rest,
for my yoke is easy
and my burden light (Mt. 11:28-30).

His yoke is easy and His burden is light because He is with us to help us carry them. As our Lord and God He gives us His joy, His peace and His strength. Without Him we could not carry any burden whether it be His, ours or another's. Fortified by His strength we can do so with confidence and courage. In fact, it is a privilege to carry His burden which is to love and serve the Father above all and to love and serve all others because of the Father. But we must keep ever in mind that in all our relationships, in carrying life's burdens and in enjoying life's good things, it is from Him we learn, because He is gentle and humble of heart. If we keep our eyes and ears open, we learn from Him how to live when we meet Him in His Church.

6. JESUS REVEALS TO US THAT HE WILL GIVE HIS LIFE FOR US

Jesus, who is the Way, the Truth and the Life, teaches that He is our Lord and Brother, our Friend and Guide. From the following words, let us learn how close He is to us and how close He wants to be in truth, in love and in life:

I am the good shepherd.
I know my sheep and my sheep know me
in the same way that the Father knows me
and I know the Father;
for these sheep I will give my life.
I have other sheep
that do not belong to this fold.
I must lead them, too,
and they shall hear my voice.

There shall be one flock, then,
one shepherd.
The father loves me for this:
that I lay down my life to take it up again.
No one takes it from me;
I lay it down freely.
I have power to lay it down,
and I have power to take it up again.
This command I received from my father
    (Jn. 10:14-18).

We should read these words again and again. They are life-giving! They are a well-spring of love and true freedom!

Do you see how close Jesus is to each one of us? He knows each one of us intimately, just as we are, in all truth. He loves us to the point of giving His life for us just as He finds us in order to save us. Jesus lays down His life for us freely because He loves us unreservedly. It is His most Holy Will that each of us be united with Him in love. And so He invites us to respond freely to His love and to imitate His generosity as we serve one another in His Name. In our response of love, we are sorry for all our sins, as well as determined, with His grace, never to offend Him again. In this way too we build up His Church in love and strengthen it in unity.

7. JESUS TEACHES
THAT WE MUST IMITATE HIM

Jesus teaches that if we open our lives to His person, our minds to His message, and our hearts to His love, we will become His friends and learn to love as He loves. Try to taste the gentle power of these words:

As the Father has loved me,
so I have loved you.
Live on in my love.
You will live in my love
if you keep my commandments,
even as I have kept my Father's
    commandments,
and live in his love.
All this I tell you that my joy may be yours
and your joy may be complete.
This is my commandment:
love one another as I have loved you.
There is no greater love than this:
to lay down one's life for one's friends.
You are my friends
if you do what I command you.
I no longer speak of you as slaves,
for a slave does not know what his master
    is about.
Instead, I call you friends,
since I have made known to you all that I heard
    from my Father.
It was not you who chose me,
it was I who chose you to go forth
and bear fruit.
Your fruit must endure,
so that all you ask the Father in my name
he will give you.
The command I give you is this,
that you love one another (Jn. 15:9-17).

My dear young brothers and sisters, do you not see the real, true and honest caring that issues from this love? This love is the source of all justice and peace and joy within us and among us. It is worth everything else. At least I think so, and I hope you do too. It is this kind of love which is from God that makes us more human because it makes us more like Jesus who is the perfect Man, who is God made Man, the Son of God who became man in order to save us because of God's loving care for us. Jesus, the Tremendous Lover, teaches us the true meaning of compassion, caring and concern. He invites us to be united in love, recognize each other's needs and give glory to the Father in heaven by serving our brothers and sisters. He invites you and all to meet Him in His Church and to carry on with Him the work given Him to do by His Father: To reconcile the whole world with the Father through the blood of His Cross, through His loving sacrifice (cf. Col. 1:20).

8. THE RESPONSE OF THE YOUNG

Isn't it sad that some young people do not appreciate their value and dignity in the light of God's loving care for them? Isn't it tragic that they do not realize how much God loves them as His sons and daughters? Isn't it pathetic that some of them turn to alcohol and drugs to overcome boredom or that they confront loneliness by involvement in illicit sexual activity? Although they may not realize it, such destructive behavior is not worthy of their dignity as children of God. Yet, God never ceases to love them in Christ and to reach out to them with compassion and forgiveness, because in spite of their sinfulness and misery God knows their real value and dignity. God invites them to turn to Him in repentance and accept His love and forgiveness. Recall the message of Jesus contained in the parables of the Lost Sheep and the Prodigal Son.

I thank God with all my heart that so many of you young people in our Archdiocese are anxious to listen to the words of Jesus, to accept His grace and to respond to His love. You may experience sad moments, but you do not give up or give in. Your Faith in God is enabling you to have confidence in yourselves too. Your trust in God is assisting you to develop this self-confidence. Your love for God is inspiring you to express legitimate love for yourselves—and for all others. In a variety of ways you are trying to meet Christ in His Church. Keep it up. As Pope John Paul II says to you, "Allow Christ to meet you." Get ready to answer His loving invitation, "Come, Meet Me in My Church."

II.

The Church: a Caring Community

During my recent conversations with the young people who came to visit me, we not only talked about the person and message of Jesus in relation to the youth of today, but we also discussed the meaning and the place of the Catholic Church in the life of the young person.

The Catholic Church is a marvelous gift of Jesus Christ, who is its Head. This brief letter cannot possibly exhaust the deep Mystery of the Catholic Church which the Sacred Scriptures call the Bride of Christ and the Body of Christ. Christ loves His Church. He gave Himself up for it (cf. Eph. 5:25). I regret that we can only dwell now very superficially on some aspects of the Church which it is my privilege to love and to serve with all my heart and all my strength. However, I welcome the opportunity of reflecting with you upon the Catholic Church as a "Caring Community," where Christ invites you to meet Him.

1. JESUS PROMISES TO SEND THE HOLY SPIRIT

When Jesus was preparing to return to the Father He promised He would never abandon His friends and followers. Let us listen to Him:

> I did not speak of this with you from the
> beginning
> because I was with you.
> Now that I go back to him who sent me,
> not one of you asks me,
> "Where are you going?"
> Because I have had this to say to you,
> you are overcome with grief.
> Yet I tell you the sober truth:
> It is much better for you that I go.
> If I fail to go,

the Paraclete will never come to you.
Whereas if I go,
I will send him to you (Jn. 16:5-7).

Jesus was sent by the Father to reveal His
love for us, to gather us around Himself in
Faith, Hope and Love, and thereby save us for
the Father through His blood. During His
public ministry Jesus formed a community of
friends and disciples. He taught them that one
of the reasons He came among them was to
share His life and love with them. Jesus invited
them to respond to His love by imitating Him as
their Teacher and Model. He reminded them
that if they were to be His loyal friends and
disciples they must become, among other things,
a caring community. Because He cares, they
too must care. Jesus assured His disciples
that He would send His Holy Spirit, the Paraclete, to support and strengthen them in all
their efforts. Through the ages the Holy Spirit
would sanctify and guide the Church as she
fulfills the mission entrusted to her by Jesus
Christ.

2. THE PROMISE OF JESUS IS FULFILLED

And so on Pentecost Sunday the Catholic
Church was born when the Holy Spirit came
upon the Apostles and those assembled with
them, among whom was the Church's most
blessed member, Mary, the Mother of Jesus.

When the day of Pentecost came
it found them gathered in one place.

Suddenly from up in the sky
there came a noise like a strong, driving wind
which was heard all through the house where
      they were seated.
Tongues as of fire appeared,
which parted and came to rest on each of them.
All were filled with the Holy Spirit (Acts 2:1-4).

3. SOMETHING ABOUT THE CHURCH

How would you describe the Church?
What is the Church in your view? Your answers
to that question may vary, depending on what
you have heard and what you have seen some
members of the Church do. Some describe the
Church as the Pope or bishops, priests or
religious sisters or brothers, or lay people;
others view the Church as the Archdiocese or
the parish. Some might think that the Church is
a building; others say that they are the Church.
Which description is correct? In a sense, each of
them is part of the total Mystery of the Catholic
Church. Because Christ lives on in His Church,
and because Christ cared so much for all of us so
as to lay down His life for us, the Church which
lives by Him, from Him, and for Him, must, of
necessity, be a caring community. To be faithful
to Him it must care as He cared and forever
cares. Even though some members of the
Church may not care, still the Church as a
Community is indeed a "Caring Community."
Witness the countless variety of works it en-

gages in to promote human dignity in the name of Jesus who is the Way, the Truth and the Life.

4. THE CHURCH
AS A CARING COMMUNITY

The Church is a caring community when it shares with us Christ's message, teaching us faithfully what He taught, since we need the word of His truth to live. He said, "Man does not live by bread alone, but by every word that comes from the mouth of God" (cf. Mt. 4:5).

The Church is a caring community when the successor of St. Peter, the Pope, and the successors of the other Apostles, the bishops, guarantee the authenticity of what is preached and taught as being the truth coming from Jesus.

The Church is a caring community when it makes clear to us that God loved us so much that He sent His Son upon earth to redeem us from our sins and to teach us how to live.

The Church is a caring community when it guides and directs us so that we may pattern our lives upon the life of Jesus.

The Church is a caring community when it brings us to the means that Christ instituted, both for our happiness here on earth and for our eternal happiness in heaven: the Sacraments, especially Penance or Reconciliation, and the Eucharist, and all other means of receiving grace.

The Church is a caring community when it assists us to grow, develop and mature in the new life into which we were reborn in Baptism.

The Church is a caring community when it helps us to love and serve God and to love and serve our neighbor in countless works of justice and mercy for the glory of God and the advancement of His Kingdom of life, love, peace and joy.

5. THE CHURCH IS A COMMUNITY WHERE PEOPLE BELONG

None of us enjoy being abandoned and alone, forgotten and ignored, unchallenged and bored. I certainly don't. (However, we can accept all these as penance for our sins and the sins of others and so redeem the world with Jesus.) Each of us is anxious to be accepted and appreciated. We all want to be wanted, to be needed. All of us desire to be recognized and respected, to be comforted and challenged, even if we are not always willing to admit this to one another.

Now, Christ who loves and cares for us has founded the Church so that these needs might be fulfilled for each of us—partially in this world, and totally in heaven. He has established the Church as a community of His followers who should be caring persons so that we, whether young or old, might be enriched and enlivened personally with the spiritual riches that come from Him and from one another. He has established the Church to be a community of caring persons so that we, whether young or old, might be willing and able to share His truth with others by word and action.

Within the community of the Catholic Church, Jesus Christ shares with us His life and love, His teachings and values—His light. Within this community He invites us to discover our meaning, to appreciate our value, to develop our talents and to cultivate our lives. Within this community He calls us, each of us, whether young or old, to accept His Gospel, to respond to His love, to share His peace with the freedom of God's children and true human responsibility. The Catholic Church is a community in which each of us belongs as an important person in the mind and heart of Jesus Christ.

6. THE CHURCH IS A COMMUNITY WHERE PEOPLE RECEIVE STRENGTH AND POWER TO DO GOOD

Do you ever become discouraged and downhearted? Do you ever feel that you are fragmented and disjointed, bewildered and confused? At times you may question the meaning and value of life itself. On occasion you might worry about your popularity and wonder if you're accepted by others. Possibly you are concerned about your studies, your ability to achieve and whether or not you'll be happy in the future. As you no doubt suspect, other young people have experienced these feelings, asked similar questions and raised comparable concerns. What is important is how you deal with them. One thing we are sure of is that Jesus deals with them for us in His Church. Do you remember the parable of the birds of the air and the lilies of the field?

I know that the pace of life today can be hectic for all of us. It is for me. You, as young people, are gifted with energy and vitality. However, it would be wise for you to be aware that your strength can become your weakness. Because of your youthful spirit you may neglect to set aside precious moments to slow down, to think and pray, to talk to God through Jesus and even to talk honestly with others and listen to their advice.

Remember the words of Jesus, "Come to Me and I will refresh you." And as your Archbishop and brother who loves you, I am saying to you for Him, "Come, Meet Me in My Church." That invitation is directed to each of you. The Catholic Church is a community in which we meet Jesus as He speaks to us in the Scriptures; in the Liturgy; in the Sacraments; in the teaching of the Holy Father, the Pope and of the bishops with him; in the lives of others and in prayer. The Church is a community in which we learn about the meaning and value of our lives, in which we are guided and supported, forgiven and healed. Just as the roots of the tree, though below the surface, are so important for its life and growth, so as we are rooted in the community of the Church, and fortified by the Sacraments which give life, each of us receives the strength and power to live our lives today with enthusiasm and joy as we prepare for tomorrow with confidence, and for eternity with hope.

And this is so in spite of the fact that everyone in the Church does not appear to make every effort to follow Christ. Some may even attempt to destroy the work of Christ by what they say and by the way they live. We need to have great compassion for these wounded members of Christ's Body which is the Church and help to heal them with our loving concern. This is part of the mission of the caring community whose spirit is the Spirit of Christ.

7. THE CHURCH IS A COMMUNITY IN WHICH PEOPLE CULTIVATE FRIENDSHIP

Where would we be without good friends? Friends are persons whom we respect and admire and love. Because we know them to be good and truthful, we trust them and so share our thoughts, our feelings, and our hopes with them. When we meet Jesus in His Church, He invites us to open our minds to His truth and our hearts to His love: to get to know Him better and love Him more. Jesus invites us to grow in friendship with Him. He asks us to listen to Him, to learn from Him as He speaks to us in the Church, and to imitate Him. Jesus has assured us that each of us is special to Him as His friend and that He will always be at our side with a loving heart, as our Friend.

Jesus has founded the community of the Church for many reasons, but this is certainly one of them: that each of us might cultivate friendship not only with Him but with one another. We, no matter what our age or position, are asked by Jesus to respect one another, to listen to one another, to support and encourage one another. The Church is a community of people like you and me called to be and do many things, but certainly to be good and loyal friends of Jesus and of one another. Unfortunately, some of us fail to follow Jesus closely. We use poorly and unwisely our gift of freedom. Our unwise choices hurt us and also the Church as a Caring Community.

8. THE CHURCH IS A COMMUNITY IN WHICH PEOPLE ARE COMFORTED AND CHALLENGED

It is important for all of us to realize that we are valuable and responsible. Some people seem to think that their value is measured by their material possessions. How much money in the bank? How many cars in the garage? A cottage on the shore? A big-paying job? Unfortunately, contemporary culture tends to reinforce this view. However, the Gospel of Jesus stresses that even if we have nothing we are valuable before God, because we have been made in His image and likeness and have been redeemed by the blood of Christ. We, as His sons and daughters, are invited each day to grow in His life and to promote His love, justice and peace by what we say and do. The community of the Church shares the message of Jesus that each of us, whether young or old, is called to worship God, and assist others to discover real and true meaning and happiness in life. We fulfill this responsibility by living out our true relationship with God and one another in Christ Jesus Our Lord.

It is not surprising that you, even if you are aware that you are valuable and responsible young people, may become tired and frustrated on occasion. In spite of this, I am convinced that you really desire to grow in Faith, Hope and Love. You are anxious to respect your sexuality and to cultivate your talents and gifts in spite of your weaknesses.

You try to be generous and kind despite many temptations to selfishness and anger.

You want to understand and forgive others.

But sometimes all this is not easy.

Most of us know the tension involved in knowing what Jesus asks and doing what He expects—and what He requires!

Jesus understands that all of us experience moments when we really cry out for help.

And so He invites each of us to come to Him, to meet Him within the community of the Church—especially in His Eucharistic Presence. He is always eager to welcome us there.

We may be hesitant to turn to Him because we have not been as loyal and responsible as we should have been. We may have violated His commandments. We may have caused scandal to others and even led them into sin. No matter what our situation, we should never hesitate to meet Jesus Christ in the Church. He longs to forgive and fortify us in the Sacrament of Reconciliation, to enrich and encourage us in Holy Communion, to strengthen and support us in prayer. In spite of all our faults, Jesus promises that He will give us the power and strength to carry on with courage. With Him we can do all things (cf. Phil. 4:13).

9. THE CHURCH IS A COMMUNITY IN WHICH PEOPLE ARE FORGIVEN

It is not always easy to follow Jesus. I should know. I have been trying for 67 years. On occasion—or even frequently—we may fail to live as we know we should. After sinning, we should experience a healthy sense of guilt and sentiments of sorrow. When we have done wrong we should be honest enough to admit it. We should recognize that we have sinned and ask God for healing and forgiveness. Jesus, as Savior, is always eager to reach out to us with compassion and understanding—with His caring love. He wants to be Jesus for us! He has founded the Church as a saving community. He has instituted in it the Sacrament of Reconciliation so that we, as repentant sinners, can receive His healing and forgiving love. We, as His friends and followers, are called to turn to Christ and then to share His healing and forgiveness with others.

10. THE CHURCH
AS THE BODY OF CHRIST

I thank God for this opportunity of reflecting with you briefly upon another beautiful aspect of the Catholic Church. Neither you nor I can view the Church simply as an institution outside of us. Following the mind of Christ, St. Paul reminds us that we are the Church. He tells us that if we do not accept Christ's invitation to be His faithful friends and followers, then the Church as a caring community will be all the weaker. Whether we want it or not, the Church of Christ in this world is made up of people like you and me who love Him and try to obey His commandments. Let us pay very close attention to the great Apostle's inspired teaching:

The body is one and has many members,
but all the members,
many though they are,
are one body; and so it is with Christ.
It was in one Spirit that all of us,
whether Jew or Greek, slave or free,
were baptized into one body.
All of us have been given to drink of the one
Spirit.
Now the body is not one member,
it is many.

If the foot should say,
"Because I am not a hand I do not belong to the
   body,"
would it then no longer belong to the body?
If the ear should say,
"Because I am not an eye I do not belong to the
   body,"
would it then no longer belong to the body?
If the body were all eye, what would happen to
   our hearing?
It it were all ear, what would happen to our
   smelling?
As it is, God has set each member of the body
in the place he wanted it to be.
If all the members were alike,
where would the body be?
There are, indeed, many different members but
   one body.
The eye cannot say to the hand, "I do not need
   you,"
any more than the head can say to the feet, "I do
   not need you."
Even those members of the body which seem
   less important
are in fact indispensable (1 Cor. 12:12-22).

St. Paul teaches clearly that the Church is
not an unruly mob but a well-organized institution—like a body. He stresses that each member is valuable. In accordance with God's plan
each member is expected to exercise specific
responsibilities within the Church for the good
of the whole Body. It is important that we
understand our place within the Body of Christ
and take it if we are to contribute to the
Church's mission.

One member of the Church has been chosen by Jesus Christ to be the successor of St. Peter. That person is the Pope. The Pope's responsibility is unique and cannot be exercised by any other member. He is the Vicar of Christ. He is the visible head of the Church, while Christ remains its invisible Head.

I, as your Bishop, have been called by the Lord to fulfill a particular role within the Church. The priests, because of their vocation and ordination, have been assigned to participate in a specific manner in the work of the Church. And the religious have an irreplaceable witness to render in the Church for the sake of the Kingdom. Your parents and teachers have been given a valuable and unique place within the Church. Actually, no one can adequately carry out their mission for them. When they are missing, something vital is missing. You, because of your Baptism and Confirmation, have been called by the Lord to grow in Christian maturity and to be responsible members of the Church, assigned to bring the Gospel message at least to your peers. I believe no one can do it better.

All of us have an important place in the Body of Christ. Each has been given a particular role to fulfill—a role we are not at liberty to abandon. None of us may exercise tasks or responsibilities within the Body that have not been assigned to us by the Lord. For this we have received no power. Besides, it would be presumption. It would be a usurpation. But

Jesus invites us all to be united in His Spirit and to cooperate with one another as mature members of His Body, the Church, each in his or her assigned task. As we fulfill our proper responsibilities faithfully, the Church is seen by others as a Caring Community—which it then actually is.

11. MY PRAYER FOR YOU

It is a joy for me to reach out to you by means of these simple words. I pray that you will place your hands in mine and walk with me in the service of the Lord and our brothers and sisters. I pray that you will not attempt to overcome boredom by turning to liquor and drugs; that you will not confront loneliness by playing at love, by cultivating detrimental friendships or by striving to be popular at any price; that you will not avoid decisions for the future by living and acting as if tomorrow or eternity will never come. Rather, I pray that you, as friends and followers of Jesus, will overcome boredom by cultivating your gifts and employing your talents in the service of God and on behalf of others; that you will confront loneliness by accepting Christ's call to become active, responsible members of His caring community; that you will prepare for the future by living, thinking and acting as mature Christians in the present; that you will instill hope in this our generation. You can do it.

Listen to Pope John Paul II addressing the young people of Sicily just two months ago:

Have courage! Christ is your hope. Be on the side of Christ, my dear young people, and you will be on the side of hope.... And then share this hope with others, especially with the young who have lost heart, and share it through the example of your life. Courage!... Together with them learn how to build a new future and a new society, in which there will be justice and peace for all (unemployment is the death of young people), a future and a society without drugs (drugs deal a death blow at the roots of being), a future and a society without violence and war. Peace is possible.... Christ gives you the hope of sharing in this great human, social, moral and spiritual reconstruction of society. Christ is the God of hope, of newness, of the future....

Finally, live and build up this hope with the Church. Love the Church, your Bishops, your priests. With them learn how to be instruments of the mystery of salvation, witnesses and doers of the beatitudes, of service, of humility, of poverty, and of self-giving. The hope of the Christian is a joyful witness of the Church which announces the resurrection and prepares for this resurrection with those who weep, who are weak, who are small, poor, marginalized, but whom God, who loves everyone, trusts in order to break the bow of those who believe themselves to be strong (cf. 1 Sm. 2:4)....

With the Church, pray to Christ for hope. It is He who guarantees hope because He is our hope (cf. 1 Tm. 1:1).

When you look at yourselves, at your own mystery, when you think of your fears, your problems, your uncertainties, look to Him.

When you look at others, at their pain and sorrow, at their reactions, at their fatigue, when you think of the future of the earth, look to Him, to Christ, "the hope of glory" (Col. 1:27).

He is the hope that overcomes. He is the one calling you day after day to work with all your strength for the coming of His eternal and universal Kingdom among men,...a kingdom of truth and life, a kingdom of holiness and grace, a kingdom of justice, love and peace (*L'Osservatore Romano,* November 22-23, 1982, page 7).

I pray that you will respond to Christ generously and so will always be happy. True happiness, real joy, is the echo of God's presence in our lives. Through Baptism we have entered into Christ's Life which is strengthened in us by His Word and Sacraments within the Church.

12. YOUTH: RESPONSIBLE MEMBERS OF A CARING CHURCH

As your Archbishop and friend I acknowledge with gratitude that many young men and women are accepting a responsible role within the Church in Boston as a caring community. Many of you have met Christ in His Church and are teaching CCD classes, visiting the sick and elderly and participating in programs to assist the poor and needy. Large numbers of you are active in parish youth programs, involved in parish councils, fulfilling the roles of servers, lectors and ushers at parish liturgies. Some are members of retreat teams and are exercising a peer ministry within the high schools of the Archdiocese.

I realize that many of you are numbered already among these outstanding young people who have met Christ in His Church and are effective messengers of His hope. I am confident that others too might be asking timely and important questions. What can I do? How can I become more actively involved in continuing the work of Jesus Christ? How can I be the Church for others? How can I bring hope to my peers, to my generation? You do see, I trust, that in practice each of us represents the whole Church for others. Many people come to know the Church as a Caring Community because of the manner in which we reflect faithfully the teachings and the example of Jesus Christ.

If these questions are on your mind and in your heart, I am pleased to offer the following suggestions for your consideration.

Contact a priest in your parish and discuss ways in which you can become more actively involved in the life and work of the parish as a caring community.

Investigate areas of service in which you can assist others by using your talents and gifts.

Formulate and implement a practical approach to assist your peers to appreciate their lives as gifts from God, to understand and accept the message of Christ—His vision and values, to cultivate their friendship with Jesus and follow Him as their model, to fulfill the purposes for which God placed us upon this earth.

Pray daily for an increase of vocations to the priesthood and religious life. If the Lord is calling you to serve in this manner, meet with a priest or religious to receive guidance and support.

13. CONCLUSION

I am happy to share these prayerful thoughts with you as we celebrate the wonderful feast of Christmas. As you know, each of you is very special to me. Whenever I am with you I am encouraged and enriched by your Faith and enthusiasm. My prayer is that you will grow in this Faith, in your understanding of God's love for you, and continue to respond to the gifts of Faith, Hope and Love received at Baptism.

Listen to Jesus as He speaks to you in the Scriptures as explained in the Church that He founded, and where we all meet Him and one another. Appreciate the significance of the Sacrament of Reconciliation in your lives. Meet the Lord frequently in that wonderful sacrament and ask Him to forgive, heal and strengthen you. Open your hearts to the Lord as He comes to you in the Eucharist. Cooperate with the graces of the Eucharist as you develop unity, serve the cause of justice and respond to the love of God in spirit and in truth for the advancement of His Kingdom of peace and joy.

Recognize the presence of Jesus within your parish community where you truly meet Him, and become ever more involved in the life and work of your parish no matter what the faults and shortcomings of any of its members. Remember that we are all sinners on pilgrimage trying to become saints. Some of us are slower than others. Open yourselves to receive the peace of the feast of Christmas. Dedicate yourselves, as Church, to sharing that peace with those people whose lives you touch. God bless and be with you always.

Mary, Mother of Jesus, and Mother of the Church, pray for us.

St. Joseph, Patron of the Universal Church, teach us to follow Christ and lead us to meet Him in His Church.

A peaceful and joyful Christmas to all.

The Ministerial Priesthood

Easter Week, 1971

My beloved brother priests:

1. I stand among you as a father, a brother and a friend, and I am writing only after having listened, reflected and prayed. I do not write to you from a walled hermitage or from a distance. What I express are my own thoughts and words. I want to speak to your hearts, to what is innermost within you, implanted there by God Himself.

2. You and I share, according to our different roles and capacities, the work of building up the Church of God here in the Archdiocese of Boston. We know that it is the sovereign will of the Lord that there be perfected here a Church first gathered together by the proclamation and acceptance of the Word of God in faith, hope and love — a sign to all, among whom we journey, of God's intimacy and of His loving concern for all men. It is given to you and to me as

priests of the New Testament to bend every effort to the arduous but indispensable task of building up that community so that it will be a beacon in the dark night of our times to all around us. We believe this to be a work of divine grace but God has always called and will continue to call men for the singular task of drawing other men to intimacy with Himself.

3. It is understandable and proper that the people should look to us for direction, example, leadership and for that peace which comes from Christ. It is to us that they look especially in a time of confusion about the very meaning and purpose of the Gospel. Having this in mind before beginning to prepare these reflections, I have tried to do something which is very close to my heart. I believe that it is something the Bishop is called to do by the very nature of his office. I have tried to listen. I want to continue to listen.

4. After prayerful reflection, two convictions have been growing within me. First of all I am aware of and I thank God for the many gifts with which God has blessed you. It is my responsibility to foster and nourish these manifold and diverse gifts for the building up of the whole Body of Christ in love. In the second place I am deeply

moved by your anxieties. In fact they are in my thoughts all the day long and well into the night.

5. A prime anxiety comes from the very nature of our service to the obedience of faith. The daily thoughts and actions of a priest place him in a tension between what is seen and unseen. He loves and gives his life to the One Whom he does not see. Further, he is constantly calling other men and women — some older, some wiser than himself to live by faith. The priest feels the burden of his own faith struggle and he is also keenly aware that the people look to him for the nourishment of their own belief. He is commissioned to repeat the "hard saying" of faith in the midst of a culture which stresses the immediate rather than the distant, pleasure rather than inner peace, and the instant satisfaction of all needs rather than the more durable contentment which comes from trust and service of others.

6. Intertwined with this "tension of faith" there is that anxiety experienced by Christ Himself, by St. Paul and indeed by all who preach the gospel.[1] It is the experience of rejection. Rejection—the most painful of all human sorrows. Rejection of the priest today seems to take the form not so much of

outright persecution as of real neglect and indifference. This indifference is directed not just at the priest but at the message which he brings and it comes to us from both young and old.

7. There is also the anxiety which comes from change. So many of us have given our lives heartily and joyfully to the work of the Lord. At present our life as we have known it seems to be slipping away from us and where once there was security and peace, there is now uncertainty and even fear. We do not seem to walk with that steady gait which marked our path in days gone. by. Some have lost that sense of direction, that experience of wonder which they knew in the past. A few brother priests who once bore the burden of the day with us have given up the ministry, causing us to experience a certain loneliness and sense of loss.

8. A convergence of many factors has caused some of us to feel more keenly our own needs. We are human beings after all. We feel the need for acceptance, the need for security, the need for belonging, the need to love and be loved. Such needs are accentuated in our lives which call for dedication and availability to all. Priests know well that God intends their happiness and

yet they often find it difficult to integrate their human experience with the full day-to-day living of the priestly vocation.

9. Others raise the question of the priestly life-style. Struck by the directive of the Second Vatican Council that the priest should "deal with other men as with brothers,"[2] they feel themselves encumbered by a style of life which in their judgment does not encourage their presence among men.

10. Finally there is the emphasis of the recent Council on the call of the whole Church to holiness in the love of charity. The focus on the dignity and role of the laity combined with the clarification of the role of the bishop has caused some priests to question their own vocation and ministry in the Church and in the world, even while they pour themselves out daily for the flock.

11. We are tempted today to seek the quick and easy answer. I am convinced, however, that questions like the above, which go to the heart of what it means to be a man and a priest, cannot be answered superficially. Indeed each of us must work out the answers prayerfully, over a long period of time — often with the help of another priest. Reflection on these questions involves confrontation with the person of Jesus Christ,

with the vocation of the whole Church and with ourselves. Such a confrontation I believe can animate and strengthen us for the work that the Lord Himself has set out for us.

I.

The Ministerial Priest in the Church

THE PRIMACY OF JESUS CHRIST

12. What is the meaning of your life and mine? We can only begin to face this most central question by turning to Christ. It was Christ "whose humanity united with the Person of the Word was the instrument of our salvation." [3] In simple terms this means that when a man is in union with Christ through faith he reaches into and experiences the abyss of love which is God Himself. Christ possessed an inner strength which made possible His serenity in the midst of unbelievable turmoil and rejection. What was the source of His security? It is found in His loving union with His Father— a union made manifest in Christ's love for His disciples. From this ineffable union came acceptance of the Father's will, and total devotion to all men everywhere. From that loving union as manifest on the cross came the foundation of the Church. "When I am lifted up from the earth I shall draw

all things to myself." [4] Thus the Lord of creation and history, the Lord of redemption Who has risen from the dead is also the Lord and Head of the Church. There is no other. The apostle Paul realized how important it was for Christians to understand this if they were to recognize and appreciate their own dignity and their mission.

> He is the image of the unseen God, and the first born of all creation for in Him were created all things in heaven and on earth, everything visible and invisible...all things were created through Him and for Him. Before anything was created He existed and He holds all things in unity. [5]

Significantly, the apostle then speaks of Christ's association with the Church.

> Now the Church is His Body, He is its head. [6]

THE CHURCH AS GIFT OF GOD

13. The Church then depends absolutely on Christ to carry on His mission. His loving union with the will of the Father must be present in the Church. His efforts to bring divine love to all men must constantly take place in the Church. "By her relationship with Christ, the Church is a kind of sacrament or sign of intimate union with God

and of the unity of all mankind. She is also an instrument for the achievement of such union and unity."[7] Accordingly, "it is the vocation of the whole Church to show to its members and through them to the whole world the tender loving face of Jesus Christ."[8] We are called to become in space and time the visible, tangible extension of the crucified and risen Christ. All our activity for a greater communion among ourselves must take its origin in the mystery of Christ. All ecumenism begins and ends here. Our work to bring peace, to enrich and defend human life, to ease economic burdens finds its source here. The unfathomable mystery of Christ and the dignity He brought to all men must be made manifest throughout the whole Church and through the Church to the world.

14. This can be done and in fact it is already being done through the power of the Holy Spirit being poured out on the whole Church in the form of varied gifts and charisms.[9] Thus the example of Christ brought to mind through the work of the Holy Spirit prompts religious to live redemptively; it urges husbands and wives to move beyond selfishness and make a true gift of themselves to each other; it beckons some to work untiringly for the sick and the aged.

These are but a few examples of the work of the Holy Spirit Who calls all to follow Christ by means of faith, hope and love.[10] So in this sense we can see that the whole Church is called to be priestly — to be totally offered to God and to give an example of fraternal love for all men.

MINISTERIAL PRIESTHOOD

15. How is it possible for such a Church to continue? How can men in all their weakness trust so completely in God? How can men overcome that subtle selfishness, that silent narcissism which lodges within? How can they be hopeful and joyful in the midst of apparent depression? How can the Church be a true sign and a visible instrument for good in the world? It is the grace of Christ which makes all this possible in the Church. The priest by his life, by preaching the Word, by his sacramental ministry, mediates this grace to the members of the Church, helping them to see their vocation of faith, hope, and love. Working in the power of Christ, the priest stands in the midst of the Church to show her what she should be, to renew her wonder at the great acts of God, to lead her thanksgiving and to show by his manner of life the intimacy of God with man. The

priest by what he is as well as by what he does must make evident the loving care of Christ for the whole Body.

> To the degree of their authority and in the name of their bishop, priests exercise the office of Christ the head and the shepherd. Thus they gather God's family together as a brotherhood of unity, to lead it through Christ to the Father. For the exercise of this ministry as for other priestly duties, spiritual power is conferred on them for the upbuilding of the Church.[11]

16. Therefore, even though we ourselves are in constant need of redemption and are aware of our own sinfulness, yet we stand before and in the midst of our people as their shepherds—as the visible embodiment of the risen Lord's desire for a community of faith, hope, and love. I urge you with all my heart to embody for your people the loving concern of Christ for all. Such a mission calls us to be out among men in order to invite them to become disciples of Christ.

1) Preacher of the Word

17. We begin the work of building up the Church by preaching the Word of God. It is first of all in this area that the people have a special right to expect well of us. In

a certain sense their faith depends on our preaching. "Since no one is saved who has not first believed, priests as co-workers with their bishops, have as their primary duty the proclamation of the gospel of Christ to all." [12] Before he can preach effectively, the priest must subject himself to a two-fold listening. First, he must listen attentively and prayerfully to God's Word in the Church and allow himself to be transformed by it. His fidelity to the Word and to the personal love of God in Jesus Christ acts as an anchor. Such a man breathes authenticity. He comes before his people with a message which he himself has absorbed while realizing that he can never grasp it fully. Thus the pure Word of God, especially when preached by a man who himself believes it, brings life. It prepares the people to enter into the mystery of Christ in the Eucharist. This Word when preached and accepted builds up our flock in love. Preach this Word, I beg you, in season and out of season. Subject yourselves to it. Meditate on Paul's conviction that we are called to an "obedience of faith." [13] Otherwise your preaching and mine will ring hollow and will fail to inspire. When we prepare our homilies for that sacred moment on Sunday morning or when we prepare parents for the baptism of their children, or for the crucial

work of catechetics, we should first ask ourselves: "What is God trying to communicate
in His revealed Word?" For Christ is the
self-communication of the Father. "To see
Jesus is to see His Father."[14]

18. There is a second kind of listening. The
preacher must try to look deeply into the
hearts of his contemporaries. By looking
into himself, by regular dialogue with his
people, by the reading of contemporary
authors and by many other means, he
should come to appreciate his brothers. He
should try with special insight to understand their weaknesses and those present
currents and forces which seem to make it
difficult for many to accept the gospel. The
priest should search for that approach which
is most likely to be understood by his people. For while God is present in the Word,
he is also present in those who are listening, enabling and helping them to say,
"yes," to what is presented to them in
faith. The preacher must know and hear and
embrace the revealed Word. He must also
know and hear and embrace the flock. How
beautifully such a man mediates God's
saving presence!

19. Through constant prayer let this Word
be imprinted in your hearts. Then preach it
everywhere. Preach it in your pulpit and in

your life. Speak it to unbelievers as well as to your own flock. Preach it by the way you respond to the great issues of the day thoughtfully, courageously and above all as men to whom the gospel is real.[15] Make every effort to prevent your own weaknesses or deficiencies from getting in the way of God's Word. We all have our own personal areas of blindness. It is part of our human frailty but we must not let it hamper God's Word and God's work.

2) Minister of Sacrament

20. The Word comes to fulfillment in the celebration of the sacraments. Here it is that men, having heard and embraced the Word, are enriched and elevated by the touch of God Himself. The sacraments focus attention on that ineffable divine dimension of human life which so easily escapes us. Through the visible, we experience in faith the invisible unchanging God now vitally acting in us and among us. For the sacraments—especially when administered with sensitivity and faith—proclaim and make present the saving acts of Jesus Christ. The more we understand and savor the sacraments and our role in them, the more we will experience the joy of true ministers of Jesus Christ.

EUCHARISTIC SACRIFICE

21. To a world starved for true love and acceptance, the Church presents again and again the total love of Jesus Christ as signified and made present in the Eucharist. We all know from the experience of recent years that the offering can remain empty and shallow for many people. Even our extensive liturgical reform only opens the door. It makes possible a climate for Eucharistic renewal. It does not and cannot of itself bring about the holy, offered community of faith sensitive to God's presence and God's work.[16] For this to happen the Eucharist and indeed all the sacraments must be celebrated in faith.

22. My own conviction after years of pastoral life is that the people come to us with goodwill. They are open-minded, sincere, willing to learn, eager to understand and embrace their own role in the Church's life. Yet we will have little joy and effectiveness in inspiring them unless we ourselves have entered with our whole heart into the faith mystery which is the Eucharist. I have noticed and I endorse with all my heart the efforts in so many parishes to effect active and authorized programs of worship. I expect every parish to make progress in this direction and to include full participation

in every Mass. All of this, however, must be accompanied by efforts to help the people become immersed into the mystery of the Lord's death which is re-presented in the Eucharist. Word and Sacrament are a unity.[17] They show forth the Lord's death until He comes again.[18] He is given *for* us. Let us not offer the Eucharist without discerning and reaching the sacred event through an ever deepening faith.

23. Still, even this is not all. The Mass sends us on a mission. It calls the community to contemplate in faith the Lord's loving death and then to cooperate in making it vitally present in their own lives. This proper and precise catechesis of the Eucharist is what Paul presented to the Corinthians as an antidote to their divisions and self centeredness. When the offering is internal, sacrificial, from the heart, it will bring healing and joy in place of division and depression. "The blessing-cup that we bless is a communion with the blood of Christ and the bread that we break is a communion with the body of Christ."[19] What is the result in the community of such an attentive offering? "Nobody should be looking for his own advantage but everyone for the other man's."[20] Such an offering of the Eucharist moves against division, egotism, fear. It

fosters unity, thanksgiving, love, faith, joy and trust. Let us work to call our congregations to an offering of the Eucharistic sacrifice in which they will realize their union with one another and with their Lord Jesus Christ. Let us also help them to see by the example of our own lives the demands which the *event* of the Eucharist makes of them.[21] If Christ's self-giving is discerned in faith at every Mass, then all of us will be moved to give ourselves to the Father and to one another in the measure of the giving of Christ. Let us work together to make true of the whole Church what the Council has indicated for priests: they "by uniting themselves with the act of Christ, the Priest, are offering their whole selves every day to God. While being nourished by the Body of Christ, their hearts are sharing in the love of Him who gives Himself as food for the faithful ones."[22]

24. As I reflect with you on these mysteries which we can never fully grasp but which give meaning and direction to our lives, I must say a word about the manner of celebration. We all know from the Church's tradition and from our own experience that the sacraments can be efficacious even when not celebrated well. Nevertheless, the right kind of Eucharistic celebration (and this

applies to all the sacraments) is a vital force in the transformation of the community. The liturgy must be offered according to the Church's directives and in such a way that it will alert the people to its meaning, incline them to enter into the mystery and touch their innermost being.

25. The union which we experience in faith at every Eucharist is meant to be abiding. It should endure and grow. The sacrament of the Eucharist calls the community and especially the priest to a lasting union of loving friendship with Christ. That is why, following the Second Vatican Council, with all my heart I urge priests to offer the Eucharist regularly even when the community is not present.[23] It is still the act of Christ and the Church. Every Mass, public or private, affords the priest a most significant occasion to grow in the knowledge and strength of Christ. A further indispensable aid to this abiding union with the Lord is faithful prayer in the presence of the Holy Eucharist. By this kind of prayer the union effected at Mass is made strong and lasting. Is not this what the Lord Himself had in mind when He said:

> I am the vine; you are the branches. Whosoever remains in me, with me in him bears fruit in plenty; for cut off from me you can do nothing.[24]

SACRAMENT OF RECONCILIATION

26. If one could describe the theme of the Second Vatican Council in one word, that word would be "renewal." "The Church incessantly pursues the path of penance and renewal."[25] "Every renewal of the Church essentially consists in an increase of fidelity to her own calling."[26] "All are led to examine their own faithfulness to Christ's will for the Church, and wherever necessary, undertake with vigor the task of renewal and reform."[27]

27. We must be careful not to ascribe the need for renewal to structures only. In this context the priest finds himself constantly made aware of his own weaknesses and needs. He must continually approach God for his own forgiveness and redemption even as he seeks to be a minister of reconciliation to others. The age in which we live is marked by alienation. No alienation is deeper or more agonizing than the distance we experience between ourselves and God when we sin. The message of Jesus Christ is that redemption is available to us.

28. There is a great deal of confusion today about the nature of sin and the develop-

ment of a mature Christian conscience. We are being challenged to rise above a merely legalistic morality to embrace and live by a law implanted by God in the hearts of men. This is not that easy to do in practice. We fail often. If we do not admit this we are liars and the love of God is not in us.

29. Only sincere on-going repentance opens the human heart to God and the following of Jesus Christ. In the sacrament of penance we affirm that we are being called to a life beyond what we are now living. It is an expression of our sinfulness and of our need for God's healing presence. It is this kind of confession that frees us gradually from our egotism and enables us to be better ministers of reconciliation for others both in the sacrament itself and in the various life situations where we are called upon to be healers.

30. Let us help others to understand anew this call to personal renewal and resurrection. In our ministry we can help many to take that extra step which releases them from a heavy burden of sin and guilt and enables them to experience the merciful and redeeming glance of the Savior.

3) Faith — Leader in the Community

FOUNDATION OF CHRISTIAN COMMUNITY

31. If we are attuned to the hearts of men and if we look into our own hearts we find a genuine longing for communion with others. This longing which is everywhere evident and which the recent Council has seen as "a sign of the times"[28] may be accepted by the man of faith as a reflection of the life of the Trinity where there is constant love and communion. This desire for acceptance, for being part of something larger than oneself, is detected in God's plan for salvation. For "it has pleased God, however, to make men holy and save them not merely as individuals without any mutual bonds, but by making them into a single people, a people which acknowledges Him in truth and serves Him in holiness.[29] The risen Lord is among us. It is His constant desire that His followers be formed into a truly human community of faith, hope and love. As God has accepted and loved all of us in and through Christ, so we must love and accept one another.[30] You and I have a mission and a commitment to work towards the formation of this kind of community which finds its foundation in the total giving of Christ, and at the same

time achieves visibility in the most human acts of kindness and graciousness.

CHURCH AS FAITH-COMMUNITY IN WORLD

32. From her earliest days, the Church stood apart as a brotherhood of people who proclaimed Jesus as Lord and therefore discovered a way to share and pray in communion with one another.[31] The first Christians evoked the admiration of those who did not yet know Christ. While the Church was still a persecuted people, there was an inner nourishment and strength derived from the moments of life shared together. With her emergence from the underground experience of the first centuries, the Church developed in earnest her mission to transform the secular. Since then there have been oscillations between periods of deep secular involvement and periods of retreat. The Catholic spiritual tradition has always tried to keep alive the tension between the call to the city and the call to the desert.

33. Primarily it is the call of the whole Church community to live in and for the world. The Church's uniqueness rests in her experience of God in Jesus Christ through the power of the Spirit. From this

flows her mission to town and city, to country and world. Persons who call themselves Christian cannot hold themselves aloof from the strife and tension that tear men apart. Of all people, they are called to break down barriers of race, creed, ethnic background, wealth and poverty, etc., which separate men from one another.[32] Their experience of a shared sonship in God impels them to work diligently to promote the brotherhood of all men. They are concerned about the scandalous inequality in the distribution of the world's wealth, the criminal deprivation suffered by large segments of mankind, the up-side-down priorities often adopted by national governments in the pursuit of their own selfish goals. They are anxious about the growing callousness toward human life from fetal development to old age. They seek to promote a deeper appreciation of that kind of sexual love which integrates the whole person and therefore enables man and woman to live according to the spirit rather than the flesh. They bend every human effort to increase the possibilities of peace at home and abroad.

34. The whole Church must also be moved with anguish and sorrow at the human degradation found in a world of pain and

groans—the world of the poor. Hers cannot be a disinterested zeal for a doctrinaire ideal. And the long spasmodic cry rising and falling from the lips of the poor—their desperate plea for human dignity—calls the Church into the heart of the gospel: "...insofar as you did this to one of the least of these brothers of mine you did it to me." [33]

35. Vatican II has proclaimed that the poor—the noble descendants of Christ, the Poor Man of Israel—are the Church's special concern. And it would be cruel to remain content with a disinterested zeal for principle alone in the face of the harsh reality of the life of the poor. Indeed, Pope John XXIII condemned those spiritual cataracts which blind even the faithful so that they do not recognize that some action must follow upon the Church's teaching. [34]

36. I have seen with my own eyes in my pastoral visits through large areas of the Archdiocese that the poor have taken on the characteristics of their environment. At a very early age the priceless dignity of the person—even of children—becomes nothing more than a human relic of a life that remains broken, disconnected and cluttered with psychological debris.

37. Thus arises the opportunity for the Church, together with Paul, to pay a high

personal and communal tribute to Jesus Christ: "It makes me happy to suffer for you, as I am suffering now, and in my own body to do what I can to make up all that has still to be undergone by Christ for the sake of His body, the Church." [35] It is the cross alone, freely embraced on behalf of the poor, which is the key to personal and social redemption. It is this cross—the cross of true sacrificial giving, not merely the giving of the casual gleanings of our "extras"— which I call upon the whole church in Boston to embrace with us.

PRIEST AS FAITH LEADER IN THE CHURCH

38. In order that we might be in the world as Christ wants us to be, it is necessary that we who are priests be truly sensitive to the mission of the whole Church—the worship of the Father through self-sacrifice for the world. It is ours to be so deeply immersed in the Christ mystery that we can sense the urgency of this mission. Our attention to God's saving word and our celebration of God's redeeming presence in sacrament must constantly face us with our responsibility to lead the brethren in faith-responses to the needs of men. It is the Word and the Sacrament when properly preached and

celebrated which bring together and build up the truly Christian community.[36] But we do not mediate Christ's love only at the time of the Sunday Eucharist. The priest is called by the nature of his office to make Christ's love visible in his every day existence. The priest should make evident in his very person Christ's enduring desire for a community of faith, hope and love. Hence it will never be enough for the Church to have priests who celebrate the Eucharist merely on Sunday and then return to totally secular work during the week. For this was not the way in which Christ went among men. He wished to make His saving presence felt in the entire community. You and I by our pastoral example must inspire our people — according to their capacity and to the grace given to each one — to live and work for a life of communion with all men.

"Christ went about all the towns and villages, curing every kind of disease and infirmity as a sign that the Kingdom of God has come.[37] So also the Church, through her children, is one with men of every condition but especially with the poor and the afflicted." [38]

39. Let us then examine our pastoral concern and interest. Do we truly understand the pain in people's hearts? Are we really

acquainted with the families of our parishes? Are their needs and problems in our minds and hearts when we reflect prayerfully in the silence of our own rooms or churches?

40. Do we actually reach out to the young? They are full of enthusiasm and idealism. They experience hopes and fears. Can we show them understanding, confer on them a sense of dignity by our sincere concern, and call them forth to adult responsibility?

41. In a period that tends to hide from old age and approaching death, can we give attention to the older men and women who are preparing, often in great loneliness, for their passover to the Lord? They call out for a new sense of belonging and for help in transforming their last years into constructive living.

42. Is our heart truly touched, as I have said before,[39] by the cries of the poor? Christ reveals Himself to us in His suffering humanity in a special way through the poor.[40] Do we, by the simplicity of our life, allow the poor to identify with us? Do we, by our tangible concern for their plight, give them hope for the future? Do we help them find their own dignity in Christ by giving them a sense of their own mission in life?

43. Can we visit the homes of the affluent who need the example of dedication and abnegation? Do we recognize their hunger and thirst for a deeper spirituality and a more enriching purpose in life?

44. How do the anxieties of the vast middle class become our own? They often feel their economic gains in jeopardy by the pressures of the poor and are not yet secure enough to assume more responsibility for the sharing of wealth. Can we speak of the gospel to them?

45. There are always the outcasts in every community. Who are they for us? The retarded child? The alcoholic? The drug addict? The outsider because of race, creed or social background? Do we walk in their midst? Can they sense just a bit more that their lives are worth living because of our presence and interest?

46. Are we aware of the larger issues which trouble the city or town, the nation and world? Can we call suffering caused by injustice, inequality, unjust aggression and brutality, our own?

47. The priest is not expected and cannot hope to be personally involved in all of these concerns. It *is* his mission, however, to uncover the Christian dimension in

these real-life problems and issues. It *is* his duty to help the entire Church be more responsive to the gospel message in these various areas of involvement. It *is* his task to encourage and facilitate the appropriate responses to agonizing questions and to suffering people. It *is* this *faith-leadership* that must characterize the distinctive and unique service that the priest can give by virtue of his office in the community today.

48. Such a pastoral life, when lived in season and out of season, makes visible the tender care of our Savior for all men. It makes more credible our standing in the place of Christ at the Eucharistic sacrifice. It furthers that communal life which was the Lord's dying wish and His legacy to His disciples.[41] I spoke earlier of our own need to love and to be loved. I am convinced that this kind of pastoral life if lived simply and warmly, will bring from the people a response of love, affection and respect which will be a source of consolation, and which is part of God's gift to us His priests.

49. This going out to others is the mission of the whole Church. As the Christian community was formed by the Lord's self-giving, so its members must continue to give to one another and to all men. Always the example of Christ urges and impels us

to a thoughtful generosity. The priest, indeed, is called to encourage each one to do his part. Especially today there is need for the continuation of a very ancient tradition—that the Christians of one community should go out of themselves to support their brothers who are in less fortunate circumstances. Here I would dare to make my own the words of St. Paul. The motive which he gives for the gifts to the poorer churches is the example of the Lord Himself: "Remember how generous the Lord was; He was rich but He became poor for your sake, to make you rich out of His poverty.... This does not mean that to give relief to others you ought to make things difficult for yourselves; it is a question of balancing what happens to be your surplus now against their present need, and one day they may have something to spare that will supply your own need."[42] This going out to others springs from the very nature of the Church. Thus many priests, sisters and brothers among us—fully aware of this —have given of themselves with great zeal and dedication to the poorer churches in Latin America or to the ghetto parishes in our own cities. In addition, many suburban parishes make regular financial contributions to poorer urban parishes. I am thrilled to find such efforts among you, and I want to work with you for their expansion.

50. Many of our efforts at building a stronger community of faith, hope and love will face great difficulty today because of the dehumanizing culture in which we find ourselves. We are all aware of the rootlessness of so many suburban families who, because of circumstances, are constantly moving. The depression of so much of our urban life further complicates the problem. Such conditions only call for a deeper commitment from you and me to the constant manifestation in our lives of the Lord's desire for a community — truly human and truly divine — reaching out, by the quality of its life, as a ray of hope and joy to all men.

(1) Shared Responsibility

51. To accomplish this we must work together. As your bishop I am completely committed to close collaboration with you who are my appointed co-workers. Happy and grateful to follow the directives of Vatican II,[43] I recognize the Senate of Priests as a brotherly and effective means of being in communion with you. This is something which I want and need in order to become a better shepherd. Your real union and constant communication with your senator will alert all of us to present needs and opportunities and will make possible a true spirit of orderly ecclesial

cooperation. I have tried and will try to listen well to my senate. It is a practical means of priestly cooperation. Let us all work together to increase our sharing and communion. Please understand my desire to go forward together with you. I am confident that you will not misinterpret a delay, a modification or even an occasional no to a given recommendation. Be assured that whenever possible I will try to share my reasons and my views with you. Ours is a shared responsibility in accordance with our respective offices for the whole Church of Boston. The Bishop bears responsibility for all — priests and people — and must keep in mind the edification of the entire flock. But I do not bear this alone. Moreover, we must also be attuned to the universal Church. Indeed this universality is in the best tradition of the Archdiocese of Boston.

52. I am very conscious of the need for more adequate sharing of responsibility in the parochial situation. Because I am a priest first and foremost, the parish ministry is very close to my heart. It is there, especially, that salvation comes to most of us. Every priest by virtue of his ordination shares in the bishop's role in the local area. Pastors are commissioned to exercise a leadership-role of inspiration and coordination of

parish activities. They cooperate with the bishop in a very special way.[44] Still, all priests must participate in establishing parish priorities, policies and programs.[45] Above all it is my urgent prayer that a genuine spirit of cooperation and Christ-like charity continue to develop among priests of all ages and varying backgrounds no matter what their position or special function may be in the Archdiocese or on the parish level. As Vatican II has put it: "Each and every priest, therefore, is joined to his brother priests by a bond of charity, prayer and every kind of cooperation. In this manner they manifest that unity with which Christ willed His own to be perfectly one, so that the world might know that the Son has been sent by the Father. Consequently, older priests should receive younger priests as true brothers and give them a hand with their first undertakings and assignments in the ministry. They should likewise try to understand the mentality of younger priests, even though it be different from their own and should follow their projects with good will. For his part a young priest should respect the age and experience of his seniors. He should discuss plans with them, and willingly cooperate with them in matters which pertain to the care of souls."[46]

53. Moreover, all the priests in a given parish are expected to serve Christ by working not only for the people, but with them, without ever abdicating that priestly and pastoral role of leadership proper to them alone. They should collaborate in a special way with religious who may be working in their parishes. Priests and religious share a common ministry in many respects. Unity in this endeavor can reveal much of Christ's love to the people.

54. Archdiocesan policy makes the parish council the normal vehicle for this purpose. This kind of shared responsibility enhances rather than diminishes the priest's irreplaceable position in the community. The fact of his sacred authority can never be questioned but he must be careful to exercise it in humility, love, compassion, wisdom and knowledge after the manner of Jesus Christ. Working closely with the parish council in the decision-making process as it affects the pastoral life of the people can—at least for now—make the priest more vulnerable and more subject to criticism and even opposition. Yet it also provides him with the opportunity to concentrate his efforts in that area which is more directly of priestly concern. In effect he should work within the parish council

to stimulate sound Christian response. Whoever approaches these discussions with the charity of Christ can prevent disagreement from becoming personal.

55. A great part of the priest's role within the parish council is a formative one which should be carried out with a strong awareness of those faith-responses which God is now seeking and making possible within the parish. To be valid and inspired by the Spirit the whole process must build up rather than tear down and should foster Christian life and unity.

(2) Special Ministries

56. In this context it is easier to see how important it is to have parish priests with a heart open to all and a willingness to work generously with one another. The parochial ministry must, therefore, always be at the center of the Church's life.

57. At the same time, I know that some of you desire newer approaches to serve our people. It is important that you submit information in this area to my Personnel Office or to others appointed by me so that I may be able to benefit from experience and good judgment in arriving at wise pastoral decisions. I encourage you to be creative —

in communion with your bishop — especially in attempts to reach the poor while recognizing the primacy of preaching the gospel of Jesus Christ. Just as I am called to discern and encourage the various gifts of the Spirit in the whole Church of Boston, so I must recognize and nurture the gifts which are given to so many of you, my "prudent cooperators"[47] in the work of the Lord.

58. In the appreciation of these gifts it is necessary to understand that they are given primarily for the building up of the whole Body of Christ.[48] If they are authentic they will not be injurious to that unity of which the priesthood itself must be a sign. Hence the ultimate criterion for decision in this area cannot be personal interest alone, but primarily the good of the people as a whole. It must be a pastoral criterion and hence inspired and guided by faith. It is not always easy to decide in these matters. There are many factors which must be weighed, but the more we try to do this together the more the Church will become a true household of faith and a community of love.

(3) Availability

59. Whatever may be the specific way in which we are engaged in our priestly minis-

try, our life, lived in openness to the anguish of men, leaves us very vulnerable. The more sensitive we are to human need, the more we can be hurt. Open our hearts to all we must.[49] Once we do, however, we must be realistic about the consequences. We will become a prisoner of our brothers. It takes a man with a deep interior life to walk with faith and courage among the sick, the handicapped, the neglected, the im- prisoned, those sinned against because of racial, ethnic, or credal bigotry.[50] Some of us are afraid to take this step, because we may be misunderstood by others, or may have to surrender some of the luxuries we have come to consider necessities. Some of us may have taken the step and lost our way in spite of the generous desire to render truly Christian service to our broth- ers in special need.

60. In pursuit of our goal, we should be aware always that our mission is to bring Christ to every man by word, sacrament and pastoral charity.[51] If we can communicate to all men a sense of Christian hope by our conviction that their lives are worth living, grace may touch a yet unhardened heart and release boundless redemptive energy in the community. It is our experience of God's love for men that animates our concern and hope for them. Our solicitude cannot be

merely to alleviate human misery for a time, but also must include serious attempts to get at the causes which unnecessarily perpetuate such misery. This takes faith, intelligence and the capacity to suffer. Above all it presumes a realistic understanding of the power of evil in the world and the limited victory which is to be ours prior to the final consummation.[52] Suffering, agony, death can never spell defeat for us, because we believe that Christ has made them redemptive for those who are faithful. Let us then join with all men of good will both **within** and beyond the Christian community in an effort to awaken the conscience of man in our society to the injustices and inequities that beset the human condition. It is our mission to lead men, like the Good Shepherd,[53] gently but firmly to the freedom of the children of God and not to the sham liberty advocated by so many today. Let us also be mindful that our particular responsibility is to try to discern in prayer and fasting what God is unfolding for us in each human situation that man encounters and to grasp it in the light of faith as given to us in and through the Church.

(4) Communal Living

61. To support and strengthen one another in this endeavor, we do need to come together.[54] It always seems unfortunate to me that some priests must live alone without the strengthening companionship of other priests. We need to explore ever more fully the possibilities for greater sharing of life together. The more we enrich one another by joint reflection on what the Church points out as the meaning, hopes and goals of our ministry, the more support we can be to one another. To this end some shared prayer in our life together can root us in deeper communion with one another in the Lord.

II.

The Priest's Call to Spiritual Maturity

SENSE OF VOCATION

62. This kind of priestly ministry presumes that we have received a call that touches the core of what we are. As we look back on the very ordinary way in which we were led to come to the seminary and to the priesthood, we can be tempted to see only the human factors which were at work. But the eyes of faith can discern God gradually unfolding the call to us. Even the apostles were invited at first only to come and see what association with Christ's work could mean.[55] They were attracted to Him for rather superficial reasons that gradually had to be refined and deepened as they came to know Him and to suffer with Him. When the suffering came, one betrayed Him,[56] another denied Him,[57] most of them ran away,[58] all had their very convictions severely tested. They even had difficulty in accepting the resurrection.[59] The coming of the Spirit strengthened them although

even then they had to struggle to determine
precisely what the Lord meant and what
He wanted them to do.[60] How much like
ourselves they were! The inner call, then,
is not always that easy to discern in the
beginning and can be difficult to answer
with fidelity. In our more honest moments
we recognize how vacillating we can be.
Only the experience of God's grace makes
some degree of fidelity to the call possible.
Grace always nudges us to greater generosity. It reveals to us the deeper desires in
our heart and draws us to follow even if
we cannot at the moment see where He is
leading.[61] The more we recognize the slow-
ness of our response, the more we are in-
clined to trust the strength that comes from
Him alone.

63. May I also encourage those of you who
are preparing for the priesthood in the
seminary. These are sacred years in your
life for maturing in your response to God's
call. I beg you to continue to seek honestly
and openly for the enlightenment to know
God's will and the strength to respond to it.
Consult your faculty in confidence and
trust. It is in working together now that
you clarify the goal and lay firmer founda-
tions for further growth and development
later on.

PRAYER

64. The reason why Jesus first invites us to intimacy with Him[62] is that He wants us to come to know Him personally — His thoughts, His ideals, His struggles, His deeds. Most of all, He lovingly persists in urging us to be of one mind with Him[63] and to share more deeply His life.[64] It is through Him that we come to call God, "Father," in the Spirit.[65] Hence the priest is called to walk before God,[66] i.e. to be a man of genuine prayer. He is not just called to lead others in prayer or to say prayers for others, but also in a deeper sense to become a man who prays — a man who lives in some degree of loving communion with the Triune God.

65. It is not by accident that we embraced the responsibility of praying the breviary at the time of our subdiaconate. The Church, as the People of God, asked us then, and asks us now perhaps more than in the past, to see prayer at the heart of what it means to be a priest: "During His life on earth, He (Jesus) offered up prayers and entreaty, aloud and in silent tears, to the One who had the power to save Him out of death, and He submitted so humbly that His prayer was heard. Although He was Son, He learnt to obey through suffering; but

having been made perfect, He became for all who obey Him the source of eternal salvation and was acclaimed by God with the title of high priest *of the order of Melchizedek.*"[67]

66. Like Jesus we are asked to pray constantly,[68] but also to go off regularly to some place where we can be alone and pray.[69] We are asked especially to become men of biblical prayer that we may come to recognize how God customarily reveals Himself and His will in human life. No man can experience the sustaining joy of his ministry unless he prays often. Here it is that we discover, with the help of the Spirit, fresh insights into the message of God and experience what it means to be taught by God.[70] This prayer must not be a selfish prayer. It has to be a vital prayer that urges us to be concerned for the things of God[71] and His people.[72] I do urge those of you who may have supplanted explicit moments of prayer with apostolic activity to re-embrace this urgent and serious responsibility. What a power prayer gives to the heralds of the gospel! The experience of prayer transforms the preacher, and as a result his preaching is more likely to bring a response of faith in the people. This is why the responsibility of praying is assumed, not for our

own sakes primarily, but rather for the sake of the people.

67. Let me urge you to pray to God's Mother and ours. "Sincere devotion to the Virgin Mother of God becomes necessary to every faithful person, but above all to the priest, because in addition to all the other singular benefits, she is the model of our love for God, for Christ and for the Church." [73]

DISCIPLESHIP

68. Until intimacy with God is experienced through faith, hope and love, we cannot begin to appreciate the demands of the gospel. The attractions of the life surrounding us are enticing, and can suffocate the spirit. The more real our experience of God is, the more sense the gospel-call to total priestly ministry can make. It never makes complete sense in the eyes of a calculating world; it does make sense to the man who has met Christ in faith, hope and love. As prayerful men, we no longer see the call of discipleship in terms of what we have to give up. Rather we begin, even in our weakness, to appreciate, at least in part, the greatness of spirit to which we are called.

69. Let us never forget that we are invited to a relationship with Christ that transcends the master-servant model[74] and yet recognizes Him as the Lord of our life and ministry.[75] Christ reveals to the man called to be an apostle the special demands of discipleship which go beyond those to which all Christians are called.[76] When He issues the call, He does not want the man to vacillate even to fulfill a sacred responsibility at home.[77] Nor does He want the disciple, once the response is begun, to turn back.[78] There must be a single-mindedness that makes the life of priestly ministry all-consuming.[79] There must be a willingness to forego wealth and possessions,[80] even though he may be guaranteed a moderate income. Most of all the disciple should never expect to be free from hardship. The apostles considered hardship as a logical consequence of their ministry.[81]

70. It is hard for me, therefore, to understand our call except as a call for a permanent commitment. The Church must always show pastoral love and mercy where an adjustment is necessary by way of exception. But the call to discipleship to which the priest responds affirmatively contains an inner logic which is expressed in fidelity. In fact, it is the priest who is especially

called to witness to God's faithful love for men. God is always faithful. The priest is asked to show this forth in his own fidelity. This call to fidelity is not fulfilled merely by remaining in the active ministry until death or retirement. It is a call to grow and develop a more profound spiritual maturity and self-giving. This is our call even though we often have difficulty in grasping it and responding to it in practice. Yet He who has begun the good work in us will bring it to perfection.[82] It is not only through our own fault that we have difficulty these days in understanding all this. The temper of the times can befog our minds and keep us from a clearer grasp of these profound mysteries. But the conditions and events of our day also challenge us to mature in a way we probably never dreamed possible before.

CELIBACY

71. It is a joy for me to dwell if only for a moment on the call to celibate love which marks our ministerial priesthood in the West. I do this, not unmindful of the anguished cries of some who seem to find celibacy an unbearable burden in this age of renewal — an age which is beset by so many philosophies contrary to the spirit of the gospel.

72. It is sometimes helpful to situate the call to celibacy, as the New Testament does, in the context of the complementary call to marriage.[83] The Scriptures unfold for us a very attractive picture of marital love. In fact God's covenant with man is frequently described in the Old Testament in terms of a marriage relationship.[84] But in the New Testament it is not marriage that reveals God's love for man. Rather, God's love for man as made visible in Jesus' love for His Church, in turn sheds light on both marriage and celibacy.[85] Each manifest a dimension of Jesus's love for His people. The respect for celibacy in the New Testament seems to grow out of a desire to imitate Christ's own celibate love for men and the growing awareness of the implications of the belief in the resurrection of the body.[86]

73. Although I recognize that in apostolic times celibacy and priesthood were not always conjoined, yet the roots of a celibate priesthood can be found as far back as Saint Paul who saw a special value in a celibate ministry as based on his own experience: "I should like everyone to be like me...."[87] Moreover, due largely to what today we would call a grass-roots movement in the Church of ancient times, there has been a real development over the centuries

which discerns a true evangelical appropriateness in the celibate commitment of the priest. This ascetical and disciplinary development, although expressed in different practices in East and West, has perdured to our day. Pope Paul has indicated that the question of ordaining some mature married men may be treated at the next Bishops' Synod in Rome. Already we have several married priests who had formerly been ministers in other Christian Churches and communions. However, this does not necessarily mean that the Church will abandon such valued witness in men already ordained. No reversal of a Church law can abruptly change the inner commitment made with hope and in great generosity by the subdeacon, and nourished gradually over the years of the priesthood. I encourage those preparing for ordination to be more and more receptive to this divine gift. For when joyfully and freely received, this gift can only enhance and enrich their manhood.

74. It is man who changes. God is always faithful. It should not surprise us that He is now inviting and enabling us to come to a more mature commitment of ourselves to Him. Church law becomes a mere formality if it just allows or forbids external behavior.

Church law is intended to be an external expression of a deeply internal reality, given by the Spirit and fostered in faith and hope. The call to consecrated celibacy in the priesthood is a divine gift.[88] It is important to pray for this gift in order to open the heart to receive it and to grow in an appreciation of it.[89] It is, of course, true that man is always tragically free to reject the divine gifts he has received.

75. This is why, under the present Church practice, it is important to see celibacy as involving a profound form of discipleship intimately connected with the priestly ministry. Most men are not called upon to give up a wife and family for the sake of the Kingdom.[90] But we are privileged to receive this call in order to witness to the mystery of the divine marriage which God has entered into with His people, and to allow us to adopt as ours the larger human family in Christ.[91] Our call is to serve Christ by serving in love the universal Church, without binding ourselves to any small segment of it, such as a family which we might constitute or the family from which we sprang.[92]

76. At the same time we live in an era of turmoil which naturally enough affects and involves the Church. Those who lead and represent the Church must make every

effort to understand fully the problems and difficulties of the individual person — whether he be a layman or a priest. As your bishop, I want to be available to give whatever help I can to anyone suffering anguish in this regard. I do insist on searching in prayer and the seeking of competent spiritual counsel. I recognize that many human factors affect man's decisions. I do not try to judge another man. Jesus Christ is our judge — yours and mine. Nevertheless — as I am sure you understand — I must take all factors into consideration. My mission — as assigned to me by Christ in the Church — requires me to make decisions based also on the common good of all the faithful. The shepherd must tend the whole flock while also responding to the need of the individual brother.[93] We are profoundly aware of the great message of hope that is preached not just in word, but in life by the priest who grows and matures in celibate love for his brothers in the world. We are deeply in need of men who have so experienced in their lives the transforming power of God's personal love that they can forego the joys of marital love for the joys of celibate self-giving for the sake of the Kingdom.[94] The contemporary world needs neither the manichaeistic condemnation of sex nor the pagan hedonistic and unnatural glorification of it. It needs people who can proclaim by their lives that the human spirit has a wondrous capacity for consecrated love in the service of the gospel. In this connection the witness of a celibate love which is warm and human should be coupled with the willingness of priests to embrace at least a relative poverty.[95] If the celibate refuses to share his goods or if he becomes introverted and complacent in his own little world, his selfishness works counter to the Kingdom that he seeks to announce and to promote.

REFLECTIVE STUDY

77. May I also share with you my fond hope that from a position of belief, we continue without failing to read and reflect on our faith and our ministry. The rapid pace of development in all areas of knowledge makes the intellectual life seem overwhelming. This is one reason why we find on the one hand so many academicians specializing, and on the other hand the non-academicians abandoning study altogether. We *do* have a specialty. It is the life of the spirit—"the obedience of faith." All the work of our priestly ministry must be integrated into our mission to foster, develop and nurture the life of faith in us

and in others. We must read in faith in order to grow in understanding.[96] Scripture and theology can help us to come to a richer grasp of God; religious psychology and sociology can help us understand man. But the priest is expected with the help of Divine grace to integrate his knowledge of these wonderful sciences into his basic life-project — the following of Jesus Christ. So we must stand back from the demands of our daily service to the brethren in order to reflect and put things together.

78. It is my hope that the Pastoral Institute will continue to provide an important service in this area. Often it will be helpful to share with another priest. Those of us who are able to keep up with the complexities of modern day living while nurturing and developing an inner sense of direction and purpose are going to be of greatest service to our fellowmen.

Concluding Remarks

79. As you know, your bishop does not own a house. His place of residence belongs to the people of God. It is our home. Consequently it is open to all. I hope that you will feel free to come and go when you can; break bread with us — even when I may be

absent on duty. I trust that it may be possible to see you especially during the weeks which you spend annually at the Pastoral Institute.

80. Be of good heart, my beloved brother priests. Do not be afraid.[97] The Lord is with us.[98] Let us rejoice in Him and try to bear one another's burdens.[99] He has promised that the victory will be ours.[100]

81. Let us thank the Lord Jesus for granting us the privilege of living in these times of challenge and opportunity for the gospel. I pray humbly and fervently that the Holy Spirit will renew and unify still more the presbyterate of the Archdiocese of Boston for the glory of God and the service of the Church.

82. Once again it is a great joy for me to place myself, my mission, and all of you, my beloved brother priests, under the maternal care of Mary, the Mother of the Church which we love and serve.

NOTES

[1]Cf. Jo. 1.10-11; Act 17.33-34.

[2]Decree on the Ministry and Life of Priests, *Presbyterorum ordinis*, 3.

[3]Constitution on the Sacred Liturgy, *Sacrosanctum concilium*, 1.

[4]Jo. 12.32.

[5]Col 1.15-17.

[6]Col 1.18.

[7]Dogmatic Constitution on the Church, *Lumen gentium*, 1.

[8]"...obeying the will of Christ, who delivered Himself to death 'that He might present Himself the Church, not having spot or wrinkle...but that she might be holy and without blemish,' (Eph 5.27), but as pastors devote all our energies and thoughts to the renewal of ourselves and the flock committed to us, so that there may radiate before all men the lovable features of Jesus Christ, who shines in our hearts 'that God's splendor may be revealed' (2 Cor. 4.6)." (*Message to Humanity* issued at the beginning of Vatican II by the Council Fathers with the endorsement of Pope John XXIII).

[9]Cf. 1 Cor. 12.4-11; Rm 12.3-8.

[10]Cf. *Lumen gentium*, 7; 12; 33.

[11]*Presbyterorum ordinis*, 6.

[12]*Ibid.* 4.

[13]"'The obedience of faith' (Rm 16.26; cf. Rm 1.5; 2 Cor 10.5-6) must be given to God who reveals an obedience by which man entrusts his whole self freely to God, offering 'the full submission of intellect and will to God who reveals,' (First Vatican Council's Dogmatic Constitution on the Catholic Faith, chpt. 3) and freely assenting to the truth revealed by Him. If this faith is to be shown, the grace of God and the interior help of the Holy Spirit must precede and assist, moving the heart and turning it to God, opening the eyes of the mind, and giving 'Joy and ease to everyone in assenting to the truth and believing it.' (Second Council of Orange, Canon 7)."

Dogmatic Constitution on Revelation, *Dei verbum*, 5.

[14]Cf. Jo. 14.9.

[15]*Presbyterorum Ordinis*, 4.

[16]Rm 15.16.

[17]"The two parts which, in a certain sense, go to make up the Mass, namely, the liturgy of the word and the Eucharistic liturgy, are so closely connected with each other that they form but one single act of worship." *(Sacrosanctum concilium, 56).*

[18]1 Cor. 11.26.

[19]1 Cor. 10.16.

[20]1 Cor. 10.24.

[21]"Such is especially true of the liturgy of the Word during the celebration of Mass. In this celebration, the proclamation of the death and resurrection is inseparably joined to the response of the people who hear, and to the very offering whereby Christ ratified the New Testament in His blood. The faithful share in this offering both by their prayers and by their recognition of the sacrament for what it is." *(Presbyterorum ordinis, 4).*

[22]*Ibid.,* 13.

[23]Cf. *Presbyterorum ordinis,* 13.

[24]Jo. 15.5.

[25]*Lumen Gentium,* 8.

[26]Decree on Ecumenism, *Unitatis redintegratio,* 6.

[27]*Ibid.* 4.

[28]Pastoral Constitution on the Church, *Gaudium et spes,* 4.

[29]*Lumen gentium,* 9.

[30]Cf. Phil. 2.1-18; 2 Cor. 8.8-9.

[31]Cf. Act 2.42-47; 4.32-35.

[32]Cf. *Gaudium et spes,* 27; 29.

[33]Mt 25.40.

[34]"We do not regard such instructions as sufficient, unless there be added to the work of instruction that of the formation of man, and unless some action follow upon the teaching by way of experience." *Mater et magistra,* 231.

[35]Col. 1, 24.

[36]Cf. *Lumen gentium,* 3.

[37]Cf. Mt. 9.35; Act 10.38.

[38]Decree on the Church's Missionary Activity, *Ad gentes,* 12.

[39]Cf. *supra,* p. 16 ff.

[40]Cf. *Ad gentes,* 12.

[41]Cf. Jo. 17.20-23.

[42]2 Cor. 8.9-13.

[43]Cf. *Presbyterorum ordinis,* 7.

[44]Cf. *Christus Dominus,* 30.

[45]Report passed by the Boston Priests' Senate in May, 1970 regarding renewal in parish and rectory life. (Cf. *Presbyterorum ordinis*, 8).

[46]*Presbyterorum ordinis*, 8.

[47]*Christus Dominus*, 16.

[48]Cf. 1 Cor. 12.1-31; Rm. 12.3-8.

[49]"In our times a special obligation binds us to make ourselves the neighbor of absolutely every person, and of actively helping him when he comes across our path, whether he be an old person abandoned by all, a foreign laborer unjustly looked down upon, a refugee, a child born of an unlawful union and wrongly suffering for a sin he did not commit or a hungry person who disturbs our conscience by recalling the voice of the Lord: 'As long as you did it for one of these, the least of my brethren, you did it for Me.' Mt. 25.40 (*Gaudium et spes*, 27).

[50]"True, all men are not alike from the point of view of varying physical power and the diversity of intellectual and moral resources. Nevertheless, with respect to the fundamental rights of the person, every type of discrimination, whether social or cultural, whether based on sex, race, color, social condition, language, or religion is to be overcome and eradicated as contrary to God's intent." (*Ibid.*, 29).

[51]Cf. *Presbyterorum ordinis*, 4; 5; 6.

[52]"On the other hand, it is a sad spectacle when confronted with the abuse and compromise of the liberty of man, who, not knowing the open heavens and refusing faith in Christ the Son of God, redeemer of the world and founder of the Holy Church, turns his search entirely to the pursuit of so-called earthly goods, under the inspiration of him whom the Gospel calls the Prince of Darkness and whom Jesus Himself in His last discourse after the Supper called the prince of this world. This Prince of Darkness organizes the contradiction of and the battle against truth and welfare, the nefarious position which accentuates the division between those called by the genius of Saint Augustine the two cities, and he keeps ever active the effort to confuse so as to deceive, if possible, also the elect and bring them to ruin." (Pope John's Announcement of Vatican II, January 25, 1959).'

[53]Cf. Jo. 10.10.

[54]Cf. *Presbyterorum ordinis*, 16.

[55]Cf. Jo. 1.39.

[56]Cf. Mk. 14.43-45.

[57]Cf. Mk. 14.66-71.
[58]Cf. Mk. 14.50.
[59]Cf. Mk. 16.14.
[60]Cf. Act 11.1-18.
[61]Cf. Hb. 11.
[62]Cf. Mk. 3.14.
[63]Cf. Phil. 2.5.
[64]Cf. Jo. 10.10.
[65]Cf. Rm. 8.15.
[66]Cf. Gn. 17.1.
[67]Hb. 5.7-10.
[68]Cf. I Thes. 5.17.
[69]Cf. Lk. 5.16; 6.12; 9.18; 9.28; 11.1; 22.41.
[70]Cf. Jo. 6.44.
[71]Cf. 1 Cor. 7.32.
[72]Cf. Jo. 17.9.
[73]Pope Paul VI, Apostolic Letter on the Fourth Centenary of the Birth of St. Francis de Sales, Jan. 29, 1967.

[74]Cf. Jo. 15.14-15.
[75]Cf. Mt 6.24; 10.24.
[76]Jesus did not distinguish explicitly between "apostle" and "disciple" in His teaching as recorded in the Gospels. However, it is clear that the Twelve understood that the demands of discipleship applied to them in a very unique way.
[77]Cf. Mt 8.21-22.
[78]Cf. Lk 9.62; 14.28-33.
[79]Cf. Lk 14.26
[80]Cf. Mt 4.22; 19.16-22; 19.27.
[81]Cf. 2 Cor 4.7-18.
[82]Cf. Phil 1.6.
[83]Cf. Mt 19.1-12; 1 Cor 7.1-40
[84]Cf. Dt 4.24ff; Is 1.21-26; Jr 2.2; 3.6-12; Ez16 & 23; Os 1-14.
[85]Cf. Eph 5.21-33; 1 Cor 7.32-35.
[86]Cf Lk 20.27-40.
[87]1 Cor 7.7.
[88]"This holy Synod likewise exhorts all priests, who, trusting in God's grace, have freely undertaken sacred celibacy in imitation of Christ to hold fast to it magnanimously and whole-heartedly. May they persevere faithfully in this state, and recognize this surpassing gift which the Father has given them, and which the Lord praised so openly." (Presbyterorum ordinis, 16).

[89]"Many men today call perfect continence impossible. The more they do so, the more humbly and perseveringly priests should join with the Church in praying for the grace of fidelity. It is never denied to those who ask. At the same time let priests make use of all the supernatural and natural helps which are available to all. Let them not neglect to follow the norms, especially the ascetical ones, which have been tested by the experience of the Church and which are by no means less necessary in today's world. And so this most holy Synod beseeches not only priests, but all the faithful to have at heart this precious gift of priestly celibacy. Let all beg of God that He may always lavish this gift on His Church abundantly." (*Presbyterorum ordinis*, 16.)

[90]Cf. Mt 19.12

[91]Cf. *Presbyterorum ordinis*, 16.

[92]Cf. Lk 14.26

[93]Cf. *Christus Dominus*, 16.

[94]Cf. Mt 19.12.

[95]Cf. *Presbyterorum ordinis*, 17.

[96]"I acknowledge, Lord, and I give thanks that You have created Your image in me, so that I may remember You, think of You, love You. But this image is so effaced and worn away by vice, so darkened by the smoke of sin, that it cannot do what it was made to do unless You renew it and reform it. I do not try, Lord, to attain Your lofty heights, because my understanding is in no way equal to it. But I do desire, Lord, to understand Your truth a little, that truth that my heart believes and loves. For I do not seek to understand so that I may believe; but I believe so that I may understand. For I believe this also, that unless I believe I shall not understand." (Anselm, *Proslogion*, ed. M. J. Charlesworth, Oxford: 1965, p. 115.)

[97]Cf. Jn 14.28.

[98]Cf. Matt. 28.20.

[99]Cf. Gal. 6.2.

[100]"...anyone who has been begotten by God has already overcome the world; this is the victory over the world — our faith." (1 Jo. 5.4.)

The Sacrament
of Penance
and the Priest

Lent, 1981

My dear Brother Priests:

I write to you at the beginning of the ancient season of repentance. It is Christ's season, the special time when His merciful love reaches out more eagerly to every person. It is a time of unusual grace. It is a special season for priests too, because we take up again in a new way that word of life for which men and women hunger as never before, the word which alone restores the dignity of every human person, the word of God's merciful, forgiving love.

You and I—Christ's chosen shepherds— have received a very precious gift this Lent. For we have been presented by our Holy Father with fresh and deep insights into God's relationship with man. We may well call Pope John Paul II "the Pope of divine mercy" or "the Pope of the dignity of man." His brilliant penetration into God's merciful love and the Church's mission to proclaim it prompt me to write this

317

letter to you, my brother priests, as we begin once again our specific work, the calling of people to conversion, or rather that of Christ calling them through us.

The Holy Father's two remarkable encyclicals show us the indispensable place of the Sacrament of Penance in this work; and they show also the hunger of every person for this close encounter with Christ, the Good Shepherd. But how will they meet the forgiving Lord unless priests, in many different ways, but especially through this sacrament, allow Christ to touch the hearts of each one in a unique, personal way? Christ depends on you and me for this, and God's people of all ages and conditions depend on us also. We are not allowed arbitrarily to invite some for forgiveness and to exclude others. Rather, looking to Christ and to the teaching and practice of the Church, we must seek out those for whom Christ shed His blood. It was Peter who said to Christ, "Depart from me, O Lord, for I am a sinful man" (Lk. 5:8), and Peter it is who speaks of forgiveness to us today.

Pope John Paul II writes:

"In faithfully observing the centuries-old practice of the Sacrament of Penance—the practice of individual confession with a personal act of sorrow and the intention to amend and make satisfaction—the Church is therefore defending the human soul's individual right: man's right to a more personal encounter with the crucified forgiving Christ, with Christ saying, through the minister of the Sacrament of Reconciliation: 'Your sins are forgiven; go, and do not sin again.' As is evident, this is also a right on Christ's part with regard to every human being redeemed by Him: His right to meet each one of us in that key moment in the soul's life constituted by the moment of conversion and forgiveness. By guarding the Sacrament of Penance, the Church expressly affirms her faith in the mystery of the Redemption as a living and life-giving reality that fits in with man's inward truth, with human guilt and also with the desires of the human conscience. 'Blessed are those who hunger and thirst for righteousness, for they shall be satisfied.' The Sacrament of Penance is the means to satisfy man with the righteousness that comes from the Redeemer Himself" *(The Redeemer of Man,* no. 20).

"It is the Sacrament of Penance or Reconciliation that prepares the way for each individual, even those weighed down with great faults. In this sacrament each person can experience mercy in a unique way, that is, the love which is more powerful than sin" *(On the Mercy of God,* no. 13).

This truth that sins can be forgiven, that God is touched by our confusion and loss of direction, that He is filled with "anxious love" (cf. *On the Mercy of God,* footnote 52), is central to the Gospel of Jesus Christ, to the work of the Church and to priestly ministry. You and I can never fully appreciate this mystery and yet we are called to be ministers of God's gift of forgiveness and healing to the men and women of our time.

Sacred Scripture reveals and the Church teaches that our sins can be forgiven in many ways: baptism (Acts 2:38), a devout, prayerful offering of the Eucharist (Mt. 26:28), a prayer for forgiveness (Mt. 6:14), pastoral concern for others (Jas. 5:19-20), the admission of our fault and the petition for forgiveness from the person we have offended (Mt. 5:23-24). But we also believe that Jesus has given us a special sacrament of His forgiveness in the Sacrament of Reconciliation (Jn. 20:22-23). It is in this sacrament that He continues to be present and active, inviting us to repentance, conversion, confession and forgiveness, just as He invited others during His earthly life (Lk. 5:18-26; 7:36-50; 15:1-7, 8-10, 11-32; 19:1-10; 23:34, 39-43). The Church has made it clear that we are held to submit our serious sins to this sacrament for full reconciliation (C.I.C., can. 901). The importance of this sacrament has been reaffirmed by Vatican II (*Sacrosanctum concilium*, no. 72; *Presbyterorum ordinis*, no. 5).

In a wondrous way the Sacrament of Reconciliation makes tangibly visible and accessible to us the mysterious initiative of our Trinitarian God. Is it not the Father who joyfully welcomes the repentant sinner on his return, the Father who first loved all of us? Is it not the Son who gently carries the lost sheep back to the fold, the

Son who sacrificed Himself on Calvary for all of us? Is it not the Holy Spirit who once again makes holy His temple or dwells therein in a more intense way, the Holy Spirit who is the Sanctifier? (cf. Letter of Cardinal Secretary of State to Italian Liturgical Week, August 25-29, 1975)

We know that in recent years fewer faithful have been approaching this Sacrament of Reconciliation. There are undoubtedly many reasons for this—the increased awareness that God's forgiveness is sometimes available in other ways, the secular temper of our times, the diminished sense of sin and even the difficulties which some people have encountered in the past in the confessional.

I write to you now because of my great desire that the riches uniquely available in this Sacrament of Reconciliation may be increasingly more accessible to our people. As stewards of God's mysteries, we have a responsibility to do our part to make sure that people are not deprived of the consoling and healing power of God's sacramental forgiveness.

Regular Availability to the Faithful

First of all, it is pastorally important for us to make ourselves available in the confessional on a regular basis at a designated time which is convenient for those seeking the sacrament. It is never sufficient for us merely to announce that we are available by appointment. Most parishioners are hesitant to take that kind of initiative and look for us. Even if few take advantage of the opportunity, our continuing presence in the confessional speaks eloquently of our own faith conviction regarding the centrality of this priestly ministry to others. It is a witness to Christ's availability and readiness to forgive. He came to save sinners at any time and at all times!

Moreover, our attempts to spell out the fuller meaning and richness of this sacrament in our preaching can touch the hearts of so many who seem to hunger for God's forgiveness, but often do not know how to experience it. Furthermore, our own prayerful celebration of the sacrament with them can assist so many to move beyond any formalism in confession to deeper conversion of heart and greater receptivity to God's healing grace.

The new Rite of Penance presents us with the opportunity to offer communal penance services as a way of assisting our people to hear God's invitation to conversion in community and to sense more fully the communal dimensions to both sin and grace. It is particularly appropriate to plan such services in Lent and in Advent or in connection with major feasts. The opportunity for private confession and personal absolution must always be preserved when these services are offered.

Initiation of Children
to First Penance

Secondly, I would like to draw special attention to the mandate which is ours to help children become appropriately initiated to this sacrament of forgiveness. Jesus Himself, despite the protestations of many around Him, always wanted to make it easier for children to come to Him (Lk. 18:15-16), and pointedly indicated to the surrounding adults that the children had a special claim to redemption (Lk. 18:17).

In the light of the teaching of the Church on the value and importance of the Sacrament of Reconciliation, it would be a tragedy if any obstacles were placed in the way of a child, preventing him or her from receiving the grace of this sacrament.

It is not enough merely to refrain from preventing children from receiving First Penance before First Eucharist. The Church, deeply conscious of the value and the importance of the Sacrament of Penance, clearly teaches that it is the norm that confession should precede First Holy Communion. Our *National Catechetical Directory* states, "The Sacrament of Reconciliation normally should be celebrated prior to the reception of First Communion." This directive was explicitly written at the request of the Holy See (cf. *Origins*, December 7, 1978, p. 394).

This instruction from the Sacred Congregation was not something novel. On numerous occasions during the past decade, the Church has seen fit to reaffirm and to emphasize this teaching.

The *General Catechetical Directory*, issued by the Holy See in 1971, pointed out that:

"The Supreme Pontiff, Pius X, declared, 'The custom of not admitting children to Confession or of never giving them absolution, when they have arrived at the use of reason, must be wholly condemned.' One can scarcely have regard for the right that baptized children have of confessing their sins, if at the beginning of the age of discretion they are not prepared and gently led to the Sacrament of Penance" (*General Catechetical Directory*, Appendum, no. 5).

Subsequently, this teaching was reaffirmed by several other documents emanating from the Holy See. Then, in April of 1978, our late Holy Father, Pope Paul VI, speaking to a group of American bishops "on a fundamental aspect of the Gospel: Christ's call to conversion," declared:

"Another important aspect of the penitential discipline of the Church is the practice of First Confession before First Communion. Our appeal here is that the norms of the Apostolic See not be emptied of their meaning by contrary practice" (cf. *Origins*, May 4, 1978, p. 724).

Our present Holy Father, Pope John Paul II, in an address to a group of bishops, in which he reminded them of Pope Paul VI's reaffirmation of the Church's teaching on the practice of First Confession before First Communion, went on to state:

"In a spirit of exemplary fidelity, numerous bishops, priests, deacons, religious, teachers and catechists set out to explain the importance of a discipline which the supreme authority of the Church had confirmed, and to apply it for the benefit of the faithful.... I ask you to continue to explain the Church's solicitude in maintaining this universal discipline, so rich in doctrinal background and confirmed by the experience of so many local Churches. With regard to children who have reached the age of reason, the Church is happy to guarantee the pastoral value of having them experience the sacramental expression of conversion before being initiated into the Eucharistic sharing of the Paschal Mystery" (cf. *Origins*, December 7, 1978, p. 395).

I am aware that a contrary practice has emerged in some parishes of our own Archdiocese as well as in other parts of the nation and world. This practice often postpones the fuller catechesis and the celebration of the sacrament until after First Holy Communion, usually to the fourth grade. I want to make clear that the directives of the Holy See (incorporated in the guidelines of our own Office of Religious Education) require that this formal experiment cease (Congregation for the Sacraments and Divine Worship and the Congregation for the Clergy, May 24, 1973. Cf. *Origins*, July 27, 1973, p. 100).

Some of the positive fruits of this experiment can still be preserved while following our traditional practice of initiation to First Penance and First Eucharist in the same year: separate catechesis and celebration of each sacrament; involvement of the parents in the preparation and the decision on the precise time the child is ready for each sacrament; the gradated catechesis for the Sacrament of Penance so that new insight into the depths of this sacrament can be appreciated at each succeeding stage of the child's development in faith and conscience.

It is our pastoral responsibility neither to deprive young children of their *right* to be initiated into this rich experience of God's healing grace, nor to coerce them into the exercise of this right. It is the duty of parents, priests and religious instructors to educate children as to the teaching of the Church, to inspire them with an appreciation of and a love for the sacraments instituted by Our Lord Jesus Christ, and to see to it that they are "gently led to the Sacrament of Penance." As one theologian has so aptly expressed the thought: "On a supernatural plane, the Church's judgment should also be trusted: that a child of seven...needs the inflow of divine grace which Christ bestows on all who receive His sacrament of peace.

"We do not consider it coercion to suggest and, if need be, insist that a child get a balanced diet of food or adequate sleep and clothing. No parent believes he is unduly tampering with a child's liberty by sending it (perhaps reluctantly) to school. A Catholic cannot afford to follow a double standard where the spiritual needs of God's children are concerned. After all, they belong to Him" (John A. Hardon, S.J., *First Confession, an Historical and Theological Analysis,* pp. 41-42).

It is, of course, necessary that children be properly prepared to receive the Sacraments of First Penance and First Holy Communion. Parents, as the primary religious educators of their children, should be involved in the preparations of their children for the first reception of the Sacraments of Penance and the Holy Eucharist, not only as teachers of the sacraments, but also as models in their own faith-lives through their appreciation and frequent reception of the sacraments. To aid their children in this preparation, parents are encouraged to participate in the formal parish programs (Teachable Moments Programs) designed to enable them to assume their responsibility in preparing their children for the reception of the sacraments.

Catechesis (religious instruction) for children must always respect the natural disposition, ability, age and circumstances of individuals. It must also seek to make clear the relationship of the Sacrament of Penance to the child's life, help the child recognize moral good and evil, repent of wrongdoing and turn for forgiveness to Christ and the Church, encourage the child to see that, in this sacrament, faith is expressed by being forgiven and forgiving, and encourage the child to receive the sacrament freely and regularly.

First Confession should be separated from the reception of First Holy Communion "by an appropriate lapse of time" (cf. Letter of the Cardinal Secretary of State to Italian Liturgical Week, August 25-29, 1975).

When the catechesis for these sacraments is kept distinct, the child will become aware of the specific identity of each sacrament. If this catechesis presents God as a merciful, loving and forgiving Father, the child will learn to be at ease with the reception of the Sacrament of Penance.

Because continuing, lifelong conversion is part of what it means to grow in faith and in the virtue of penance, catechesis for the Sacrament of Penance should be ongoing. Children, as well as adults, have a right to fuller catechesis on this sacrament, and indeed on all sacraments, year by year.

Implications for Ourselves

Lastly, I would like to mention an obvious implication of all that the Church asks of us in our priestly responsibility with regard to offering this sacrament to others. The best confessors are those who are good penitents themselves. If we do not experience the special grace of this sacrament regularly in our own lives, we are going to run the risk of becoming hardened to the possibilities for others. True repentance in ourselves will move us to greater humility, patience and compassion in mediating God's merciful forgiveness to others. I urge you, my brother priests, to approach this sacrament regularly with humble and sincere hearts.

As I bring this letter to a close, I ask all of you, my brother priests, to meditate with me on the beautiful description of divine mercy found in the new *Rite of Penance*. Here we read of Christ touching sinners through the Sacrament of Penance:

"Jesus...not only exhorted men to repentance so that they should abandon their sins and turn wholeheartedly to the Lord, but He also welcomed sinners and reconciled them with the Father.... He Himself died for our sins and rose again for our justification. Therefore, on the night He was betrayed and began His saving passion, He instituted the sacrifice of the new covenant in His blood for the forgiveness of sins. After His resurrection He sent the Holy Spirit upon the Apostles, empowering them to forgive or retain sins and sending them forth to all people to preach repentance and the forgiveness of sins in His name.... The Church has never failed to call men from sin to conversion, and by the celebration of Penance, to show the victory of Christ over sin" *(Rite of Penance,* Introduction, no. 1).

With priestly affection and a hearty blessing, I remain

Devotedly yours in Our Lord,
✠ Humberto Cardinal Medeiros
Archbishop of Boston

Pastoral Care
for the Homosexual

Feast of the Sacred Heart, 1979

My dear brother priests:

I have chosen the Feast of the Sacred Heart as the occasion for this letter to you because it focuses our attention on the love of the priestly Heart of Jesus for all people. He was sent into the world to reconcile all His brothers and sisters with His Father and lead them to salvation. Since, through sacramental ordination, we share in a unique way in His priestly service, this Feast which celebrates His compassionate and healing love has a singular meaning for us, His priests. We believe He has chosen us not only to accept His special love for us, but also to continue His mission of renewing the human family in Him until He comes in glory. This, I think, is what St. Paul had in mind when he wrote:

> And for anyone who is in Christ, there is a new creation; the old creation has gone, and now the new one is here. It is all God's work. It was God who reconciled us to Himself through Christ and gave us the work of handing on this reconciliation. In other words, God in Christ was reconciling the world to Himself, not holding men's faults against them, and He has entrusted to us the news that they are reconciled. So we are ambassadors for Christ; it is as though God were appealing through us, and the appeal that we make in Christ's name is: be reconciled to God. For our sake God made the sinless one into sin, so that in Him we might become the goodness of God. As His fellow workers, we beg you once again not to neglect the grace of God that you have received (2 Cor. 5:17-21; 6:1).

Looking with faith at the Heart of Christ pierced for us, we come to realize how vividly God wishes to reveal to us His loving will that all His children be reconciled to

Him. Out of infinite love, symbolized by the human heart, the Father sent His only Son into the world so that through the blood shed by Jesus on the cross, God might reconcile all to Himself (cf. 1 Jn. 4:9-10: Eph. 2:11-18). This is a marvelous mystery indeed! And perhaps more marvelous still is the fact that God calls us to join Him in this stupendous work of divine love, as if He "were appealing through us." *God appealing through us!*

Pastoral Concern for Homosexual People

Because as priests we are not merely ambassadors for Christ, but stand in the midst of the people *in the person* of Christ, we are the ministers of His reconciling and healing love and the bearers of the light of His truth. As human beings, we need His healing and light. As priests we bring His healing to the wounded and His light to those in darkness and confusion. For this reason, I wish to speak with you on an issue of considerable concern, especially in our time. You know of the confusion in doctrine and pastoral practice which has arisen in recent years regarding those of our brothers and sisters who have homosexual tendencies or engage in homosexual behavior.

I have written at length to you on this matter in the past, and there are several official Church documents which have dealt with it. Nevertheless, the confusion seems to persist. Hopefully, these observations of mine will assist you to help dispel the confusion which seems to afflict the minds and hearts of some, perhaps many.

First of all, we know that there is a segment of our human population who experience significant homosexual inclinations, drives and attraction. In fact, many people experience some such feelings temporarily during their adolescence or in situations where they are living in a *homosocial* environment for an extended period of time. For some, the inclinations seem to persist and are stronger than heterosexual feelings and attractions. It is important to note that human drives, feelings and attractions are ultimately rooted in natural impulse. Unless they are deliberately nurtured and strengthened, they are morally neutral.

The cultural environment in which we live, however, seems to offer confusing advice. Film, drama, literature, television and radio sometimes tend to suggest that homosexual behavior is a morally legitimate alternative in sexual expression.

In recent months, some of us have received a letter from an organization called *Dignity*. In this and other documents including books and tapes, the authors make strong recommendations to us regarding our ministry to homosexual people. For instance, sometimes we are counselled to minister to homosexual brothers and sisters in a special group, to allow only certain priests to minister to them, to accept the theory that homosexuality differs from heterosexuality just as being right-handed differs from being left-handed, to accept the contention that the Church has condemned not only homosexual acts but also the homosexual orientation, to provide liturgies, prayer services, even parishes which are exclusively or primarily for those who are homosexual and, as official representatives of the Church, to accept homosexual unions as preferable to promiscuity. At times, it is even suggested that we are guilty of harming those who are homosexual when we adhere to the moral teaching of the Church.

The attitudes reflected in these recommendations do appeal to the pastoral love of the Church, because basically they bespeak a yearning, however hidden, for healing, for reconciliation. This is true both of those who experience these tendencies and those who try to help them. May we not say that whatever the more specific origin of these attitudes and inclinations may be, fundamentally they arise from the "wounded" human person of whom St. Paul speaks so feelingly? (cf. Rom. 7:14-25)

The Second Vatican Council addressed itself to this source of confusion within us and in our social life. The Council is a reflection of St. Paul's analysis and a fruit of the Church's experience. Allow me to quote it:

> The truth is that the imbalances under which the modern world labors are linked with that more basic imbalance rooted in the heart of man. For in man himself many elements wrestle with one another. Thus, on the one hand, as a creature he experiences his limitations in a multitude of ways. On the other, he feels himself to be boundless in his desires and summoned to a higher life.
>
> Pulled by manifold attractions, he is constantly forced to choose among them and to renounce some. Indeed as a weak and sinful being, he often does what he would not, and fails to do what he would. Hence he suffers from internal divisions, and from these flow so many and such great discords in society (*Constitution on the Church in the Modern World*, 10).

It appears that confusion and discord come naturally from our "internal divisions," but we seek forever to find new ways to heal this basic wound of our nature. It is not surprising, therefore, that some would press special plans for action on the Church to heal those who experience homosexual pain.

Appreciation of True Dignity in Christ Jesus

The Church listens to the appeal because she is sent to all to heal them, to save them in the power of Christ. That is her mission. On this point we have the eloquent and inspiring words of our Holy Father, Pope John Paul II:

> Jesus Christ is the chief way for the Church. He Himself is our way 'to the Father's house' (cf.

Jn. 14:1ff.) and is the way to each man. On this way leading from Christ to man, on this way on which Christ unites Himself with each man, nobody can halt the Church (*The Redeemer of Man*, 13).

He also says:

The Church cannot abandon man, for his 'destiny,' that is to say his election, calling, birth and death, salvation and perdition, is so closely and unbreakably linked with Christ (*The Redeemer of Man*, 14).

And, finally, Pope John Paul II writes:

This man is the way for the Church—a way that, in a sense, is the basis for all the other ways that the Church must walk—because man—every man without any exception whatever—has been redeemed by Christ and because with man—with each man without any exception whatever—Christ is in a way united, even when man is unaware of it: 'Christ who died and was raised up for all, provides man'—each and every man—'with the light and the strength to measure up to his supreme calling' (*The Redeemer of Man*, 14).

Precisely who is this man? For the Pope he is not an abstraction. He is a concrete, living human being "in all the truth of his life, in his conscience, in his continual inclinations to sin and at the same time in his continual aspiration to truth, the good, the beautiful, justice and love..." (*The Redeemer of Man*, 14). And the Holy Father describes this man or woman for us, lest we think the Church is to deal with man as he might be and not as we find him every day in ourselves and in others. Forgive me the length of this quotation, but it is good for us to keep it in mind in connection with our subject. Pope John Paul II writes:

We are speaking precisely of each man on this planet, this earth that the Creator gave to the first man, saying to the man and the woman: 'Subdue it and have dominion!' (Gn. 1:28) Each man in all the unrepeatable reality of what he is and what he does, of his intellect and will, of his conscience and heart. Man who in his reality has, because he is a 'person,' a history of his life that is his own and, most important, a history of his soul that is his own. Man who, in keeping with the openness of his spirit within and also with the many diverse needs of his body and his existence in time, writes this personal history of his through numerous bonds, contacts, situations, and social structures linking him with other men, beginning to do so from the first moment of his existence on earth, from the moment of his conception and birth. Man in the full truth of his existence, of his personal being and also of his community and social being—in the sphere of his own family, in the sphere of society and very diverse contexts, in the sphere of his own nation or people (perhaps still only that of his clan or tribe), and in the sphere of the whole of mankind—this man is the primary route that the Church must travel in fulfilling her mission: *He is the primary and fundamental way for the Church*, the way traced out by Christ Himself, the way that leads invariably through the mystery of the Incarnation and the Redemption (*The Redeemer of Man*, 14).

There is no doubt that man and woman as we find them anywhere at any point in history are the center of the pastoral love and concern of the Church. This is every one of us wounded by original sin and our own personal sins and suffering from "internal divisions" which lead to alienation from God, from self and from others. From the basic wound and its consequences Jesus came to heal us. Moreover, we, His priests, have been entrusted with the mission to extend His healing and saving service to everyone of our brothers and sisters without exception, no matter what the pain, what the division, what the alienation. Man in his actual condition is the path for the Church and so He is the path for the priests of the Church.

Pastoral Response

There is no question, therefore, that we are called to minister with pastoral love to those of our brothers and sisters who have homosexual inclinations or enter into homosexual behavior. To them as to all others without exception we must bring the riches of the healing love and mercy of the Good Shepherd. We do this in the Church and through the Church to whom the Lord Jesus has entrusted the dispensing of His mysteries and the authentic proclamation of His saving word. Let us listen together to the Second Vatican Council:

> Since the priestly ministry is the ministry of the Church herself, it can be discharged only in hierarchical communion with the whole body. Therefore, pastoral love demands that acting in this communion, priests dedicate their own wills through obedience to the service of God and their brothers. This love requires that they accept and carry out in a spirit of faith whatever is commanded or recommended by the Sovereign Pontiff, their own Bishop, or other Superiors *(Decree on the Ministry and Life of Priests, 15).*

We know what the light of Christ through the Church is with regard to our brothers and sisters under consideration. Let us listen to the Holy See:

> At the present time, there are those who, basing themselves on observations in the psychological order, have begun to judge indulgently, and even to excuse completely, homosexual relations between certain people. This they do in opposition to the constant teaching of the Magisterium and to the moral sense of the Christian people.

A distinction is drawn, and it seems with some reason, between homosexuals whose tendency comes from a false education, from a lack of normal sexual development, from habit, from bad example, or from other similar causes, and is transitory or at least not incurable; and homosexuals who are definitely such because of some kind of instinct or a pathological constitution judged to be incurable.

In regard to this second category of subjects, some people conclude that their tendency is so natural that it justifies in their case homosexual relations within a sincere communion of life and love analogous to marriage, insofar as such homosexuals feel incapable of enduring a solitary life.

In the pastoral field, these homosexuals must certainly be treated with understanding and sustained in the hope of overcoming their personal difficulties and their inability to fit into society. Their culpability will be judged with prudence. But no pastoral method can be employed which would give moral justification to these acts on the grounds that they would be consonant with the condition of such people. For according to the objective moral order, homosexual relations are acts which lack an essential and indispensable finality. In Sacred Scripture they are condemned as a serious depravity and even presented as the sad consequence of rejecting God. This judgment of Scripture does not, of course, permit us to conclude that all those who suffer from this anomaly are personally responsible for it, but it does attest to the fact that homosexual acts are intrinsically disordered and can in no case be approved (*Declaration on Sexual Ethics*, 8—Sacred Congregation for the Doctrine of the Faith).

For us as priests to sustain this teaching of the Church and to present it with peace and confidence, we must ourselves accept the Church as bearing in herself the light of Christ. We must also nurture in our own hearts a strong resistance to any self-centered forces in the culture which claim to foster human dignity, but which in fact inhibit and debase it. In the faith of the Church we must see the homosexual person as one whom Christ loves and wants to heal in the light of truth through genuine love.

The homosexual person must be free to seek help from any and all of Christ's priests. On our part, each of us must be ready to respond to such needs. This is a ministry for all of us and we must be prepared to make serious efforts to fulfill it as we do all other aspects of our priestly calling. We do not want to push them aside or cut them off from the mainstream of Catholic and parochial life by encouraging them, even if indirectly, to worship only in a few designated churches or allowing them to be counselled only in a special group or instructing them that they are only to approach one or at most several designated priests for spiritual support. On the human level, such a course on our part would be demeaning. It would deprive them of their rightful place in the whole Church community. And on the spiritual level, this attitude is unchristian. Such segregation would not be sound psychologically, spiritually or pastorally. It is important that we reach out in sacramental ministry to them and give the time and effort of personal counselling and guidance when they need this.

Sometimes such counselling must be done against a background of social pressure that presents the notion so prevalent in our culture today, and even in some theological writings, that homosexual relationships and homosexual acts are not sinful as long as they are "personally enriching." My brother priests, if we accept such a notion, we degrade the person we are counselling—a person for whom Christ shed His blood. Moreover, we destroy the possibility of truly helping the person. You and I must resist this pressure and retain in our hearts the same respect for this individual man or woman that Christ Himself has. Basically, what you and I must desire as we engage in conversation with the individual needing help is that through us he or she can meet Christ. Because of this goal, any acceptance on our part of homosexual acts in themselves or of homosexual life-styles as consonant with Christian living is foreign to our pastoral practice. Such acts and the life-styles which sometimes lead to them debase the human person. They are objectively immoral, even if certain people experience difficulty in moving beyond them. We want to avoid various errors as we try to lead this person to Christ. We must avoid the extreme of the Pharisee; we must resist our own desire for acceptance and popularity on the part of this person or other homosexual people; we must resist the desire to give an easy answer; we must resist the growing thrust toward undiscerning tolerance in our times.

Perhaps we can learn a great deal from an episode in the life of Jesus which is preserved for us in John's gospel (Jn. 8:1-11). When the woman caught in adultery was brought to Jesus, it soon became obvious that the Scribes and Pharisees wanted to trap Jesus with a pastoral dilemma. He had preached mercy toward the sinner; yet the Law was utterly clear in cases where the adultery of a woman could be publicly attested. Jesus refused to be forced to choose between the two proposed alternatives: condone or condemn. In effect, he asked the accusers to look into themselves: "If there is one of you who has not sinned, let him be the first to cast a stone at her" (Jn. 8:7). And they slipped away, one by one. Then that remarkable and touching exchange transpired: "Jesus looked up and said, 'Woman, where are they? Has no one condemned you?' 'No one, sir,' she replied. 'Neither do I condemn you,' said Jesus, 'go away and do not sin anymore' " (Jn. 8:10-11). In this simple episode Jesus revealed how God shows mercy without condoning sin. We, His priests, are called to do in like manner.

If we model our approach on Christ Jesus, we will be moved to share in His compassion and understanding, while remaining firm in our adherence to the Church's teaching despite pressures to the contrary. In this connection let us recognize humbly, yet discerningly the significant gift that theologians offer us in the Church. They are called upon to explore new ways of understanding and interpreting God's message for contemporary people. Their probing work is always tentative until tested and refined in and by the Church. In pastoral practice, we must adhere to the theological positions which have been officially incorporated into Church teaching. Thus we are called to do what we can to help the homosexual person lead a chaste life. In doing so, we are accepting a homosexual man or woman as a full member of the Church and of society. When we do this, we are calling the person to that same life of chastity which we try to live. We are calling and helping this person to the same virtue of chastity to which we are encouraging married persons or single members of our flock. We are giving them their full place in the Church. We refuse to relegate them to a "separate but equal" category which ultimately denies them their basic human dignity and Christian nobility.

Experience tells us that in working with homosexual people, we will realize the very great difficulty that many of them—whether married or single—have in avoiding homosexual behavior or in avoiding the places or circumstances which so easily lead to these acts. What will we do? The answer we already know. We will bring them to Christ who alone has the power to strengthen and heal them. We bring them to the person of Christ most directly when they approach us in the Sacrament of Reconciliation. This sacrament is never out of date because Christ always wishes to redeem, to forgive, to release from sin, to heal what is wounded. We bring them to Him in the Holy Eucharist. We bring them to Him by leading them to personal prayer, to the prudent practice of penance and self-denial and to the avoidance of the occasion of sin. We encourage them to sound spiritual reading. We are their friend. We love them—but as Christ loves them—with an intelligent, disciplined and pastoral love.

Some Implications
for Our Common Pastoral Practice

I hope that these thoughts are helpful to you. Since this is a pastoral question which touches the whole Archdiocese, I have the responsibility to indicate some specific norms for implementing Church teaching in the local pastoral situation.

(1) All priests are to be open to assisting homosexual people along the lines outlined above. If all of us adopt a stance toward homosexual people which is truly Christ's and the Church's approach, they will be affirmed and drawn to Christ at the same time. If we as priests accept them as Christ accepts them, receive their words with respect, as the words of brothers and sisters, and also observe strict confidentiality as is our duty, we can help them to find their rightful place in the parish without drawing attention to this in a public way. It is this full membership and activity—when coupled with a deep spiritual and sacramental life—which will help them to avoid sin and enable them to grow both spiritually and psychologically. Hence there is no priest specifically assigned to ministry to homosexual people. If there has been any confusion in the past as to what was the actual situation, I trust that this matter is now clear. This is part of the overall ministry of every priest in the Archdiocese of Boston.

(2) We do not want to encourage our people to join so-called "gay groups." Experience also shows that such groups can lead young people who are anxious or confused about their sexual drives to embrace a homosexual

culture and even a homosexual way of life. It is possible that the very fact of banding together in such groups for social and religious purposes could include the recognition and even the fostering of homosexual activity. Moreover, I do not authorize any priest in the Archdiocese of Boston to offer the Eucharist for a group who band together as homosexuals. Such groups tend to impede true human and spiritual development. We want to integrate all men and women into the life of our parishes.

(3) We also want to be discerning in this area in recommending candidates for the seminary and ordination. A man who experiences difficulty in handling homosexual drives and feelings will find himself attempting to live a celibate life in an environment which only heightens his struggles. Sometimes such men experience serious liabilities in relating comfortably with women. Or they may find themselves arrested in their emotional development. Only those who have moved beyond genital sexual preoccupation and found a real capacity for marital life and love, can proceed to a celibate life with a reasonable possibility for truly oblative love. I realize that there are varying degrees of homosexuality. Obviously, I am not including the young man who is still struggling to grow and who may experience some homosexual feelings, but gives assurance of moving beyond his tendencies. But it should be our practice to lead an individual person with all his special traits to that state of life where he will find the most peace and be personally best able to live a life of true and unselfish love without having to overcome almost insurmountable obstacles or difficulties.

Conclusion

Pope John Paul II has indicated to us the way we should follow. Let us reflect together on his pastoral guidance, on how to all we must always be priests and shepherds:

It may sometimes seem to us that they do not want this, or that they wish us to be in every way 'like them'; at times it even seems that they demand this of us. And here one very much needs a profound 'sense of faith' and 'the gift of discernment.' In fact, it is very easy to let oneself be guided by appearances and fall victim to a fundamental illusion in what is essential. Those who call for the secularization of priestly life and applaud its manifestations will undoubtedly abandon us when we succumb to temptation. We shall then cease to be necessary and popular. Our time is characterized by different forms of 'manipulation' and 'exploitation' of man, but we cannot give in to any of these. In practical terms, the only priest who will always prove necessary to people is the priest who is conscious of the full meaning of his priesthood; the priest who believes profoundly, who professes his faith with courage, who prays fervently, who teaches with deep conviction, who serves, who puts into practice in his own life the program of the Beatitudes, who knows how to love disinterestedly, who is close to everyone, and especially to those who are most in need.

Our pastoral activity demands that we should be close to people and all their problems, whether these problems be personal, family or social ones, but it also demands that we should be close to all these problems in 'a priestly way.' Only then, in the sphere of all those problems, do we remain ourselves. Therefore, if we are really of assistance in those human problems, and they are sometimes very difficult ones, then we keep our identity and are really faithful to our vocation. With great perspicacity we must seek, together with all men, truth and justice, the true and definitive dimension of which we can only find in the Gospel, or rather in

Christ Himself. Our task is to serve truth and justice in the dimensions of human 'temporality,' but always in a perspective that is the perspective of eternal salvation. This salvation takes into account the temporal achievements of the human spirit in the spheres of knowledge and morality, as the Second Vatican Council wonderfully recalled, but it is not identical with them, and in fact it goes higher than them: 'The things that no eye has seen and no ear has heard...all that God has prepared for those who love Him.' Our brethren in the faith, and unbelievers too, expect us always to be able to show them this perspective, to become real witnesses to it, to be dispensers of grace, to be servants of the word of God. They expect us to be men of prayer (Letter of John Paul II *To All the Priests of the Church on Holy Thursday,* 1979).

My dear brother priests: this has been a long letter when perhaps a few words of direction might have sufficed. Yet I wished to place this issue, as all other issues affecting the human person and our pastoral love for one another, in the context of the more extended teaching of the Scripture, the Council and our Holy Father. I feel I have not done justice to any of these, but I have tried hard, I prayed and suffered, and I consulted in order to be clear, just and faithful to our mission in Our Lord Jesus Christ. You know that in dealing with the human person, we find each man and each woman to be a mystery hidden with Christ in the God who created us for Himself. Because of this we must appeal to faith to know what to say and what to do in the process of healing any of our brothers and sisters. In the last analysis we must walk in faith. The Council tells us:

Since all of these realities are hidden with Christ in God they can be best grasped by faith. For the leaders of the People of God must walk by faith, following the example of the faithful Abraham, who in faith 'obeyed by going out into a place which he was to receive for an inheritance; and he went out, not knowing where he was going' (Heb. 11:8). The dispenser of the mysteries of God can be truly compared to the man who sowed his field and of whom the Lord said: 'Then he slept and rose, night and day; and the seed sprouted and grew without his knowing it' (Mk. 4:27) (*Decree on the Ministry and Life of Priests*, 22).

And so we walk by faith in the Son of God who loved us and gave Himself up for us (cf. Gal. 2:20) as we embrace in pastoral love all our brothers and sisters we can reach to bring the healing grace of our Divine Redeemer.

Walking
in Light

Excerpts from Christmas Homily, 1972

The true Christian senses a mysterious joy. Something has happened to him that he does not fully understand but can never forget. He believes that he has passed from darkness into light and from death to life (cf. 1 Jn. 2:10-11; 3:14). He feels free with the freedom of the children of God.

This sense of freedom, however, is always associated with living the truth in love (Eph. 4:15) as revealed by God and proclaimed by the living voice of His Church. He has accepted the words of the Lord who said, "You will learn the truth and the truth will make you free" (Jn. 8:32). He always links his freedom with the love of God which places on his personal life the demands of faithful discipleship to His crucified Son. Our blessed Lord says to all of us, "If anyone wants to be a follower of mine, let him renounce himself and take up his cross and follow me" (Mt. 16:24). And again he says, "If anyone loves me, he will keep my word, and my Father will love him, and we shall come to him and make our home with him" (Jn. 14:23).

It is with a far more than human sense of joy and gratitude that we Christians strive to keep these words of the living God operative in our everyday life-situation. We find strength to live out the will of God in our lives in every blessing we receive from the hands of our heavenly Father, both great and small. The greatest of these we believe to be the gift of His only Son to us.... The Son of God became the Son of Mary, ever a virgin, a man like us in all things except sin, but always God. As the Creed puts it, He is "God from God; Light from Light; true God from true God...."

We need the gift of faith to seek and to find this Savior in Bethlehem's Cave. And once we find Him, we need the same faith to stay with Him through life. We need this gift of the Father to begin to look for His Son, because we can never go to the Son unless the Father draw us to Him (cf. Jn. 6:44). It is also through this same gift of faith that the Son leads us to the Father Himself (cf. Jn. 14:6). It is all the gift of God!...

We thank the Father, through Jesus Christ our Lord, in the Holy Spirit, for this gift, for this necessary gift of faith, without which we would walk in darkness as we make our painful pilgrimage on the face of the earth, with eyes filled with hope in the happiness and peace promised by the Redeemer of the world to all those who believe in His name. To such as these God has given the power to be children of God.

As God's children we are to walk in the light given us by the Father, and that light is His Son our Lord Jesus Christ who has proclaimed Himself the Light of the world (cf. Jn. 9:5). That light has been shining for us from Bethlehem ever since the first Christmas. St. John writes in his Gospel concerning Christ, the Son of God and the Word of God, that:

"All that came to be had life in him and that life was the light of men, a light that shines in the dark, a light that darkness could not overpower.... The Word was the true light that enlightens all men; and he was coming into the world. He was in the world that had its being through him, and the world did not know him. He came into his own domain and his own people did not accept him. But to all who did accept him he gave power to become children of God, to all who believe in the name of him who was born not of human stock or urge of the flesh or will of man but of God himself. The Word was made flesh and lived among us, and we saw his glory, the glory that is his as the only Son of the Father, full of grace and truth" (Jn. 1:4-14).

The darkness of evil in the world has not overpowered the Light of the Son of God; nor will the devil, the evil one, with the darkness of confusion he labors relentlessly to sow in the minds and hearts of men, ever prevail against the kindly light of the Son of Mary Immaculate, the sinless and grace-filled new Eve, the new Mother of all the living with the new life brought to men by her Son's death upon the cross. This guarantee we have from God.

Nevertheless, the Prince of this world, Satan, wages constant war against the children of light, the new children of God born of water and the Holy Spirit (cf. Jn. 3:5). In this fight, however, not every child of God comes out unscathed or victorious. Many a victim lies moaning or dead on this dismal battlefield. Such as had neglected to put on the breastplate of justice, the shield of faith (cf. Eph. 6:14-17), have perished or are mortally wounded.

But even these, if still with us in the struggle, have the opportunity to lift their eyes to the Lord, to repent and receive the light that dispels the darkness of confusion which tortures them, and begin anew to believe that Jesus Christ is the Light of the world. It is He, the Prince of

Peace, who reconciled all men with God
and with one another through the shedding of His blood (cf. 1 Cor. 5:18-19).

It is these aimless children of God, confused and bent on confusing others, doing
the works of "the father of lies" (Jn. 8:44),
believing all the while, in their confusion,
that they are doing a service to God
(cf. Jn. 16:2) — it is these who must
especially approach in humility and simplicity of heart the mystery of the Incarnation and birth of the Son of God and the
Son of Mary, and moved by the Father,
open their hearts to the light of Christ
present in us and with us as the Head of
His holy Church. They must come to believe once more, or for the first time,
that it is the Spirit of the Infant Savior who
speaks in the Church, to the Church and
through the Church which He has made a
beacon of light to all the nations (cf.
Vatican I, *Dei Filius*, Denziger, 1744).

It is for such as these within the Church
and outside of it that I implore you, my
dearly beloved brothers and sisters in
Christ, to pray fervently now and always.
I am not the first one, nor shall I be the
last to make this plea, because brothers
and sisters such as these have always
lived in our midst and shall always be
with us.

Writing in the very first years of the life of the Church, St. Paul said what I make my own as I humbly and lovingly turn to them:

"In particular I want to urge you in the name of the Lord, not to go on living the aimless kind of life that pagans live. Intellectually they are in the dark, and they are estranged from the life of God, without knowledge because they have shut their eyes to it. Their sense of right and wrong once dulled, they have abandoned themselves to sexuality and eagerly pursue a career of indecency of every kind. Now that is hardly the way you have learned from Christ, unless you failed to hear him properly when you were taught what the truth is in Jesus. You must give up your old way of life; you must put aside your old self, which gets corrupted by following illusory desires. Your mind must be renewed by a spiritual revolution so that you can put on the new self that has been created in God's way, in the goodness and holiness of truth" (Eph. 4:17-24).

Is it not true that so many among us need to hear this exhortation of St. Paul? The new self created in God's way, in the goodness and holiness of truth avoids the works of darkness and is busy with the works of light.

How many among us have dulled their sense of right and wrong and rationalize now their lamentable condition in order to justify it by appealing to what they claim to be the latest findings of the behavioral sciences, quite possibly misunderstood by them! But even if rightly understood, should finite and always imperfect human science be placed by a Christian above the revealed truth and light of God in His Son Jesus Christ? What a tragedy for those who do it and so teach others to do! What a scandal! Would it not be better for them that a millstone were tied around their neck and that they should be thrown into the sea!

How they sin against love who lead others astray, trusting in their own darkness rather than in the light of God! The man of faith realizes that Christ is foolishness to the wise men of this world, but like Paul he is certain that the foolishness of God is better than the wisdom of man. It is through the ultimate folly of the cross that God brings men from death to life and from darkness to light (cf. 1 Cor. 1:17-18).

How many among us today have shut their eyes to the true knowledge which is found fully in the Church of the living God and have preferred the darkness outside of it, with frightening consequences for themselves and for those whom they seduce with pleasant words and easy morals! (cf. 2 Tim. 4:3-4) St. Paul tells us that such have "abandoned themselves to sexuality and eagerly pursue a career of indecency of every kind":

—the sexual permissiveness of our age with its insensitivity to sin of every sort;

—the insensibility of so many to the real spiritual and material needs of men;

—the cruel and depersonalized attitude of large numbers of people towards others;

—the mad pursuit of money and profit without regard for justice;

—the loathesome profiteering in sex, in pornography, in drugs and alcohol;

—the exploitation of men and women solely for pleasures condemned by the Gospel of Christ as sinful and leading to everlasting damnation while disrupting the orderly and peaceful progress of human society;

—the morbid and debilitating egotism of so many who live only for themselves because their sense of right and wrong has been dulled (these have forgotten that man cannot live for himself alone and ever hope to develop the full potential of his nature healed by the grace of the Savior);

—the degradation of human dignity seen all around us because of alienation from God and His Church;

—the myopic view that many have of the Church, expecting all her members, except themselves, to be perfect, especially her leaders, such as the Pope and

the bishops — unaware, it seems, in spite
of all their learning, that in God's infinite
wisdom and mercy His Church was to
be made up of saints and sinners, of sinners striving to be saints with every possible degree of enthusiasm: some with
much, some with little, and still others
with none at all. Pride and anger blind
them and they are shut off from the knowledge that makes men humble and simple
with the simplicity of the Christ Child.

Such as these have suffered corruption
by following illusory desires, removed as
they are from the realities of the human
condition, unsympathetic towards it, impatient with sinners, devoid of love.

St. Paul told us so beautifully that "Love
is always patient and kind; it is never
jealous; love is never boastful or conceited; it is never rude or selfish; it does
not take offense and is not resentful.
Love takes no pleasure in other people's
sins, but delights in the truth; it is always ready to excuse, to trust, to hope and
to endure whatever comes" (1 Cor. 13:4-7).

It is this love, not love of our own invention, that must renew our old selves by
a spiritual revolution so that we can put
on the new self that has been created in
God's way in the goodness and holiness
of truth.

The Courage
of Peace

Excerpts from New Year Homily, 1973

In all things, my dear brothers and sisters, Our Blessed Lord sought to do and did His Father's will. He never sought to do His own. He said again and again, "My aim is not to do my own will, but the will of him who sent me" (Jn. 5:30). In His agony in the Garden, He prayed, "Not my will but yours be done" (Lk. 22:43). It is absolutely true that it is in seeking and doing God's will that man finds his peace, peace for himself and for the universal family of mankind.

Mary, the Mother of God, followed her Son in seeking and doing the will of God. She became the Mother of God precisely because she wanted nothing more and nothing less than to do the Divine Will. We see this disposition of her heart and mind in the simple answer she gave to the angel who announced to her the Good News that the Almighty wished her to be the Mother of His Son. It was a joyful answer springing from the loving freedom which pervaded her whole being, "Behold the handmaid of the Lord, let it be done

unto me according to your word" (Lk.
1:38). Mary enjoyed fullness of peace
because she was perfectly in tune with the
will of God. Jesus saw in the will of His
Father the only source of the order that
can bring peace to man. Mary in turn saw
in her Son the perfect manifestation and
accomplishment of the Father's will, the
perfect acceptance in joy and in freedom
of the order the Creator had established
in His infinite wisdom for all His creatures. It is in knowing this order and in
accepting its demands freely that men as
individuals and as a society will find the
peace which is the fruit of justice.

Pope John XXIII opens his famous encyclical letter *Pacem in Terris*, with these
words, "Peace on earth, which men of
every era have most eagerly yearned for,
can firmly be established only if the order
laid down by God is dutifully observed"
(*Pacem in Terris*, Introduction). Free men
fall within this order of the Creator. To
try to avoid it, to try to escape it, to ignore
it, to substitute another order of man's
own making, is to go mad, because it is
to abandon the things that are for man's
peace (cf. Lk. 19:42); it is foolish for man
to close his eyes to the very source of
his peace as an individual and as a member of the human family. Pope John also
says, "How strongly does the turmoil of

individual men and peoples contrast with
the perfect order of the universe! It is
as if the relationships which bind them
together could be controlled only by force.
But the Creator of the world has imprinted
in man's heart an order which his conscience reveals to him and enjoins him to
obey, 'They show the work of the Law
written in their hearts. Their conscience
bears witness to them' (Rom. 2:15). How
could it be otherwise? For whatever God
has made shows forth His infinite wisdom,
and is manifested more clearly in things
which have greater perfection (cf. Ps.
18:8-11)" (*Pacem in Terris*, Introduction).

What is it that God has written in the
tablets of man's heart? We all know what
it is, my brothers and sisters, or at least
we used to know it and be conscious of it.
What God has written in the fleshly tablets
of our hearts He also engraved in the tablets of stone He gave to His Chosen People through Moses. I am going to recall it
here for you:

I am the Lord your God who brought
you out of the land of Egypt, out of the
house of slavery.

You shall have no gods except me....

You shall not utter the name of the
Lord your God to misuse it, for the Lord
will not leave unpunished the man who
utters his name to misuse it....

Remember the sabbath day and keep it holy....

Honor your father and your mother so that you may have a long life in the land that the Lord your God has given you....

You shall not kill.

You shall not commit adultery.

You shall not steal.

You shall not bear false witness against your neighbor.

You shall not covet your neighbor's house.

You shall not covet your neighbor's wife, or his servant, man or woman, or his ox, or his donkey, or anything that is his (cf. Ex. 20:1-17).

In these commandments God manifests openly to all what He has written in secret in the hearts of all. This is His order for the life of man. It is the basic order of justice and love. This is His law simply and clearly stated for us all to understand and to obey. Our Lord Jesus Christ did not come to abolish this Law but to complete it and make it even more demanding, more perfect (cf. Mt. 5:17). The will of His Father made known to us in the Old Testament is the will of His Father in the New, but manifested to us even more clearly through the infinite love of the Father for all of us as revealed in the Incarnation, death and Resurrection of Jesus, the Son of Mary.

Whenever man deviates from the basic order of justice and love established by God and chooses his own order, he violates the first Commandment and begins the process of his personal and collective ruin. It should not be difficult for you, my brothers and sisters, to see what arrogant and defiant violations of all of God's Commandments plague modern society. God simply is not wanted by millions of us as the Lord of lords, the King of kings, the Supreme Lawmaker and Ruler of all things and of all men. In this country we are making at present frightening advances in the gradual destruction of all morality, both private and public, in the name of freedom and under the protection of the law! What a travesty of freedom—and of law! Is it not the very existence of freedom which gives birth to morality? The God who gave us freedom has given us also the moral law to protect it and to guide us in its use. To destroy one is to destroy the other. Ignore the moral law and you destroy freedom. Destroy freedom and the only law left is the law of the jungle, the law which says that might makes right, the law that endorses the survival of the fittest physically. With the neglect of the moral law or the order established by God for men, the law of passion takes over and holds sway. It is the death of peace!

But the order written in men's hearts by God will never be completely erased from them, my brothers and sisters, even though it may become dim and blurred at times such as our own. For this reason we can assert with confidence that peace is always possible and, as Pope Paul VI has it in his message for the 1973 Day of Peace: "It must be possible. It must be possible," he explains, "because this is the message that rises from the battle-fields of the two world wars and the other recent armed conflicts by which the earth has been stained with blood. It is the mysterious and frightening voice of the fallen and of the victims of past conflicts; it is the pitiable groan of unnumbered graves in the military cemeteries and of the monuments dedicated to the Unknown Soldiers; peace, peace, not war. Peace is the necessary condition and the summing up of human society."

And the Holy Father goes on, "Peace must be based on reason not passion; it must be magnanimous, not selfish. Peace must not be inert and passive but dynamic, active and progressive according as the just demands of the declared and equita-ble rights of man require new and better expressions of peace. Peace must not be weak, inefficient and servile, but strong in the moral reasons that justify it and in the solid support of the nations which must uphold it.... It is necessary to repeat once more the basic statement that peace is possible, in these two complementary affirmations:

Peace is possible, if it is truly willed; and, *If peace is possible, it is a duty.* "This involves," the Pope says, "discovering what moral forces are necessary for resolving positively the problem of peace. It is necessary to have — as we said on another occasion — the courage of peace. Courage of the highest quality; not that of brute force, but that of love. We repeat: every man is my brother; there cannot be peace without new justice."

This new justice, my brothers and sisters, I dare to say is the old justice of the Ten Commandments enlivened and perfected by the love revealed in the Gospel of Jesus Christ. This justice is a duty for all men because it is the source of peace; and peace, since it is possible is also a duty we have towards God and towards one another. Justice is the will of God for us. Peace is the will of God for us. But it takes tremendous courage to seek and do the will of God. That is what Christ did. That is what Mary, the Mother of God, did. That is what all true peace-makers have done and will continue to do. It takes the courage to love as God loves! It is vain to seek peace outside the moral order established by our loving Father.

Man needs to live in the light of this life-giving Law of grace, justice and love, if he is to find enduring and true peace.

As of now it seems to me that our efforts for achieving true peace have not been too successful in spite of much hard work and good will. Could it be that we do not deserve the peace we yearn for as individuals and as a nation because of our abandonment of the basic moral order established by God for our peace? We need to search our souls in the light of God's Commandments and of the Law of Christ, and be humble enough to admit our failures and our sins. Any deliberate violation of God's will by any one of us is sinful and wounds peace. There is little use in shouting accusations at one another when the culprit is the unrepentant and self-righteous ego in each one of us.

When was the last time we dared to face God in sincerity and humility and tell Him with true sorrow, like King David, "Have mercy on me, O God; in your great tenderness wipe away my faults; wash me clean of my guilt, purify me from sin"? (Ps.50:1-2) How many of us—and we are all sinners—have the "courage of peace" to return to our Father's house, to fall on our faces before Him and say, like the prodigal son, "Father, I have sinned against heaven and against you, I no longer deserve to

be called your son"? (Lk. 15:18-19) How
many of us sense the need for forgiveness,
for redemption, for help from God? Those
of us who do are just beginning to be
filled with the courage of peace, because
we are beginning to want to seek the will
of God and to do it. We are beginning truly
to love as God loves.

My brothers and my sisters, peace is
not the work of man alone; it is the work
of man with God, or rather the work of God
in man and with men. I, for one, believe
that tragedies like Vietnam in all their terrifying significance for mankind will
never really end until we accept God in
our lives as He is, with all the demands
for justice and love expressed in the Ten
Commandments and in the Law of Christ.
Not until we seek His will for peace in
the order He has established for us His
creatures and His children, shall we have
true peace. We must understand that a
ceasefire or an armed truce is not the true
peace of God. In fact it is not peace at all.

Mary, the Mother of God, asks us to seek
the will of God and do it if we wish to
have peace. This is the message she
delivered from God to the three little
shepherds at Fatima in 1917, during the
First World War: We must stop sinning,
we must repent, we must do penance
for our sins and the sins of others, and
we must pray. She pleaded especially

for the devout recitation of the rosary for the conversion of Russia. for peace, and for the conversion of sinners. We have not yet done our part. We have only half-heartedly heeded her simple request which is in keeping with the teachings of the Gospel and of the Church. I exhort you, dearly beloved brothers and sisters, to take your rosary every day and say it with faith and fervor so that men will return to free and loving obedience of the will of God. Say it alone, say it especially with your family, say it with your neighbors, say it together in our churches. If you meditate upon its mysteries you will come to know the will of God, you will come to appreciate the order He has established for our peace....

The Gift of American Religious to the Poor

*Address given at the Conference
of Major Superiors of Men,
on June 21, 1971,
in De Pere, Wisconsin*

My dear brothers:

I am deeply grateful for the privilege of addressing this Assembly of the Conference of Major Superiors of Men and for the opportunity it affords me to reflect with you upon the gift which American Religious make to the poor.

The Church's Bishops and Religious

Occasions such as this enable us to "bear one another's burdens" (Gal. 6:2) and to express in joyful communion the life and mission of the Church. The Spirit of the Lord who unites us also preserves a balance between the Church's divinely given power to govern and her mysterious and almost limitless capacity to inspire (cf. 1 Cor. 12:4). As Bishops and Religious, we are servants of the Gospel of Christ who is "the peace between us" (Eph. 2:14). Because we are united in faith and in our love for Christ, we are drawn together by one hope of everlasting life. Hence, there must be no competition between us, and certainly no deceit. Everyone is to be self-effacing. Our minds must be the same as Christ Jesus "who, though He was in the form of God, did not count equality with God a thing to be grasped, but emptied Himself, taking the form of a servant, being born in the likeness of men. And being found in human form He humbled Himself and became obedient unto death, even death on a cross" (Phil. 2:6-8).

Religious life has always been the result of the action of the Spirit present in the Church, giving birth to new religious families to meet the needs of the times and breathing fresh inspirations within the religious communities of men and women. Religious are prophets in the biblical sense, i.e. persons whose special gift or charism, as we like to call it today, is to witness to what they know from personal experience of the power and love of God. Their words and deeds daily proclaim the "Mirabilia Dei," those saving achievements which have already taken place within them and which continue to transform their lives into that of Christ. Hence, when a religious talks about his call and gift from God, and when his own

life is one of total dedication to God —
binding himself as he does by an act of
supreme love to the evangelical counsels of
poverty, chastity and obedience that characterized Christ's earthly life — then his words
and deeds have a compelling and convincing value as a sign of God's presence
among men.

Like the Community of the Twelve
around Jesus whom He prepared to be
witnesses of His death and resurrection to
the ends of the earth, so religious communities are formed in the spirit of their great
founders — Augustine, Pochomius, Benedict, Dominic, Francis, Ignatius, Vincent
de Paul, John Bosco and countless others
— each of whom, as history has shown,
sought to express a unique insight into the
rich life of Christ: His contemplation on the
mountain, His preaching to the multitudes,
His healing of the sick, His love for sinners,
His blessing of children, His concern for
poor widows and orphans, His "doing good
to all, and always obeying the will of the
Father who sent Him." (*Lumen Gentium*,
46)

A Problem of Religious Life

While these are charismatic ideals of
religious communities, yet it seems that all

too many individual religious fail to achieve them. Father John Courtney Murray, S.J., in an article printed after his death, candidly spoke of such failures among those who take religious vows (Woodstock Letters, 1968, pp. 421-427). As he looked about he saw many religious who had lost their manhood, whose integrity was incomplete and whose character was immature. He noted that such failures arise not from the vows themselves, but from those religious who use their vows as a shield and as an escape—a shield which gives them the appearance of being religious, and an escape from any personal encounter with the three elemental forces of life. In each of these primal conflicts with earth, with woman, and with his own spirit, every Religious must struggle to attain his manhood or else he dies as a man. Many who enter religion, thought Father Murray, avoid this struggle. The vow of poverty spares them from the battle for survival because the community assumes this responsibility for them. They know no want nor the fear of want; they remain irresponsible like a child living off the security of its family. The vow of chastity allows them to decline any encounter with women, and again, the risk is manifold. Not infrequently, as the Church Fathers warned, the danger one faces in choosing virginity is pride: either a hardness of heart that withdraws into a world of unreality, or a relapse into softness and sentimentality that wanders and wastes itself. In both instances one fails to have integrity. The vow of obedience protects them from the most bruising encounter of all — that of a man with himself, his own spirit, his power of choice and his purpose. When a religious without reflection before the Lord yields to the community or to the will of his superior, he enjoys the comfortable feeling of making no decisions for himself and likewise of assuming no responsibility for his failures.

Father Murray points to a problem very clearly, yet he only hints at a possible solution. The solution, he suggests, must be founded on a paradox which will somehow show that being poor is to be truly responsible, being chaste is to be really mature, and being obedient is to have purposeful self-direction.

Toward a Solution

If I were to pursue his suggestion and search for such a paradox of responsible poverty, integral and mature chastity, and enterprising obedience, I would turn intently to Jesus, the God-man, Who "being rich, made Himself poor for our sake that we might become rich out of His poverty" (2 Cor. 8:8-9). And I would reflect quite seriously upon the powerful and paradoxical style of His earthly life and upon the strange and enigmatic contrast which He made between the poor and Himself: "Pauperes semper habebitis." The poor you will always have with you. In fact, the Second Vatican Council recommends this same approach: "Let religious follow Him as their one necessity. Let them listen to His words and be preoccupied with His work" (*Perfectae Caritatis*, 5).

Neither the Old nor New Testament knew anything of our industrial middle-class. Wealth was concentrated in the hands of the few. Widespread poverty was taken for granted politically and socially, simply because the poor could legally and religiously expect the rich not to take undue advantage of them. The prophets, however, realized that a rich man is all too prone to harden his heart at the distress of his brother and to abuse his power to exploit others. And so, while the prophets frequently spoke out against those wicked rich who deliberately oppressed the poor, at the same time they spoke quite compassionately to the poor as God's chosen ones, as deserving of God's special predilection and protection.

Only with Christ does the religious significance of poverty become fully clear. Socially Christ belonged to the poor working class. He made no attempt to improve or to disguise His lot, nor did He advocate it as the ideal for all to follow. He preached no false detachment; He advocated no political or social revolutions, although He was accused of it, and His personal attitude toward wealth was most simple: it can constitute a burden and obstacle for those who would enter the kingdom of heaven. He loved the poor primarily because they embodied in a most evident and embarrassing way every man's need of God, and because they were impoverished enough even to listen to His Good News. And so, Jesus took the poor quite seriously and actually shared their plight. He repeatedly identified Himself and His saving mission with them: "Go and tell John what you hear and see; the blind receive their sight and the lame walk, lepers are cleansed and the deaf hear, the dead are raised up and the poor have the good news preached to them. And blessed is he who takes no offense at me" (Mt. 11:4-6).

His penchant for the poor and the oppressed, His preoccupation with the outcasts of society, was not a passing fancy nor a superficial concern. The very heart and purpose of His life on earth, the reason for His coming and for His sacrifice unto death, was "to search out and save what was lost" (Lk. 19:9-10). Moreover, the unique love He had for the poor was to be the pattern and the ultimate measure by which His followers would be finally judged: "For I was hungry, and you gave me food; I was thirsty and you gave me drink; I was a stranger and you made me welcome; naked and you clothed me; sick and you visited me; in prison and you came to see me" (Mt. 25:35-36). These words exhort us not to occasional acts of heroic charity, rather do they constitute a most solemn warning that insofar as we neglect one of the least, we have to that degree neglected Christ (cf. Mt. 25.15)

Characteristic of our time is an extremely active social consciousness, a responsiveness to works of justice and charity. There is a corresponding temptation to imagine Christ as a towering social worker who seeks to relieve all human suffering and to make all men equally happy and successful in earthly terms. Jesus had no such apostolate in mind. "It does not run counter to His wishes, but He Himself was not concerned with this. He saw too deeply into suffering. For Him the meaning of suffering, along with sin and estrangement from God, was to be found at the very roots of Being. In the last analysis, suffering for Him represented the open road, the access back to God—at least the instrument which can serve as access. Suffering is a consequence of guilt, it is true, but at the same time, it is the means of purification and return. We are much closer to the truth if we say: Christ took the sufferings of mankind upon Himself. He did not recoil from them, as man always does. He did not overlook suffering; He did not protect Himself from it. He let it come to Him, took it into His heart. As far as suffering went He accepted people as they were, in their true condition. He cast Himself in the midst of all the distress of mankind, with its guilt, want, wretchedness. This is a tremendous thing, a love of the greatest seriousness, no enchantments or illusions —and therefore, a love of overwhelming power because it is a 'deed of truth in love,' unbinding, shaking things to their root" (R. Guardini, *Jesus Christus*, p. 40-41).

Because He saw all poverty as a consequence of man's sin and alienation from God, and at the same time as a possible way to salvation, Jesus proclaimed the poor as "blessed" and promised even to them — in spite of their grinding needs — the possession of "the kingdom of God" (Mt. 5:3). He enjoined material poverty upon those who would consecrate their lives to Him: "Give to the poor...then come, follow Me" (Mk. 10:17). But the saying of Jesus which is most pertinent to our reflection and most difficult to understand is the one recorded in all four Gospels, when at a dinner in the house of Simon the Leper a woman broke an alabaster jar of costly ointment and anointed Christ's head. Some of those present protested against this outrageous waste, because it could have been sold and the money given to the poor. But Jesus sternly rebuked them for harassing this woman's faith and loving attention to Him: "You have the poor with you always, and you can be kind to them whenever you wish, but you will not always have me" (Mk. 14:7). His remark recalls the wisdom of the Old Testament: "The poor will never cease from the land" (Dt. 15:11), and echoes that mystery of God's providence according to which poverty and oppression will

never be completely eliminated from the
earth. Whatever our efforts and successes
in civil and technical domains, each step
of progress creates new problems and
unsuspected dangers. Man can never make
his life on earth perfectly secure (cf.
Sacramentum Mundi V, p. 67). In this
paradox of man's inevitable poverty—
with all its sinful causes—and His own
fleeting presence among men, Christ
praises the woman for her act of adoration
of Him (Mk. 14:9), and He precisely distin-
guishes between mere humanism and the
Christian apostolate of faith.

Application to the Church and Religious Life Today

Christ provided no social panacea for
the problems of His day and His followers
of today have no special competence to
resolve the great problems of our times.
Our only competence against violence, fear
and oppression is to reconcile each man to
God, and then, with one another. "If the
Church is silent when the world proclaims
its own salvation through human progress,
it betrays Him who alone is the way. If it

encourages men in the belief of a world made perfect through human effort alone, it trades Jerusalem for a tower of Babel. If in the excitement of helping men live, it forgets to tell them how to die, it abandons Him who is the resurrection and the life. Its involvement in the affairs of men can never deliver it from its divine commission to remind men that they stand under God's judgment; that without the grace of Christ they are senseless, faithless, heartless, ruthless" (J. Rohr and D. Luecke, art. in *America,* Nov. 16, 1968, p. 480 sq.). Who can say these hard sayings except the Church? Who can show men that these hard sayings, when accepted interiorly and lived exteriorly, become a "blessed burden" and a "yoke that is light"? – the Religious.

The gift which American religious offer to the poor is simply the Christ of the Church. The riches you have received are the riches you must share with them: your faith in Him, your hope beyond all human hope, and your sacrificing love unto death. The challenge which the poor present to you is to live the mystery of Christ's poverty, to live it by authentic religious lives, so that even the poorest who have the most reason to doubt and to disbelieve are convinced that Christ loves them today.

Undoubtedly the members of this assembly in the days ahead will propose ways in which American religious, as individuals and as communities, can more effectively reach out to and help the poor in our land. Their number is legion: they are the aged and lonely, the sick in mind and in body, the addicts and alcoholics, the prostitutes and prisoners, the fatherless and homeless, the undesirable and unemployed, the estranged and wandering youth. Give all that you can to these broken bits of humanity, these poorest fragments of life.

Imitate Christ who embraced a life of external poverty to teach us that internal values are always more important and to repudiate the false assumption, still common in our day, that a poor man is less than good and that a successful man is always better. Be truly poor and "poor in spirit" so that you neglect no one who needs God, for only the freely detached and dispossessed can clearly hear the cries of the poor and honestly prove to them that they are brothers. As St. Paul says, "Nihil habentes, sed omnia possidentes"...."Be regarded as paupers though you make others rich, as having nothing though you possess all things" (2 Cor. 5:10). Enter into the mystery of the cross, so that you might

share Christ's power over poverty and
triumph over death. He conquered them
only by surrendering Himself to them
freely and with confidence, knowing that
the Father loved Him more, even as He
let Him die.

I wish to close with a quotation from the
opening speech of Pope John XXIII to
the Fathers of Vatican Council II: "The
Catholic Church, raising the torch of
religious truth by means of this Ecumenical
Council, desires to show herself to be the
loving mother of all, benign, patient,
full of mercy and goodness toward the
brethren who are separated from her. To
mankind, oppressed by so many difficulties,
the Church says, as Peter said to the poor
who begged alms from him: 'I have neither
gold nor silver, but what I have I give you;
in the name of Jesus Christ of Nazareth,
rise and walk' (Acts 3:6). In other words,
the Church does not offer to the men of
today riches that pass, nor does she promise
them a merely earthly happiness. But she
distributes to them the goods of divine
grace which, raising men to the dignity of
sons of God, are the most efficacious
safeguards and aids toward a more human
life. She opens the fountain of her life-
giving doctrine which allows men, enlightened by the light of Christ, to understand

well what they really are, what their lofty dignity and their purpose are, and, finally, through her children, she spreads everywhere the fullness of Christian charity, than which nothing is more effective in eradicating the seeds of discord, nothing more efficacious in promoting concord, just peace, and the brotherly unity of all."

Christian Hope
and Joy

*Keynote address during the New England Conference
of Religious Education, August 20, 1971*

My brother bishops, my brother priests, Your
Honor the Mayor of Newton, Your Honor the
Mayor of Boston, distinguished guests, beloved
religious, and my dear brothers and sisters in
Our Lord Jesus Christ:

"We announce to you the eternal life
which was with the Father, and has appeared to us. What we have seen and
have heard we announce to you, in order
that you may have fellowship with us, and
that our fellowship may be with the Father,
and with His Son, Jesus Christ. We are
writing this to you to make our own joy complete" (1 Jn. 1:2-4). In writing this, St.
John shows himself to be a faithful messen-
ger of the Son of God who said to His
Apostles, "If you keep my commandments
you will remain in my love, just as I have
kept my Father's commandments and remain in his love. I have told you this so that
my own joy may be in you and your joy
may be complete" (Jn. 15:10-11).

Paul, the faithful and fearless apostle to the gentiles, tells us in simple and concise language where lies the source of our hope. He writes to the Romans that, "Through our Lord Jesus Christ, by faith we are judged righteous and at peace with God, since it is by faith and through Jesus that we have entered this state of grace in which we can boast about looking forward to God's glory. But that is not all we can boast about; we can boast about our sufferings. These sufferings bring patience, as we know, and patience brings perseverance, and perseverance brings hope, and this hope is not deceptive, because the love of God has been poured into our hearts by the Holy Spirit which has been given us" (Rm. 5:1-5). Paul's prayer for the Romans was, "May the God of hope bring you such joy and peace in your faith that the power of the Holy Spirit will remove all bounds to hope" (Rm. 15:13).

Guided by the teachings of holy scripture as well as sacred tradition, the Fathers of Vatican II set forth authentic teaching about divine revelation and about the Church's mission to proclaim Christ's message of salvation so that "the whole world may believe; by believing, it may have hope; and by hoping, it may love" (*Divine Revelation*, 1).

On behalf of all the Bishops of New England, I want to express my heartfelt greetings to all of you who dedicate yourselves to preserve and to hand on that sacred tradition which Christ Himself commissioned the apostles to preach to all men. I am happy to welcome you as teachers of "that gospel which is the source of all saving truth and moral teaching" and as preachers of that living tradition of the apostles which we have all received by faith, and which we must all faithfully defend. Your efforts contribute to the teaching life of the Church, to an increase of faith and holiness of life among the People of God. With your generous help, the Church perpetuates and hands on to future generations "all that she herself is, all that she believes" (*Divine Revelation*, 8).

This tradition which comes to us from the apostles continues to develop in the Church. The Council Fathers tell us that, "Through the contemplation and study made by believers, who treasure these things in their hearts (cf. Lk. 2:19), through the intimate understanding of spiritual things they experience, and through the preaching of those who have received through episcopal succession the sure gift of faith," there is a growth in the understanding of the sacred realities and of the divine truths which we have received. The Church constantly advances toward a fuller understanding of divine revelation. God converses uninterruptedly with the Bride of His beloved Son, the Church; "and the Holy Spirit, through whom the living voice of the gospel resounds in the Church, and through her, in the world, leads unto all truth those who believe and makes the word of Christ dwell abundantly in them" (*Divine Revelation,* 8).

My dear brothers and sisters, it is essential for all believers but especially for those who share as you do in the teaching mission of the Church to keep in mind at all times the following words of Vatican II: "The task of authentically interpreting the word of God, whether written or handed on, has been entrusted exclusively to the living teaching office of the Church, whose authority is exercised in the name of Jesus Christ. This teaching office is not above the word of God, but serves it, teaching only what has been handed on, listening to it devoutly, guarding it scrupulously, and explaining it faithfully by divine commission and with the help of the Holy Spirit. It is clear therefore," as the Council Fathers concluded, "that sacred tradition, sacred Scripture, and the teaching authority of the Church, in accord with God's most wise design, are so linked and joined together that one cannot stand without the other, and that all together and each in its own way under the action of the one Holy Spirit contribute effectively to the salvation of souls" (*Divine Revelation*, 12).

But the good news of the Gospel of faith, hope, love, joy and peace which the Church has received must be proclaimed to the men of this age with all their "griefs and anxieties." The Church must bring to contemporary mankind in the modern world that "light kindled from the gospel" and to place at their disposal "those saving resources which the Church herself received from her Founder"; the Church must teach man to realize the sacred dignity of human life in society (cf. *Gaudium et Spes*, 1 and 3). And so we are challenged to scrutinize "the signs of our times," to look especially, but not exclusively, into the solemn and grim faces of many of our youth and, with God's help, to bring about a return or conversion of their minds and hearts to God and a renewal of their faith in the Christ of the Church, and not in some pseudo-Christ made more in man's image and likeness in order to suit the passing whim of the day. We are called to answer in a language which men can understand the perennial questions which every generation asks about this life and the life to come – to respond to their fears and their longings, their joys and their hopes, and to lead them out of their empty isolation into the midst of God's People, the Church.

In an analysis of the trends of our day, Rollo May has described the prevailing mood of our times as one of apathy – an inability truly to love and to will anything. "We cling to each other," he says, "and try to persuade ourselves that what we feel is love; we do not will because we are afraid that if we choose one thing or one person, we'll lose the other and we are too insecure to take the chance.... The individual is forced to turn inward; he becomes obsessed with the new form of the problem of identity, namely, Even-if-I-know-who-I-am, I-have-no-significance, I-am-unable-to-influence-others. The next step is apathy. And the step following that is violence. For no human can long endure the perpetually numbing experience of his own powerlessness" (*Love and Will*, pp. 13-14).

It seems to me that much of our contemporary drama and works of art support this analysis. They depict a broken image of man, alienated and alone, unable to give any meaning to his life because of his despairing fear that nothing really matters.

And so many of our youth seem deliberately to "play it cool"; they refuse to display their true feelings, and withdraw from meaningful and constructive involvement. They become another anonymous member of David Riesman's "lonely crowd."

A somewhat comparable evaluation was offered by another psychologist who characterized this generation as inward, fatherless and convulsive (H. Nouwen, art. "Christian Leadership of Tomorrow" in *Louvain Studies*, Spring, 1971, p. 175 sq.). Despite their apparent activism and protest, their psychedelic and exotic dress, their rock music and smoking stick, many of the youth are now turning to meditation and contemplation. Yogas and "Jesus People" are withdrawing into the self to find something solid and meaningful, perhaps to an inward discovery of the unseen God. Moreover, this generation has rejected any fatherly authority over them, and therefore, any dignity or identity which God or any other father figure might have bestowed on them. The worth of man is not what is given to him from above, they insist, but rather what he freely makes of himself and of his future. And that future is now threatened by instruments of death and war, by eroding poverty and screams of hunger, by all the painful and persistent evidence of man's injustice, of man's inhumanity to man. In rejecting the legitimate claims made by authority upon them, contemporary men of all ages face the danger of becoming captives of themselves. Their peer groups become their new dictators, demanding scrupulous allegiance to what they think and feel about society. It seems that their indifference is often calculated, their casualness carefully studied, and their sloppy appearance a copied imitation of the contempt of their friends. Whatever guilt feelings they once might have felt for disobedience to authority have now been overcome by a stronger feeling of shame if they fail to conform to the dictates of their peers. This shift from guilt to shame has serious consequences; it means that they no longer aspire to become adults and to take on the responsibilities of their fathers in society. This attitude explains the third aspect of the new generation: its characteristic convulsiveness, its deep-seated unhappiness with everything in society, its feeling that there is something radically wrong with the world and for which they are not responsible. Small wonder that these feelings explode at times into acts of undirected violence and purposeless waste — of escape through drugs and suicide. So much of their compulsive behavior reveals their complete lack of any vision or worthwhile goal.

My dear brothers and sisters, it goes without saying that all true religious education must be concerned with man as he is and with man as God wants him to be. For us as Catholic believers the impossible distance between the reality and the ideal, between what we are and what we ought to be, has already been bridged once and for all in the person of Christ Who is the living Head of His Body, the Church. Our faith in Him and our sacramental life in His Church have prompted all of our energies and inspired all of our efforts to proclaim to this generation and all others the saving mysteries of Christ's redemption. As St. Paul said, "People must think of us as Christ's servants, stewards entrusted with the mysteries of God. What is expected of stewards is that each one should be found worthy of his trust" (1 Cor. 4:1-2).

Today more than ever before those who devote themselves to teaching others the sacred mysteries of our Catholic faith must necessarily apply various methods and techniques. They must confront current issues, such as ecology and war, poverty and population control, but always in the light of the risen Christ Who alone illumines and guides our understanding of every human problem on earth. Our faith in the risen Christ encourages us to hope, to rest confident and to trust in His promises of life over death: "I am the light of the world" (Jn. 8:12). "I have come so that they may have life and have it to the full" (Jn 10:10). "In the world you will have trouble, but be brave: I have conquered the world" (Jn. 16:33).

It seems to me that in addition to our various religious educational programs and techniques, what is especially needed in the catechetical apostolate of the Church today, and a need which is becoming increasingly and perhaps unconsciously felt by the young and old alike, is for religious teachers who are truly spiritual leaders. The articles of our faith are not simply truths directed to the head; they are mysteries which address themselves to the whole man. The teaching and learning of religious truths is not only or primarily an intellectual exercise, but rather an invitation to a prayerful study and shared reflection upon the mysteries of the gospel. "What was written of old," says St. Paul, "was written for our instruction, that by patience and the consolation of Scripture we might have hope" (Rom. 15:4). We need in our schools and catechetical centers today teachers who are spiritual leaders, who are familiar with and even somewhat afraid of deeply significant movements of the Spirit of God, who have that delicate discernment to distinguish between merely human impulses and authentic inspirations of God's Spirit in the soul.

But to become a spiritual leader, one must first enter himself into the center of his own existence and become thoroughly familiar with the complexities and subtleties that arise in the depth of one's soul, the conflict between self and Christ. One must, like St. Paul and all great men of prayer, slowly and consistently remove those demonic desires that prevent him from doing what the Spirit wills. He must daily pray "Grant to us, O Lord, a heart renewed; recreate in us your own Spirit, Lord." Only the one who is able to articulate his own authentic experience of God can offer himself as a teacher, a source of clarification, to others. A spiritual leader is willing to put his own articulated faith at the disposal of those who ask his help. In this sense he is the servant of the servants, telling those who are still afraid of what he himself has already seen and heard and touched. He is able to help others recognize the promptings of God within them and to affirm God's reality as the Source of their own existence. In this way, he leads others through an endless series of conversions of the heart to the ultimate affirmation that without Christ man cannot be man.

A spiritual leader lives the life of Christ; he thinks and acts like Christ; and his whole life teaches Christ. He commands that kind of authority which marked the earthly life of Jesus; he has compassion for the multitudes. He stands in the middle of his people; nothing human is alien to him, no joy or sorrow, no way of living or dying. He does not identify with pressure groups; he is neither a liberal nor a conservative. He transcends all boundaries of languages and cultures, of the powerful and weak, because of his limitless capacity to forgive the faults of others. Forgiveness is a sure sign of spiritual leadership; it arises only from those who are conscious of their own sins and of their constant need of the forgiveness of God. Like the prodigal son who one day "came to his senses," our young generation needs a compassionate father to meet them on their way home and to show them that forgiveness is the endless possibility of the Church. Training and techniques in religious education are necessary, to be sure, but there is always a danger that professional people become entangled in their specialization and consequently avoid facing the much more difficult challenge of being a compassionate man. Professionalism without compassion exploits, rather than heals, the truant heart of youth.

Contemplation and compassion are qualities of true spiritual leadership, and they are qualities which should characterize the lives of all those who are involved in religious education: personal contemplation of the mysteries of God and deep compassion for the miseries of man. Such a combination preserves the religious educator from all prevailing cynicism and destroying sarcasm that believes in nothing at all, while preventing his complete absorption by the latest and most urgent needs that demand satisfaction here and now. Such a religious educator is able to direct others beyond their immediate concerns and individual impulses to see the face of Him in whose image we are all made and to know the heart of Him in whose love we have been made anew. He does not crave popularity nor fear rejection. He depends instead upon his own gift of faith through and in the Church and upon his unique call from God. He does not run after the latest novelty nor allow others to worship idols, but remains in constant contact with that One Reality which is central and ultimate to life: the triune God.

Hence, he never curses the present in favor of future dreams, rather will he critically discern in the concrete circumstances of his life those precious signs of hope that already contain a reflection and a promise of that greater life to which we are called by Christ. He will do all these things because he is a man of daily prayer, for only a man of prayer is able to make visible what is hidden by God and to recognize in his brother the face of Christ. Only a man of prayer can truly love, and give himself generously to the Church's mission on earth: to teach all nations that "Jesus is Lord" and to incarnate them into Christ's sacramental life.

In the days ahead I am confident that you will give serious consideration to many of the problems and possible solutions advanced for the much needed improvement of religious education. You have the privilege of sharing ideas with very competent and notable persons concerning a wide range of topics, some quite crucial, such as text books, the preparation of catechists and teachable moments, various approaches and skills, the levels of learning and the extension of catechetics to adults, the personal and ecclesial dimensions of faith. I realize that your task is especially difficult during these challenging times, and I am truly grateful to all for your inspiring assistance and zeal. In the words of St. Paul, "That will explain why I, having once heard about your faith in the Lord Jesus, and the love that you show towards the saints, have never failed to remember you in my prayers and to thank God for you. May the God of Our Lord Jesus Christ, the Father of Glory, give you a spirit of wisdom and perception of what is revealed, to bring you to full knowledge of Him. May He enlighten the eyes of your mind so that you can see what hope His call holds for you, what rich glories He has promised the saints will inherit, and how infinitely great is the power that He has exercised for us believers" (Eph. 1:15-19).

On Prayer
for Priestly Vocations

*Feast of the Visitation
of the Blessed Virgin Mary
May 31, 1981*

My dear brothers and sisters in Christ:

1. One day when Jesus saw the crowds that followed Him, He went up the hill, sat down with His disciples and then began to teach all of them. Some of His teaching that day was on prayer. It was then that He gave us the "Our Father." He taught us to pray from the heart, in sincerity and in truth, aware that God knows all our needs long before we feel them ourselves. He said to the people on that day what He tells all of us today:

> Ask, and it will be given to you;
> search, and you will find;
> knock, and the door will be opened to you.
> For the one who asks always receives;
> the one who searches always finds;
> the one who knocks will always have the door
>   opened to him.

Is there a man among you who could hand his
    son a stone
when he asked for bread?
Or would he hand him a snake
when he asked for a fish?
If you, then, who are evil,
know how to give your children what is good,
how much more will your Father in heaven
give good things to those who ask Him?
    (Mt. 7:7)

When Jesus finished what He had to say
that day on the hill, His teaching had made a
deep impression on the people, "because he
taught them with authority" (Mt. 7:29).

We who believe that Jesus is the Son of
God, sent by the Father to be our Teacher,
believe also that all we have heard from Him
is true.

Jesus speaks the truth.

Jesus cannot lie.

Jesus is faithful to His word.

Jesus cannot and will not fail in His promises to us.

It is because of God's faithfulness to His
love for us that we even dare to pray—and so to
hope for an answer to our prayer. And it is
because the gift of priestly vocations is so
dependent on prayer that I have begun this
Pastoral Letter by reflecting on the words of
Jesus concerning prayer.

2. I regret to tell you that for the last fifteen years at least, there has been a dramatic drop
in priestly vocations in many parts of the world
where such vocations had been considered

plentiful twenty-five years ago. The many and varied changes that have taken place especially in western society provide a partial explanation for the decline in these vocations. This decline is alarming because the number of young men preparing for the priesthood now in these countries taken as a whole is less that one half what it was fifteen years ago! And yet the Catholic population in the world has increased by over one hundred million faithful in this same period! And the number of God's children on earth who seek Him in a thousand ways and whom He loves and whom He wills to know Jesus Christ their Savior is over four billion!

3. In the Archdiocese of Boston—which has been rich in vocations for the missions in this country and abroad—the decline in priestly vocations is a grave danger for us and a source of profound sadness for the Church. Suffice it to say, in order to alert you to the danger, that this year we are ordaining only seven young men from St. John's Seminary and two from Pope John XXIII! Twenty-five years ago we ordained over fifty! At present we lose through death, retirement, illness, incapacity and other causes between twenty-five and thirty of our priests every year! In four years we could lose over one hundred priests! We have in Theology at Saint John's fewer than fifty students and only nine at Pope John XXIII for Boston for the next four years! This means that in four years we will have lost at least fifty priests without a replacement for them!

4. The picture is clear—but it is not as joyful as it was twenty-five years ago, or even ten years ago. At least it does not appear to be. Priests and people come and write to me, pleading for more priests to serve in their parishes! Obviously you understand that unless young men from the parishes come to our seminaries to prepare, I cannot ordain them priests and send them in the Name and Person of Christ Jesus to our people to be their shepherds.

All this notwithstanding, there is always solid hope for us because we are never alone! Our work is always undertaken and carried out with Our Lord Jesus Christ, the High Priest and "Shepherd of our souls" (1 Pt. 2:24). It is to Him we look for direction, because it is Him we believe; it is in Him we hope; and it is Him we love, and everyone because of Him.

5. What does He say to us now? Let us consult the Gospel according to St. Matthew. In it we read that

> Jesus made a tour through all the towns and villages, teaching in their synagogues, proclaiming the Good News of the kingdom and curing all kinds of diseases and sickness.
> And when He saw the crowds, He felt sorry for them, because they were harassed and dejected, like sheep without a shepherd. Then He said to His disciples, "The harvest is rich but the laborers are few, so ask the Lord of the harvest to send laborers to His harvest" (Mt. 9:35-37).

The Lord was filled with compassion when He saw the thousands in the towns and villages of Palestine in His day, looking to Him for relief from their distress and confusion. Today there are millions and millions stretching out their hands all over the face of the earth in an endless effort to touch Him, hoping to be healed! The harvest was never so vast—the workers were never so few for the vastness of the harvest! How deep His compassion must be!

And so it is from the depths of His divine compassion for all His brothers and sisters in the world that Christ urges all of us to pray to the Father to send more laborers to continue His saving work.

Prayer to the Father is first.

Prayer through Jesus Christ our Lord in the Holy Spirit.

Prayer that the Father send us laborers.

The Father is the One who is to send them.

Laborers are to be sent.

Laborers do not send themselves.

The Father sends them

when and if

the disciples pray to the Father

to send them.

6. A vocation to the Holy Priesthood is a gift from God.

It is a call from God.

It is a sending from God.

It is a sending, after a choosing. "You did not choose me, no, I chose you; and I commissioned you to go out and to bear fruit, fruit that will last; *and then the Father will give you anything you ask Him in my name.* What I command you is to love one another" (Jn. 15:16-17).

Vocations to the Holy Priesthood are gifts from God, but it appears that God will *send* us these gifts only when and if we ask for them. And so we need to pray for vocations, if we want more priests laboring in the harvest of the Lord. Certainly we need more priests to evangelize, in the Person and power of Christ, the billions who search for Him and have yet to find Him. But we need more priests also in our country and in our Archdiocese of Boston where the shortage of priests will soon be critical.

7. My brothers and sisters in Christ:

It seems to me that to pray sincerely and in truth at any time for what we need, we have first really to feel the need. We have to realize that what is missing in our life is not simply a surplus commodity or a luxury item, but something we dare ask the Lord to give us because without it we will be in sore distress, and only God can help us.

To pray effectively to the Lord for priestly vocations, we must be convinced that we need priestly service in our life with God and with one another. In faith we must see the priest standing in our midst in the person of Christ— and we need Christ! If we sense this need, we will pray for priestly vocations!

The priest himself must sense in faith his place in the Church and realize that without his *presence* and *service* the community of faith will disappear—unless God intervenes in some special way. The faith of the Church must enlighten the prayer of priests and people when we pray for priestly vocations.

The priest belongs to the mystery of the Church—his *presence* and *service* share in this mystery and are accepted in faith by the believing Church.

8. But the priest also comes from the midst of our families. He is a man taken from among men (cf. Heb. 5:1).

> A priest is not an angel.
> In fact, an angel cannot be a priest.
> God Himself, in desiring to be a priest, had to become Man!
> It is the Son of God as Son of Mary,
> Jesus Christ our Lord,
> and our brother,
> Who is a priest forever.
> Priests are born in families, as Jesus was.
> It is within the family that God first calls anyone,
> because He calls from the beginning.
> Those whom God destines to be His priests
> He calls even from their mother's womb!
> (cf. Jer. 1:4-5)

Hence the first and most basic *obligation* to discern and foster a priestly vocation rests with the parents at home. It is also the *privilege* of the mother and the father to be the first to hear the voice of God—in whatever way He calls—

together with their son, and *prayerfully* and *gratefully* to *guide* him to answer the call in *love* and *freedom*.

Family prayer is a necessity to obtain priestly vocations because the family is the "home church," reflecting, in its own way, the whole church at prayer for vocations. The Rosary recited devoutly to Mary, the Mother of the Church, is a most powerful means to help parents and children know the will of the Lord and follow it in faith and love.

9. We, the Church of God in the Archdiocese of Boston, must become vividly aware of our need for priests to serve our parishes and to serve all God's children who need their *presence* and *life-giving ministry*. This awareness of our need must drive us to our knees to implore the Father to send more laborers into His harvest and to spare mercifully those we have and give them good health and strength, joy and peace to bear the burden of the day out of love for Him and for His people.

As we pray in our homes, schools, institutions and churches, in private and public, we must carry out with persevering trust in the Good Shepherd the plans of our Archdiocesan Commission for Vocations, and be creative and imaginative in our approach to our young people to challenge them with Christ's loving invitation: "Come, follow me."

We must not allow the oppressiveness of our pagan, secular culture to stifle their freedom to answer with faith and courage the call of the Good Shepherd to lead His people in love to peace and joy with Him and one another.

Because we believe in Christ and love Him, we are a people of hope. And so we know that if we truly pray to the Lord of the harvest, He will send more laborers to do the harvesting. We have His word for it. He is forever faithful to it! Blessed be His name!

Filled with confidence, we place all our vocation work under the loving guidance of Mary, the Mother of the Good Shepherd and Queen of Apostles.

With a hearty blessing, I am

Devotedly yours in Our Lord,

✠ Humberto Cardinal Medeiros
Archbishop of Boston

Stewards
of This Heritage

*Religious and Moral Reflections
on the Dignity
and Responsibility
of Public Office and Citizenship*

July 4, 1983

My dear friends in Christ:

I have long desired to write this letter to you, my fellow citizens of the Catholic community of the Archdiocese of Boston, and to all who may be willing to listen to the message I bring as I approach you with sincere love for you, filled with hope in our future together because of the common ideals we share and strive to realize in this land which is our home.

I have an especially keen interest in reaching the hearts and minds of youth among us. When I look at you, my dear young friends, I am compelled to cry out from deep within me, "We need one another." To be honest with you, to be frank, to be truthful, to be open with you, "I need you and you need me." How I wish all of us could deeply realize this fact of life and make it operative in living out our lives! We need one another because of who we are! We do not live *to use* one another, but *to be* a source of joy and strength to one another; to be of service to one another freely and willingly. You, the young, seem to specialize in wanting to serve in this way, for a time at least. You are generous. In this you exhibit one of the best qualities or endowments of the human person. What a resource for justice and peace you can be! That is why the caliber of your vocational choices as well as the quality of your public service are of profound concern to us all.

My dear friends, allow me the privilege to profess publicly that I love our country and its ideals, that I love all our people deeply as we continue to strive to realize these ideals in our personal lives and in the life of the nation as a whole. It is my conviction that, given the varied circumstances of our backgrounds, and in spite of our many shortcomings, past and present, our country is still the noblest and most successful experiment in human living achieved so far. It may be of interest to you that when Pope John Paul II visited Boston in the deluging rain of early October, 1979, as I drove down with him from the Boston Common to our residence, and thousands upon thousands of people were crowded on the sidewalks in the torrential downpour to greet him with outbursts of sincere enthusiasm, I heard him say almost to himself in response to the spontaneous welcome of young and old alike, "This is a free people, this is a free people." Yes, my dear friends, we are a free people. Our freedom may not be complete; at times, in fact, we may be rather confused about true freedom, but we are a free people striving constantly to be more truly free, more truly human. While enjoying this freedom, we manifest together as a people a tremendous effort to seek the truth and to live by it, to search for the ways of justice and follow them, to find the path of mutual love and solidarity and take it, to be inspired by true freedom and to respect and promote it in everyone everywhere.

I find that these ideals flow from the Faith given freely to me by God in the land of my birth, the town of Arrifes on the island of St. Miguel in the Azores, Portugal. Soon after I arrived in Providence, Rhode Island, as a fifteen-year-old immigrant with my mother and my two younger brothers and sister, to join my father, on April 18, 1931, I found out as a "green horn" teenager that the land of plenty which we had eagerly sought was also a land of poverty and unemployment for many—even a land of ethnic discrimination! It was the height of the depression and Fall River, where we came to live, was suffering the decline of its textile industry. But I also found that a great spirit of solidarity and freedom breathed over all. The problems of those far-off days were many in this country and all over the world, but the free and determined people of this land were able to find their solution in part at least. In spite of obvious difficulties, my family believed, and I believed along with them, that this was still the land of opportunity. It was in January, 1935, that my father was able to allow me to enter high school—I was almost twenty years old—so that I could begin the long preparation for the priesthood.

We were very poor. My friends too were poor. But all of us had determination and faith that God would supply the rest, which was most of it. And so, in spite of much hardship—at least by today's standards—and privation, I realized that I had come to a country rich in blessings, even if money did not grow on trees, as we had expected! It was out of grateful love that I embraced my new country and decided to become a citizen. I was not and I am not blind to its faults, but I am so grateful for its goodness to me and to all of us, and I entertain such high hopes for its future, that I burn with a desire to help those I love to know better what we are and what we have. In doing this, I hope to show further my gratitude to my adopted country as we all strive in freedom and love to improve ourselves personally and as a nation for the good of the human family.

We, the people of the United States of America, have come from everywhere in the world seeking an ideal which we alone can realize in this country, but only with the help of God and never without it. We have advanced toward it together through the years, but we still have a long way to go. And we are neither afraid of nor deterred by the obstacles on the way, nor by the distance yet to be covered. We know we need a clearer vision of our common good; we need greater courage, deeper wisdom, more calm reflection, more unselfish love and much more understanding, patience and compassion. This noble and fascinating experiment which is the United States of America must continue for the sake of world peace. I believe we owe it to the rest of the human family and to the Father of mercies who brought us here as part of His providential plan for His children. With His grace, we can find the solution to our common problems and help the rest of the world lessen the evils that beset us and so attain the justice and peace we need for the pursuit of happiness in true human freedom. The words spoken by Pope John Paul II about Boston when he visited us in 1979 are appropriate here and should lift up our spirits:

In the city of Boston, I am greeting a community that, through the many upheavals of history, has always been able to change and yet remain true to itself—a community where people of all backgrounds, creeds, races and convictions have provided workable solutions to problems and have created a home where all people can be respected in their human dignity. For the honor of all the citizens of Boston, who have inherited a tradition of fraternal love and concern, may I recall what one of the founders of this city told his fellow settlers as they were aboard ship en route to their new home in America: "We must love one another with a pure heart fervently, we must bear one another's burdens." These simple words explain so much of the meaning of life—our life as brothers and sisters in our Lord Jesus Christ.[1]

Because of my Faith and because of my love for this City, for this Commonwealth, for my adopted country and for the human family, and because of the many blessings I have received as Archbishop of Boston, I feel compelled humbly to share these thoughts with you on this Fourth of July. May they bring us closer together in our common effort to realize our cherished ideals.

The Fourth of July is a day on which we Americans give thanks to God for the rich and noble history of our nation. It is an occasion for remembering the many blessings of freedom and justice that our forebears have handed on to us. It is also a day on which we need to examine our stewardship of this heritage. Like you, I have deep respect and love for our country and for the freedom and opportunity that it has made possible for so many of us. When I came to the United States as a teenager from the Portuguese Azores, I saw neighborliness and compassion in a community of people from different ethnic, religious and racial heritages. Through the years, I have been a beneficiary of the practical application of many of the highest ideals of our country. For me, these ideals are not mere platitudes. They have been a source of inspiration and a cause for gratitude to God. At the same time, as an immigrant to this my adopted country, I saw firsthand also the evil effects of discrimination and economic injustice. My experience has taught me much about both the promise and the perils of the American experiment. When Pope John Paul II addressed the assembly on Boston Common during his pastoral visit to the United States four years ago, he called us to remember "the past achievements of this land" and to rededicate ourselves "to a more just and human future."[2] Both remembering and rededication are essential if we are to achieve the promise and avoid the perils of this daring and necessary American experiment.

On this Independence Day, I want to speak with you about an aspect of our public life that I feel to be especially important in 1983. This pastoral letter is meant to call public officials and citizens to a deeper sense of their vocation to public service and a stronger fidelity to this vocation. The success of our efforts to secure freedom and justice for all largely depends on the answers we give to two questions: Do we esteem the work which the men and women who serve our community in public office are called upon to do? How deep is our sense of the dignity and responsibility of our activity as citizens?

There is reason for concern as we consider these questions today. A decreasing percentage of Americans has been exercising the right to vote in recent years. Also, an increased cynicism about the motivations and integrity of our public leaders has sometimes led to the lessening of esteem for the noble role which they exercise in our regard. A number of explanations, with varying degrees of validity, have been offered for these trends.[3] Such efforts at explanation are important. But my purpose in this pastoral letter is to call men and women of goodwill to a fresh consideration of the great dignity and responsibility carried by those who devote their lives to public service in our nation and our communities, as well as by all citizens of our country.

Public life, politics and citizenship, when approached properly, are not principally the spheres where individuals or groups pursue power and self-interest. Rather, politics and citizenship are above all concerned with the common good of our social life together. As Christians we know that we are called by God to an active concern for the freedom and well-being of our neighbor. This call to serve our neighbor is both deeply Christian and profoundly human. Participation in public and political life is therefore a genuine Christian vocation. If we recognize the great dignity of public service and active citizenship, we will hold both our leaders and ourselves to a high standard of responsibility and integrity. The pursuit of the common good is not optional; it is a duty. The Second Vatican Council has clearly stated, "In loyalty to their country and in faithful fulfillment of their civic obligations, Catholics should feel themselves obligated to promote the true common good."[4]

The Massachusetts Tradition of Public Responsibility

The conviction that public service, political activity and responsible citizenship can truly be vocations from God is one of the richest threads running through the history of Massachusetts and the City of Boston. The vision which inspired the Founders of the Massachusetts Bay Colony was based on a lively sense that they were called by God to unite together in a community of mutual support and service. The Founders' vision of Massachusetts was based on the Bible and drawn from faith in Christ. But theirs was not a form of faith that restricted the influence of religion to the inner heart or the private sphere of family. For the Founders of Massachusetts, religion was to help form the life of the community by inspiring believers to active service for the common good. As John Winthrop, the first governor of the colony put it, "the care of the public must oversway all private respects...for it is a true rule that particular estates cannot subsist in the ruin of the public."[5] And another early Massachusetts leader, John Cotton, concluded that an occupation or way of life was a true vocation from God only if it "should tend to the public good."[6]

Response to God's call is inseparable from response to the needs of the community. Thus Cotton declared that "this is the work of every Christian in his calling, even then when he serves man, he serves the Lord."[7]

The Second Vatican Council, reaffirming the constant Christian tradition, has urged all Christians to appreciate

> their special and personal vocation in the political community. This vocation requires that they give conspicuous example of devotion to the sense of the common good.[8]

The Founders of our Commonwealth had a noble vision of public service, politics and citizenship because they were profoundly convinced that Christians could keep fidelity to one another in public life only if they were faithful to God and His law. Government, law, the judiciary, education—all major parts of our public life together—were spheres where honesty, fidelity and love for one another were to be active. Our forebears had a view of public and political life which led them to put their energy of mind and heart into building up the nation, cities and towns in which they lived. Their convictions about the dignity of public life and citizenship led them to a deep sense of civic duty. Just as public servants were highly esteemed, so were they held to high standards of integrity and excellence. The cynical notion that political activity is "dirty" and that citizens are simply the victims of the actions of power-hungry politicians was far removed from the minds of the early Massachusetts colonists. Rather, they were convinced that to enter government service and to participate in the political life of the community was to respond to God's call to build a society of solidarity, justice and freedom.

The Challenge to Public Life Today

Our political roots are here, and they are obviously religious and moral! Can we honestly and sincerely say that our generation is faithful to them?

This noble view of government and citizenship makes high demands on us all, not only on those who lead, but on all who take their citizenship seriously.

The complexity of the life of American society today makes the fulfillment of this great vision of government and citizenship especially difficult to sustain. The Founders of Massachusetts lived in a society that was much simpler than is our own. Issues of public importance were easier to define and the means for addressing them were more readily proposed. Today many citizens feel powerless—powerless to understand the public life of our community and powerless to influence it. We face a crisis of citizenship itself.[9] Citizenship is in danger of losing its meaning, of being reduced to a "cheap commodity,"[10] rather than valued as a noble vocation. If we are to maintain the best traditions of our Commonwealth and to act in accord with Christian principles of political life, we must ask: How can we regain a vision of the common good of our community? How can we regain a sense that it is within our power to work actively and effectively to realize this common good? How can we restore to politics and citizenship that dignity which makes them truly human activities? How can we prevent public life from becoming a competition of private interests against the common good? Both public officials and individual citizens have major roles to play in finding the answers to these questions.

The power of government in our lives is great. The Founders of our nation established constitutional provisions such as the separation of the powers of the executive, the legislative, and the judiciary, to keep this power in check. Such constitutional checks are essential means for the protection of our freedoms, and they are fully supported by Catholic social teachings. Pope John XXIII, drawing from the age-old teaching of the Church, stated in his encyclical *Pacem in terris,*

> it is in keeping with the innate demands of human nature that the state should take a form which embodies the threefold division of powers corresponding to the three principal functions of public

authority.... (This) in itself affords protection to the citizens both in the enjoyment of rights and in the fulfillment of duties.[11]

John XXIII went on, however, to point out that the structure of governmental institutions is not itself a guarantee that the government will realize the goals of justice and freedom. Attaining these purposes is also dependent upon the moral vision of both leaders and citizens. In the words of the Pope, we must become persons of "great equilibrium and integrity, competent and courageous."[12] We must, in other words, be persons of public vision and public virtue if we expect our communities to be places of freedom and justice. These demands are given vivid expression in Article XVIII of the Declaration of Rights in the Constitution of the Commonwealth of Massachusetts.

A frequent recurrence to the fundamental principles of the Constitution and a constant adherence to those of piety, justice, moderation, temperance, industry, and frugality are absolutely necessary to preserve the advantages of liberty, and to maintain a free government. The people ought, consequently, to have particular attention to all those principles, in the choice of their officers and representatives; and they have a right to require of their lawgivers and magistrates an exact and constant observance of them in the formation and execution of the laws necessary for the good administration of the Commonwealth.[13]

The Moral Foundation
of Government

The principles and virtues to which the Constitution refers are based on that quality of mind and heart which leads us to direct our actions by a concern for the good of all persons. This means that our life together in a civic community is not merely a balancing of the competing interests of different individuals and groups. Public well-being is not simply the sum total of all these private interests. No, social and political life is itself based on values which are moral. That is to say, it is built on values which create community and which can only be realized when citizens are committed to something larger than their own private interests and concerns. As Pope John XXIII put it,

> The order which prevails in society is by nature moral. Grounded as it is in truth, it must function according to the norms of justice, it should be inspired and perfected by mutual love, and finally it should be brought to an ever more refined and human balance in full freedom.[14]

These four great values of truth, justice, mutual love, and full freedom are the moral core of the public and political life of society. When citizens and public officials strive to realize them, a just social, political and economic life can thrive. But when commitment to them is

replaced by narrowly defined interests and lack
of concern for the rights of all, we witness a loss
of trust in political leaders and cynicism about
the meaning of citizenship. My dear friends, the
foundation of a free society is nothing less than a
constant seeking for the truth, a sustained
desire for justice, a living sense of mutual love
and social solidarity, and a deep respect for the
freedom and rights of all.

As we reflect on the history of our country
and of Massachusetts we see that these ideals
have been present among us. But as Pope John
Paul II has reminded us, "Past achievements
can never be an acceptable substitute for present responsibilities toward the common good of
the society you live in and toward your fellow
citizens."[15] Moreover, we know that in some
important areas of public life our history has at
times deviated from the ideal of religious, racial
and ethnic justice. As Christians we know that
persons and societies are touched by sin and
weakness and will often fail. But we are called
by God to a change of heart and to continue in
our efforts to secure justice for all. The memory
of the limits and distortions in our history
should challenge us to reflect on ways in which
our own vision needs to be expanded today. As
we reflect on our vocation to participate in
public life, we need to ask how this vocation can
be genuinely lived by us today. Truth, justice,
mutual love and freedom are the values against
which our public life and public virtue must be
tested.

Truth, Justice,
Mutual Love and Freedom

In the political sphere there are many questions on which diverse opinions about public policy can quite legitimately exist. But there are also crucial convictions about the basis of our civil community whose truth is not in doubt. The Declaration of Independence ringingly affirmed that, "We hold these truths to be self-evident, that all men are created equal." Pope John Paul II has lauded the Declaration as a

> remarkable document containing a solemn attestation of the equality of all human beings, endowed by their Creator with certain inalienable rights: life, liberty and the pursuit of happiness, expressing a "firm reliance on the protection of Providence." These are sound moral principles formulated by your Founding Fathers and enshrined forever in your history. In the human and civil values that are contained in the spirit of this Declaration there are easily recognized strong connections with basic religious and Christian values. A sense of religion itself is part of this heritage.[16]

One of the most important truths on which our Commonwealth is founded is the equal human dignity of every person. This imposes on us all an obligation to protect and promote the fundamental human rights of every human being. The truth of the equal human dignity and human rights of all persons remains a great

challenge both to our political leaders and to us
as citizens in the United States today. Political
leadership will fulfill its vocation and be worthy
of admiration to the extent that it is directed to
translate this truth into policy and action. Similarly, the vocation to responsible citizenship is a
call to all of us to act on the truth that no
genuine commonwealth can exist when the
rights of some persons are denied.

It is from this truth of human dignity—
which is rooted in the fact that we are created in
God's image—that the meaning of the values of
justice and active mutual love must be determined in our communities. Justice in public life
is not simply the protection of self-interest or
individual independence. It is a structured
order of public life by which we realize our
worth as persons *together*. There can be no
secure justice for an individual person or a
single group so long as there is not justice for all.
Our Catholic tradition has always taught us that,
as Martin Luther King wrote while imprisoned
in an Alabama jail,

Injustice anywhere is a threat to justice everywhere. We are caught in an inescapable network of
mutuality tied in a single garment of destiny.[17]

Because of this network of mutual inter-
dependence that binds us together, political
leadership and active citizenship must be based
on a sense of responsibility not only for one's
own rights or the rights of one's close neighbors,
but for the well-being of the larger community

as well. Responsible citizens can and should speak out when the legitimate claims of their human dignity are denied or overlooked. Similarly public officials have the right to demand respect and support from their fellow citizens in the conscientious performance of their duties. But if the public life becomes a sheer contest between the governing and the governed because of competing group interests and narrowly focused visions, we then move away from being a civic and civil community toward a society which is internally at war. When this happens both the vocation of public service and the dignity of citizenship are endangered. We must ask ourselves today: How can we protect and foster these great values in our Commonwealth?

Dialogue: a Sign
of Political Maturity

A community based on the values of truth, justice, freedom, and mutual love or solidarity, is one where public leaders and citizens alike are committed to genuine dialogue about the public good, not simply to pressing a predetermined agenda. The vigorous pursuit of such dialogue is a sign of maturity in political life. When it is lacking, politics may become authoritarian and insensitive to the common good. The truth is that our love and service must be directed to all—not exclusively to some individuals or to some groups. And the reason is clearly set forth by Pope John Paul II:

> Authority in the political community is based on the objective ethical principle that the basic duty of power is the solicitude of the common good of society and that it serves the inviolable rights of the human person. The individuals, families, and various groups which compose the civic community are aware that by themselves they are unable to realize their human potential to the full, and therefore they recognize in a wider community the necessary condition for the ever better attainment of the common good.[18]

Sacred Scripture reveals to us

> that there is no authority except from God, and all authority that exists is established by God (Rom. 13:1).

This truth of faith enhances enormously one's appreciation of the nobility of public office. It also enhances the dignity and responsibility of citizenship in our system of government because we, as citizens, designate the public officials who are to wield the authority that comes from God. God shares this authority with His creatures not simply for the benefit of the office-holder or for special interest or favored groups, but rather for the common good. Hence, the proper exercise of this authority will be reflected in its service to the whole community, not just part of it. So, a commitment to the truth of the dignity and rights of all persons, to the achievement of justice for all, and to the building up of civic friendship and solidarity is a precondition for a humanly mature form of politics. It demands of us a deep respect for one another. In the pursuit of my mission as teacher may I ask the question: Does the dialogue about the real implications of our basic beliefs sometimes fall below this level in our public life today? The warning of the Second Vatican Council is a pertinent reminder of the importance of this question. We should "always try to enlighten one another through honest discussion, preserving mutual charity and caring above all for the common good."[19]

Politics and the Media

It seems to me there are several characteristics of our public life in the United States today that especially threaten the quality of the dialogue about the common good of our community. Our political life has long since left behind the intimacy of the town meeting, the great oratory of a Daniel Webster, and the whistle-stop campaign as the chief means for the formation of public consensus. We live in the day of the public opinion poll, the era of the media campaign, and at a time when the distinction between news reporting and public entertainment is sometimes hard to draw. The mass media hold great potential for increasing public knowledge of the crucial issues in our community. They can enable the voices of all citizens, both rich and poor, powerful and powerless, to be heard in vivid new ways. They can contribute to public education and dialogue about the full meaning of the common good.

But there is also a dangerous side to the relationship between the mass media and political life. As Pope Paul VI pointed out, "what is coming into being is an original mode of knowledge and a new civilization: that of the image."[20] Despite the genuine values contained in this development, there is a danger that that "image" will replace substance in our political dialogue today. We must ask ourselves if the urgent questions of the public good can be communicated in thirty-second TV spots or in news broadcasts edited for their mass entertainment value. We must reflect on the ways that the high cost of long political campaigns built around opinion polls and media advertising affect our officials and the integrity of government. Do they lead them to tailor their views to the interests of those who are willing to pay for such campaigns rather than to the needs of the community as a whole? When politics is largely based on "image" building, can it really respect the intelligent and responsible freedom of the people?

Respect for this intelligence and freedom calls on our public officials, both elected and appointed, to resist all temptations to pursue their goals through distortion of the truth or manipulation of public opinion. It seems to me that political freedom requires that various views on how to achieve the common good be forthrightly expressed and cogently argued before the public. The mass media can provide a powerful vehicle for the expression and argument of such views, provided the temptations of simple "image" making are avoided. Such free and thoughtful discussion is an important part of the vocation of politics and the dignity of citizenship. But most important of all, this process must be grounded on truth. Both public officials and the media should remember the extremely vital role they play in respecting the right of all "to be informed truthfully about public events."[21]

The Fundamental Questions Today

These reflections, I believe, show some of the implications of the values of truth, justice, mutual love and freedom for our political life in 1983. They are quite general in nature, but because they are so fundamental they are perhaps that much more important for the long-term health of our community. They show that one of the great challenges facing us now is that of attending to the fundamentals of our political morality. These are not new questions. The Catholic bishops of the United States addressed them in a pastoral letter some thirty-two years ago. Their words bear repeating today:

In politics, the principle that "anything goes" simply because people are thought not to expect any high degree of honor in politicians is grossly wrong. We have to recover that sense of personal obligation on the part of the voter and that sense of public trust on the part of the elected official which give meaning and dignity to political life. Those who are selected for office by their fellow men and women are entrusted with grave responsibilities. They have been selected not for self-enrichment but for conscientious public service. In their speech and their actions they are bound by the same laws of justice and charity which bind private individuals in every other sphere of human activity.[22]

These moral laws which govern political life set limits which cannot be transgressed without sin to the individual and great danger to the common good.

The Catholic Church, by its participation in public discussion, wants to continue to bear witness to truth, justice, mutual love and real freedom. This is why we have tried consistently to address the right to life, to religious freedom, to decent housing, to a just wage, and to ethnic and racial equality. It is also why we want to encourage generous and responsible participation in public life. These are questions which deserve the most careful and thoughtful consideration of public officials and all citizens of the Commonwealth.

Can we really regard ourselves as a people committed to the common good of all citizens sincerely, if we sit by and see the basic rights of the weakest among us violated? The public discussion of great human and social issues of our day, such as unemployment, the provision of adequate shelter and security for the homeless, the protection of the unborn and the elderly, must always be grounded on the worth of the human person made in the image of God. The dignity of public office and responsibility of citizenship demand serious reflection on these and many other problems of our day. For Christ indeed declared, "Insofar as you did this to one of the least of these brothers of mine, you did it to me."[23]

These considerations show how high the stakes are in the public life of our community. They also show the urgent importance of the quality of public discussion and active citizenship. Public service and active citizenship build up the human community and are expressions of love for our neighbor. The vocation to political life and active citizenship invites each of us to deepen our vision of truth, justice, mutual love and freedom in our community. The choices we must make will often be difficult. As the Second Vatican Council stated, "many different people go to make up the political community, and these can lawfully incline toward diverse ways of doing things."[24] The members of our community come from many backgrounds, and have different pressing needs. These differences must be addressed in ways that are both rational and civil. Such civility is not superficial politeness. Rather it is a condition for the existence of community and the achievement of the common good in a pluralist society like ours.

In the public life of a pluralist society, political compromise will be necessary if we are to advance justice and freedom in our complex world. But political compromise and moral capitulation are vastly different things. Public officials and citizens alike will remain faithful to their principles and to themselves when they strive through intelligence, dialogue, and persuasion to insure the protection of the rights of all in a community based on truth, justice and mutual love and freedom.

The Church's Contribution

My dear friends, I have offered these reflections on the vocation of politics and the dignity of citizenship as my contribution to the life of our community in gratitude to God and my Country. They are based on the Church's understanding of how the gospel of Christ calls us to work for the common good and the protection of human rights. They are based also on the public traditions of Massachusetts and of our Country as well as on a philosophy of public life which I trust is acceptable to all people of goodwill. I hope these reflections will help us always to choose our leaders wisely, deepen our sense of the responsibility that comes with political freedom and encourage our political officials to greater commitment in their important and noble work.

The success of these efforts is intimately linked with the development of a deeper faith in God and in Jesus Christ. The quality of the spiritual life of our people will be reflected in the larger public life of our community. We need to turn to God to ask for wisdom, help and guidance as we seek justice and freedom and as we struggle with the complex problems of our society. As Pope John Paul II reminded our nation,

> In order to bring this undertaking to a successful conclusion, fresh spiritual and moral energy drawn from the inexhaustible divine Source is needed.... Christ is our Justice and our Peace, and all our works of justice and peace draw from this Source the irreplaceable energy and light for the great task before us.[25]

And so let us turn to God in fervent prayer and ask that the Holy Spirit guide the work of our public officials as well as all our actions as citizens. I extend this invitation to you because I am convinced that civic society, as such, has an obligation to acknowledge its dependence upon God. It is the Holy Spirit Who will guide us to that city where we have our only true and lasting citizenship: the City of God in which every tear will be wiped away, the city of which it will truly be said: "Behold the dwelling of God is with men" (Rv. 21:3).

Mary Immaculate, Patroness of the United States and Queen of Peace, pray for us.

NOTES

1. Pope John Paul II, *U.S.A., The Message of Justice, Peace and Love*, St. Paul Editions, 1979, pp. 22-23.

2. Pope John Paul II, Homily on Boston Common, October 1, 1979, in *Pilgrim of Peace: The Homilies and Addresses of His Holiness Pope John Paul II on the Occasion of His Visit to the United States of America* (Washington, D.C.: United States Catholic Conference, 1979), p. 7.

3. See the analysis of these developments in the October 26, 1979, statement of the Administrative Board of the United States Catholic Conference, "Political Responsibility: Choices for the 1980's," in J. Brian Benestad and Francis J. Butler, eds., *Quest for Justice: A Compendium of Statements of the United States Catholic Bishops on the Political and Social Order 1966-1980* (Washington, D.C.: United States Catholic Conference, 1981), p. 204.

4. Vatican Council II, *Decree on the Apostolate of the Laity*, no. 14.

5. John Winthrop, "A Model of Christian Charity," in Perry Miller and Thomas A. Johnson, eds., *The Puritans*, Vol. 1, revised edition (New York: Harper Torch Books, 1963), p. 197.

6. John Cotton, "Christian Calling," in Miller and Johnson, Vol. 1, p. 320.

7. *Ibid.*, p. 332.

8. Vatican Council II, *Pastoral Constitution on the Church in the Modern World (Gaudium et spes)*, no. 75.

9. See Michael Walzer, "The Problem of Citizenship," in *Obligations: Essays on Disobedience, War and Citizenship* (Cambridge: Harvard University Press, 1970), pp. 203-228.

10. See Sheldon Wolin, *Politics and Vision* (Boston: Little and Brown, 1960), p. 353.

11. Pope John XXIII, *Pacem in terris*, no. 68.

12. *Ibid.*, no. 72.

13. In Robert J. Taylor, ed., *Massachusetts, Colony to Commonwealth: Documents on the Formation of Its Con-*

stitution, 1775-1780 (Chapel Hill, N.C.: University of North Carolina Press, 1961), p. 130.

14. Pope John XXIII, *Pacem in terris*, no. 37.

15. Pope John Paul II, Address at Battery Park, New York City, October 3, 1979, in *Pilgrim of Peace*, p. 55.

16. Pope John Paul II, Homily for Eucharistic Celebration at Logan Circle, Philadelphia, October 3, 1979, in *Pilgrim of Peace*, p. 65.

17. Martin Luther King, Jr., "Letter from Birmingham City Jail," in Staughton Lynd, ed., *Nonviolence in America: A Documentary History* (Indianapolis: Bobbs-Merrill, 1966), pp. 462-463.

18. Pope John Paul II, Address at the White House, Washington, D.C., October 6, 1979, in *Pilgrim of Peace*, p. 140.

19. *Pastoral Constitution on the Church in the Modern World*, no. 43.

20. Pope Paul VI, *Octogesima Adveniens*, no. 20.

21. Pope John XXIII, *Pacem in terris*, no. 12.

22. Bishops of the United States, "God's Law: The Measure of Man's Conduct," no. 28, in Hugh J. Nolan, ed., *Pastoral Letters of the American Hierarchy, 1792-1970* (Huntington, Indiana: *Our Sunday Visitor*, 1971), p. 457.

23. Mt. 25:40.

24. *Pastoral Constitution on the Church in the Modern World*, no. 74.

25. Pope John Paul II, Homily at Yankee Stadium, New York, 1979, in *Pilgrim of Peace*, pp. 47 and 49.

A Call
to a Consistent Ethic
of Life and the Law

Sermon delivered at St. Patrick's Cathedral,
New York, on July 4, 1971

"We hold these truths to be self-evident:
that all men are created equal; that they
are endowed by their Creator with certain
inalienable rights; that among these are
life, liberty and the pursuit of happiness."

We recall today these truths which our
Founding Fathers held, and handed on to
us. The cardinal characteristic of their
Declaration of Independence is the clear
affirmation that the political order is based
upon and governed by a prior moral order
—a moral order of rights, freedoms, and
responsibilities, whose proximate source
is man himself and whose ultimate source
is God.

The genius of our American experience
has been its ability to create and sustain
this proposition that the moral and political
orders are essentially related, and that
this relationship obtains in the face of our

strong religious pluralism. Pluralism has always posed and continues to present, a challenge to our unity as a nation. The challenge of forging from these divergent religious views an ethical consensus is the challenge which we continue to face today.

The primary articulator of our developing ethical consensus is civil law. The law is a limited but indispensable instrument between our political process and the moral purposes which direct our life as a people.

We gather today also to invoke the inspiration and power of the Holy Spirit upon this annual assembly of judges, lawyers, and public officials who stand in the tradition of our laws and in the service of justice.

As men of the law, you know the invaluable significance Law has had in the American experience, the role it has played and constantly must play in implementing our moral ideals into our political life. You know that Law is the common defender of man: it protects him from arbitrary powers; from injustices to his person and property; from deprivation of his human and civil rights; and from social and political inequalities that degrade his worth.

Limited Role of Law

On the other hand, you also recognize Law's limits, its inability to generate an interior freedom and love for what is good. Law alone does not produce that freedom which, in Acton's words, is "not the power of doing what we like, but the right of being able to do what we ought." Many, today, advocate an exaggerated individualism which betrays man's social nature and acknowledges no law higher than his own subjective conscience. Others identify morality with the prevailing laws. They confuse law and morality, and thereby advance the popular misconception that our only social evils are the crimes punishable by law.

To understand the significance of the law is to know its parameters and its possibilities. Pope Paul, in his recent Apostolic Letter, spoke of the limited role of law in the following way: "In many cases legislation does not keep up with real situations. Legislation is necessary, but it is not sufficient for setting up true relationships of justice and equality. In teaching us charity, the Gospel instructs us in the preferential respect due to the poor and the special situation they have in society: the more fortunate should renounce some of their rights so as to place their goods more generously at the service of others. If, beyond legal rules, there is really no deeper feeling of respect for and service to others, then even equality before the law can serve as an alibi for flagrant discrimination, continued exploitation and actual contempt. Without a renewed education in solidarity, an over-emphasis of equality can give rise to an individualism in which each one claims his own rights without wishing to be answerable for the common good" (*Octogesima Adveniens*, May 14, 1971).

The limitations of law necessitate a greater increase of the political responsibility for men of the law. From colonial times until our day, lawyers and statesmen have always served as custodians of our political culture in the widest sense of the term. You likewise are called to concern yourselves not only with procedures of justice but also with the progress of people. Therefore, I address you both as servants of the law and as agents of our political process.

New Light of Gospel

Like thousands of other immigrants who have come to this country each year, I left

my native village of Arrifes in the Portuguese Azores at the age of fifteen to become
a naturalized American citizen. What has
distinguished my otherwise quite ordinary
life has been my faith and God's calling
me to the priestly ministry of Christ's
Church. As priest and bishop, I am compelled by humble submission to God's
will to reflect upon the political, social,
cultural and moral "signs of the times" in
the ever new light of the Gospel. The
Council Fathers remind us that "men are
not deterred by the Christian message
from building up the world, or impelled
to neglect the welfare of their brothers.
They are, rather, more strongly bound to
do these very things."

In fulfilling this social mission of the
Church, my purpose today is to propose to
you, as professional jurists and men professed in the faith, a specific task and
urgent need of the moment, to which the
whole Church is called and in which you
have a decisive role to play. The need is
to continue a work which has been that of
the Church for centuries, but which today
must be taken up with new courage and
creativity. It is to develop with precision
and to practice with determination an
"Ethic of Life" drawn from our Catholic
tradition and designed to support a more

humane civil law of life. I do not speak of a "new ethic," as if I were saying something new. I speak rather of a renewed ethic of life, based on the moral law of the Gospels, yet challenging the realities of our time. These realities contain some issues that are very old, but appear to have new faces, such as abortion and war, and other issues that are new and which arise from the rapidly developing life sciences, such as genetic research and manipulation.

In fashioning an ethic of life equal to our post-industrial times, two problems immediately confront us. The first is the problem of constructing such an ethic, the second is the problem of communicating this ethic to our pluralistic society.

Value of Life Today

An ethic of life which will appeal to the consciences of men today must be constructed in a way that is both comprehensive in scope and consistent in substance. It must be comprehensive, in order to speak with concern to all issues where life is threatened today; and it must also be consistent, sufficiently refined and sophisticated so as to speak with precision to the different kinds of problems which touch upon the value of life today.

To construct a viable ethic is not our only task: political and moral pluralism make the medium as important as the message. While our ethical position is rooted in the Catholic faith and illuminated by the Church's view of life, the communication of this view has to be translated into the secular fabric of our political and legal heritage. While the ethic is religious in its roots, its manifestations must be secular and religious in their capacity to appeal to the broader conscience of our society.

Without claiming to have constructed or hereby to communicate such an ethic of life, I only suggest what our Catholic contribution might be in the wider civil dialogue concerning the value of life today. I appear with no ready-made solutions, but only with a suspicion of their religious perspective and a suggestion of their significance.

Religious View of Man

I wish to speak, first, of a religious insight of life. A central theme of both the "Constitution on the Church in the Modern World" and the "Declaration of Religious Liberty" of Vatican II was that all human life is sacred; that the sacredness of human life is rooted in man's call to communion with God, which confers upon man his human dignity; and that this dignity is protected in civil society by a complex of rights and freedoms. These rights, in turn, are expressed, protected and promoted by law according to the changing needs of the time. Our legal system similarly reflects this view. The Declaration of Independence affirms that every man is created by God and constituted with a dignity that is antecedent to every personal or political evaluation of a man's worth. Because God has given man dignity, government must preserve and foster it.

This religious view of man was expressed by Paul Ramsey, who states: "One grasps a religious outlook upon human life only if he sees that this life is 'surrounded' by a sanctity that need not be in a man; that the most dignity a man ever possesses is a dignity that is alien to him; ...a dignity that is an overflow from God's dealing with him, and not primarily an anticipation of anything man will ever be by himself alone" (Morality of Abortion, p. 71).

Both Ramsey and the Fathers of Vatican II base man's dignity in his creation by a free and loving act of God. This is the reason for our common religious attitude of reverence and respect before the value of life. This religious reverence also has serious ethical implications: the duty of every man, and of all societies, to protect and promote the right to life and the quality of life of each man.

To foster such a respect for life, there is a need to cultivate the conviction that all human life is at once indivisible and interdependent: indivisible, in the sense that each man is unique, and his life is a delicate thread that runs with chronological continuity from the womb to the tomb; and interdependent, in the sense that every man's life is lived on a sacred spectrum of life which is tied to other men's lives by bonds of mutual trust and common respect.

War and Abortion

It follows that to attack the sacredness of life at any one point on the spectrum of life is to threaten all life itself. This conviction gives consistency to our ethic of life. It enables us to see that all isolated and indiscriminate attacks upon life, or the quality of life, serve only to destroy the bonds of mutual respect and common reverence which are necessary for men who wish to live together in security and in civil peace. Thus, to be vitally concerned about the rights of innocent human life at one point, as in the case of war, while being quite indifferent to the destruction of innocent lives in the case of abortion, is evidence of our inability to see the unity of those bonds of trust and respect which support a consistent ethic of life. The converse is also true. It is evidence of our failure to see that one who attacks human life indiscriminately at one point exposes himself to similar indiscriminate attacks by others, thereby creating cycles of violence and a climate of fear among men.

Such a short-sighted and pragmatic view of the spectrum of life is as unworthy of life itself as it is unable to defend it, especially in the face of those threats to life which emerge from our culture and endanger it.

The fundamental ethical and political problem which our technological culture has created was prophetically raised by Father Romano Guardini at the end of World War II. The basic question he asked was whether we could develop the moral wisdom to control the powers which man was creating with such astonishing speed. The legitimacy of this question can be illustrated by at least two prominent issues, one that has dominated our life for a quarter of a century, and the other which threatens to exert even greater influence upon our future.

The first issue is that of the nuclear sword which has been hanging over the head of mankind since nuclear weapons were first used, in 1945. Perhaps this spectre provoked Guardini to ask his question. In any case, diplomatic history for the past 25 years records the frantic attempts of our national leaders to devise moral constraints to control this destructive power. Through great effort and skill, we have thus far managed to constrain this power but only after the power itself had been created. We still have little reason to rest content, for our constraints are fragile and our control is feeble. Our moral capacity to control must not lag in false security behind our technological power to create.

Another and newer evidence of this gap between what we can create and what we can control is the problem and possibilities posed for man by developments in genetic research. The vast potential for good in this field makes it an appealing frontier to conquer, but its possibilities for abuse, on both the personal and social levels, make it likewise imperative for us to anticipate our ability to control what we create. Before the technique of genetic manipulation is perfected, we must think about the ethical problems it can pose for our medical and legal professions, and for the political process as a whole.

Mechanical Shield

In light of these examples, our Post-Modern problem is that man's ever-expanding power over our physical environment, our biological and psychological constitution, and our social processes, have placed in man's hands a variety of technological instruments which can be used either in the service of life or against it in all its stages. And the problem is complicated by the technological nature of these instruments, which impose a "mechanical shield" between the user and the moral consequences of his action. In the words of Pope Paul: "It can thus rightly be asked if, in spite of all his conquests, man is not turning back against himself the results of his activity. Having rationally endeavored to control nature, is he not now becoming the slave of the objects he makes?" *(Octogesima Adveniens*, no. 9) A consistent and comprehensive ethic of life obliges us to control man's power over life and death, from world-wide destruction by nuclear weapons to the least significant implications of genetic research.

I would now specify some of the major points in terms of their ethical content and their moral implications for the law, and for men of the law. At the beginning of the spectrum of life, we are confronted with the ethical and constitutional issue of the right to life and to beget life. No one here needs to be reminded that the inviolability of this right is seriously questioned today by the contraception and abortion debates in our land. Rather than repeat the details, I would limit my appeal for a consistent ethic of life to abortion. Consistency demands that the way we evaluate the conflicting elements of this debate should influence the way we resolve other issues that affect human life. Should the law serve life or be neutral in conflicts over life? In the face of conflict, can society remain humane if the law does not protect those who are the least able to defend themselves? Does the intensely personal character of an abortion decision thereby make it an issue of merely private morality? A Catholic ethic of life has tried to respond to these issues in the abortion debate. It does so not only because of its concern for the fetus and its rights, but also because of the drastic implications it fears for society as a whole if these concerns are not answered correctly. In this unique city of New York 165,000 human lives have been snuffed out by legalized abortion in the last year. This is a horrendous situation crying to heaven for vengeance!

We believe as the Founding Fathers believed that the right to life is man's most important gift. We believe, as our constitutional tradition has held, that the urgency of this right demands protection by the law. We believe, moreover, that man's God-given dignity lays a prior claim against the state. It is not the state's prerogative to decide who shall live or die; it is the state's responsibility to see that the life of every innocent human being, weak or strong, young or old, born or unborn, is protected from unjust attack. We believe that abortion is not a matter of private morality alone, but a public issue with political implications which deserve far more consideration than they are now receiving in the courts and legislatures of our land.

Communication

Yet, to say what we believe does not solve the problem of how to communicate this belief in a convincing way to the wider society. We recognize that other reasonable men of good will do not start with our religious premises about life. We must illustrate why and how public decisions on abortion affect other areas of the spectrum of life. I offer two guidelines for our participation: we must keep our Catholic faith as a guide and we must maintain our civil courtesy. Our faith adds to the debate a dimension which is being smothered today; we owe it to society to argue the case of fetal life. On the other hand, maintaining civil courtesy is a demand not only of ethics but also of Christian charity. We must challenge the arguments and assumptions of those who disagree, and not impugn their motives or beliefs.

As we proceed to the midpoint of the spectrum of life, we move to those ethical questions which concern the quality of human life. We speak of those political, social, and economic rights which all must enjoy if they are to live as brothers in dignity. Pope John XXIII elaborated these rights in his encyclical, *Pacem in Terris*, and the Vatican Council reaffirmed their necessity: "There must be made available to all men everything necessary for leading a life truly human, such as food, clothing, and shelter; the right to choose a state of life freely and to found a family, the right to education, to employment, to a good reputation, to respect, to appropriate information, to activity in accord with the upright norm of one's conscience, to protection of privacy and to rightful freedom in matters religious too" *(Gaudium et Spes,* no. 26).

The combined efforts of social reformers, legislators, and jurists in American society have structured a system of law which protects many of these rights. And what remains to be achieved in many areas—such as housing, education and employment—for the black, the brown, and many whites in our society—is the continuing translation of law into reality. The quality of life in these areas is threatened not by our constitution or laws, but by our common failure to live up to their ideals. I would confine myself, first, to congratulate you on the progress that has been made in the past ten years by laws which promote the quality of life for all. Secondly, to call upon you as agents of our political process to advance those programs and policies which in fact enable all citizens to share, equally and impartially, the benefits of the law of our land. I refer to open housing policies in suburban areas, to educational exchanges which offer urban children the possibility of sharing suburban quality in their schools, to the recognition of the inevitable defects of our present welfare system, and the need to provide some system of assistance which places the power and policy of the state at the service of those least able to provide for themselves.

Consistency in an ethic of life requires an equal concern for the right to life and for those rights that foster the quality of life, which to be worthy of man must conform to the moral law of God. A strong stand on abortion demands a consistently strong stand on social issues. If we support the right of every fetus to be born, consistency demands that we equally support every man's continuing rights to a truly human existence. The connection between these two segments of the spectrum of life is real and concrete law. You are particularly called to protect man's right to life and the quality of his life. Man has a right to develop all his potential to reach God, his Creator, and thus enrich the entire human family.

Just War Tradition

When we look to the international signs of the times, we see the ultimate threat to life in our day: modern war. A Catholic defense of life will be neither comprehensive in scope, nor consistent in substance, if we fail to speak in favor of life in the face of war. We live in one of the two super-power states. As a democratic nation the moral responsibility for how we use our power rests not only upon our military leaders, but ultimately upon all of us as citizens.

The Catholic moral tradition has been one of the prime constituents of the Laws of War. Recently, together with the other Catholic bishops of the Boston province, I tried to apply the principles of our ethic of war to the American involvement in Vietnam. Our statement stressed the prin-ciple of the Just War tradition: the defense of civilian life from direct attack. Whenever this principle is ignored or subordinated to mere military strategy, the savagery of modern technological warfare has no limits.

The Pentagon Papers released last week revealed that, according to our CIA reports, 80 per cent of the bombing casualties in North Vietnam was absorbed by civilians. If these reports are true, and I am in no position to vouch for their accuracy, then our Catholic ethic of life requires that we consistently reaffirm that all direct attack upon innocent life is murder. It is, as Vatican II has said, a "crime against God and man, calling for unequivocal condemnation" (cf. *Gaudium et Spes*, no. 80). This principle applies to all human life, born or unborn, friend or enemy, regardless of race or color, regardless of ideology or condition. Either all human life is sacred, or else no human life is ever safe from indiscriminate attack.

The possibility of a continuing use of massive bombing in Vietnam, long after American ground forces are withdrawn, raises serious questions about further destruction of civilian life and with less apparent justification for it. As American casualties decline, the American conscience cannot afford to be apathetic to the deadly costs of technological war for others. As we stated in our Pastoral letter: "We must in conscience criticize the ethical validity of any doctrine, attitude or policy which seems to give American lives an intrinsic superiority over those of other people. Every human life, regardless of nationality, color or ideology is sacred, and its defense and protection must be of deep concern to us."

The respect for innocent life will never be reflected in our policies, domestic or foreign, if it is not first rooted in our convictions. If we are vocal about the rights of innocent life in the womb yet indifferent to the destruction of equally innocent life in warfare, we destroy the consistency of our ethical posture: either all life is always sacred, or no segment of life is ever secure from indiscriminate attack.

The problems we face regarding the value of life today are not solely the concern of religious men, nor do religious men have a monopoly regarding their solution. In the task of building a moral consensus on the value of life in our political process we do not labor alone. We believe with Pope Paul that "the Lord is working with us in the world" and "that other men are at work to undertake actions of justice and peace, working for the same ends. For beneath an outward appearance of indifference, in the heart of every man there is a will to live in brotherhood, and a thirst for justice and peace which is to be expanded...each one must determine, in his conscience, the actions in which he is called to share" (*Octogesima Adveniens,* nos. 48-49).

Choose Life

With Discussion Questions

A Pastoral Letter on the Threat of Nuclear War,
Easter, 1982

Easter and Life

My dear brothers and sisters in Christ:

This Easter Sunday I want to speak to you about a question which is of the highest importance for each of us, for our country and for the whole world. I wish to raise your consciousness to the question of how we should think, pray, and act in a world that lives in increasing fear of nuclear war.

Easter, the feast of the resurrection of Jesus Christ, the Savior and Redeemer of the human race, is God's promise that our destiny is life and not death. Easter is God's call to each of us to love life and promote all that enhances life. Easter calls us all to work among all peoples for peace, for peace protects and fosters life. When the Risen Christ came to His assembled disciples in Jerusalem on the first Easter Sunday, His greeting conveyed the gift of peace, "Peace be with you" (Jn. 20:19, 21; Lk. 24:36). These words were spoken to people who were deeply afraid. The Evangelists tell us that on the morning of the first day of the week, before the Risen Lord appeared to them, the disciples had gathered fearfully behind locked doors (cf. Mk. 16:10; Jn. 20:19).

They had good reason for their grief and fear. Just three days earlier death on the Cross had taken from them the One from whom they had expected fullness of life and freedom (cf. Lk. 24:20-21). The resurrection of Christ transformed their grief into joy and their fear into hope. The event we celebrate at Easter led the first believers in Christ to proclaim, "It is he who is our peace" (Eph. 2:14). We join them in this proclamation of faith and joyfully announce to all that He is also our life.

The Hopes and Fears of Humanity

As I listen to the hopes and fears of the people of the Archdiocese of Boston, I sense that, like them, the hearts of men and women throughout the world today are caught in a state very much like that of Jesus' followers in the time between Good Friday and the first Easter. The disciples looked back on three short days and saw death seemingly destroy the One who had become the source and foundation of all their hopes.

In 1982, when we look back on scarcely more than three short decades, we remember an event which I believe to be the most portentous symbol of death's power that the human race has ever witnessed: the atomic attack on the cities of Hiroshima and Nagasaki. When we remember this horrendous destruction of over a hundred thousand human lives in a few short hours, we, like Jesus' first followers, are afraid, and our fear leads us to seek protection against the awesome power of death that nuclear weapons have placed in the hands of human beings. But unlike the disciples as they remembered Good Friday, we have not gathered in doubt, fear, and shock behind locked doors to grieve and weep. Rather, the fear of nuclear obliteration has led some nations of our world into an increasingly feverish production of more and more of the very weapons of which we are so deathly afraid.

Our choices and our policies seem to be based increasingly on distrust, fear, anxiety, and insecurity. As a consequence, we appear to be led into military postures which increase the human cost of the arms race. Are we convinced that if we want to avoid catastrophe, this escalation of destructive fear must be reversed?

The feast of Easter calls us to a way of living in which hope overcomes anxiety and in which our commitment to building a civilization of life and love upon this earth becomes stronger than our drive to manufacture instruments for the destruction of our planet. Belief in the resurrection of Jesus Christ our Savior not only calls us to life and love, it makes such a way of living possible. Easter is the Day of the Lord longed for by the prophets. It is the day on which they foresaw that, "Kindness and truth shall meet, justice and peace shall kiss" (Ps. 85:11). The resurrection of Christ is the fulfillment of the words of Zechariah, "The day shall dawn upon us from on high, to give light to those who sit in darkness and in the shadow of death, to guide our feet in the way of peace" (Lk. 1:78-79).

From the Shadow of Death Into the Light of Peace

I want to speak to you with the hope that this Easter can be the beginning of the movement of our nation and of our world out of the shadows of the threat of nuclear death into the light which shows us the way to peace. In the words of Pope John Paul II, I wish to exhort all of us "to make a continuing and even more energetic effort to do away with the very possibility of provoking war, and to make such catastrophes impossible by influencing the attitudes and convictions, the very intentions and aspirations of governments and peoples." [1]

I wish to search with you for a pathway we can follow that will enable us to survive the knowledge of how to construct nuclear weapons, and I wish to announce some initiatives of the Archdiocesan Justice and Peace Commission to help in that search.

I need not tell you that faith in the resurrection of Christ does not blind us to the real animosity, antagonism and aggression which threaten the peoples of this world today, but I want to profess openly with you that this faith gives us hope which is deeper than all these forces of destruction. Jesus Christ, risen from the dead, is the source of this hope. He can break the iron grip of fear which today seems to drive us ever closer to nuclear catastrophe. I want, above all, to talk to you in the spirit of the hope He gives us for our common future.

I wish to speak to you according to the mind of the Holy Father Pope John Paul II. Please listen to him as he points out how it is God alone who can fulfill our hopes for lasting peace—for peace is a gift of God:

"Christian optimism, based on the glorious Cross of Christ and the outpouring of the Holy Spirit, is no excuse for self-deception. For Christians, peace on earth is always a challenge, because of the presence of sin in man's heart. Motivated by their faith and hope, Christians therefore apply themselves to promoting a more just society; they fight hunger, deprivation and disease; they are concerned about what happens to migrants, prisoners and outcasts (Mt. 25:35-36). But they know that, while all these undertakings express something of the mercy and perfection of God (Lk. 6:36; Mt. 4:48), they are always limited in their range, precarious in their results and ambiguous in their inspiration. Only God, the giver of life, when He unites all things in Christ (Eph. 1:10), will fulfill our ardent hope by Himself bringing to accomplishment everything that He has undertaken in history according to His Spirit in the matter of justice and peace.

"Although Christians put all their best energies into preventing war or stopping it, they do not deceive themselves about their ability to cause peace to triumph, nor about the effect of their efforts to this end. They therefore concern themselves with all human initiatives in favor of peace and very often take part in them; but they regard them with realism and humility. One could almost say that they 'relativize' them in two senses: they relate them both to the sinful condition of humanity and to God's saving plan. In the first place, Christians are aware that plans based on aggression, domination and the manipulation of others lurk in human hearts, and sometimes even secretly nourish human intentions, in spite of certain declarations or manifestations of a pacifist nature. For Christians know that in this world a totally and permanently peaceful human society is unfortunately a utopia, and that ideologies that hold up that prospect as easily attainable are based on hopes that cannot be realized, whatever the reason behind them. It is a question of a mistaken view of the human condition, a lack of application in considering the question as a whole; or it may be a case of evasion in order to calm fear, or in still other cases a matter of calculated self-interest. Christians are convinced, if only because they have learned from personal experience, that these deceptive hopes lead straight to the false peace of totalitarian regimes."

Yet each one of us individually and all of us collectively must work unceasingly for peace. For peace is a constant challenge to Christians. Our Holy Father makes it clear that even a realistic view of all the tensions and conflicts in modern society does not render ineffective our striving for peace. He says:

"This realistic view in no way prevents Christians from working for peace; instead, it stirs up their ardor, for they also know that Christ's victory over deception, hate and death gives those in love with peace a more decisive motive for action than what the most generous theories about man have to offer; Christ's victory likewise gives a hope more surely based than any hope held out by the most audacious dreams" (1982 World Day of Peace Message).

For Pope John Paul II, genuine peace does not consist in aggressive pacification. Hence he writes:

"This is why Christians, even as they strive to resist and prevent every form of warfare, have no hesitation recalling that, in the name of an elementary requirement of justice, peoples have the right and even the duty to protect their existence and freedom by proportionate means against an unjust aggressor" (*Gaudium et spes*, no. 79).

Without infringing upon this principle we can see how, in a world that is threatened by total nuclear destruction, the need for patient and persistent negotiation is ever more urgent. Our Holy Father expresses the thought in this way:

"However, in view of the difference between classical warfare and nuclear or bacteriological war—a difference so to speak of nature—and in view of the scandal of the arms race seen against the background of the needs of the Third World, this right, which is very real in principle, only underlines the urgency for world society to equip itself with effective means of negotiation. In this way the nuclear terror that haunts our time can encourage us to enrich our common heritage with a very simple discovery that is within our reach, namely that war is the most barbarous and least effective way of resolving conflicts. More than ever

before, human society is forced to provide itself
with the means of consultation and dialogue which
it needs in order to survive, and therefore with the
institutions necessary for building up justice and
peace.

"May it also realize that this work is something
beyond human powers!"[2]

As we proceed in our considerations of nuclear
armament and nuclear war, let us keep in mind this
teaching of the Holy Father. It is central to our
thinking and meditation.

The Horrors of Hiroshima

At the outset we realize the terrifying fact that
the spiral of nuclear arms production has led the
human race into a situation of the gravest peril. On
August 6, 1945, the news that the first atomic bomb
had been dropped on Hiroshima had a profound
effect on me when I was still in the seminary
preparing to be a priest. The awareness that an
awesome and utterly dangerous power had been
discovered by humanity has been with me ever since
that day. For over thirty-six years I have seen this
awareness hover like a storm cloud on the horizons
of the minds of all of us. I have had discussions with
many of our young people who fear they have no
future because they expect a nuclear war to occur
before their future arrives.

Recent developments in the quantity and kind
of weapons which are being produced now prompt
me to repeat the warnings and the plea of Vatican
Council II *(Gaudium et spes*, no. 80) and to note
that the danger of nuclear destruction is constantly
being intensified. With this in mind, I have engaged
in dialogue and consultation with many individuals, including experts in the scientific and medical
aspects of the nuclear arms race.

As a result of this effort, I have prepared this pastoral letter to help us understand the dangers of nuclear war, to urge all to pray fervently with me that these dangers never become realities, and to encourage educational programs throughout the Archdiocese that will help us to make morally responsible decisions. I can offer the teachings of the Church and raise questions to call your attention to this most serious issue. My responsibility as Archbishop will allow me to do no less for the sake of peace, justice, and human life. I therefore address these words to the members of the Catholic community in the Archdiocese of Boston and to all who hope in God and the human future.

The Magnitude of Nuclear Destructiveness

The overriding urgency of the nuclear arms question is most clearly evident from the sheer magnitude of destruction these weapons are capable of inflicting upon the human race. It is difficult to consider, without becoming numb with fear and even despair, the scope of human suffering and death these weapons can cause. Yet I am convinced that our hope in the Risen Christ and our reverence for human life compel us to face, with full awareness, the dangers which confront humanity.

My brothers and sisters in Christ, it is quite clear to me that the potential effects of nuclear war lead us to this somber conclusion: the decision makers in the governments of nations which possess nuclear weapons today hold in their hands the power to cause or to prevent the greatest disaster ever to occur in human history. Moreover, the decisions which will either prevent or bring about nuclear catastrophe are not like those made by governments and generals in previous wars. A full-scale nuclear war could be conducted in a few hours. In such an exchange, decisions would have to be made almost instantaneously. The margin of time for deliberation could be minutes, not hours, days, or months, as is the case in conventional wars. Thus the policies which are being programmed into the computers of the nations will almost completely determine the split-second choices that will have to be made should a nuclear exchange begin.

For this reason, I am convinced that the time for us as citizens to consider our responsibilities in helping to shape nuclear policies is the present. I regard it as both my right and my responsibility to make what contribution I can to help raise and form public awareness of the moral and human stakes in the nuclear arms race. I make no claim to special competence in the military, scientific or political spheres, but as a human being, a citizen, a Christian, and because of my special responsibilities as Archbishop, I cannot relinquish the task of inquiring into, reflecting upon, and giving expression to the moral implications of the military, scientific and political questions which touch the rights of God and the sacredness of human persons as deeply as do the questions of nuclear armament and nuclear warfare.

In speaking with you on these topics, I am fully aware of the practical separation of Church and state in our country. I ask only that both my fellow Catholics and my fellow citizens consider prayerfully and deeply our moral responsibility as human beings in a world armed with these deadly weapons. In a democracy, citizens bear a responsibility which comes with freedom: the responsibility of helping to shape the direction of their nation's policies. As Pope John Paul II put it in his 1982 World Day of Peace Message, "Peace cannot be built by the power of rulers alone. Peace can be firmly constructed only if it corresponds to the resolute determination of all people of good will. Rulers must be supported and enlightened by a public opinion that encourages them or, where necessary, expresses disapproval." [3] To help us carry responsibility together, some reflection on criteria for the moral evaluation of the use of military force which have been developed in the Christian and humanistic traditions of our civilization can be of great assistance.

Catholic Moral Teaching on War

My brothers and sisters in-Christ, I ask you to consider prayerfully with me the theological framework for the moral evaluation of the resort to military force which has been developed through the centuries by the Catholic tradition. To begin with, this framework is based ultimately on the teaching and example of Christ our Lord, who is for us the Way, the Truth, and the Life (cf. Jn. 14:6). It is simultaneously rooted in a fundamental conviction about the dignity and sacredness of every human life, a dignity made all the greater by the life, death and resurrection of Christ our Lord who has called all of us to love our neighbor, even when this neighbor is an enemy (cf. Mt. 5:44). He has stated that all who are peacemakers shall be called children of God (cf. Mt. 5:9).

This love of neighbor and vocation to peace leads Christians to profound aversion to war and violence in all its forms. Indeed from the time of Christ the use of non-violent means for redressing injustice has been a goal set forth by Christian teaching. In recent years the Second Vatican Council has reiterated this deep conviction of the Christian tradition: "We cannot fail to praise those who renounce the use of violence in the vindication of their rights and who resort to methods of defense which are otherwise available to weaker parties too, provided this can be done without injury to the rights and duties of others or of the community itself."[4]

The Council went on to acknowledge the legitimacy of conscientious objection to participation in all war and called for nations to acknowledge this legitimacy in laws that "make humane provisions for the case of those who for reasons of conscience refuse to bear arms, provided however, that they accept some form of service to the human community."[5] While respecting the right of individuals to refuse to shoot or fire at someone, the Council has words of praise for members of the armed forces: "All those who enter the military service in loyalty to their country should look upon themselves as the custodians of the security and freedom of their fellow countrymen: and when they carry out their duty properly, they are contributing to the maintenance of peace."[6]

A more complex moral framework has been generally characteristic of Catholic thought through much of its history—the form of moral reasoning known as the just war theory.

This approach to the morality of the use of force continues to be viewed by the Catholic Church today as a significant help both in guiding individual consciences and in evaluating public policy in accordance with the gospel of Christ and the sacredness of human life. It is a stance which rests on the central obligation to love one's neighbor and to respect the dignity of every human person.

The just war theory acknowledges that this love and respect can, in some circumstances, call for the defense of human life and dignity even by the limited use of force. Its overriding goals are the protection of human persons and the preservation of peace. This teaching recognizes that the demands of justice and the complete avoidance of violence are not in all cases simultaneously realizable in a world touched by human arrogance and sin. Thus the Second Vatican Council has stated that, "as long as the danger of war remains, and there is no competent and sufficiently powerful authority at the international level, governments cannot be denied the right to legitimate defense once every means of peaceful settlement has been exhausted."[7] Therefore, "governmental authority and others who share public responsibility have the duty to protect the welfare of the people entrusted to their care and to conduct such grave matters soberly."[8]

The Council presupposed the traditional Catholic teaching on conditions that must be fulfilled before resort to war can be considered as justified. The conditions are the following:

1) The action must be for the purpose of defending persons who are being unjustly attacked.

2) The use of force must be a last resort.

3) There must be a reasonable hope that the use of force will succeed in righting the wrong it resists.

4) The human cost of the force used must be proportionate to the evil it seeks to overcome.

5) Finally, in the actual course of hostilities the means used must be such that non-combatants are immune from direct attack.[9]

Actions which fall outside the limits of these conditions are judged incompatible with the demands of justice and Christian love. The criteria of the just war theory are held in common by the Catholic moral tradition and the humanistic tradition of the West, for they are the criteria which safeguard the dignity of the human person under the circumstances of conflict.[10]

In light of the possible consequences of nuclear war, and the moral criteria just outlined, I ask you to consider carefully the following most urgent questions, and I ask you to search your own consciences for answers.

First: Can there be a justification for the "first use" of nuclear weapons? Is such a "first use" to be judged good or bad, fair or unfair, moral or immoral, just or unjust, compatible or incompatible with the teachings of the Church, with the fundamental respect for human dignity, and with the demand that force never be used aggressively?

Second: Is there a reasonable hope of success in righting the wrong which a nation resists by launching a full-scale attack on another nation, even in retaliation for a nuclear attack which has already been launched against one's own country? Is there such a hope in launching a lesser attack under the same conditions? What would be the moral goodness or the moral evil of such actions?

Third: Is there a proportion between the use of even a small fraction of nuclear forces stockpiled on the earth today and the good to be achieved?

Fourth: Is it possible to use nuclear weapons against an adversary without violating the principle of non-combatant immunity?

Fifth: What is the morality of the use of strategic weapons against military targets on land if such use causes "collateral damage" in the form of deaths, injuries and radiation of vast numbers of innocent persons? What is the morality of the use of strategic weapons if such use does not cause such extensive "collateral damage"?

Sixth: What is the moral goodness or evil of the use of nuclear weapons, strategic or tactical, against any target, civilian or military, if such use is likely to lead to escalation to a full-scale strategic exchange? What is the moral goodness or evil, if such a use is not likely to lead to such a catastrophe?

My dear brothers and sisters in Christ, we are indeed reflecting on a most fundamental issue of our day. It is as fundamental as life and death. As Christians we must give it our prayerful attention. After all, we choose life! That is why the Christian community is called to help in the formation of an international consensus to reject ultimately the use of all nuclear arms. I cannot adequately stress this important truth. Let me repeat it from the bottom of my heart and with all the vigor at my command: the Christian community is called to help in the formation of an international consensus to reject ultimately the use of all nuclear arms.

The Responsibility of Catholics for Peace in the World

Christians are citizens of all the nations of the world. As citizens, American Catholics are rightly concerned with the preservation of freedom and justice in the land which is our home. The call of Christ, however, is not limited by national borders. The community to which Christians owe their ultimate loyalty is the whole family of God's children, the entire human race. The Church is "a kind of sacrament or sign of intimate union with God, and of the unity of all humankind. She is also an instrument for the achievement of such union and unity."[11] The vocation of the Church to work for the achievement of the greater unity of the peoples of the globe meets an especially urgent need in the nuclear age. This vocation does not mean that Christians can naively ignore the profound threats to their own nations and to the world as a whole that nuclear armaments have created. Rather, it means that we have a duty to take a stand which promotes the safety of all nations, including our own, by working for the rejection of these weapons of destruction.

I have reached into my conscience, as I pray you are reaching into yours, and I find that such a stand is the only and ultimate response that holds any promise of breaking the spiral of mutual fear which is driving nations into ever greater peril. It is my personal belief that this is a realistic response to our situation and the only response, at present, that is an expression of hope for the human family on our planet.

The Question of Deterrence

The conviction that nuclear weapons must be banished from the earth should press us to the utterly urgent issue of how to prevent their use from ever occurring while we still have them. The moral legitimacy of the production and development of nuclear arms in order to deter an adversary from using its nuclear force against us has become one of the most controverted questions in the nuclear debate in our day. Even if there were agreement on the unacceptability of any use of nuclear weapons, that agreement could co-exist with disagreement about the morality of possessing nuclear weapons for purposes of deterrence.

There are at least two kinds of deterrence— deterrence by pain and deterrence by denial. The deterrence theory by pain is built upon the supposition that a nation can prevent another's use of nuclear weapons by itself possessing such massive destructive force that only an adversary bent on suicide would dare launch an attack against it. It seeks to prevent nuclear war by creating a situation where no one could rationally consider starting such a war. There is another deterrence, the deterrence of denial, predicated on the idea that the possession and placement of more sophisticated low-yield nuclear weapons aimed at strategic military targets involving only those few civilians who are working in the nuclear field, can in fact deter an enemy because it denies the possibility of first strike capability (either of a conventional or nuclear nature) with impunity.

In following a deterrence strategy, nations threaten and prepare to take actions which can have catastrophic effects upon life in this world. At the same time the intention which leads to such threats and preparations is the intention to prevent nuclear war.

The danger and ambiguity of any deterrent strategy are immediately evident when one considers the possibility of an accidental initiation of a nuclear exchange. On the other hand, there are many persons who maintain that the possession of nuclear arms by each of the superpowers has in fact deterred any nuclear attack upon one by the other. These persons also suggest that an atomic attack would never have been launched against Hiroshima and Nagasaki if Japan had possessed an atom bomb and the United States was convinced that Japan was ready to use it.

In any case, the dilemma is real: does a system which seeks to prevent nuclear war by threatening nuclear attack truly prevent the use of these weapons, or does it make nuclear war more probable? If a concrete policy and strategic posture are actually means to the prevention of war and to the development of arms control, then the ambiguity inherent in the possession of nuclear weapons can be tolerated, even though not approved as a desirable situation. [12] On the other hand, if such a policy and posture are judged to make nuclear war more likely and the goal of abolition of nuclear weapons less attainable, then this policy would be difficult to justify on moral grounds.

Whatever the ambiguities about deterrence may be, one thing I believe is certain: the only way to prevent nuclear war for the children of today and for unborn generations to come is the abolition of nuclear weapons from the earth and the creation of a world order and a civilization of love that will insure that they are not again produced, much less used.

The Cost of the Nuclear Arms Race in Human Resources

Dearly beloved in Christ, when considering the nuclear arms race and nuclear war, we cannot ignore the immense cost in human resources. This factor has moral implications. The combination of deterrence theory, strategies which prepare for actually fighting nuclear wars, and sophisticated technological innovation in weapons programs constitute an immensely costly mixture. The total of the world's present conventional and nuclear military expenditures is $550 billion per year. [13]

This outlay is the equivalent of the total annual income of the poorer half of the entire population of the earth. In a world of over 4 billion human beings, where one-third of all people lack the necessities of life, the huge amounts of money that prevailing strategies have driven us to expend on weapons are an outrageous affront to human life, to the rights of the poor and therefore to God Himself.

As the Holy See declared at the U.N. Special Session on Disarmament in 1976: "The obvious contradiction between the waste involved in overproduction of military devices and the extent of unsatisfied vital needs (both in developing countries and in the marginal and poor elements in rich societies) is itself an act of aggression which amounts to a crime, for even when they are not used, by their cost alone, armaments kill the poor by causing them to starve."[14] Moreover, these expenditures for arms are not only a threat to the poor. They reduce the resources available for housing, medical care, human services and education of all of us and all of our children. The immense drain of human resources represented by the unprecedented arms build-up now underway robs the whole of God's family of possibilities for social and intellectual development and fulfillment. Indeed the economics of present arms policies around the world in itself raises serious moral questions.

An Appeal to the Leaders of Nations

Dearly beloved in Christ, the drift towards destruction must end! And so, in the name of God, in the name of the Risen Christ in whom we place our hope, in the name of humanity, I ask you to join with me in raising an urgent appeal to leaders of nuclear nations, and to all citizens of these lands to turn back from the strategies of death.

Together let us call on the United States and the Soviet Union to consider carefully the wisdom of bilateral and even multilateral negotiations leading to a mutual halt on testing, production and deployment of nuclear weapons and of missiles and aircraft designed primarily to deliver nuclear weapons. Serious consideration of this action I believe to be the minimal moral response to the present highly dangerous circumstances. I realize that this is a complex matter and falls far short of the goal of disarmament, but it could hopefully have the effect of breaking the spiral of fear and hostility which daily carries us closer to disaster. Obviously the process would have to be verifiable in order to yield trust and remove fear. We make a similar urgent appeal to the scientific and technological communities involved in the discovery, development, and production of nuclear weapons. After all, without them, the weapons would not have come into existence and could not be developed and produced.

More importantly, let us call on the leaders of all nations possessing nuclear arms, including our own, to heed Pope John Paul's appeal for peace, as enunciated in his message of January 1, 1982, and enter into negotiations which seek in all good faith to bring about an actual reduction in arms. Because of the utterly grave threat posed by nuclear arms, arms control and disarmament negotiations should not, in my judgment, be made dependent on previous resolution of the other serious differences which divide us. Indeed let us call on our government as well as the governments of other lands to approach the conflicts between us in a way which protects the integrity of negotiations on genuine arms control and reduction.

In a world threatened with nuclear catastrophe, do the superpowers dare risk any other way of dealing with their differences? As I have noted

above, Pope John Paul II has wisely pointed out
that the nuclear threat leads us to recognize "that
war is the most barbarous and least effective
way of resolving conflicts. More than ever before,
human society is forced to provide itself with the
means of consultation and dialogue which it needs
in order to survive and therefore with the institutions
necessary for building up justice and peace."[15]

I believe then that a positive appeal for negotiation, consultation, dialogue and for the strengthening of international institutions which foster a
peaceful and just world order should accompany
our call for the abolition of nuclear weapons from
the earth.

Seeking Peace: the Task of All of Us

In the exercise of my responsibilities as Archbishop of Boston, I ask all members of the Catholic
community to consider carefully and conscien-
tiously the course of action each of us should take in
light of the teachings and of the concerns set forth in
this letter. Above all, we need to pray together at all
times, but especially in this Easter season, that the
Lord of life will give us the wisdom, the courage,
and the hope to act on the basis of our commitment
to Jesus Christ and to all our brothers and sisters in
the human family.

The peace we seek is God's own peace. Without God's help it is beyond our power to attain it.
But the Easter message is God's promise that this
help is constantly offered to us by the Holy Spirit,
the comforter. So let us pray daily that the Spirit
will strengthen us in the bonds of peace. Let us pray
that through the Risen Christ, who is our peace,
every dividing wall of hostility may be broken down
(cf. Eph. 2:1). St. Paul has assured us that "to set

the mind on the Spirit is life and peace" (Rom. 8:6). So let us turn our minds and hearts to God and ask for peace and hope with all our being.

The good news of Easter also calls each of us to examine our own attitudes toward conflict and violence. Have we allowed ourselves to slip quietly into a kind of despair, a state of mind that accepts the inevitability of nuclear war? Easter challenges us to renewed hope and to renewed commitment to peace, both as individuals and as nations.

As shepherd of the flock, I have tried in this letter to let the message of Christ's resurrection renew and deepen my own service of the God of peace. I call on all the priests, deacons and religious of the Archdiocese to consider how the Easter proclamation can bring true renewal of your ministries in a nuclear world. I invite parents and families to let the hope of Easter become the foundation of your lives together so that the children of the next generation may have greater hope in their future. I ask that all of us examine how the labor of our hands and the work of our minds might become not only a means of earning our livelihood but a real contribution to the peace of the world.

The area of the Boston Archdiocese is a center of scientific, technological, medical, financial and artistic achievement which is second to none in our country. In all these areas of human creativity, we need to examine how we can direct our talents to the service of life, peace and hope rather than the spiral of fear and nuclear despair. And finally, I call on teachers and educators from kindergarten to the most advanced levels of learning to look at the future which awaits your students as you pursue your noble task. Let the words of Isaiah become your own: "They shall not learn war anymore" (Is. 2:4).

A Response of the Archdiocese to the Appeal for Peace and Life

In order to help the Catholic community of Boston in our efforts to deal with these urgent questions and needs, the Archdiocese plans to take a number of specific steps in the months ahead. An Archdiocesan conference on the response of Christians to the issues raised by the arms race will be convened on June 26. Its purpose will be further examination of questions dealt with in this letter and exploration of concrete ways for the Boston Catholic community to respond to them. In September we will begin organized programs on these questions in the parishes of the Archdiocese. Also in September educational programs in Catholic schools and parish religious education programs will begin.

It is my hope that this letter and these specific steps will be a source of renewed faith and hope that war can be avoided and that we can truly live as peacemakers in a fear-ridden world.

Conclusion: Prayer for Peace and Life

Before I bring this letter to a close, I wish to address all those who believe in God and who respect life, with the words of Moses to God's people: "I set before you life or death, blessing or curse. Choose life then, so that you and your descendants may live, by loving the Lord your God, heeding his voice and holding fast to him. For that will mean life for you, a long life for you to live on the land which the Lord swore he would give to your fathers, Abraham, Isaac, and Jacob" (Dt. 30:19-20).

Because we choose life, we choose peace, peace which is ultimately God's gift to us; and for this gift we must pray according to the mind of His Holiness, Pope John Paul II:

"Yes, our future is in the hands of God, who alone gives true peace. And when human hearts sincerely think of work for peace, it is still God's grace that inspires and strengthens those thoughts. All people are in this sense invited to echo the sentiments of St. Francis of Assisi, the eighth centenary of whose birth we are celebrating: Lord, make us instruments of Your peace: where there is hatred, let us sow love; where there is injury, pardon; when discord rages, let us build peace.

"Christians love to pray for peace, as they make their own the prayer of so many psalms punctuated by supplications for peace and repeated with the universal love of Jesus. We have here a shared and very profound element for all ecumenical activities. Other believers all over the world are also awaiting from Almighty God the gift of peace, and, more or less consciously, many other people of good will are ready to make the same prayer in the secret of their hearts. May fervent supplications thus rise to God from the four corners of the earth! This will already create a fine unanimity on the road to peace. And who could doubt that God will hear and grant this cry of His children: Lord, grant us peace! Grant us Your peace!"[16]

I leave you with the words Jesus addressed to the two women who came to the tomb on the first Easter morning: "Peace! Do not be afraid" (Mt. 29:9-10). And in the words of the liturgy in which we celebrate our hope, I pray for all of us and for our world: "May the light of Christ, rising in glory, dispel the darkness of our hearts and minds. Christ yesterday and today, the beginning and the end, Alpha and Omega, all time belongs to him and all the ages, to him be glory and power through every age forever. Amen." [17]

Mary, Queen of Peace, pray for us.

A peace-filled Easter to all.

NOTES

1. Pope John Paul II, "Address to the General Assembly of the United Nations," October 2, 1979, no. 11, in *Pilgrim of Peace: The Homilies and Addresses of His Holiness Pope John Paul II on the Occasion of His Visit to the United States of America* (Washington, DC: United States Catholic Conference, 1980).

2. Message of His Holiness Pope John Paul II, *For the Celebration of the Day of Peace*, January 1, 1982, From the Vatican, December 8, 1981, no. 12, pp.17-18.

3. Pope John Paul II, *1982 World Day of Peace Message*, no. 6, p. 10.

4. *Gaudium et spes*, no. 78.

5. *Gaudium et spes*, no. 79.

6. *Gaudium et spes*, no. 79.

7. *Gaudium et spes*, no. 79. See Pope John Paul II, *1982 World Day of Peace Message*, no. 12.

8. *Gaudium et spes*, no. 79.

9. For a full discussion of the just war theory as understood in contemporary Roman Catholic moral teaching, see J. Bryan Hehir, "The Just War Ethic and Catholic Theology: Dynamics of Change in Continuity," in Thomas A. Shannon, ed., *War or Peace?* The Search for New Answers (Maryknoll, NY: Orbis Books, 1980), pp. 15-39.

10. This humanist tradition is admirably exemplified in Michael Walzer, *Just and Unjust Wars: A Moral Argument with Historical Illustrations* (New York: Basic Books, 1977).

11. Vatican Council II, *Lumen gentium* (Dogmatic Constitution on the Church), no. 1, in Abbott and Gallagher, op. cit.

12. See John Cardinal Krol, "Testimony before the Senate Foreign Relations Committee, September 6, 1979, *Origins 9* (September 13, 1979), pp. 195-199.

13. Ruth Leger Sivard, World Military and Social Expenditures 1981 (Leesbury, VA: World Priorities, 1981), p. 5.

14. *The Holy See and Disarmament* (Vatican City: Tipographica Poligotta Vaticana 1976).

15. Pope John Paul II, *1982 World Day of Peace Message*, no. 12.

16. Pope John Paul II, *1982 World Day of Peace Message*, no. 13, pp. 20-21.

17. Liturgy of the Easter Vigil, *The Sacramentary of the Roman Missal*.

SOME SUGGESTIONS TO AID DISCUSSION
ON THE PASTORAL

1. How is it possible to say: "Easter is God's promise that our destiny is life and not death"? What is the relationship of Easter to life for the world?

2. Obtain some information on the destruction of Hiroshima and Nagasaki: the power of the bomb used, the number of people killed, the number of people maimed for life, the material destruction, etc.

3. Pope John Paul II says, "For Christians, peace on earth is always a challenge, because of the presence of sin in man's heart." Why does the presence of sin in the human heart make peace on earth a real challenge? What is meant by "the presence of sin in man's heart"?

4. In what way can peace be said to be the work of justice? How are both peace and justice related to the pursuit of Christian love?

5. What are the reasons that would move the spiritual leader of an archdiocese to give expression to the moral implications of nuclear armament and nuclear warfare?

6. When Cardinal Medeiros asks us to "consider prayerfully and deeply our moral responsibility as human beings in a world armed with these deadly weapons," is he violating "the practical separation of Church and state in our country"?

7. The Church, while stressing the Lord's command that we love our neighbor—even our enemy—also upholds the right of self-defense. Explain this teaching of the Church.

8. Cardinal Medeiros, quoting a passage from the Second Vatican Council, stated: "While respecting the rights of individuals to refuse to shoot

or fire at someone, the Council has words of praise for members of the armed forces." Discuss these points.

9. Enumerate the conditions which in Catholic teaching could justify resort to warfare. Try to present the reasons behind each condition.

10. How would you respond to the questions posed by the Cardinal on pages 13-14? Give the reasons behind your answers.

11. Why is it essential that the Catholic community cooperate in the formation of an international consensus to reject ultimately the use of all nuclear arms?

12. Discuss the morality of possessing nuclear weapons for purposes of deterrence. Evaluate the arguments pro and con.

13. Explain the theories of deterrence by pain and by denial.

14. What reasons are proposed by those who believe that a policy of deterrence prevents nuclear warfare? By those who believe that a policy of deterrence makes nuclear warfare more probable?

15. Discuss the huge expenditure of funds involved in maintaining a nuclear armament, especially in the light of: a) world hunger and poverty; and b) the obligation to protect the lives and freedom of citizens from attack.

16. Given the seriousness of the contemporary situation regarding the proliferation of nuclear arms, what do you think the moral response of concerned persons should be?

17. Some of those opposed to nuclear proliferation have urged unilateral disarmament. Discuss the implications of such a position and comment on its validity.

18. Discuss the Cardinal's appeal that we "call on the United States and the Soviet Union to con-

sider carefully the wisdom of bilateral and even multilateral negotiations" with the hoped-for effect of "breaking the spiral of fear and hostility which daily carries us closer to disaster."

19. How does "choice for peace" make "choice for life"?

20. Pope John Paul II has declared: "In the final analysis, when we consider the question of peace, we are led to consider the meaning and conditions of our own personal and community lives." How can we foster peace in our own hearts and in our individual relations with one another and with our community?

APPENDIX ONE

"Prevention Is Our Only Recourse"

On October 7-8, 1981, under the chairmanship of Professor Carlos Chagas, President of the Pontifical Academy of Sciences, at the headquarters of the Academy (Casina Pius IV, Vatican City), a group of 14 specialized scientists* from various parts of the world assembled to examine the problem of the consequences of the use of nuclear weapons on the survival and health of humanity.

Although most of these consequences would appear obvious, it seems that they are not adequately appreciated. The conditions of life following a nuclear attack would be so severe that the only hope for humanity is prevention of any form of nuclear war. Universal dissemination and acceptance of this knowledge would make it apparent that nuclear weapons must not be used at all in warfare and that their number should be progressively reduced in a balanced way.

The above-mentioned group discussed and unanimously approved a number of fundamental points, which have been further developed in the following statement.

Recent talk about winning or even surviving a nuclear war must reflect a failure to appreciate a

---

* Carlos Chagas, Rio de Janeiro; E. Amaldi, Rome; N. Bochkov, Moscow; L. Caldas, Rio de Janeiro; H. Hiatt, Boston; R. Latarjet, Paris; A. Leaf, Boston; J. Jejeune, Paris; L. Leprince-Ringuet, Paris; G. B. Marini-Bettolo, Rome; C. Pavan, Sao Paulo; A. Rich, Cambridge, Mass.; A. Serra, Rome; V. Weisskopf, Cambridge, Mass.

medical reality: any nuclear war would inevitably cause death, disease and suffering of pandemic proportions and without the possibility of effective medical intervention. That reality leads to the same conclusion physicians have reached for life-threatening epidemics throughout history: prevention is essential for control.

In contrast to widespread belief, much is known about the catastrophe that would follow the use of nuclear weapons. Much is known too about the limitations of medical assistance. If this knowledge is presented to people and their leaders everywhere, it might help interrupt the nuclear arms race. This in turn would help prevent what could be the last epidemic our civilization will know.

The devastation wrought by an atomic weapon on Hiroshima and Nagasaki provides direct evidence of the consequences of nuclear warfare, but there are many theoretical appraisals on which we may also draw. Two years ago, an assessment undertaken by a responsible official agency described the effect of nuclear attacks on cities of about two million inhabitants. If a one-million ton nuclear weapon (the Hiroshima bomb approximated 15,000 tons of explosive power) exploded in the central area of such cities, it would result, as calculated, in 180 km² of property destruction, 250,000 fatalities and 500,000 severely injured. These would include blast injuries, such as fractures and severe lacerations of soft tissues; thermal injuries such as surface burns, retinal burns and respiratory tract damage; and radiation injuries, both acute radiation syndrome and delayed effects.

Even under optimal conditions, care of such casualties would present a medical task of unimaginable magnitude. The study projected that if 18,000 hospital beds were available in and around one of these cities, no more than 5,000 would remain relatively undamaged. These would accommodate only 1 % of the human beings injured, but it must be stressed that in any case no one could deliver the medical service required by even a few of the severely burned, the crushed and the radiated victims.

The hopelessness of the medical task is readily apparent if we consider what is required for the care of the severely injured patients. We shall cite one case history, that of a severely burned twenty-year-old man who was taken to the burn unit of a Boston Hospital after an automobile accident in which the gasoline tank had exploded. During his hospitalization he received 140 liters of fresh-frozen plasma, 147 liters of fresh-frozen red blood cells, 180 milliliters of platelets and 180 milliliters of albumin. He underwent six operative procedures during which wounds involving 85 % of his body surface were closed with various types of grafts, including artificial skin. Throughout his hospitalization, he required mechanical ventilation. Despite these and many other heroic measures, which stretched the resources of one of the world's most comprehensive institutions, he died on his 33rd hospital day. His injuries were likened by the doctor who supervised his care to those described for many of the victims of Hiroshima. Had 20 score of such patients been presented at the same time to all of Boston's hospitals, the medical capabilities of the city would have been overwhelmed. Now, consider the situation if, along with the injuries to many thousands of people, most of the medical emergency facilities had been destroyed.

A Japanese physician, Professor M. Ichimaru, published an eyewitness account of the effects of the Nagasaki bomb. He reported: "I tried to go to my medical school in Urakami which was 500 meters from the hypocenter. I met many people coming back from Urakami. Their clothes were in rags and shreds of skin hung from their bodies. They looked like ghosts with vacant stares. The next day I was able to enter Urakami on foot and all that I knew had disappeared. Only the concrete and iron skeletons of the buildings remained. There were dead bodies everywhere. On each street corner, we had tubs of water used for putting out fires after air raids. In one of these small tubs, scarcely large enough for one person, was the body of a desperate man who sought cool water. There was foam coming from his mouth, but he was not alive. I cannot get rid of the sounds of the crying women in the destroyed fields. As I got nearer to the school there were black, charred bodies with the white edges of bones showing in the arms and legs. When I arrived some were still alive. They were unable to move their bodies. The strongest were so weak that they were slumped over on the ground. I talked with them and they thought that they would be OK, but all of them would eventually die within two weeks. I cannot forget the way their eyes looked at me and their voices spoke to me forever...."

It should be noted that the bomb dropped on Nagasaki had a power of about 20,000 tons of TNT, not much larger than the so-called "tactical bombs" designed for battlefield use.

But even these grim pictures are inadequate to describe the human disaster that would result from an attack on a country by today's stockpiles of nuclear weapons, which contain thousands of bombs with the force of one million tons of TNT or greater.

The suffering of the surviving population would be without parallel. There would be complete interruption of communications, of food supplies and of water. Help would be given only at the risk of mortal danger from radiation for those venturing outside of buildings in the first days. The social disruption following such an attack would be unimaginable.

The exposure to large doses of radiation would lower immunity to bacteria and viruses and could, therefore, open the way for widespread infection. Radiation would cause irreversible brain damage and mental deficiency in many of the exposed in utero. It would greatly increase the incidence of many forms of cancer in survivors. Genetic damage would be passed on to future generations, should there be any.

In addition, large areas of soil and forests—as well as livestock—would be contaminated, reducing food resources. Many other harmful biological and even geophysical effects would be likely, but we do not have enough knowledge to predict with confidence what they would be.

Even a nuclear attack directed only at military facilities would be devastating to the country as a whole. This is because military facilities are widespread rather than concentrated at only a few points. Thus, many nuclear weapons would be exploded. Furthermore, the spread of radiation due to the natural winds and atmospheric mixing would kill vast numbers of people and contaminate large areas. The medical facilities of any nation would be inadequate to care for the survivors. An objective examination of the medical situation that would follow a nuclear war leads to but one conclusion: prevention is our only recourse.

The consequences of nuclear war are not, of course, only medical in nature. But those that are compel us to pay heed to the inescapable lesson of contemporary medicine: where treatment of a given disease is ineffective or where costs are insupportable, attention must be turned to prevention. Both conditions apply to the effects of nuclear war. Treatment would be virtually impossible and the costs would be staggering. Can any stronger argument be marshaled for a preventive strategy?

Prevention of any disease requires an effective prescription. We recognize that such a prescription must both prevent nuclear war and safeguard security. Our knowledge and credentials as scientists and physicians do not, of course, permit us to discuss security issues with expertise. However, if political and military leaders have based their strategic planning on mistaken assumptions concerning the medical aspects of a nuclear war, we feel that we do have a responsibility. We must inform them and people everywhere of the full-blown clinical picture that would follow a nuclear attack and of the impotence of the medical community to offer a meaningful response. If we remain silent, we risk betraying ourselves and our civilization.

APPENDIX TWO

Results of a
Nuclear Attack on Boston

by Dr. James Muller

We drift quietly toward destruction because the effects of a nuclear weapon are difficult to imagine. To develop the strength to alter our course we must first ask God for the courage to see the coming disaster. I ask you to join me in a painful but necessary consideration of the results of a nuclear attack on the Archdiocese of Boston. The results presented are based on the report entitled "The Effects of Nuclear War" which was prepared by the Office of Technology Assessment of the United States' Congress.

Let us assume that a one megaton bomb, a bomb equivalent to one million tons of TNT, is detonated at ground level on the Boston Common. This is an average sized bomb in a modern arsenal but over 60 times larger than the Hiroshima bomb. The explosion occurs in fair weather at 3 p.m. on a spring day.

The immediate blast produces a crater 20 stories deep and two blocks in diameter. Within 1.7 miles of the center, all buildings, including heavily reinforced concrete structures, are demolished. This includes total destruction of the State House, the Massachusetts General Hospital, the Quincy Market, Faneuil Hall, South Station, the John Hancock and Prudential Towers, Fenway Park, the Museum of Fine Arts, Northeastern University, Boston City Hospital, Cardinal Cushing High School, the Massachusetts Institute of Technology and parts of Charlestown and East Boston. Virtually all individuals within this area are killed instantly.

At a distance of 2.7 miles, including parts of Chelsea, Somerville, Cambridge and South Boston, all frame and brick buildings are severely damaged. Over 50% of the people in this area are killed immediately and most of the remaining are injured. At 4.7 miles from the center, including all of Logan Airport and parts of Winthrop, Revere, Everett, Watertown, Brighton and Brookline, there is moderate damage to commercial buildings, and severe damage to homes. Seven miles from the center, as far as Revere Beach, Winchester, Boston College and parts of Milton and Quincy, moderate blast damage occurs to homes.

The bomb causes destruction not only by its blast effects but also by the release of thermal energy. Six miles from the center, individuals whose skin is exposed receive second degree burns. Hundreds of thousands of individuals have severe burns with no hospital to go to and no physicians to provide even minimal pain relief. In the area within Route 128 many secondary fires ignite from ruptured gas mains and oil stores.

The third type of injury inflicted by the explosion results from radioactive fallout. Its extent and severity depend upon unpredictable wind conditions, but it greatly enlarges the area of danger over the weeks following the blast.

These are the early effects of a single one megaton bomb on Boston. It is likely that in an all-out US-USSR nuclear war the city would be hit by 10 such bombs. Furthermore, it is probable that other targets in the Boston area would be attacked such as the Pilgrim Nuclear Power Plant, Otis Air Force Base and Hanscomb Field. Neighboring cities such as New Bedford, Providence, Hartford, Worcester and Manchester would also be devastated by separate attacks.

Such a description of the effects of a nuclear weapon on a city provides an idea of the scope of a nuclear explosion, but it fails to convey the personal meaning of the tragedy. We can come closer to understanding this by focusing on its effect on a family. The following fictional account is based on stories related by Hiroshima victims.

The family lived in a frame home two miles inside Route 128. At the time of the nuclear explosion the father was at work in his office in Boston. The mother was at home, the fourteen-year-old son was in the high school building three miles from ground zero and the seven-year-old daughter was walking home from school with her friends six miles from the center.

The father saw a flash of white light, felt intense heat and was incinerated within seconds. The son also saw a flash of light, felt the warmth, and saw shattered glass, bricks and people hurled about by winds exceeding two hundred miles per hour. The ceiling of the building crashed down on him and his classmates. Deafened and trapped in the rubble, he remained alive for several hours with multiple fractures and lacerations until the firestorm which coalesced incinerated all in the area.

The daughter and her friend turned reflexly toward the fireball and were blinded and then knocked to the ground by the blast. Their exposed faces, arms and legs were burned immediately by thermal radiation.

The mother was in the basement at the time of the attack. She saw a flash followed by an explosion. The lights in the basement went out as all electric power to the area failed. She ran outside in search of her daughter. Amidst the burned and wounded, she recognized her daughter by her shoes and book bag. She took her home. The car could not be used because the streets were thronged with the wounded and dying. She attempted to call her pediatrician for advice about the burns but the phone was dead. There was no water from the faucet because the water main was broken, but the mother was able to give the daughter a soft drink through a straw.

One week later the daughter died of infection complicating her burns. In addition to the psychologic trauma caused by the loss of her family, the mother, exposed to fallout, began to experience the nausea, vomiting and diarrhea of radiation sickness. If she survived several months she would face starvation, epidemics and probably death in the cold of a winter without fuel.

In summary, the Archdiocese would be a scene of unimaginable horror following a nuclear war. The churches, schools and universities in which we labor would be devastated, the children we nurture incinerated, and entire parish communities annihilated. The few surviving priests and religious would be unable to minister to most of the dying or to comfort even a small fraction of the wounded. In most cases there would be no individual funerals, only mass burials. In many instances there would be no mourners to comfort because entire families from grandchildren to grandparents would have been killed. The church would be unable to conduct God's work in any form resembling the usual manner following the holocaust.

Our primary task must be to work now to spread the message of Christ's love so that such an utterly evil event will never occur.

Pastoral Reflections on Conscience

Feast of St. Simon and St. Jude
October 28, 1980

Dearly beloved in Christ:

A few weeks ago I had the opportunity to reach you at home through *The Pilot*,* our respected Archdiocesan newspaper. I had occasion then, as your spiritual father, to remind you of your obligation to be attentive to your conscience in the discharge of a very serious civic duty.

Today I would like to reflect with you about conscience itself—that uniquely human power we call "the voice of God within us." It is not my intention to make this an exhaustive theological treatise on the subject, but I believe we must think about it seriously, especially at this time.

Some years ago I was given a book of memorable quotations from the works of American writers. Among them I found this one from George Washington, the Father of our beloved country:

> Labor to keep alive in your breast that little spark of celestial fire—conscience.

---

* See pp. 500-502.

1. *Conscience*

In searching for the source of this most basic advice, a priest friend found it in the Appendix to the second volume of *The Writings of George Washington*, published in Boston in 1834. This Appendix contains fragments from manuscripts written in his boyhood and youth. The youthful Washington may have copied the maxim from another author, but be that as it may, the young Virginian appears to have been deeply concerned with the formation of his conscience.

We know that it was Washington's conscience—his keen sense of duty—that led our infant nation to freedom with responsibility and honor. His countrymen appreciated the superlative qualities of his character—developed under the guidance of a good conscience, a conscience anchored on basic moral principles—and elected him the first President of our country. To his conscientious judgment they entrusted with confidence the destiny of the newly-born United States of America.

Somehow folks realize that people with a good conscience can be trusted: they are loyal; they will not compromise with evil; they are courageous.

But like all good men and women, Washington had to labor to keep alive in his breast the "little spark of celestial fire" called conscience. As the Second Vatican Council was to say almost two centuries later, the young Washington had discovered deep within himself—as most of us should—"a law which man does not lay upon himself but which he must obey." This is how the Council speaks of conscience:

Its voice,
ever calling him to love
and to do what is good and to avoid what is evil,
tells him inwardly
at the right moment: do this, shun that.
For man has in his heart a law inscribed by God.
His dignity lies in observing this law,
and by it he will be judged.
His conscience is man's most *secret core,*
and his *sanctuary.*
There he is *alone with God*
whose voice echoes in his *depths.*
By conscience,
in a wonderful way,
that law is made known
which is fulfilled in the love of God
and of one's neighbor.
Through *loyalty* to conscience
Christians are joined to other men
in the search for truth
and for the right solution
to so many moral problems
which arise both in the life of individuals
and from social relationships.
Hence, the more a *correct* conscience prevails,
the more do persons and groups turn aside
from *blind* choice
and try to be guided by the *objective standards*
of moral conduct.

Yet it often happens
that conscience goes astray
through *ignorance*
which it is unable to avoid,
without thereby losing its dignity.
This cannot be said of the man
who takes little trouble
to find out what is true and good,
or when conscience is by degrees
almost blinded through the habit of committing
    sin
(Gaudium et spes, no. 16).

2. *Conscience and Error*

As the Second Vatican Council points out, it
can often happen that conscience goes astray. I
believe young Washington was aware of this
danger, and that is why he felt that we must
labor to keep it alive within our breasts.

Dearly beloved in Christ, allow me to be a
little philosophical or theological if you like,
but please stay with me for the sake of conscience—for the sake of justice and peace in
your heart and in our society.

I think it is clear—
or should be clear after some reflection—
that anyone who acts on the basis of a
    conscience
that he or she knows to be in error,
cannot be said to be acting blamelessly.
To be without blame, therefore,

everyone has the obligation
to take whatever steps are necessary
to assure that the dictates of his or her
    conscience
present the morality of an act
as it really is objectively.
Surely a person cannot be held to be
    blameless
if he or she is responsible
for the ignorance which led to the erroneous
    conscience,
or if he or she actually chooses
to permit his or her conscience to go astray.

We must remember that conscience has need of guidance, for conscience is *not* infallible. Indeed we call it the "voice of God within us," but it is not God. We can actually almost drown out the voice of God with the noise of other voices. That is why we must labor hard and never lose sight of the fact that no one has the right to form his or her morality for himself or herself, independently of the holy will of God, which is His law. It is a sure personal tragedy to fall into the habit of thinking that true freedom permits a person to establish his or her own morality.

3. *Badly Formed Conscience*

Unfortunately, as we know, it can also happen that "conscience goes astray through ignorance which it is unable to avoid." *Subjectively*, a person who acts on the basis of such a conscience cannot be accused of guilt, even though the act which he or she performs is, in the *objective* order, morally wrong. And yet, all of us know that despite the *good faith* of the individual, to act in consequence of a conscience that is in error can result in the perpetration of the most atrocious crimes. Slavery, for example. The Holocaust.

May the person with an erroneous conscience continue thus to act?

For example, if the action is seriously unjust against his or her neighbor, is the person free to persist in doing it, simply because he or she is in good faith?

The fact is, dearly beloved in Christ,
that any conscience
which dictates the performance of an
    objectively evil act
is a *badly formed* conscience.
And so, if at any time
the individual begins to have reason
to believe that the act may be wrong,
or if the wrongness of the act is called
to his or her attention,
then there exists *the obligation*
of making every effort to bring one's
    conscience
into conformity with the objective truth.

In this connection the Second Vatican Council spoke very clearly in a passage that is deserving of our prayerful consideration. Please reflect on it with me:

...In forming their conscience
the faithful must pay careful attention
to the *sacred* and *certain* teaching
of the Church.
For the Catholic Church is by the will of Christ
the teacher of truth.
It is her duty to proclaim and teach with
    authority
the truth which is Christ
and, at the same time,
to declare and to confirm by her authority
the principles of the moral order
which spring from human nature itself.
In addition, Christians should wisely
approach those who are outside,
"in the Holy Spirit, genuine love,
truthful speech" (2 Cor. 6:6-7),
and should strive,
even to the shedding of their blood,
to spread the light of life
with all confidence and apostolic courage
(Declaration on Religious Liberty, no. 14).

The sage advice of the Father of our country is as valid and as relevant today as it was when he first wrote:

Labor to keep alive in your breast that
little spark of celestial fire—conscience.

Pray God that we may hear that advice with attentive ears and heed it with magnanimous hearts.

May the American conscience never forget the basic truths enshrined in the Preamble to our Declaration of Independence. We all have God as our Creator, from Whom we have all our rights. He is the Father of all and the Lord of life. With all this in mind we can conclude that:

To violate one's conscience is to violate one's humanity.

To violate one's conscience is to diminish one's human dignity.

To violate one's conscience is to dare disrupt one's human relationships.

To violate one's conscience is to strain or break one's relationship with God.

To violate one's conscience is to sin.

To violate one's conscience is to invite serious damage to those civic relationships that we should enjoy as citizens of this nation dedicated to the pursuit of liberty and justice for all.

Our conscience will make or break our nation!

May the American conscience be upright, just, and truthful, anchored on the God of our Fathers and His Law. In God we trust!

Vote
"To Save Our Children"

*From the September 12, 1980
issue of* The Pilot

Dearly beloved in Christ:

As all of you know, since becoming Archbishop of Boston ten years ago, I have written
and spoken to you many times about the most
vital concerns of our day. I have joined with
millions all over the world and in our country to
condemn the evil of abortion. I have testified
before the Senate Judiciary Committee in
Washington favoring the passage of a Human
Life Amendment; I have spoken and written in
defense of innocent human life on any number
of occasions, and it is my constant prayer, alone
and with my people, that the United States
would reaffirm what the Declaration of Independence proclaims as a fundamental human
right—the right to life.

Living in a society that puts such faith in
statistics, it is frightening to realize that
1,000,000 unborn children have been legally
aborted in the United States every year since

the death-dealing decision of the Supreme Court on January 22, 1973. As of this date, more than 8,000,000 of our very own children have been destroyed in the womb, strangely described as a "medical procedure."

Presently, we are faced with primary contests in our own districts, and a few weeks later, the final election which will determine those individuals who will vote on the law which will govern the conduct of the Commonwealth and the entire country. Through this letter, as your Archbishop, I wish to restate my unalterable opposition to legalized abortion as an offense against God and humanity, against our Maker and His people.

With pastoral concern for the spiritual welfare of the faithful who are both heirs of God's Kingdom and citizens of this noble nation, I plead with you to exercise your right and duty to vote in the upcoming elections; and, to bring your own conscience—the voice of God within you—to the ballot box with you. We are a nation *under God*, as we are a *nation of law*, and we must be as consistent with our concern for the unborn as we are for all those people from far and near who look to us for aid and comfort. We must work to change our nation from its blood-drenched current condition to a sacrificing society that welcomes life at every stage of human development. That might makes right by court ruling can never be the last word when human life is the issue.

The Second Vatican Council declares that abortion is "an unspeakable crime." Those who make abortions possible by law—such as legislators and those who promote, defend and elect these same lawmakers—cannot separate themselves totally from that guilt which accompanies this horrendous crime and deadly sin. If you are for true human freedom—and for life—you will follow your conscience when you vote; you will vote to save "our children, *born and unborn.*"

Your answer to this call to vote must not be taken lightly since it could be a matter of life or death for millions yet to come. May our values be a living witness of the faith and hope and love we share.

Morality in Our Time

Given at the Churchman's League for Civic Welfare,
April 20, 1972.

I am very honored indeed to have been
invited to address this annual banquet
of the Churchman's League for Civic
Welfare, and pleased to share with this
distinguished assembly whatever light I
have on the perplexing moral problems
which challenge all religious groups in our
day. I accept this gracious invitation with
all humility and with all the respect I have
for you as spiritual leaders in our common
pastoral concern for the religious and
moral perfection of God's children.

Even the most casual observer of our
times would readily admit that ours is a
society in which diversity of ideas has
often led to division, disorder and discord.
Poets and social psychologists tell us that
a mood of anxiety and alienation has seized
the soul of our nation. People sense they
are fragmented, forgotten and systematically abandoned to the mounting waves
of senseless crime and fatal moral disintegration. And lest we deceive ourselves
by the volume of our own rhetoric about our

society's unique and unprecedented concern for persons, the overwhelming evidence to the contrary gives us every reason to question more and more our self-righteousness and presumed sincerity. The painful fact remains that we are a nation that is severely divided and singularly un-united in almost everything. We are separated into mutually opposing camps by virtue of all the divergent elements through which a society is normally destined to succeed — by virtue of age, color, wealth, politics, and even religious practices. The promise of pluralism seems to have become instead the problem of pluralism.

Since we share in the effect — and perhaps in the cause — of the problem of religious pluralism in American society, as religious leaders of various backgrounds and different convictions, we must be among the first to try to live peacefully with one another. We are all aware that religious diversity of its very nature can provide an enormous potential for good or for failure. The Christian unity within which our own religious diversity exists, is at best a tenuous and fragile bond easily shattered by human weakness. Our conversation and confrontation can become trying at times, and sometimes even abrasive. Surely the last example we should wish to give to society is one of open hostility and mutual bitterness.

Since dissension generally originates in misunderstanding, the task of clarification is a particularly urgent and important need for us, and it is to this task that I wish to address myself tonight. Before doing so, however, I would first point out that resolving our mutual misunderstandings should not be confused with dissolving our religious differences. These differences represent deep convictions and strong commitments that touch the very heart-stone of God's revelation to man. They penetrate the very depths of the currents of the Christian faith and its contents. Certainly it would be an incalculable disservice to deny these differences for the sake of superficial unity or to explain them away in the name of ephemeral brotherhood. The many real needs we have for one another oblige us not to engage in personal polemics nor to hide our truly religious beliefs — but rather to reverence each other and to achieve a certain unity in the midst of this diversity.

Among the many theological and moral issues which are regarded as the source of much troublesome and taxing debate is the Catholic Church's mission and manner of ethical decision-making. In directing your attention to this issue, my purpose is simply and entirely to provide information. I have no intention to defend my belief by apologetic arguments. My desire is to present as clearly as I can the position of the Catholic Church in the hope that in our future conversations and mutual encounters you may better understand my Church. I realize that this issue may hold little interest for the members of this League who are so active in the field of moral and social welfare, and so vitally concerned about such issues as alcoholism, drug abuse, crime and pornography in terms of our Commonwealth's present legislation and educational programs. Obviously I have grave concern about these and other matters, but I must also confess to you how limited I am to speak about these specific problems. I am by profession a Bishop of the Roman Catholic Church. As such, my competence as a moral teacher and leader flows principally from my faith and professionally from my ordination to the teaching office of my Church. Thus, it seems to me that an understanding of my Church's role in the moral order and its normative manner of making ethical decisions will be helpful to all of us. It is true that issues like pornography, alcoholism, homosexuality and others are important and should be discussed among us. But it is precisely because these are all so closely related to and essentially dependent upon the larger issue of the Catholic Church's moral stance in a pluralistic society, that I have chosen to expound upon this central issue tonight.

The Christian ethic is the New Testament love revealed by Christ (Cf. C. Spicq, *Agapé in the New Testament*). The one Christian imperative is that we are to love God and one another as He showed us how to love. To say this is to say everything, and yet very little. Unhappily, love can mean many different things to men. Actions that some people commend in the name of love, others merely condone and still others condemn. Little wonder that there is so much confusion and debasement of Christian love in our society. Clearly this commandment needs constant articulation and clarification, lest Christian love be lost in a sea of subjectivism. The words and actions of Jesus provide the perfect example of what Christian love is. The question to be raised is how do these words and actions find their formulation as moral principles in the Catholic tradition? How do we avoid inconsistencies and conflicting practices of love? How do we select certain actions which are to be promoted and condemn other actions which are opposed to them? There must be an inner logic to the law of love, and the question is: How do we as believers discern this logic?

I would answer this question by indicating immediately how Roman Catholics do not discover these moral truths or principles. First, we do not believe that the truths of morality emerge from any political process such as a consensus or compromise. However unpopular and unenlightened this position may appear, especially in a democracy like ours, we reject the notion that the religious and moral truths of Christianity are determined by popular vote. Social surveys and pollsters do give us some insight into what people generally feel may be morally right or wrong, and to a certain extent this opinion is interesting and useful. But the popular will of the people is not necessarily the holy will of God, as the history of revealed religion has shown. Secondly, we equally reject the much more reasonable view that Christian moral principles can be determined by the dictates of reason alone. Again, in an age which is newly enamored with the insights of the human mind and the achievements of science, this rejection on our part is not popular. To be sure, we believe that it is the task of man's reason to discover Christian moral truths, but it is not in man's power to create them. To maintain that man is the sole creator of

his values is ultimately, we believe, to
deny God's revelation. And even if we were
to suppose that it was a question of a
rational search for moral principles unfor-
tified by faith, then whose reason would
become the standard for all? Would it be
yours, or mine, or ours? Perhaps it would
be the reason of the philosopher or the
historian? perhaps the reason of the psychologist or the social scientist? But which
philosopher or which social scientist?
Our reason, both individually and collectively, is so evidently limited and
fallible that any sure reliance upon it in
matters so grave as salvation should cause
us serious concern. Thirdly, we do not
accept the even more popular idea advanced by moral philosophers in favor of
"liberty of conscience," namely the freedom of the individual to decide infallibly
for himself what is absolute and morally
right. Conscience, they say, is known to
the individual in the depths of his soul —
an intuition of love, it is called — and it is
supposed to be superior to all other laws
and the ultimate guide for making moral
choices. But the individual who appeals
solely to the sovereign autonomy of his
conscience in order to advance his personal freedom from all responsibility, has
totally passed from the Christian moral
order. "Individual conscience," as Cardinal

Wright explains, "is not always on the side of freedom, nor of life, nor of God, nor of man" ("Reflections on Conscience and Authority" in *The Critic*, April-May, 1964). Similarly, Professor C. A. Pierce contends in his book *Conscience in the New Testament* that it is one thing to teach that conscience is inviolable, but that it is another thing to suppose that conscience is infallible. He protests, therefore, that when the Church offers men no better guidance than "act according to conscience," she is abdicating the office to which she was appointed and surrendering the first article of her creed, i.e. Jesus is Lord. To say this is not to deny what the Fathers of the Second Vatican Council expressed, that in the depths of his conscience man detects a proximate and practical law which summons him to love what he believes is good and to avoid what seems to be evil. But since conscience frequently errs and since man's freedom has been damaged by sin, they add, each man must render an account of his own life before the final judgment of God (*Gaudium et Spes*, 16 and 17).

Now I would like to indicate how Catholics do believe religious truths find their formulation. For us, the Christian truths of faith and morality are revealed by the Spirit in the Church and to the Church.

We believe that the Church is of God and that the Lord Jesus works in and through His Church in ways which are not always detected by man. God's ways are not our ways, but these ways of God must be discovered and expressed in a manner which can be understood in some degree and interiorly accepted as truths of faith. At this point we face the problem of Catholic teaching in a pluralistic society.

Let me say parenthetically that as Americans we all cherish sincerely and strongly our political democracy. We are all willing to live and die for a democracy, which in spite of its imperfections, tries to assure all men their basic human rights and freedoms, and strives to give them an equal share in the forming of national policies and international practices. Although American society constitutionally endorses our freedom of belief, nevertheless the religious authority of the Catholic Church is frequently accused of infringing upon the legitimate freedoms of others. Yet, the history of our government teaches that those in political authority are to insure the right and freedom of religious leaders to express their views on moral matters which affect the health of the body politic. Our collective contributions to this moral discourse, therefore, and our collective influence upon the course of moral events are all the more urgent and necessary.

Tonight, however, my interest is not the contribution of Catholic thought to civic discourse, but the role of religious authority within the Catholic Church. We believe that every religious society needs an authoritative voice which continues to articulate its founding spirit to the changing consciousness of its members. The authoritative voice of the Catholic Church's teaching in matters of faith and morals, we believe, is the divinely instituted successor of St. Peter, Pope Paul VI, and united with him and under him all the members of the episcopate. Each Bishop is also divinely empowered to exercise within his own diocese the magisterial authority of the Church as teacher of faith and morals in union with the sovereign Pontiff. As the Fathers of the Second Vatican Council stated: "This sacred Synod teaches that by divine institution bishops have succeeded to the place of the apostles, as shepherds of the Church, and that he who hears them, hears Christ, while he who rejects them, rejects Christ and Him who sent Christ" (*Lumen Gentium*, 20). "Among the principal duties of bishops, the preaching of the gospel occupies an eminent place. For bishops are preachers of the faith...authentic teachers, that is, teachers endowed with the authority of Christ, who preach to the people committed to them the faith they must believe and put into practice.... In matters of faith and morals, the bishops speak in the name of Christ and the faithful are to accept their teaching and adhere to it with a religious assent of soul. This religious submission of will and mind must be shown in a special way to the authentic teaching authority of the Roman Pontiff, even when he is not speaking ex cathedra. That is, it must be shown in such a way that his supreme magisterium is acknowledged with reverence, the judgments made by him are sincerely adhered to, according to his manifest mind and will" *(Lumen Gentium, 25)*.

The hierarchy, Pope Paul recently explained, is not free to teach what it likes in the religious field nor to follow the latest whim of certain doctrinal or antidoctrinal movements of modern opinion. The episcopate is invested with a primary duty to transmit faithfully and fully the body of truths which Christ revealed and entrusted to the Apostles for the salvation of men. "From this point of view," Pope Paul said, "the Church is tenaciously conservative, therefore she does not grow old." Yet, there is also the authentic and authoritative development of the Church's original teaching and a constant and consistent application of the living faith to the practical experiences of life. This dual office of doctrinal fidelity and pastoral understanding, the Pope concluded, is the mission and responsibility of the bishops. In their pastoral care, the bishops are assisted by the efforts of professional theologians, so that the indispensable relationship between the bishops and the theologians cannot be minimized at any time. But the final decisions of faith and morals are left to the bishops to whom has been divinely entrusted the pastoral care of the flock of Christ.

In the area of Catholic morality there will always be discussion and inevitable diversity of opinions on certain issues. There will always be personal views and schools of thought. Given this diversity, the Church articulates her official moral teaching by the bishops who decide not on the basis of consensus, or rational arguments, or conscience alone, but on the basis of faith and their teaching office. And our common Catholic belief is that these means were established for the Church by Christ Himself.

I would add to these remarks one important qualification. Those who share in the teaching authority of the Catholic Church must always be Christ-like; they must always be humble, sincere and open to the inspirations of the Spirit. For someone, like myself, the purpose of authority is primarily to inspire, to encourage, to direct and to challenge others to new levels of Christ-likeness; seldom should authority be used to rebuke and never to oppress. As an instrument of this authority, I stand as a spokesman for my Church and for what my Church believes. I do so neither to alienate nor to cause anger, but simply because I believe this has been willed by Christ for His Church until the end of time.

In conclusion, it appears to me that moral problems today are basically religious problems. No doubt these problems are being addressed with all the resources of reason and love that we can command. Our idealism, however, should occasionally be tempered with theological realism, as the Jesuit John Rohr and the Lutheran David Luecke observed: "Prejudice, violence, selfishness, fear, ignorance and oppression are all grounded in the basic predicament of man. The cause of that predicament is theological, not sociological. The judgment of God on sinful men and their societies cannot be wished away" (Art. "The Church's Proper Task and Competence" in *America*, Nov. 16, 1968). Man's problem today is not only that he has failed to adjust to his environment, but that he has also lost sight of his religious worth, his spiritual origins and his supernatural end. He is root-less and goal-less. And so modern moral theologians, Protestant and Catholic alike, are presently preoccupied with restoring man's aware-ness of the spiritual sources of his moral behavior. Worshipping at the altar and paying one's debt to his neighbor, accord-ing to James Gustafson, are essentially related. "The more problematic that experience and belief in God become" he writes, "the more fragile the tone and quality of the moral life of the Christian become...persons become means rather than ends, sin becomes infraction of moral rules rather than a denial of God; the end of action becomes an increased quantity of moral goodness rather than the glorifica-tion of the goodness of God.... Without the experience of the Holy, Christian moral life withers" (Art. "Spiritual Life and Moral Life" in *Theology Digest*, 19; 1971). Paul Ramsey also reminds us that there can be no morality among men unless there is belief in God. "The whole modern world," he writes, "may without too great exag-geration be described as a vast and ghastly concentration camp in which social forces and movements of thought combine to destroy for the individual the divine significance of his name" (Art. in *Nine Modern Moralists*). And Father Stanislaus Lyonnet, S.J. offers us a classic analysis of

Pauline Theology and suggests the deeply religious consequences that flow from living in the Spirit of Christ (Art. "St. Paul: Liberty and Law" in *The Bridge*, Vol. IV, 1962).

I share the view that loyalty to the Christian gospel and a living faith in Christ evoke distinctively Christian insights and attitudes, goals and norms (Cf. J. Gustafson, *Christ and the Moral Life*, p. 238-271). As the Fathers of Vatican II stated: "Whoever follows after Christ, the perfect man, becomes himself more of a man" *(Gaudium et Spes*, 41). It is love of Christ which makes us holy and binds us together to do what is good. Like all love, it is hard sometimes; but for Christians it is the only way.

Man's Cities
and God's Poor

Feast of the Assumption,
August 15, 1972

My dear brothers and sisters in Christ:

For almost two years I have been Archbishop of Boston and have met many people and have seen many problems. Now I feel that it is my duty to speak about certain situations in the light of the mission and teaching of the Church. The Gospel is clear. Christ has come into the world "that men may have life, and may have it in all its fullness" (Jo. 10:10). All of life is a gift of God: the life of creation and the life of redemption. All of life is from God and for God.

But life in its totality today is being cruelly strangled, especially in many of our cities. "Life in all its fullness" is far from reality to the elderly who are imprisoned in their apartments because of fear, and its bright hope does not shine on the bitter faces of those who are unemployed and restless or sitting in empty silence. Robert Coles records a rather pathetic view of city life seen through the eyes of a black

child from Roxbury. "This here city isn't
for us. It's for the people downtown.
We're here because, like my mother said,
we had to come. If they could lock us up
or sweep us away, they would."[1] In the
face of such evils moral indignation is not
enough. Moreover, the doctrine of the "new
creation" rejects that unhealthy attitude
which would remove the Church from effective service to the world around it, and
reminds us that we are continually called
by God to re-create this world in accordance with His will, His justice and His
love.

It is a long way from first-century Jerusalem to twentieth-century Boston and
other large urban centers of America, but
the words of Christ are still so applicable:
"If when you are bringing your gift to the
altar, you suddenly remember that your
brother has a grievance against you, leave
your gift where it is before the altar. First
go and make your peace with your brother,
and only then come back and offer your gift"
(Matt. 5:23-24). It is in the context of these
words of the Gospel, coupled with Christ's
compelling example of compassion, that
Thomas Merton could say: "One cannot be
a Christian today without having a deeply
afflicted conscience. I say it again: we are
all under judgment."[2] The very existence
of the poor in our cities who lack the material, intellectual and spiritual necessities
of human decency is a frightful accusation

against all who are apathetic or indifferent to their plight. In my installation homily I said, "It is impossible to be a Christian without being concerned for every man, without being involved in the now real life-situation of every brother."[3]

It is not with the hope of bringing complete solutions to the seemingly insoluble problems of urban America that I begin this letter. It is rather to project some insights in the light of the Catholic tradition and of the Church's mission of reconciliation that I prayerfully undertake this urgent, though difficult, task.

A. THE ROLE OF THE CHURCH IN THE SOCIAL SPHERE

The mission of the Church and the aspirations of all mankind are indissolubly linked. As the Fathers of the Second Vatican Council observed, "the joys and hopes, the griefs and the anxieties of the men of this age, especially those who are poor or in any way afflicted, these too are the joys and hopes, the griefs and anxieties of the followers of Christ. Indeed, nothing genuinely human fails to raise an echo in their hearts."[4] The Church and society are involved in the total development and well-being of all men. Society works toward this common goal by constantly improving the practice of its just laws. The Church does this by proclaiming the revealed truth that every man is created in the image and likeness of

God. In this way, the Church anchors the dignity of human nature against all tides of opinion, for as the Fathers of the Second Vatican Council taught: "By no human law can the personal dignity and liberty of man be so aptly safeguarded as by the gospel of Christ which has been entrusted to the Church."[5] And the Fathers went on to explain: "For faith throws a new light on everything, manifests God's design for man's total vocation, and thus directs the mind to solutions which are fully human."[6] Christ has commissioned His Church to free men from their sin and to alleviate for all the dire consequences of pride, arrogance, selfishness, lust, greed, injustice, oppression, prejudice and hatred.

In the words of Pope John XXIII, "the Church does not offer to men of today riches that pass, nor does she promise them a merely earthly happiness, but she distributes to them the goods of divine grace which raises men to the dignity of sons of God and are the most efficacious safeguards and aids toward a more human life. She opens the fountain of her life-giving doctrine which allows men, enlightened by the light of Christ, to understand well what they really are, what their lofty dignity and their purpose are, and finally, through all her children, she spreads everywhere the fullness of Christian charity, and there is nothing more effective than this charity in eradicating the seeds of discord, nothing more efficacious in promoting concord,

just peace and the brotherly union of all."[7]
Hence, it is imperative that the Church
through all its members, in accordance with
their role in it, effectively appeal to and
relate all of our human resources — political,
economic, social and institutional — to
God's divine purpose.

For our society to grasp the simple wisdom of God's complex plan being worked
out in conformity to that timeless purpose
which is centered in Christ Jesus, our Lord
(Eph. 3:10), the Church must express to
mankind what is always and everywhere
inconsistent with the "Kingdom of God."
By divine mission, the Church must appeal
to and challenge the conscience of society.
Long before the evangelist John put these
words into writing, Christians had already
learned that the Church and the world were
to be related in a constant dialectic of identity and non-identity:

> "Do not set your hearts on the passing godless
> world or anything in it. Anyone who loves the
> world is a stranger to the Father's love. Every-
> thing the world affords, all that panders to the
> appetites, or entices the eyes, all the glamour
> of its life, springs not from the Father but from
> the passing godless world."[8]

Precisely because the Church has been
sent by Christ to serve mankind, the Church
must continually proclaim the judgments of
Christ upon human society. Thus, for
example, because of the recent report of
the President's Commission on Popula-

tion Control and the Future, calling for abortion on demand, we must question and judge the opinion of many modern men who feel they are the final judges in the worldly realm. Church and society can never be perfectly identified until this world is no more. Until then, the Church is Christ present in the world in order to reconcile the world and all men to the Father, and part of God's plan concerning the establishment of His Kingdom imposes the sacred responsibility of bringing His judgment even upon the complex issues of the social or political arena.

B. THE EXPANSIVE POWER
OF THE MYSTERY OF CHRIST

Yet, I am not, and with God's grace will never be, an advocate of negativism, defeatism and doubt. God's Word is bound up with the history of this world and continually confronts us as His Church through the events of life. It is in His Word in its multiple forms, as discerned by the Church, that I place my trust. Amid today's confusions it is His Word that offers a hope, a vision of what yet may be, by freeing us from our slavery to what actually is.

It must never be forgotten that God's dialogue with man receives its complete expression in Christ: "When in former times God spoke to our forefathers, He spoke in fragmentary and varied fashion through the prophets. But in this final age He has spoken to us in the Son whom

He has made heir to the whole universe..."
(Heb. 1:1-2). It was this profound consciousness of the expansive power of the
Christ-Mystery which prompted Paul to
write the first pastoral letters. As a believer,
I also confess that it is the paschal mystery
of Christ—the living Wisdom of the Father,
the inexhaustable source of Truth and
Love—which must be inserted into concrete situations as the key to all human
problems. It is from this graced insight
which sees the whole field of human activity as finding its fulfillment in Christ that
I wish to evolve this pastoral letter. It is in
Christ, the Revealer, and Lord of the Universe, in whom we discover the total design of the world; Christ the Servant, in
whom we serve our fellow men; Christ the
King, whom we must obey; Christ our God,
whom we must adore.

C. METHOD AND PLAN

I humbly submit that the urgency of
this letter cannot be doubted. The violent
future grimly depicted in the report of
*The National Advisory Commission on
Civil Disorders* and *The National Commission on the Causes and Prevention of
Violence* makes it clear to me at least that
the immediate resolution of conflicts, both
psychic and material, within America's
scarred cities and metropolitan areas is
necessary for our country's claim to future
greatness. Otherwise, ours will be a country
drowning in passion and blood. A complete-

ly doctrinaire approach, however, does not penetrate the roots of our urban ills. As the Pastor of the Archdiocese of Boston, my constant effort has been to suggest and to enforce the spiritual perspectives of our faith. I have no doubt that these perspectives, especially as they are generously lived and realized by the faithful, will aid in the arduous task of shaping our world according to the Gospel.

I have divided this letter into three major sections. Beginning with the image of the "Tower of Babel," I have tried to capture the "feel" of the City of Man today. At this point, it is not so much any particular geographical area upon which I am concentrating; rather I am focusing on the prevailing spiritual atmosphere in America today which, I believe, is responsible not only for many of our urban ills but also for some of the confusion within the Church. The second section of this letter will be addressed to the Church in the Archdiocese of Boston. Unless the Word of God is enfleshed in our lives, we are in danger of leading our fellow men to regard us as impostors. Memorable phrases, even eloquent interpretations of the Word of God, must always and everywhere be made explicit in good deeds. Because the Christian and all men of good will can never assume an a-political, and thus ineffective, stance before the evils of the time, I have attempted in the third section to make some practical suggestions to our wider political and social communities. I realize that facile self-righteousness can shatter trust and friendship, and this is not my intention. My honest desire to promote social justice and to safeguard the rights of the poor force me to enter these complex and sensitive areas. My judgments in these matters may be fallible, but they are the fruit of my prayerful meditation on Christ's Gospel of justice and love as proclaimed by the Church. No one should expect more. No one can demand less.

PART I
The City and the Tower of Babel

A. CONFUSION IN THE CITY

1. The "feel" of the City of Man

The American city, although almost last in the hierarchy of the intergovernmental structure that rules our nation, does maintain an operational primacy in dispensing our common resources for the common good. We must commend those who are working to resolve the problems of unemployment and under-employment, transportation, poverty, social isolation, educational deficiencies, prejudice and crime. Yet despite the talent and the sophisticated technology applied to the problem of urban America, the American city constitutes a terrible series of absurdities.

Elegant skyscrapers are tangled side-by-side with skid row—that squalid refuge for the downtrodden among our brothers. Downtown, one finds the glittering nerve-center for the relentless pursuit of profit and pleasure. Meanwhile, human beings are squeezed together in over-crowded slums where they remain unseen except by a few. By contrast, the carefully zoned bright suburban ring heightens the drab look of despair and desolation which the city sadly projects. And there are always the innocent children whose daily intimacy with senseless brutality — both institutional and personal — has often destroyed their spirit. In short, a city is a kaleidoscope of disparate, swirling images. It is a system of administrative arrangements. It is a social convenience. It is a crowd of people, each one trying to carve out of his melancholy environment an area of happiness. It is a place with a history whose contemporary enactment is so cruel to many, perhaps to all. Mingled with all these is the over-riding "feel" of the urban scene: the feeling of confusion in the mind of urban man. Mumford describes this feeling in these words: "increasingly, men in cities find themselves 'strangers and afraid' in a world they never made: a world ever less responsive to direct human command, ever more empty of human meaning."[9]

2. The curse of confusion

It is this curse of confusion which prompts me to turn to the image of the "Tower of Babel" as a fundamental symbol for urban America. I suggest that our cities' compulsory togetherness-without-community and their collective isolation provide a lucid modern commentary on the biblical meaning of Babel. So many are confused and without roots. So many are searching for meaning and lacking security. So many are pursuing a course of self-destruction in our cities today. The full horror of their torment can be seen even among the young who have already grown weary with life and turned to the streets and to narcotics. Others in their barren moments blindly grope for peace by turning to the ultimate oblivion: suicide. All of these children of God, miracles of grace and love, are seeking a sense of relief from their tragic inability to relate themselves to the world with confidence and faith in their personal worth.

We must return to this biblical symbol of confusion in order to fathom the depths of the endless irrationalities which are characteristic of the city scene: the juxtaposition of glitter and colorlessness; the quest for scandalous comfort taking precedence over human needs; the strangle hold of custom suffocating noble impulses of the heart; the dead feelings of complacency; and the abject feelings of frustration. Born from this confusion at the heart of city life today is a peculiarly intense isolation among individuals and communities. The rich, the middle-class and the poor are clearly separated from each other and divided in their own experience. They are unable to trust one another, and so pretend not to need one another. The usual catagories of religious and secular discourse seem unable to bridge the gap; and the more strident discord one hears on every side from white and black, rich and poor—in the ecclesial, political and intellectual communities—conveys the diminishing dimension of human dialogue.

Small wonder that the majority so often fail to hear, much less understand, the poor's cry for justice and equality. And justice is needed! It was, for example, an ambiguous and questionable application of justice which allowed the average assessment ratio of residential property, from January 1960 through March 1964, to remain almost twice as high in the Roxbury area of Boston than in other sections of the city.[10] And, despite disclaimers, another pernicious form of injustice—racism—still exists! Almost every national index available documents the fact that segregation still persists. America still exploits cheap black labor. Even in the middle of the country's economic boom in the mid-sixties, under-employment in Roxbury was a scandalous 24%.[11] Given the same education, the black still receives only 60%-70% of the pay of a white man, and there is always the self-reinforcing nature of racism:

"The enormous concentration of poor children at the bottom of the society is a depressing, dynamic fact. It is made all the worse by the incredible inferiority of public education in the slums, where so many children are unfitted for anything but marginal working lives. In the metropolitan-area schools of the United States, the Department of Labor reported in 1967, the average twelfth-grade Negro has a mathematical proficiency which is somewhere between the seventh- and eighth-grade level and a reading proficiency not much higher. This statistic, it should be noted, describes the fortunate black children who did not drop out of school. Since everyone from the Senate Manpower Subcommittee to the President's Automation Commission now proclaims that it takes two years of post high-school training to be a successful member of the working class, the millions of poor young Americans are at an unprecedented disadvantage."[12]

More recent estimates show that in urban poverty areas almost 75% of the children never reach the level of literacy required for available employment.[13] It is no surprise that many young blacks have united in a community of common bitterness, almost hatred, of the white world and its institutions. Any violence, even the invisible violence of apathy and indifference, causes men to clench their fists. And against violence men are instinctively joined together. Thus, the curse of confusion remains.

3. The meaning of the Tower of Babel

It was in the city where Babel was rising to the skies that men lost their ability to speak intelligently to one another: "That is why it was called Babel, because there the Lord confused the speech of all the world" (Gen. 11:9). Because they had reduced their religion to the worship of themselves and the world's goods, they were unable to acknowledge with reverence God who transcends the powers of man. No longer feeling themselves bound together in common obedience to God's Will, they quickly lost their ability to communicate meaningfully with one another.

This same theme—the confusion of images and ideologies governing our thinking, even about religion—is found also in New Testament times, as the famous Trappist monk, Thomas Merton, observed:

"The judgment of the world as, by definition, *closed in upon itself*, and therefore, closed *to any revelation that demands to break through its defensive shell*, is surely one of the key ideas of the New Testament. By the Incarnation and Cross, Christ does in fact *break through* the defensive shell not only of sin and passionate attachment, but of all ethical and religious systems that strive to make man self-sufficient in his own worldly realm."[14]

In spite of the apocalyptic sense of doom in our cities—the majority's terror of destruction, and the minority's rage for destruction—men still do not turn to the will of the Father as manifested in the Old Testament and as clearly revealed and perfectly fulfilled by Christ in the gospel. Instead, they seek solutions to our urban ills through a comfortable slavery to the many secular and political currents at work in America today.

At the outset, I must make it clear that I by no means reject, much less condemn, everything achieved by the social, economic and political sciences. But I must also try to view from another perspective in the light of the Gospel those influences which unconsciously dispose us to decide in favor of the world and against Christ, the Savior of the world.

4. America's "theology" of affluence

In his Apostolic Letter written on the occasion of the eightieth anniversary of the Encyclical "Rerum novarum," Pope Paul VI explained the meaning of Christian charity:

"In teaching us charity, the Gospel instructs us in the preferential respect due to the poor and the special situation they have in society: the more fortunate should renounce some of their rights so as to place their goods more generously at the service of others."[15]

Elsewhere in the same letter, the Pontiff points to the dangers of technology:

"Unlimited competition utilizing the modern means of publicity incessantly launches new products and tries to attract the consumer, while earlier industrial installations which are still capable of functioning become useless. While very large areas of the population are unable to satisfy their primary needs, superfluous needs are created. It can thus rightly be asked if, in spite of all his conquests, man is not turning back against himself the results of his activity. Having rationally endeavored to control nature, is he not now becoming the slave of the objects which he makes?"[16]

The Holy Father previously expressed these same ideas in another encyclical letter:

"Increased possession is not the ultimate goal of nations nor of individuals. All growth is ambivalent. It is essential if man is to develop as a man, but in a way it imprisons man if he considers it the supreme good, and it restricts his vision. Then we see hearts harden and minds close, and men no longer gather together in friendship but out of self-interest which soon leads to opposition and disunity. The exclusive pursuit of possessions thus becomes an obstacle to individual fulfillment and to man's true greatness. Both for nations and for individual men, avarice is the most evident form of moral under-development."[17]

John Kenneth Galbraith coined the phrase "economic theology" in order to indicate the idolatrous commercial value-system to which many if not most Americans unthinkingly subscribe. The word "theology" seems to have been deliberately chosen, both because the canons of this system of thought are accepted as irrevocable and because it constitutes the principal motivating-force in our nation's life-style. Geared almost exclusively to material growth, it concentrates on the idea of consuming more comfortable and better things. With the precision of a surgeon, the poet Robinson Jeffers cuts to the core of this "theology":

"We must adapt our economy to the new abundance...
Of what? Toys, motors, music-boxes,
Papers, fine clothes, leisure, diversion."[18]

The dazzling euphoria depicted in TV and magazine advertisements, and the promises of happiness which they offer, are popular expressions of this "theology." But by catering to and creating for man an insatiable appetite for more and more material things, by appealing to the desires of a consumer public, this "theology" has become divorced from the poor man's experience. In fact, the poor soon become subjected to numerous negative prejudices.

Meanwhile, poor fathers weep in tenements because their children have been bitten by rats; unscrupulous slum-lords exact the last "pound of flesh" from the helpless, weak and downtrodden, and frightened adolescents hang themselves out of desperate misery. I am beginning to believe that perhaps the social analyst, Gunnar Myrdal, was correct when he wrote: "...when the problem presents itself as a question of redistributing income and organizing collective consumption through public measures...the majority of Americans have become hardhearted and stingy."[19]

The problems still exist. As a believer in the Gospel and the teachings of the Church, I must bring the wisdom of the Word of God to this economic value-system: "This has taught us love—that He gave up His life for us; and we, too, ought to give up our lives for our brothers. If a man who was rich enough in this world's goods saw that one of his brothers was in need, but closed

his heart to him, how could the love of
God be living in him? My children, our
love is not to be just words or mere talk,
but something real and active" (1 Jo. 3:16-
18). This is the wisdom which the Church
obliges us to apply at every level of our national and individual consciousness.

I admit that generalizations are open to
divergent interpretations, but a conscientious and empirical examination of our
collective ego, appears to capture at least
this truth: we have in so many ways closed
our hearts to our poor brothers! As yet, the
massive potential of our nation's economic
power has not been turned to the monumental suffering found in our cities. A walk
from Dudley Street to Upham's Corner
verifies the accusation that the Kerner
Report has received only a token response
and implementation.

We have made real progress, but we are
apt to forget that promises of a better future
do not automatically anesthetize the pain
of the poor man's present condition. By
failing to re-organize radically our nation's
way-of-life and economic priorities, we are
displaying an insulting insensitivity to the
suffering of our brothers. In reality, we are
asking them to feel content to be the reci-
pients of whatever might be left over from
our superfluous goods—while the majority
continues to live better than ever.

But it would be wrong to place all the
blame on the government, economists, etc.
Most of us subscribe to the values of "eco-

nomic theology," even within the Church. The warning of the Apostle James is a part of our Christian heritage: "My brothers, what use is it for a man to say he has faith when he does nothing to show it? Can that faith save him? Suppose a brother or a sister is in rags with not enough food for the day, and one of you says, 'Good luck to you, keep yourselves warm, and have plenty to eat,' but does nothing to supply these bodily needs, what good is that? So with faith; if it does not lead to action, it is in itself a lifeless thing" (James 2:14-17). In answer to this challenge, and despite the evidence of degrading poverty, the average contribution to the Church's Campaign for Human Development—the response of the Church in America to Pope Paul VI's cry to "break the hellish circle of poverty"—was only 14¢!

There is another cry born from America's "economic theology" which is equally opposed to the Gospel of reconciliation. It is heard when blacks or other minority groups begin to move into a neighborhood; and it is heard when the question of low-cost housing is raised in our affluent suburban areas. It is always a variation on the theme: "Our property will devaluate." And God's poor continue to be restricted to the areas of squalor.

5. A competing absolute

Due to their sincere, often taxing commitment to areas of social concern, members of the secular community assuredly deserve America's praise. Their name is legion. In a variety of studies and through multiple media, they have exposed the unspeakable living conditions which have taken such a horrendous toll among the helpless poor. In God's mysterious providence, their efforts are having a purifying effect on the Church itself. They are challenging the Church in all its members to give ever greater evidence of the Gospel of love, justice and compassion—and to make ever deeper commitments to the human family.

Adopting the ancient ethic that "man is the measure of all things," the psychological framework of humanism can easily, if it is unqualifiedly accepted, lead men to regard the Church as increasingly irrelevant. It can at the same time beget a disdain for the supernatural, an utter rejection of any transcendent reality. This is particularly prevalent in our day:

"Perhaps the most central and significant change in human awareness involved in the secularization of life has been the great diminution both in scope and relevance, as well as in intensity and immediacy, of the experience of the sacred. This mode of apprehension has been progressively constricted and diluted for Western men and in very many instances has disappeared altogether."[20]

As the atmosphere of the City of Man becomes systematically divorced from the supernatural, a cruel paradox is, I fear, being enacted. Whenever man acts supreme, the way is opened for each individual to play God with others. Thus, the most God-like gift within man — his ability to love and appreciate the truth and goodness in God's world as it is — is slowly lulled to sleep.

I do not deny the value of passionate indignation, especially in the cause of justice and compassion, but many of the issues in the city today are distorted by man's temptation to self-righteousness. Men become so intoxicated with their own insights as to how things ought to be that all they do is criticize destructively, and this simply adds to the confusion.

6. The world of abstractions

The Fathers of the Second Vatican Council have instructed us that there can never be any true social progress apart from a sensitive awareness of the individual.

"Man's social nature makes it evident that the progress of the human person and the advance of society hinge on each other. From the beginning, the subject and the goal of all human institutions is and must be the human person, which for its part and by its very nature stands completely in need of social life." [21]

And it appears to me that there is a type of indecency in our generalized, abstract approach to so many of our social questions.

We casually refer to the "problem of public housing," or the "black problem," or the "Puerto Rican problem," or the "Chicano problem," or the "Indian problem," or the "Portuguese problem," forgetting that these children of God are expected to accept what is said about them by the majority. Soon they begin to feel that they do constitute a problem. Have we ever reflected how a man feels being "a problem"? What a potential for human degradation! Moreover, abstractions and generalizations cannot convey the appalling living conditions which make housing a matter of great urgency to millions of Americans. Anthony Downs, in summing up the situation as it exists, forcefully illustrates this point:

"...most Americans have no conception of the filth, degradation, squalor, overcrowding, and personal danger and insecurity which millions of inadequate housing units are causing both in our cities and rural areas. Thousands of infants are attacked by rats each year; hundreds die or become mentally retarded from eating lead paint that falls off cracked walls; thousands more are ill because of unsanitary conditions resulting from jamming large families into a single room, continuing failure of landlords to repair plumbing or provide proper heat, and pitifully inadequate storage space. Until you have actually stumbled through ill-lit and decaying rooms of a slum dwelling, smelled the stench of sewage and garbage and dead rats behind the walls, seen the roaches and crumbling plaster and incredibly filthy bathrooms, and recoiled from exposed wiring and rotting floorboards and staircases, you have no real ideal of what bad housing is like." [22]

To overlook or dismiss the sensitivities of individual living human beings by reducing them to abstractions or static categories inevitably leads to the devaluation and destruction of life. The recent Report of the President's Commission on Population Control advocating "abortion on demand" indicates that social planners, despite protestations, are not exempt from this tendency. Life, in this case the unprotected life of the unborn child, was simply reduced to a statistic. The problem was clearly posed in clinical and quantitative terms: "We have looked for, and have not found, any convincing economic argument for continued population growth. The health of our country does not depend on it, nor does the vitality of business nor the welfare of the average person." [23] And in a world which prides itself on such statistical analysis, it is all too easy to justify with a sociological explanation the destruction of God's unborn children!

It is unfortunate that so many Americans have placed an almost unconditioned faith in the tidy, preconceived systems of order constructed by social engineers who are frequently removed from meaningful dialogue with and awareness of the people involved. In the last analysis, man cannot be generalized or geometrized, subjected to blue-prints and time-tables that are geared to commercial pursuits. The poor above all, should not be treated as merely "objects of investigation." Approaches of this type are, indeed, subtle forms of dehumanizing aggression. Still, the "world of abstractions" continues to be a persuasive force in the City of Man today. Throughout the city of Boston, for example, the residents of many housing-projects have been subjected to countless investigations, while their life and surroundings steadily deteriorate year after year. And few of our poor, generally only the most articulate, are readily accepted by social planners as co-investigators in dialogue.

The real battlefield of the "War on Poverty" is in the human heart, and it is to the heart that the Gospel speaks.

B. CONFUSION IN THE CHURCH

1. "The Death of God" Life-Style

In this age of awkward transition, there can be no doubt that many within the people of God, even priests and religious, are confused. At the first sight of unjust and involuntary poverty, their noble instincts compel them to react against its ugliness with instant compassion and love. But even their best efforts seem unable to stem the tide of confusion in the city. Some soon feel themselves in the grip of external forces over which they have no control. Urban life is so swift that everything seems inevitable.

Feeling powerless, they are likely to lose a sense of purpose.

Frustration and failure — in the world's sense of the term — have shattered many good men and women to their psychic and spiritual depths. They desire to be of service to life. In searching for responses to basic human needs, however, they have exhausted themselves by expending energy in a hundred different directions: procuring houses, clothes, food and other basic necessities; also, counseling, visiting the sick and tending to other human needs. But needs still exist and grow ever more pressing each day. Soon, a feeling of futility arises. Others do not seem to be listening to their apostolic cries for help. Some brood over such a slight. In these circumstances a disenchantment with the so-called "institutional" Church, however they may justify it, can easily become a temptation even to those who have consecrated their lives to it.

In a sense, I understand and sympathize with what is happening to them and to all of us. Dreaming of the future, men can begin to feel that the past has outlived its usefulness. The whole world appears to them to be moving on the pivot of permanent change. There is a compulsion to identify the new with the true. Such constant change, coupled with this thrust to identify the new with the true, often contributes to a breakdown of internalized norms and personal value-systems. And men in the midst of such chaos and confusion can hardly develop to their fullest human potential. Confusion threatens a person's ego and self-identity; it challenges the creative capacity of man's supreme faculty—his mind.

The Church in the cities, however, offers us a source of great hope. We esteem and admire the many priests and religious who love their people and are so beloved by them. Theirs is a ministry of surrendering themselves to the needs of others. A singleness of purpose marks their mission: to give a more abundant life, both natural and supernatural life. They are transforming the ugliness and shoddiness of the urban world into a more beautiful opportunity to live and to love. Because of the criticism they have received from so many who fail to understand and appreciate their efforts, they have felt the mystery of the cross carved into their own hearts. My own warm, heartfelt admiration for them cannot be compressed into a few sincere words.

Even though they may never waver in intensity, they, too, find themselves emotionally buffeted by the same confusing atmosphere which befogs the clear course of the Church in the City of Man. On the surface there seem to be signals pointing to a "new Christianity." Its "doctrine" revolves around a passionate concern for healing man's body, almost to exclusion of saving his soul. However, I cannot accept the tendency to reduce the role and meaning of the Eucharist to man's quest for

earthly bread, i.e. good housing, good sani-
tation, good education, etc. Many attempt
to reduce our Sacred Tradition to a simple
phrase: "God is love." This is true as far as
it goes and in all its ramifications. But some
make the effective realization of a limited
notion of God's love the unique value in the
City of Man. They summarily dismiss and
even challenge the need for worship, religious education and prayer. Others start to
lose their enthusiasm and love for the very
Church they pledged themselves to serve
and which they can help sanctify by their
own lives of total dedication. Instead, they
sound as though they are "apologizing apostles," personally ashamed of "the system"
and unable to bear the burden of its faults.
When on every side we hear elevated to the
highest values of our times the cries of "self-
fulfillment" and "full humanity," such an
orientation is almost natural. The quest for
human fulfillment has value. But so often it
leads only to unreflective and faithless
activism.

I do not doubt the subjective sincerity of
many who have embraced the creed of self-
fulfillment. But so often, its concrete expressions lack those convincing qualities of
tolerance, patience, and courtesy which
St. Paul describes as characteristic of true
Christ-like love. Commenting upon our
modern tendency toward a similar type of
religionless Christianity, C. B. Armstrong
warns us: "We have to know Christ before
we know what love is: Christ the historical

man who died on the Cross, and Christ the invisible King who rose into the future from the dead. And knowing him, we have to worship; and worshipping him we have to express his majesty in acts, symbols and places and words."[24]

Again, the paradoxical condition of our age appears. At the very time when men are still searching for the presence of God and have for the moment allowed themselves to be lured by the perennial idols of affluence, technology and humanism, — our Christian quest for "relevance" in the City of Man is slowly turning our churches into tombs of God. Instead of opposing modern idolatry with true worship of God, the main thrust and sometimes the central concern for some is to make God conform to the ideals of secular society. At this point, the "death of God" becomes realized by those who in the same breath loudly proclaim a living faith in the Lord.

2. Prejudice in the Church

A scholastic definition states that prejudice is "thinking ill of others without sufficient warrant." A generation ago, those charged with the care of the human spirit were both distressed and surprised that members of Christian churches in this country were more prejudiced than non-churchgoers.[25] Unfortunately the phenomenon of people being Church-affiliated and, at the same time, being highly prejudiced has not disappeared.

The well-publicized admonition of the mythical hero, Harry Yucca, to keep force-fully the "niggers" out of a local white high-school, must make everyone wonder whether the commandment of brotherhood is taken seriously, even in a strongly Catholic area of Boston.[26] No one so far has been able to explain the complex character and societal context of prejudice. Extensive studies have been and are still being made.

But in so far as it leads to segregation, discrimination and a denial of rights, it departs from the Gospel message of recon-ciliation and justice. This is wrong.

In so far as it is a matter of gross in-sensitivity and over-generalization, it de-parts from the Gospel message of respect and love for the individual person. This is wrong.

In so far as it entails contempt, rejection and condescension, it departs from the Gospel teaching that we are all children of the Father. This is wrong.

And it would be wrong to believe that prejudice is confined only to certain areas of our cities or only to certain lower-income classes. Prejudice rears its ugly head even in rather unlikely places and in seemingly harmless phrases like: "They wouldn't be happy in my neighborhood," or "I wouldn't mind selling to them, but I have to consider my neighbors," or "They are known to be lazy and uneducated," etc. The list of catch-phrases is as endless as it is depressing. In suburbia "economic theology" feeds prejudice with the fear that "property will devaluate."

Christianity was not meant to be taken in convenient, casual doses. It demands that we commit ourselves whole-heartedly to Christ's Gospel of love and justice for one another.

PART II
A Message to My People

Christ's holiness possesses the power to redeem all mankind and all of nature. He has willed that His redemptive mission be shared by us through our daily efforts. Redemption is a living work and the individual Christian is a living "sacrament" of Christ's presence in and to the world. The hard doctrine of the New Testament is that the individual believer, in living for others, must also daily die to self. "Every day we experience something of the death of Jesus, so that we may also know the power of the life of Jesus in these bodies of ours. Yes, we who are living are always being exposed to death for Jesus' sake, so that the life of Jesus may be plainly seen in our mortal lives. We are always facing death, but this means that you know more and more life" (2 Cor. 4:10-11).

Unjust poverty is a vast area where redemption is yet to be accomplished. The followers of Christ, by giving up all thought of self, must labor to make it a reality. The cities today offer a concrete invitation to continue Christ's saving work. Those who are entombed in degrading, lifeless poverty

are our brothers in Christ and, like ourselves, they are called to the fullness of His
life. And we are all called to be our brother's brother — instruments of His redemption.

Concern for reconciliation and for the
poor is an integral part of the Church's
sacred and cherished tradition. History is
my witness. From the beginning, the apostolic community practiced a common sharing of material and spiritual goods, and this
sharing represented their spontaneous
awareness of being a community of "one
heart and soul" (Acts 2:44). In a deep, unchanging way, this primitive consciousness
has remained throughout the history of the
Church's constant care and charity, especially toward the poor and the helpless.

Sacrificial sharing remains a unique, visible sign that we are "one in Christ." This
mystical reality lies at the very heart of
Christian life. St. Paul had a particular
horror of sins against the common life — of
divisions which existed between rich and
poor, of barriers of race or nationality, of
indifference of one toward another. His
consciousness of the meaning of Christian
community, a common life shared in Christ,
prompted him to organize collections of
money from the Christians in "Gentile
churches" on behalf of the poverty-stricken
Christians in Jerusalem (1 Cor. 16.). Again
and again throughout his letters, he warned
those who were wealthy that to ignore, even
materially, the common needs of others was

a sin. And St. James warned rich Christians against despising the poor, against ridiculing and abusing them in their weakness. Never would he permit them to make distinctions between classes and always, he reminded them, they are to love the brothers as they love themselves (James 2:1-9).

Elsewhere in the New Testament the reason for the Church's burning concern for the poor is even more clearly explained. The triumphant resurrection and ascension of the Son of Man does not remove Christ from the sufferings of this world. As its Savior, He is forever identified with the whole of suffering humanity—the hungry, the thirsty, the outcast—wherever they are (Mt. 25:35-36). His is an identification with every single unfortunate person. With terrifying pointedness, the Evangelist concludes that in each and every man, woman or child who claims my help, I meet my Savior, Christ Himself, and my Judge.

The heart of Christian love which has its origin in God is simply this: "You did it unto me." I love Christ by loving my brother when he is in need. And I am called to seek out those who are naked and poor, since at times their inhuman condition may prevent them from coming to me. I must search for those who are hungry and in prison, since they are too proud to beg or feel too lowly to come to me for help. I must do these things not simply because I want to do good, but rather because I wish to find Christ where He said He would be "in the least of my brothers." They are the naked and hungry and poor whom I seek to confer Christ's own blessing on me. In a most "shocking" way they make Christ real to me.

In the Bible the human person is considered in such realistic terms that hunger for food is not less important than the hunger of the spirit. Although the spiritual hunger of man was the primary concern of Christ's mission, still the measure of His judgment of us as members of His Church will also include our care and consideration for those who suffer bodily hunger and thirst and neglect. And since all men are brothers, the Church's concern must not be limited to the community of believers. Throughout Sacred Scripture God shows His constant predilection for the poor and outcasts everywhere.

Beginning with the Book of Exodus, we find that God is the Savior of the Oppressed. He threatened to punish those who afflicted the poor ones who cried out to him (Ex. 22:21-27). Apart from fear of judgment, however, a more noble motivation for helping the poor is given when God identified himself with the afflicted (Ex. 3:7-8). In the words of Edward Sunshine: "The God of Exodus, the 'God of the Hebrews' was the God of a people without rights."[27]

There can be little doubt that the City of Man today still needs examples of this same preferential love for the poor and the suffering. Redemptive truth demands living witness. Men find hard to believe what they cannot see and touch. Ultimately, the solving of our cities' problems will involve suffering for all of us. The Christ of the cross calls us to personal sacrifice and to a painful restructuring of attitudes, but this is the only way to our individual and social resurrection. Can the Church be worthy to be called Christ's Body, the bearer of His message, if it is not also willing to follow His same unaccommodating path?

In the light of what I have set down so far in this letter, I make the following recommendations:

Priests of the Archdiocese. To the priests above all has been given the awesome responsibility of proclaiming and representing the central event of our faith to the world: that God has spoken His Word in answer to mankind's search for truth. His Word was made flesh and dwelt among us. His Word is the true light that enlightens all men, and to all who accept Him He gives power to become children of God. No one has ever seen God; it is only the Son who has made Him known (Jo. 1:9-18). His Son's Gospel must be preached in season and out of season.

Recent studies of the communication-process have emphasized the importance of non-verbal language as an aid or obstacle to effective discourse: "In addition to what we say with our verbal language," Edward Hall observes, "we are constantly communicating our real feelings in our silent language, the language of behavior."[28] In other words, what a man says will be heard only to the degree that he offers himself as a convincing witness to the truth he proclaims, only as his life itself reflects his wholehearted commitment to the validity of his statements. Simply stated, the priest as "sacrament" can be the most evocative and compelling sign of the Gospel.

Thus, in the light of the problems of our cities and the Church's mission to proclaim the mystery of Christ to the world, the priest cannot be content merely to preach the need of reconciliation and sacrificial sharing. He must enflesh the Gospel in his own life. Ultimately, he must become a symbol of evangelical poverty for his people. He must oppose America's scandalous quest for comfort and elegance with Christ's simplicity of life and love for the poor.

We must all judge ourselves, our lifestyle within the rectory and the parish, as well as our consciences before God to see whether we may have personally failed to be convincing symbols and messengers of Christ's Church.

Each Vicariate. With the formation of the newly increased Vicariate system, it is the responsibility of the Archdiocesan Human Rights' Commission to set up a series of monthly discussion groups, in each Vicariate, on the general subject of "social justice" in the light of Vatican II. It is part of our heritage that the truth will make us free. As an Archdiocese, we can no longer afford to find comfort and reassurance in illusions. We must speak plainly with confidence and charity. And because a man learns best what he experiences, specific projects with realistic goals in the area of social justice are to be incorporated into our instruction.

"Within the word we find two dimensions, reflection and action, in such radical interaction that if one is sacrificed—even in part— the other immediately suffers. There is no true word that is not at the same time a praxis. Thus, to speak a true word is to transform the world."[29]

It is only through such an integrated approach that we can begin to detect our imperfections toward our suffering brothers and the inadequacies of our ideas of "justice" and "equality."

Visitors for Christ.[30] The importance of this lay movement lies in a prosaic fact: individuals demand respect. Without respect dialogue becomes little more than meaningless talk. Unfortunately, the over-powering combination of ignorance and fear in the City of Man has blunted and, at times, obliterated this respect. One of the indecipherable sins of our age is that the invisible strands which normally should bind men to their brothers—since all men are God's children—have been senselessly slashed. The geography of our cities shows that there are few common interests between the rich and poor, and even fewer shared experiences between black and white and other minority groups.

If we deny a man his place in the larger community, it is inevitable that he will come to reject those whom he feels have rejected him. This type of rejection, coupled with a deeply felt futility, gnaws at self-respect. Man has to be touched by an awareness of the possibility of hope. I have chosen the "Visitors for Christ" movement, which I inaugurated in Brownsville, to be our common pastoral approach to dissolve those ghettos of hatred and mistrust which separate men from one another. My Senate of Priests agrees with me. In the last analysis, the future shape of our society will depend basically upon the heightened concern and care man has for his fellowman, and not merely upon social conventions such as culture, education or systems of law, vital as these may be.

— To souls plunged in bitterness, the movement aims at announcing the truly Good News that God loves them.

— To individuals suffering from non-recognition and neglect it offers the presence of Christian warmth and respect.

— To a people who have been subjected to callous manipulation and exploitation, it exhibits the spirit of true love and self-giving shown to all by Christ.

— To a vague feeling of dedication which so many with sincere hearts want to express, it offers an opportunity to concretize their good will.

— To those who still do not understand the real meaning of the wound of unwanted human poverty, it reveals God's special consecration of the poor. Through their sufferings they are mystically united with Christ.

— And above all, amid the city's often depressing atmosphere, the Visitors for Christ must re-establish mutual respect.

The very root of the word respect (re-spicere, i.e. to look at) demands that we learn to see every person as he is, a unique child of God. Eric Fromm describes respect as "the concern that the other person should grow and unfold as he is. Respect, thus, implies the absence of exploitation; it is a desire that the other person grow and unfold for his own sake not just for the purpose of serving me."[31] At the heart of learning what respect is, there is always the necessity of seeing each person in the graphic terms of his actual situation. Otherwise, men find it hard to believe and their generosity remains unchallenged.

In his message of the New Year 1972 celebrated as the Day of Peace, Pope Paul VI equates this sincere feeling and true respect for man with Justice:

Difficult though it is, we must form an authentic notion of peace. It is difficult for the person who closes his eyes to the primal intuition which tells us that peace is the most human of realities. This is the royal road we should travel in trying to discover genuine peace. If we seek its true source, we perceive that it is rooted in the sincere feeling for man. A peace that does not well up from the true veneration of man is not peace in truth. And what do we call this sincere feeling for man? We call it justice.[32]

In this context, furthermore, we can appreciate that oppressive and unwanted suffering has its own peculiar language which is not always to be taken literally. Failure to understand the language of this suffering has often contributed to the breakdown in dialogue. Vulgarity, for example, is often little more than the wounded cry of someone whose spirit has been broken or whose dignity has been denied.

It is not dreaming that leads me to see in the "Visitors for Christ" a partial solution for many of our urban ills; rather is it an honest awareness of evil and of its consequences. What evil is and what it destroys demands that we conquer it by Christ's more powerful and redeeming love.

Parish Communities. The spirit of Catholicism must take on flesh in order to communicate itself. The divine Word must come alive with acts of urgent compassion in the heart of the Christian community. In conjunction with the "Visitors for Christ" movement, I ask that Parish Priests and our Parish Councils adopt in their parishes the "parish sharing" program. I believe that our common life in the Body of Christ demands this.

A bridge must be built over the double abyss of despair and degrading poverty. No one who is a follower of Christ can rest passively content commenting upon the hungry faces of children, the twisted bodies of derelicts and the hollow eyes of the aged and homeless. We must do more than stammer with embarrassment or anger, when reminded of the inferior level of citizenship which much of America has indifferently bestowed upon the helpless poor. Whatever the issue—job opportunities, educational facilities, housing, health care facilities, etc.—the poor consistently seem to come off second best.

Even if all our parishes would participate in these "parish sharing" programs, I realize that there would never be enough money to solve our many urban ills. And yet, in my role as spiritual leader of the Archdiocese, I am trying to raise the problem to a spiritual level where every dollar and every positive gesture become a symbol of hope, a sign someone cares. The Archbishop's Stewardship Appeal is made on this level. The late Senator Robert Kennedy saw something of the truth I am suggesting:

"It is from numberless diverse acts of courage and belief that human history is shaped. Each time a man stands up for an ideal, or acts to improve the lot of others, or strikes out against injustice, he sends forth a tiny ripple of hope, and crossing each other from a million different centers of energy and daring, those ripples build a current which can sweep down the mightiest walls of oppression and resistance."[33]

It is likewise for this reason that I recommend to our more affluent parishes "the adoption" of inner-city parishes not merely by remote giving, but also by learning to share experiences together. There is too often a patronizing pride in our approach to the poor. Often we feel that we are "bestowing" our favors and assistance upon them, forgetting that they are really affording us an opportunity to serve Christ in them. Such an attitude leads to a flaunting show or a listless sharing of left-overs. But, as I have said repeatedly, "We need one another." Whenever a local parish becomes self-centered, it fails to accomplish its "catholic" mission as a portion of the Church in the world. Besides, there is a beautiful simplicity to the life of the poor which the more affluent members of the Church in America very much need to incorporate into their own often superficial life-style. Elegance and extravagance should not take precedence over basic human needs. We have been conditioned to the comfortable too long, and it is my belief that the poor can teach our affluent society something it has lost—a tenderness for life.

Priests and Religious Actively Involved in the City. I have already expressed my sincerest admiration for those who work in our cities, but I must now explain a principle of Christian spirituality which is frequently overlooked: The ministry of loving and serving the poor is a gift of God. As with all of God's gifts, it demands that we spiritualize ourselves in suffering and prayer in order to appreciate it. Only when one stands in all his nakedness before God, and thus comprehends his own spiritual destitution, can he establish that mystical bond which identifies him with the least of Christ's brethren. The human heart is seldom devoid of self-interest. In order to avoid any selfish manipulation of these precious souls of the poor, true Christian love, which voluntarily embraces the cross, is necessary. But so often, when the idealized grandeur of the cross begins to take its real form of failure, we start to deny the spiritual value of suffering and turn, instead, to self-pity or self-justification. It may be natural — but it is not Christian. It amounts to an implicit denial of the truly resurrectional power of the cross and of the promises of the Risen Christ.

I do not mean to ignore, much less deny, the need at times for righteous indignation and Christian courage. Silence and timidity in the face of evil are the daughters of cowardice, hardly Christian virtues. Rather, I am emphasizing the need for inner-tranquility and peace amid the sufferings of frustration, anxiety and even temporary failure; the need to be aware of the importance of the "sacrament" of self in the City of Man. As the Apostle Paul noted, it is this consciousness of self grounded in Christ crucified which is the key to our apostolic ministry (1 Cor. 1:17). In the Christian dispensation this consciousness comes only through an interior embrace of the cross within our hearts.

In a seldom mentioned act of self-forgetfulness, many of the teaching, nursing and social servicing communities of religious within the Archdiocese have already indicated their "preferential love for the poor." Due to the obvious lack of funds in many urban parishes, these Sisters are attempting to staff "priority" schools and other agencies completely with religious and to provide them with a better quality of education. It seems that some hidden harmony between their own consecrated lives as religious and the haunting cries of poverty in the city have impelled them, under God's grace, to take this decisive and dedicated step. No one gesture, of course, will repair all the intellectual, psychological and spiritual havoc caused by urban poverty. Nevertheless, this is a first step and a clear example of self-sacrifice for the whole Church in the Archdiocese of Boston to admire and imitate.

Finally, granting that vocations are a free gift of God, still we all must make every effort to detect, encourage and foster vocations to the priesthood and the religious life. These efforts of the highest priority will include Archdiocesan programs for the permanent diaconate, especially for those who wish to serve as ministers for minority groups. Their message to the world as well as their work will be an integral part of the Church's mission to the city. Modifications in existing programs will, no doubt, have to be made and the priests and religious now serving in the core cities will have much to contribute to these programs.

The Professional Community. Although I am neither a doctor nor a dentist, I have seen too many sallow faces and neglected teeth which compel me to appeal to the members of the medical community in our city areas to donate still more of their time and professional skill to the health needs of our poverty-stricken communities. Many already have done so, but their efforts are so scattered and the needs are so great. Much more is desperately needed. As the poet, John Donne, said: "No man is an island." One cannot isolate himself in affluent comfort in the midst of a flood of physical disease and mental decay which degrading poverty brings. And this includes men of the medical professions.

I, therefore, ask the members of St. Luke's Guild and the Guild of St. Apolonia to meet with me or my representatives in order to establish new programs or to assist other existing health-programs which already contribute professional services to the poor. Ultimately, this could lead even to the training of members of poverty-stricken and minority groups in the medical professions through scholarships, technical assistance, etc.

Along other lines, St. Thomas Aquinas expressed the idea that "freedom is willing obedience to the law." In every society there must be some correlation between law and personal freedom. Many, unfortunately, are looking for simple solutions to our urban problems by their cries for "law and order." Pope Paul VI has reminded us, "Peace is not a lie made into a system. Much less is it pitiless totalitarian tyranny. Nor is it, in any way, violence."[34] Too often law has been interpreted in the past to favor more the economically advantaged, but as the Roman Pontiff said, "Since a different and better perception of his personality fills the consciousness of man, it is a dynamic justice, and no longer a static justice that is born of his heart. This is not simply an individual phenomenon, nor one reserved for select and restricted groups; it is now a collective and universal phenomenon. It demands a new expression, Justice, a new foundation for Peace."[35] Only when law is linked with this growing awareness of the dignity of all men will law serve man's innate desire to be free and live in peace.

As Americans we have accepted in theory certain principles of dynamic justice, such as those stated in our Constitution and in the United Nation's Declaration of Human Rights. These principles are still far from realization in our day. Thus, I ask the members of the legal profession and legislators to work to implement them and enact them into law so that the poor and defenseless might live in justice and with dignity as God wills us to live on earth. Only in this way will society live in peace and men will not feel the need to violate the law.

For some, this may involve defending the poor and deprived in court or giving them legal counsel. For others, it may mean joining in the laborious work of preparing "class-cases." The agony and the bewilderment of our modern age which recognizes more and more the dynamic dimensions of justice, especially with regard to the helpless and dispossessed, calls everyone to this task. The work of justice is everyone's vocation.

PART III
Dialogue with the Wider Community

The picture of poverty we have depends upon our angle of vision. Through the eyes of the majority the problems of the poor represent a study of continuous progress. The "War on Poverty," the elimination of discriminatory legislation, work-training programs, etc., have all become symbols of America's moral re-awakening.

But the landscape of the cities appears quite different when we gaze at it through the eyes of the poor man. He sees and lives realities which continue to blaspheme God's image in the human person. There is still dilapidated housing and poor education; some stores still continue to charge inflated prices for shoddy goods. The recent report issued by Senator William Proxmire, Chairman of the Joint Economic Committee, confirms the fact that inequalities and inequities still exist. The poor "are asked to pay the price necessary to stop inflation for the rest of society," and, despite cries of progress, the income gap between the poorest and richest has nearly doubled in the last twenty years.

It is because I believe in the high aspirations of the majority of the American people, who pledge themselves to the principles of justice and equality for all that I offer the following recommendations. Although a pluralism of viewpoints exists in our society, I am compelled as the spiritual leader of the Archdiocese to offer my own convictions and practical suggestions to all who are engaged in working for the common good, in order to help banish the disease of debilitating poverty and racism from our society.

Welfare. The malaise of our cities has its roots in the distance between our national ideal and our national reality. We take just pride in the fact that every American has a right to "life, liberty and the pursuit of happiness," but millions of Americans — including many who are crammed together in our urban centers — are unable to satisfy basic human needs. They lack even a frugal standard of living. True social responsibility demands that we meet the needs of men in their actual situation now. It demands that we absorb and transform the hopeless world of the poor into a society of greater security and dignity.

Welfare legislation is one positive way to meet this need. New programs of support for those whose income is inadequate are constantly being proposed. Through the same maze of legislation the principle of justice which should guide our action is this: Whatever types of programs are decided upon by our legislative bodies, the in-kind assistance (food stamps, housing subsidies, etc.) and cash assistance offered should provide every household with the equivalent of an adequate and decent income; i.e., above the officially defined poverty-level for the area. This may well vary from place to place, but it should be the goal of all legislation created to help the poor. Fundamental compassion, a virtue which presupposes we are capable of feeling with our whole being the degradation of the indigent, demands no less.

Because of this principle the United States Catholic Conference and the National Office of Catholic Charities have supported the recent Ribicoff-Bennett Amendment on welfare legislation which explicitly recognized the national goal of providing to every family, through work or assistance, an adequate income. I urge all throughout the Archdiocese to give their support towards the legal acceptance of this same principle. In this land of marvels it is insulting and humiliating to ask the poor to remain imprisoned in the vicious circle of poverty. Moreover, in keeping with the American idea of building a sense of self-determination among the poor, I would publicly favor direct cash assistance, rather than in-kind assistance, since this would provide greater freedom of choice to the individual, and consequently, a greater sense of dignity. Above all, work must be provided for them to safeguard their dignity and to promote their self-respect.

The Mass Media. No one can doubt the important role of the mass media in the arduous task of helping man develop to his full potential. In so many instances the people employed in this field have expanded our radius of empathy and understanding of our fellow man. This has been an invaluable aid to our common effort to infuse life into abstractions like "justice" and "equality."

On the other hand, there is also possible a great deal of diversity of emphasis and subtlety of meaning in our public communication media. It is notable for example that several of the demands of the "Black Manifesto" dealt directly with the communication network in America. These were not merely a matter of unbecoming photographs and the lack of sensitivity to minority groups. Rather it was argued that the affluent majority seldom see what is at stake in many areas. Demonstrators are not necessarily "trouble-makers." Generally they are people calling attention to moral rights and responsibilities which they believe are guaranteed by our Constitution or demanded by the natural law. And the appearance of militancy in the ghetto today is often only a desperate way of telling the rest of America what seems to be wrong and who is responsible. The feeling of many blacks and minority groups is that only the one who has experienced their frustrations and disappointed hopes can honestly interpret these issues to the wider community. Consequently, I endorse the idea that the mass-media incorporate members of minority groups on their staff and particularly in positions where they may interpret the "news" of the world of poverty to the larger community.

The Greeks believed that, in speech, men were most like the gods. Truthful speech — speech which reaches out to our brothers in Godlike compassion and love — should be the constant aim of the mass media.

Education. Children do not always listen to what their parents say, but they almost always imitate what they see their parents do. Despite the lip-service paid to "brotherhood," is it not true that altogether too many of us have sinned against this brotherhood by erecting a segregated society? In view of the deepening division between white and black America — a division which now breeds fear, resentment and hostility — I have publicly endorsed busing as a partial step to break what can only be called the "habit" of segregation. I now repeat my stand.

"I support the Racial Imbalance Act today for the same reasons that the late Cardinal Cushing supported the original legislation in

1965, because, in attempting to guarantee quality integrated education it is right morally. It is to this point of morality that I must adhere.... Cardinal Cushing said that he had signed the Kiernan Report because he was convinced that we had not done enough to provide an integrated education for our city school children, and he concluded... 'Let us not seek our own special advantages but the advantage of all; let no one divide us or set up rivalries among us.' It is from this point of commitment that I exhort those legally mandated to implement this Act to exert their utmost in professional competence and enlightened leadership to fulfill both the spirit and letter of the law in the manner least disruptive for all concerned."

Obviously the complex challenges of urban education must be met boldly and with vision. For example, the central problem of motivation must be confronted. Why do so many of our urban youths "drop out" of school? We are realizing more and more that emotional development, as well as working skills, must be incorporated into future educational curricula. Our educational hopes for the future must also include plans that will insure that every child who leaves school possesses the verbal and mathematical abilities necessary for his or her successful participation in the national economy. Moreover, equal educational opportunity would mean that these abilities should be taught according to the child's cultural capacities and keeping in mind the economic disadvantages of the students who want to learn. This is necessary in the growth of a child's self-esteem, although at present this is not the case—especially in our cities—as the courts in California have noted.

Even though there may not be a fundamental agreement regarding the practical steps necessary for the implementation of these hopes, almost all educators agree that change and experimentation are definitely indicated. I therefore encourage the members of the Archdiocesan Office of Education to plan and evaluate model programs, and to co-operate closely with those who staff our schools in order to utilize effectively all of our resources to meet the future needs of all our students.

Crime. One cannot speak of urban America without at the same time expressing a great sense of compassion for all those who live in areas where their own personal security is constantly threatened. The elderly, forced to live behind bolted and barred doors of their own homes, the parents who are afraid to send their children out to play, the working man who fears the theft of his wages; these and countless others are the cruel examples of the reality of urban America.

As a civilized society we cannot condone and we do not condone unlawful violent actions that lead directly or indirectly to the physical harm of a fellow human being. A civilized society cannot and we do not tolerate organized crime or the criminal activities of any group or any individual. Similarly, no one of us can condone or tolerate the unlawful use of force by those whom we, as members of society, employ by election or selection to promote our common good.

The reaction of many of us to crime in the cities is to call for the return of law and order. That call is in reality a call for repression if by it is meant the simple need of a maximum force to control criminal disruption in a neighborhood or section of a city. However, if we call for a return to order or perhaps to the creation of a new order wherein we recognize and respect the dignity of every man, then we are about our Father's business. Mr. Ramsey Clark, a former Attorney General of the United States, eloquently made this point clear when he wrote:

To insist on the dignity of the individual, to assure his health and education, meaningful employment, decent living conditions to protect his privacy and the integrity of his personality, to exercise his rights though he may be the least among us, to give him power to affect his own destiny — only then can we hope to instill in him a concern for others, for their well-being, their safety and the security of their property. Only then can we bring to him a regard for our society, our institutions and our purpose as a people that will render him incapable of committing crime. [36]

I reassert the long-standing policy of the Archdiocese by which dedicated and zealous priests are assigned as court chaplains and chaplains of correctional institutions within the Archdiocese. On behalf of these devoted men of God, I offer again their services and their expertise for the rehabilitation of those charged and those convicted of crime.

A year ago, I established the policy that all the recreational and school facilities we have in the Archdiocese were to be kept open after school hours and during vacation periods for the use of all the youth of the various parish neighborhoods. I would add to this policy that the young adult men and women already benefiting from their own parish youth programs become involved, under the direction of our C.Y.O. Office, in organizing, assisting and strengthening inner city youth programs.

Crime is the stark manifestation of disorder in our society, a disorder which indicates the serious imbalance of the material over the spiritual values of our traditions. The young in their honesty have found material values empty and the spiritual values scorned by a large number of people in our society. In their depression, as you know, many of our young turn to drugs for relief. It is in the area of drug addiction that we find the occasion for much of the criminal violence on our streets.

Parents must act. They must meet the responsibility which requires that they themselves and their children be well informed on the dangers of drugs and the horrendous consequences of drug addiction.

Within the last year, our Catholic Charitable Office, under my direction, has initiated a drug information program for the priests and sisters of the Archdiocese. These series of seminars are intended to acquaint the priests and sisters and through them, all the people in all the neighborhoods of the Archdiocese with information which, hopefully, will serve as a preventative to drug use. The drug information program shall continue and shall be expanded in the near future. We are also involved in the rehabilitation of young drug abusers in altogether too few centers recently established by us and not fully appreciated by many people.

Housing. The Housing and Urban Development Act of 1968 reaffirmed our national housing goal as: "Realization, as soon as feasible, of a decent home and a suitable living environment for every American family." The fact that this Act acknowledges that there already exist in the public and private sectors of the economy the resources necessary for the realization of this goal, makes the present living conditions in many of our urban areas an even greater national scandal.

Another scandalous indignity is suburban opposition to low and middle-income housing which in effect restricts the poor, especially minority groups, to the cities. Even in the last legislative session in Boston, there was agitation for the repeal of a law enacted to open up the suburbs to the poor. In effect, the message being received by the poor is that a comfortable majority is telling them to rebuild their lives on the hopeless decay of the past.

I have been working with the Archdiocesan Planning Office in mapping out programs for six low and middle-income housing projects throughout the Archdiocese. The Human Rights Committee will establish area programs to work positively in order to change attitudes and to counteract some of the prevailing opposition to housing programs that will help the poor. We must use all the means at our disposal in order to accomplish this work of mercy begun by Christ and entrusted to His Church on earth.

Metropolitan Government. Since the United States Conference of Mayors, in 1966, it has been acknowledged that the problems of the city cannot be solved unless we think in terms of the entire metropolitan area. No matter what the issue may be — housing, education, etc. — there is simply not enough money in our cities to meet the ever increasing needs. More and more social analysts are telling us that new structures of regional government are necessary.

The Federal Highway Act of 1962, the Housing and Urban Development Act of 1965, and the Demonstration Cities Act of 1966 have already indicated that the new problems of the 70's demand metropolitan and regional coordination. Recent court decisions have likewise shown the necessity of suburban involvement in the cities' problems. If we are ever to meet the cities' pressing needs, it appears that the establishment of area-wide planning bodies will be mandatory, as they are already by reason of federal funds in the areas of transportation, water, and air pollution, etc.

Thus far, regional planning boards have generally failed to give a proportionate voice to the people involved. Instead of the democratic "one man, one vote," they seem to have canonized as their guiding principle "one mayor, one vote." Michael Harrington has perceptively analysed the result: "The middle-class and white suburbs of 40,000 and 50,000 were 'equal' to the central city with its hundreds of thousands of black and white poor."[37] From this power base, the more affluent could legitimately continue to determine the policies that prejudice the indigent. Hence, whatever area-wide bodies are established in the future, it is morally imperative that a representative voice be given to the people involved.

Employment. It may be wrong, but in America a man is evaluated by what he does. Man's strength and self-respect seem to be measured in proportion to his earning power. The Federal Government recognized the debilitating impact of unemployment and in the Employment Act of 1946 assumed the responsibility of creating and maintaining "conditions under which there will be afforded useful employment opportunities, including self-employment for those able, willing, and seeking to work, and to promote maximum employment, production and purchasing power."

By any definition, Massachusetts' varying unemployment rate of at least 7% remains a sad reality. Of all the failures we have to face in dealing with the problems of the poor, one of the greatest is our failure to provide them with jobs.

When a nation's life-style is rigorously guided by commercial priorities, it is all too easy to overlook the poor man. A century and a half ago, John Adams wrote: "The poor man's conscience is clear; yet he is ashamed — He feels himself out of the sight of others, groping in the dark. Mankind takes no notice of him. He rambles and wanders unheeded. In the midst of a crowd, at church, in the market...he is in as much obscurity as he would be in a garret or a cellar. He is not disapproved, censured, or reproached; he is only not seen.... To be wholly overlooked, and to know it, is intolerable." [38] Self-respect and self-confidence demand that each man feels that he is making a personal contribution to the community in which he lives.

The immediate problem, then, is to enable the vast majority of the poor to achieve personal financial security where they live now. Private business should make investments that will provide a large number of productive jobs for the poor with a very real possibility of advancement. Some foresee that eventually it may be necessary to incorporate these social priorities in the tax system in such a way that businesses will be motivated to make such contributions. Employment to positions in the field of public services—in health, welfare, recreation, etc.—must also be expanded, as the President's Automation Commission suggested.

Finally, organized labor itself which has always been in the forefront of social change must critically re-examine its policies. Charges are being heard that labor has suddenly grown bureaucratic with power and become an agent of the "status quo." Honesty forces us to admit that, in the past, its policies have been discriminatory towards many minority groups.

In order to provide jobs for the poor, all of us together—including government, business and labor—must direct our energies to make "full employment" a national reality.

College students. No one in society, and especially the poor, can seriously challenge the larger community without academic ability and knowledge. I, therefore, propose that our college students offer their time to one of the Archdiocesan agencies which are already dealing with some of the challenges in our cities. Both on an individual basis, e.g., tutoring, and on the level of reforming wider structures which are responsible for so much of our urban poverty, there are opportunities to utilize their talents and good will. I refer to our Apostolate to the Spanish Speaking, the Vicar for Urban Affairs, the Human Rights Commission, and the Archdiocesan Planning Office for Urban Affairs. Perhaps several of the colleges and interested students might collaborate in a series of studies, such as the purpose and practice of "blockbusting" and the social consequences it has upon our urban areas. The "Organization for Just Housing" in Baltimore offers a practical example for this type of effort.

The landscape of much of Boston and other communities of the Archdiocese exhibits vast spaces of leveled housing where people once lived and laughed. Here and there are abandoned or charred frames of homes that still stand like sad markers over empty tombs.

In some of these cities, it is said, the poor have been confined within ghettos for the sake of profit. Without detailed evidence it would be wrong to make such an assertion about the cities throughout the Archdiocese. Moreover, we can never expect change without also proposing to the financial community alternative priorities and constructive policies.

The charting of our cities' future course, therefore, cannot be plotted with good will alone, and this is why we ask the help and expertise of those who are knowledgeable and learned as well.

Sensitivity Training. In the public-service sector efforts are now being made to provide sensitivity training programs for personnel. In essence these programs aim to teach individuals or groups to see and feel things as others do, to have compassion for one another. These efforts should be increased, especially in the delicate areas of teacher-training, the fire and police departments, and throughout the entire judicial system. Law enforcement must be firm but also humane and sensitive to particular situations. Not until we identify ourselves with the poor will we truly understand their terror and despair as they stand helplessly before the authority and the law. And, as history teaches us, to fail to understand the world of the poor is the surest guarantee of national failure.

Elderly. It is mostly our senior citizens, those whose only riches are mostly memories, who are particularly hurt by cost-of-living increases and inflation. During the past legislative session, bills were intro-

duced in the Massachusetts State Legislature calling for fifty percent reduction in the
cost of public utilities for the elderly. I
would wholeheartedly support such measures, and I look forward to further legislation in other areas which will ease the financial burden on those elderly who are
obliged to live on fixed meager incomes.

*To my brothers in the community of
suffering.* I am no stranger to the problems
of poverty. Money was never plentiful in
our immigrant family. Like so many others,
I had to interrupt my education in order to
work because my family simply needed my
help.

As this letter has tried to make clear, the
staggering evidence of unjust poverty has
called forth every ounce of my Christian
compassion. I have asked the wider community to share that suffering which a restructuring of attitudes entails. I have
urged them to grasp your sense of futility
and to pledge their support of your deepest
hopes and yearnings.

The violence of the few — be they black
or white — who have called for hatred and
revolution, for racism to meet racism, must
likewise be challenged and condemned.
When the elderly are confined within their
walls for fear of violence; when innocent
police and firemen are subjected to abuse
and threats of violence in the pursuit of
their duty; when men are called "pigs" and
racial epithets and their property is sense-

lessly vandalized because of racial or ethnic reasons; when one's bodily freedom and integrity are violated in broad day-light in our streets, these and similar acts of criminal violence must be severely condemned. Although I may be accused of raising a simplistic voice, I feel I must teach that the true way to power is the "scandal of the cross," the redemptive power of Christ who transforms all things. Dr. Martin Luther King captured this idea, when he wrote:

"Our most fruitful course is to stand firm, move forward non-violently, accept the disappointments and cling to hope. Our determined refusal not to be stopped will eventually open the door to fulfillment. By recognizing the necessity of suffering in a righteous cause, we may achieve our humanity's full stature. To guard ourselves from bitterness, we need the vision to see in this generations' ordeals the opportunity to transfigure both ourselves and American society." [39]

I, too, am fully convinced that the Risen Christ standing before us with His wounds now resplendent in glory is the only power relevant to today's urban struggles.

Conclusion. I realize that my words will bear more fruit, if I testify to them with my life. Thus, I offer the city all that I am, and such as I am. Should any crisis-situation arise, or dialogue break down or emotions escalate, I pledge that, if asked, I will offer my services directly whenever possible or through a personal delegate in the honest role of mediator. I cannot pretend to have the wisdom of Solomon, but I do have good-will and the belief that many of these problems can be eased by men of courage and vision, and by God's good grace.

＊＊＊＊＊

My beloved Brothers and Sisters in Christ:

As I prayerfully send you this rather lengthy pastoral letter on the Feast of the Assumption of Mary, Mother of the Church, I need not remind you that our one Mediator, is Christ Jesus who gave Himself as ransom for all (1 Tim. 2:5-6). But the maternal duty of Mary toward men in no way obscures or diminishes the unique mediation of Christ. Rather does it more abundantly show the divine power and pleasure. Taken up to heaven, Mary did not lay aside her saving role of continuing to intercede for us. Hence, the Church rightly looks to Her especially on this Feast of the Assumption so that through the Church Christ may be reborn and grow in the hearts of us all.

O Mary, Comforter of the Afflicted, hear us!

O Mary, Refuge of Sinners, pray for us now and at the hour of our death!

NOTES

1. Robert Coles, *The South Goes North,* Atlantic Little, Brown (Boston) 1972.

2. Thomas Merton, *Faith and Violence,* University of Notre Dame Press (Notre Dame) 1968, p. 147.

3. Archbishop Medeiros, Homily of Mass of Installation, *The Pilot,* October 10, 1970.

4. *Pastoral Constitution on the Church in the Modern World,* 1.

5. *Ibid.,* 41.

6. *Ibid.,* 11.

7. Pope John XXIII, Opening Speech to the Council, October 11, 1962.

8. 1 Jo. 2:15-16.

9. Lewis Mumford, *The City in History,* A Harbinger Book (New York) 1961, p. 546.

10. Oliver Oldman and Henry Aaron, "Assessment-Sales Ratios under Boston Property Tax," *National Tax Journal,* March 1965.

11. *Department of Labor Manpower Report, 1966.*

12. Michael Harrington, *Toward a Democratic Left,* Macmillan Company, (New York) 1968, p. 64.

13. *Counterbudget,* ed. by R. Benson and Harold Wolman, Praegar Press (New York), 1971, p. 93.

14. Merton, *op. cit.,* p. 148.

15. Pope Paul VI, *Octogesima Adveniens,* (May 14, 1971), 23.

16. *Ibid.,* 9.

17. Pope Paul VI, Encyclical, *Populorum Progressio,* 19.

18. Michael Harrington, *The Accidental Century,* Penguin Books (Baltimore) 1965, p. 161.

19. Gunnar Myrdal, *Challenge to Affluence,* Vintage Books (New York) 1965, p. 55.

20. *The Religious Situation 1968,* ed. by Donald Cutler, Beacon Press (Boston) 1968, p. 809. Guy E. Swanson in "Modern Secularity: Its Meaning, Sources and Interpretations" cites this quotation from a paper delivered by O'Dea at the sesquicentennial anniversary of the founding of Harvard's Divinity School.

21. *Pastoral Constitution on the Church in the Modern World,* 25.

22. Anthony Downs, "Moving Toward Realistic Housing Goals," in *Agenda for the Nation*, ed. by Kermet Gordon, Doubleday and Company (New York) 1968, p. 143.

23. Letter of John D. Rockefeller 3rd, Chairman of the Commission on Population Growth and the American Future, to the President and Congress of the United States announcing the findings and recommendations of the Commission.

24. C. B. Armstrong, "Christianity without Religion," *New Theology No. 2*, Macmillan Company (New York) p. 27.

25. Gordon Allport, "Personal Religious Orientation and Prejudice" in *The Person in Psychology, Selected Essays*, Beacon Press (Boston) 1968, p. 238.

26. *The Boston Globe*, March 6, 1972.

27. Edward R. Sunshine, "Religion and Revolution in Latin America," in *The Religious Situation 1969*, Beacon Press (Boston) 1969, p. 119.

28. Edward T. Hall, *The Silent Language*, Fawcett Premier Books (Greenwich) 1969, p. 10.

29. Paulo Freire, *Pedagogy of the Oppressed*, Herder and Herder (New York) 1968, p. 75.

30. The mechanism and structure of this organization is being worked out between the Archdiocesan Priests' Senate and myself and the detailed plan for its actualization will be publicized later.

31. Eric Fromm, *The Art of Loving*, Bantam Books (New York) 1967, p. 23.

32. Pope Paul VI, Message for the Day of Peace, (January 1, 1972) *L'Osservatore Romano*, December 23, 1971.

33. Robert Kennedy, *The Last Campaign*, Award Books (New York) 1968, p. 3.

34. Pope Paul VI, Message for the Day of Peace, *op. cit.*

35. *Ibid.*

36. Ramsey Clark, *"Crime in America,"* Simon and Shuster, Inc. (New York) 1971, p. 748.

37. Harrington, *op. cit. Toward etc.*, p. 133.

38. John Adams, as quoted by Robert Kennedy in his book "To Seek a Newer World," p. 33.

39. Martin Luther King, *Where Do We Go From Here?* Harper and Row (New York) 1967, pp. 46-47.

Food for the Tables of the World

Pastoral Letter while Bishop of Brownsville, Texas, April 23, 1967

Dearly beloved:

After creating man to His image and likeness, God gave him all the earth that he might use it and subdue it to his service. He created him with an inborn tendency to seek the society of his fellowmen and together with them develop all the potential for good within himself, through mutual assistance in the ever progressing conquest of the world of things over which he was appointed lord and master.

From the very beginning man lived in the family society, the basic cell of all other human communitites. As time went on, he saw the necessity for organizing extra-family societies to assist him in furthering his own development and perfection and in achieving greater domination over the material things of the universe. And so he naturally organized into professional, cultural, intellectual and even spiritual associations, for being social by nature he realized he could not reach his fullest development alone.

It is easy to see that to arrive at complete development, man must free himself at least from misery and have assurance of finding means of subsistence, health, and fixed employment. He must also assume an increased share of responsibility without oppression of any kind and in security from situations that do violence to his dignity as man. He must ever seek better education, or, in the words of Pope Paul VI, "he must seek to do more, to know more and have more in order to be more: that is what men aspire to now when a great number of them are condemned to live in conditions that make this lawful desire illusory" ("On the Development of Peoples" 1.6).

We believe the word of Holy Scripture which teaches that the whole of creation is for man and that it is his responsibility to develop it by intelligent effort and by means of his labor to perfect it for his use. "If the world," says Paul VI, "is made to furnish each individual with the means of livelihood and the instruments for his growth and progess, each man has therefore the right to find in the world what is necessary for himself.... All other rights whatsoever, including those of property and free commerce, are to be subordinated to this principle. They should not hinder but on the contrary favor its application. It is a grave and urgent social duty to redirect them to their primary finality." (Dev. of Peoples 1.3, 22)

For many years now the progress of events has made manifest that men have disturbed the order established by the Creator at the beginning. In no sector of human life is this disorder more apparent in our country and elsewhere than in the area of agriculture. Farmers leave the fields because "nearly everywhere they see their affairs in a state of depression...as regards the level of living of farm populations." (John XXIII, "Mater et Magistra" 124). Those who remain on the farm as workers or as owners,—unless these constitute large enterprises, such as corporations or cooperatives made up of smaller family-size farms—live out a precarious existence, often most unworthy of man who was made to the image of God. Under such conditions, they can hardly achieve full development.

And yet Pope John XXIII, who, like myself, was a farmer in his youth, was of the opinion that farm life was an excellent means for man to develop himself to the extent destined for him by the Creator. He taught that in rural affairs "the principal agents and protagonists of economic improvements, of cultural betterment, or of social advance, should be the men personally involved, namely, the farmers themselves. To them it should be quite evident that their work is most noble, because it is undertaken, as it were, in the majestic temple of creation; because it concerns the life of plants and animals, rich in allusions to God, Creator and Provider. Moreover, labor in the fields not only provides various foodstuffs wherewith humankind is nourished, but also furnishes an increasing supply of raw materials for industry."

Pope John saw in agriculture a dignity all its own because of its manifold relationship to the mechanical arts, chemistry, and biology. He saw scientific and technological advancement as very important to rural life. He was aware that the special nobility of farm work "requires farmers to understand well the course of the seasons and to adapt themselves to the same; that they await patiently what the future will bring; that they appreciate the importance and seriousness of their duties; that they constantly remain alert and ready for new developments." All this plays a powerful role in personal development.

But today, as always, a man cannot stand alone and hope to find his fulfillment. Neither can the farmer. Pope John insisted that "farmers should join together in fellowships, especially when the family itself works the farm. Indeed, it is proper for rural workers to have a sense of solidarity. They should strive jointly to set up mutual-aid societies and professional associations. All these are very necessary either to keep rural dwellers abreast of scientific and technical progress or to protect the prices of goods produced by their labor. Besides, acting in this manner, farmers are put on the same footing as other classes of workers, who, for the most part, join together in such fellowships. Finally, by acting thus, farmers will achieve an importance and influence in public affairs proportionate to their role. For today it is unquestionably true that the solitary voice speaks, as they say, to the winds." (Mater et Magistra 144-146).

As a final word of encouragement and advice on this matter, Pope John wrote that "since everything that makes for man's dignity, perfection, and development seems to be invoked in agricultural labor, it is proper that man regard such work as an assignment from God with a sublime purpose. It is fitting, therefore, that man dedicate work of this kind to the most provident God who directs all events for the salvation of men. Finally, the farmer should take upon himself, in some measure, the task of educating himself and others for the advancement of civilization (Mater et Magistra 149).

My dearly beloved brethren, the work of the farmer was never more necessary and useful than today when the tables of nearly three fourths of the world's population are empty of food. As Pope Paul VI says, "Today the peoples in hunger are making a dramatic appeal to the peoples blessed with abundance. The Church shudders at this cry of anguish and calls each one to give a loving response of charity to his brother's cry for help" (Dev. of Peoples 3).

And yet such is the social and economic disorder of our day that in our country we see thousands of gallons of milk dumped in the streets, vast tracts of good land lying fallow to prevent over production of food, farmworkers idle or underpaid because the farmers who hire them cannot in many instances secure a just price for the goods they produce.

We have arrived at this wretched state of affairs because on the new "conditions

of today's society a system has been constructed which considers profit as the key
motive for economic progress, competition
as the supreme law of economics, and private ownership of the means of production
as an absolute right that has no limits and
carries no corresponding social obligations." According to Paul VI, this un-
checked individualism leads to dictatorship
rightly denounced by Pius XI as producing
"the international imperialism of money."
He says that "one cannot condemn such
abuses too strongly by solemnly recalling
once again that the economy is at the service of man" (Dev. of Peoples 27).

To face the farm-workers crisis, aggra-
vated by necessary and inevitable mechan-
ization of agriculture, the introduction of
industry is a necessity for economic growth
and human progress in farming communities, and it is at the same time a sign of
development and contributes to it. By persistent work and by using his intelligence
"man gradually wrests nature's secrets
from her and finds a better application for
her riches. As his self-mastery increases,
he develops a taste for research and discovery, an ability to take a calculated risk,
boldness in enterprises, generosity in what

he does and a sense of responsibility."
(Dev. of Peoples 25).

Dearly beloved, we have no time to
waste. We must hurry with all prudence and
charity to bring about the needed reforms,
for there exist "situations whose injustice
cries to heaven. When whole populations,
destitute of the necessities, live in a state
of dependence barring them from all initiative and responsibility, and all opportunity
to advance culturally and share in social
and political life, recourse to violence, as a
means to right these wrongs to human dignity, is a grave temptation." (Dev. of Peoples 30).

We know, or should know, that a large
segment of our population, in spite of recent improvement through legislation and
the efforts of government and social-
minded groups, live under conditions
totally unworthy of man. Who is unaware
that the present plight of the migrant farm
workers of America is a constant reproach
to our way of life? Yet they do not ask for
charity. What they demand is what is theirs
by natural right. When the affluent farmers
pay a just wage to the migrant worker,
when they make it possible for him to
support himself and his family in frugal
comfort, and to provide education for the

whole family, they are not making a gift of their possessions to the farm workers; by no means! They are simply handing over to him what is his, for they had appropriated for themselves by good or evil means what had been given in common for the use of all by the bountiful Creator.

Given the national and even international depressed condition of agriculture and of farm workers and of many farm owners in particular, it is urgent that they be aware of their right to join associations which alone can procure for them the means of development which in the words of Pope Paul VI signifies peace. We know that every man has a basic natural right to form and join workers' unions which contribute to economic progress by defending his rights, but the circumstances of the times the world over indicate that for the common good of peoples it is also a duty for both migrant farm workers and for the farmers to form associations proper to themselves and to advance together in harmony, justice and peace in order to make a substantial contribution to the whole human family. God has blessed this land of ours with plenty — it is our obligation to work together as one people, workers and management united in the common cause of developing themselves through their labor, thereby sharing our superabundance with others to help them in accord with the plan of the Creator.

It is my solemn duty to urge our Catholic people and all our fellow citizens to remember the words of Paul VI that each man is part of the whole of mankind. "It is not just certain individuals, but all men who are called to this fullness of development. Civilizations are born, develop and die. But humanity is advancing along the path of history like the waves of a rising tide encroaching gradually on the shore. We have inherited from past generations, and we have benefited from the work of our contemporaries: for this reason we have obligations toward all, and we cannot refuse to interest ourselves in those who will come after us to enlarge the human family. The reality of human solidarity, which is a benefit for us, also imposes a duty." (Dev. of Peoples 17).

It is this duty which we as a nation must feel bound to fulfill first of all to our migrant farm workers and farmers by passing appropriate legislation and using other suitable and democratic means of assistance so that not only our tables but the tables of the world may be blessed with the abundance of the fruits of the earth which was given to man by the Creator for his service and as a means of achieving his personal development in fellowship with other men.

"Father, We Are Your Children"

*The Migrant Workers from the Valley...
and Texas, September, 1970*

A Migrant Bishop's Prayer

Our Father in heaven and on earth, thank You for the privilege of serving Your children of the Magic Valley. Thank You for the favor of allowing me to visit thousands of them away from home, far in the distant midwestern states of our beautiful and rich country. Thank You for the joy of seeing them and offering the Holy Sacrifice of the Mass for them and with them in fields, in churches and between rows of shanties where they spend the night after a day of honest but backbreaking work—and where they spend the days, long days, when there is no work and have to depend on the State or private charity to keep body and soul together. You know, Father, how much this dependence hurts their human dignity and how much they suffer when they cannot earn their own bread to feed their children. You made them like that, Lord. Thank You for them.

Thank You, Lord Jesus Christ, for taking me to so many of them, to their huts, sometimes unfit for animals, to speak with them,

to sit on old rickety chairs or on the corner
of a torn mattress, to chat with them and
enjoy the smile on their face, sometimes
veiled by a very subtle shade of sadness.
No one is sure of tomorrow, but they,
above all, have little or no human assurance
of tomorrow's bread. It is beautiful, edify-
ing, emboldening even to feel their trust
in You, su Diosito, their loving and tender
Father! Thank You, Jesus, for the retreat.
I know You were with me. I seldom lost
the awareness that I was with You.

You remember, Lord, that young man
who went up to the Midwest to help his
people. Here in the Valley many of our
brothers are sincere in their belief that he is
a menace to our society. He is a MAYO. But
when I left the convent where we had break-
fast one morning, he came last to say good-
bye. As he shook my hand, he said to me,
"Bishop, could I see you in private for a
moment?" Of course I could. When we
faced each other in the privacy of a small
room, he asked, "Bishop, will you please
bless me?" Of course, Lord, I blessed him
and You were there with me to bless him
from head to toe. As he gave me a big and
warm abrazo, I heard him say, "Thank
you, Bishop; I am trying my best to help
my people." Father in heaven and on earth,

thank You for him. He would suffice as my reward for all the aches and discomfort I suffered in my pilgrimage to the migrant camps of the Midwest. But, Lord, there are so many others; so many I knew all the way from Penitas to Brownsville and so many I did not know and felt so ashamed for not knowing them, because they are the sheep You have entrusted to this unworthy shepherd. Yet, if I did not know them individually I do know their collective heart and mind, I know and love the beauty of their soul, even if they do not go to Mass every Sunday. Lord, where would I be if I had had no instruction or very little instruction in the Faith like them? The mercy You have shown to me, Jesus, show it to them too. This is the heart of a father begging for his needy and beautiful children. I cannot give them a serpent, when they ask for the bread of Your word and grace; I cannot give them a stone when they ask for daily bread! You Yourself are on record as saying this about Your Father and our Father!

Father, we are Your children in the fields, toiling under the blue sky and thunder clouds, in the warm rays of the sun or the chill of a northern prairie wind, in the rain even; we are Your children and are in love with You. We trust You and we trust our brothers. In the simplicity of our hearts, we can harbor no ill will, but we pray, Lord, for those who are consciously unjust to us and in this displease You. Perhaps it may not go so well for them on Judgment Day.

We follow, as best we know and can, Your Son Jesus Christ. We do not want anyone of our brothers to be lost. We beg You to enlighten their minds and save them. We beg You to help them help us to help ourselves. You know, Lord, that we are not shiftless and lazy. You know that we are sinners like the rest of men, but You also know that we appreciate the dignity of work, especially the beautiful dignity of farm work, and that we are honorable and want to earn our daily bread. Lord, please help those in our society who are in a position to do so, to give us work. It is work we want, not alms! Please help them to see the truth, help them to see the evils in our economy and the system that governs it or fails to govern it, so that in justice to all they may renew what needs renewal, discard what must be discarded and allow themselves to be guided by the love which You manifest in Your creation but especially in the gift of Your only Son to be our brother and our Savior.

Father, we the children of the fields, ask You to bless those growers who try hard to supply us with decent living conditions and good wages but cannot because of the troubles and insecurity which they themselves endure every day. Give them the wisdom to know how to operate their temporal affairs so that the bread they eat and supply to the tables of this country and the world may not come from our oppression and degradation. We could never say that everyone of our employers is unfair, since so many of them are going bankrupt every year. But they could be unwise and proud and too independent and need to learn from You that no matter how good their intention may be, it still remains a fact that we are deprived of most of the contemporary means to develop ourselves and to take our rightful place in our society.

We thank You at this time, Lord, for the efforts of some of our legislators and our brothers of the news media for calling the attention of America to our plight and for voicing our righteous indignation for us whose voice is so weak that no one can hear it. May the numbers of our brothers who know us well increase and may they bring healing to our land which seems to be on the brink of moral disintegration and even economic disaster. You know, Lord, that we love America. After all, we work and almost slave to feed it!

In spite of our poverty, Lord, we do not bow to other men as if You had made us inferior to them. Yes, we bow to them in courtesy and respect because we see in them Your image and likeness, because we believe that every man has been bought from the slavery of sin by the blood of Our Lord Jesus Christ. Every man must be very precious in Your sight, O God, our Father. We know we are precious and demand respect for ourselves from others just as we respect them. Grant us the grace to believe this and live this belief in our daily dealings with others.

My Father, our Father, Your migrant bishop and Your migrant children thank You for Your glory and for Your love, for that Providence of Yours which watches constantly over us. We thank You for all our brothers and beg of You to open the eyes of those who do not see so that we may not in the end be led by them to be slowly alienated from You. This would be the ultimate disaster for us and for them. We know this is not Your will!

Father, thank You for the retreat! Thank You for the bishops, priests, religious and laity I met on my pilgrimage, whose devotion to the migrant workers of the Valley... and Texas is a source of strength to me. Thank You, Father, thank You! Amen.

Magisterial Teaching on Life Issues

The following is the complete text of an address at a Day of Introduction to the U.S. Catholic Bishops' Pastoral Plan for Pro-Life Activities in Worcester, MA, on March 27, 1976.

(The assembly at Assumption College was convened by the Massachusetts Catholic Conference.)

Dear Friends of Life
and so Friends of God:

I am pleased beyond words to have the opportunity of addressing an audience composed of so many dedicated and zealous men and women from every sector of Massachusetts. Your very presence here, undoubtedly at the cost of much inconvenience and sacrifice, is eloquent evidence of your profound concern for human life, and of your steadfast determination to carry on the pro-life struggle resolutely and perseveringly. May Almighty God, the Author of life, crown the efforts of all of us with success.

I say that I am pleased to be here. But I am awed as well. No one realizes more keenly than myself the awesome responsibility that is mine, as a Bishop of the Church established by Jesus Christ, to speak out clearly and uncompromisingly in explanation of the teaching of Christ as expounded by His Church, and in defense of the law of God.

Awesome? How else can this responsibility be described? Listen to the words of the Second Vatican Council: "This sacred Synod teaches that by divine institution bishops have succeeded to the place of the apostles as shepherds of the Church, and that he who hears them, hears Christ, while he who rejects them, rejects Christ and Him who sent Christ" (*Lumen gentium*, no. 20).

It is to the teaching of the Catholic Church on the dignity and sacredness of human life that I would address myself this morning: specifically to "Magisterial Teaching on Life Issues."

Is such a topic relevant? Is it important?

I am guilty of no exaggeration when I say that at no time within the memory of any person here has respect for human life reached so low a point as it has at the present. To substantiate that statement I need only point to the fact that well over one million unborn babies (perhaps even as many as a million and a half) were deliberately killed by some repulsive and painful abortion technique here in the United States last year. It is indeed frightening to reflect that each year in our nation more lives are being destroyed by abortion than were lost in all of the wars waged by our country during the entire two centuries of its existence.

Parenthetically, may I remark upon the timeliness of addressing ourselves to the topic of the right to life, in this Bicentennial year of our nation. Is it not a fact of the utmost significance that the Founding Fathers considered the right to life as the very first of the inalienable rights bestowed upon human beings by their Creator? And is it not a challenge to all of us that they were completely unafraid to affirm their belief before all the world, in ringing terms in the Declaration of Independence?

Yes, unfortunately there has been in our society a precipitous decline in respect for human life. Why? In the *Pastoral Plan for Pro-Life Activities*, adopted by the Catholic Bishops of the United States last November, the American hierarchy endeavored to identify some of the causes. Let it suffice here merely to mention the enormous harm that has resulted from the current trend toward secularization in our society, coupled with a rejection of moral imperatives based upon belief in God and His plan for creation. Then, too, the decline in respect for human life has been intensified by a widespread selfishness eventuating inevitably in a lack of concern for other persons and for society itself. And all of these factors have culminated in the enacting of laws and the issuance of judicial decisions which deny or ignore basic human rights and moral responsibilities for the protection and the promotion of the common good. One might instance the growing attempts to promote euthanasia through so-called "death with dignity" laws—and, on the judicial level, the dismaying abortion decisions of the United States Supreme Court in 1973 (cf. *Pastoral Plan for Pro-Life Activities*).

Why is it that a discussion of the official teaching of the Church on life issues is the most meaningful approach that we could employ at this juncture? The Catholic Bishops of the United States in their *Pastoral Plan for Pro-Life Activities* give the answer: "Recognizing the value of legal, medical and sociological arguments, the primary and ultimately most compelling arguments must be theological and moral. Respect for life must be seen in the context of God's love for mankind reflected in creation and redemption and man's relationship to God and to other members of the human family. The Church's opposition to abortion is based on Christian teaching on the dignity of the human person, and the responsibility to proclaim and defend basic human rights, especially the right to life."

The *Pastoral Plan* lays stress upon the fact that "human life is a precious gift from God; that each person who receives this gift has responsibilities toward God, toward self and toward others; and that society, through its laws and social institutions, must protect and sustain human life at every stage of its existence. Recognition of the dignity of the human person, made in the image of God, lies at the very heart of our individual and social duty to respect human life."

When we speak of the teaching of the Church on the dignity and sacredness of human life, it is important to realize that that teaching is as old as Christianity itself. Indeed one of the earliest Christian writings, dating back very probably to the first century, clearly warns: "You shall not kill by abortion the fruit of the womb and you shall not murder the *infant already born*" *(Didache)*.

The fact is, of course, that condemnation of killing goes back far beyond the origin of the Church. On the tablets of stone given to Moses on Mt. Sinai did not God command: "Thou shalt not kill"?

The fundamental problem, of course, is that man has arrogated to himself the power over life and death, which belongs to God alone. The Church, in her teaching, reaffirms the fundamental truth, natural as well as supernatural, that we are God's property, not our own. We have no absolute dominion over our lives. We hold our lives in trust. And, as good stewards, we must use our lives according to God's will and in fulfillment of His purposes. God created us and conserves us in existence. As the Psalmist sings:

"Know that the Lord is God.

He made us, his we are" (Ps. 99:3).

It follows that no human being has a right to "play God" by destroying human life—his

own or anyone else's. It is God alone who is the
Master of life and death. It can never be
sufficiently emphasized that, unless we realize
that all life comes from God and not merely
from the procreative act of parents, we will
never adequately understand either the dignity
and the sacredness of human life or the sover-
eignty of God over human life. "We are God's
work of art," St. Paul tells us, "created in Christ
Jesus to live the good life, as from the beginning
he had meant us to live it" (Eph. 2:10). "We are
God's work of art created in Christ Jesus...."

Have you ever paused to reflect upon the
intense personal concern of our divine Lord for
human life, natural as well as supernatural? For
three long years of His public career Jesus
Christ went about doing good, performing miracle after miracle to preserve and to prolong
human life—yes, even raising the dead to life.
And in His infinite love for us—the work of His
hands—He sacrificed His life through crucifixion on the hill of Calvary, in order that we might
have eternal life. "Greater love has no man than
this, that a man lay down his life for his friends"
(Jn. 15:13).

True to the teaching and example of her
Founder, Jesus Christ, the Catholic Church has
never ceased to proclaim her concern for human
life, and to condemn every attack upon human
life as an attack upon a person made to the
image and likeness of God and redeemed by the
shedding of the blood of Jesus Christ, the Son of
God—a person whose human nature has been

wondrously ennobled in a very special way because the Son of God Himself assumed human flesh in the womb of His Virgin Mother at Nazareth, and was born into our world in a stable in Bethlehem.

That is why, as the Church has reminded us in her recent *Declaration on Abortion,* "the person can be definitively subordinated only to God. Man can never be treated simply as a means to be disposed of in order to obtain a higher end" *(Declaration on Abortion,* Sacred Congregation for the Doctrine of the Faith, November 18, 1974, no. 9).

And that is why, also, in the words of the Second Vatican Council, "human life and the task of transmitting it are not realities bound up with this world alone. Hence they cannot be measured or perceived only in terms of it, but always have a bearing on the eternal destiny of men" *(Gaudium et spes,* no. 51).

Perhaps with greater frequency than ever before in her history, the Church during the past few decades has been reaffirming Christ's teaching on the sanctity of human life and on the evil of attacks upon human life.

Thus, in an address in October, 1951, Pope Pius XII declared: "Every human being, even the infant in the maternal womb, has the right to life immediately from God.... Hence there is no man, no human authority, no science, no medical, eugenic, social, economic or moral 'indication' which can establish or grant a valid juridical ground for the direct, deliberate disposal of an innocent human being..." (Address to the Italian Society of Midwives, October 29, 1951).

Several years earlier, in an address in November, 1944, with equal clarity and force Pope Pius XII vigorously defended human life. "As long as a man is not guilty, his life is untouchable, and therefore any act directly tending to destroy it is illicit, whether such destruction is intended as an end in itself or only as a means to an end, whether it is a question of life in the embryonic stage, or in a stage of full development, or already in its final stages" (Discourse to the St. Luke Union of Italian Doctors, November 12, 1944).

The same truth is reechoed in the Second Vatican Council: "For God, the Lord of life, has conferred on men the surpassing ministry of safeguarding life—a ministry which must be fulfilled in a manner which is worthy of man. Therefore, from the moment of its conception, life must be guarded with the greatest care, while abortion and infanticide are unspeakable crimes" (*Gaudium et spes*, no. 51).

Pope John XXIII, in his magnificent encyclical *Mater et magistra*, not only reaffirmed the sanctity of human life but also warned of the dire consequences which follow in the wake of the transgression of God's law protecting human life. "Human life is sacred—all men must recognize that fact. From its very inception it reveals the creating hand of God. Those who violate His laws not only offend the divine Majesty and degrade themselves and humanity, they also sap the vitality of the political community of which they are members" *(Mater et magistra,* no. 194).

Even more recently our Holy Father, Pope Paul VI, through a letter of his Secretary of State, Cardinal Villot, addressed to the Congress of the International Federation of Catholic Medical Associations convened in Washington, pointed to the moral identity of euthanasia, abortion and infanticide: "The same norms of good and evil apply therefore to euthanasia, abortion and infanticide. The influence of Christianity had little by little uprooted these forms of barbaric behavior, but the materialistic ideas of pagan eugenics now tend to give renewed freedom to the most abnormal practices" *(L'Osservatore Romano,* October 22, 1970).

Just a few months later Pope Paul VI again spoke out eloquently in defense of human life: "To attack human life under any pretext whatsoever and under whatever form we view it, is to repudiate one of the essential values of our civilization. In the very depths of our consciences...we affirm as an incontestable and sacred principle respect for every form of human life, life that is awakening, life that asks only to develop, life that is drawing to a close, life especially that is weak, unprovided for, defenseless, at the mercy of others.... If it be necessary to go against the current of what is sometimes being thought and said on all sides, then let us never grow weary of repeating it: all human life must be absolutely respected;

in fact, abortion and euthanasia are murder"
(*L'Osservatore Romano*, February 11, 1971).

Time and again the Church in the United
States has spoken out in defense of human life.
She has stressed that the right to life is a basic
human right. She has elaborated upon the
respect due to life. She has insisted that human
dignity must not be violated by attacks upon
life. She has underscored the grave obligation of
government to protect the lives of its citizens.

The Catholic Bishops of the United States,
in adopting the *Pastoral Plan for Pro-Life Activities* last November, called for an amendment to
the Constitution—because a majority of the
members of the Supreme Court has made it
impossible for government to fulfill its role to
protect the lives of its citizens.

The Bishops are asking for a redress of that
wrong, in the manner provided for in the
Constitution itself. As the *Pastoral Plan* points
out: "Abortion is a specific issue that highlights
the relationship between morality and law. As a
human mechanism, law may not be able fully to
articulate the moral imperative, but neither can
legal philosophy ignore the moral order. The
abortion decisions of the United States Supreme
Court (January 22, 1973) violate the moral
order, and have disrupted the legal process
which previously attempted to safeguard the
rights of unborn children."

This morning I have endeavored to point
out the continuity of the Church's teaching,
from the earliest days of Christianity, on the

dignity and sacredness of human life. As I have had occasion to remark elsewhere: "This is not some new teaching, some new development in the understanding of Christian morals; on the contrary, it is as old as Revelation itself, confirmed in unmistakable language in the solemn declaration of God from Mt. Sinai—'Thou shalt not kill!' Through all the generations of men, from the curse of Cain to this hour, God has called us to the protection of life, and that summons we must heed. Christian history is witness to the ways in which the Church brought barbarian nations to an understanding of the gospel, how they slowly put behind them their pagan ways, were taught to put on Christ and live by His precepts. The Church's witness to Christ included always a respect for human life in every form, so that ancient ways destructive of life were rejected and the civilizing creed of the Christian Church prevailed to the extent that it was accepted and lived.

"So we can see that what is happening now is not a step forward, but a step backward. It is a new barbarism, which, under whatever name it may choose to call itself, is moving ruthlessly to upset the moral order established by God as the foundation of peace on earth. All the scientific advances of modern man, all the technology that is at his disposition, should serve life, not destroy it, should protect the unborn, not eliminate them. The new barbarism is a summons to death; the Christian faith is a call to life. This call must be shouted from the housetops, spoken in the marketplace, taught in the schools and carried in the hearts of everyone who bears the name of Christian, or simply believes in God as the Lord of life and death" *(The Pilot*, January 2, 1971).

During the course of these remarks I have limited myself to a discussion of the Church's teaching on the sacredness of human life. That is the topic to which I was asked to address myself. But surely I have no intention of leaving the impression that the direct killing of innocent persons is wrong only because the Catholic Church teaches that it is wrong. The ten commandments antedated the founding of the Catholic Church, and they bind all human beings, not Catholics alone. Moreover, it is well to recall that already five centuries before the coming of Christ, the Hippocratic Oath recognized the inviolability of human life and condemned the evil of abortion. And in our own times the Geneva Medical Oath, drawn up in 1948 by the World Health Organization, declared: "I shall keep absolute respect for human life, from the moment of conception" (Quoted in Pastoral Letter of the Archbishops and Bishops of Ireland, *Human Life Is Sacred*. Cf. *Doctrine and Life*, July 1975, p. 533).

It is clear, then, as the Holy See stated in the recent *Declaration on Abortion*, that "respect for human life is not just a Christian obligation. Human reason is sufficient to impose it on the basis of the analysis of what a human person is and should be" *(Declaration on Abortion,* Sacred Congregation for the Doctrine of the Faith, November 18, 1974, no. 8).

The value that the Church places on the sacredness of human life must be considered not only in connection with the question of abortion. It is applicable to all human life. It lies at the basis of the Church's condemnation of euthanasia or mercy killing. Indeed, it is intimately connected with the Church's concern for a decent, human life, lived in the midst of conditions that are humane—the Church's concern for the poor and the needy and the destitute, for the disadvantaged and the injusticed and the retarded, for those who suffer from discrimination and oppression and persecution.

Very clearly has the *Pastoral Plan for Pro-Life Activities* articulated this concern, in stressing the awareness of the Catholic Bishops of the United States that "basic human rights are violated in many ways: by abortion and euthanasia, by injustice and the denial of equality to certain groups of persons, by some forms of human experimentation, by neglect of the underprivileged and disadvantaged who deserve the concern and support of the entire society."

Let me underscore, in this connection, the Church's recognition of the responsibility of all of us to do everything within our power to solve those problems, personal and social, that might lead a woman to seek an abortion. Four years ago the Catholic Bishops of our own state expressed this responsibility very succinctly: "No one denies—least of all, we—that the problems of modern society are many and heartbreaking. Nor are we insensitive to the anguish which they cause among their victims and in society as a whole. Churches, government, and humanitarian agencies of the private sector must combine their redoubled efforts toward the solution of these problems. As Catholic Bishops, on a national and on a local scale we are promoting and implementing many programs aimed at the alleviation of disease and poverty and distress and illiteracy and prejudice and injustice. But we must emphasize the fact that no genuine solution to these problems can be found in any action that transgresses the law of God, usurps His authority in determining who is to live and who is to die, and deprives an unborn child of his basic right to life" *(A Joint Statement by the Catholic Bishops of Massachusetts on Abortion,* February, 1972).

Our brother Bishops in another state, in a public document, have stressed the fact that "the Church extends deepest sympathy and compassion to some women who are thrown into agonizing distress by pregnancy: the mother who is in precarious health, or who is very poor, or who already has more children than she can care for; a mother in a troubled frame of mind; an unmarried mother; a woman raped or involved in incest.... She (the Church) encourages the state and private agencies to make positive efforts to help troubled mothers and to remove the evils that often are the occasion for desiring abortion. Every effort should be made to help the poor and to redeem them from helplessness, frustration and despair. Efforts should be made to afford better care for defective children and to advise and support their families. Sympathy and help should be given to unmarried mothers. Their children should be sheltered from stigmas and provided with institutional or private homes. Agencies for social service should be provided, especially for women for whom a new pregnancy creates painful burdens. Families should be helped through education for family living, counseling, family allowances, employment opportunities. By positive action, society should show respect for the sanctity of life and strive to enhance the quality of life for all" *(Statement of Roman Catholic Bishops of Illinois About Abortion,* Illinois Catholic Conference, March 20, 1969).

Perhaps no one knows better than those of us who are gathered here in defense of human life, how indescribably bitter has been and is the opposition to the teaching of the Church on the dignity and sacredness of human life. What Pope Paul VI once stated about the opposition to the Church's teaching on contraception can appropriately be applied to the question of abortion. "It can be foreseen," the Pope said, "that this teaching will perhaps not be easily received by all. Too numerous are those voices —amplified by the modern means of propaganda—which are contrary to the voice of the

Church. To tell the truth, the Church is not surprised to be made, like her divine Founder, a 'sign of contradiction,' yet she does not, because of this, cease to proclaim with humble firmness the entire moral law, both natural and evangelical. Of such laws the Church was not the author, nor consequently can she be their arbiter; she is only their depositary and their interpreter, without ever being able to declare to be licit that which is not so by reason of its intimate and unchangeable opposition to the true good of man" (Encyclical, *Humanae vitae,* July 25, 1968, no. 18).

I urge you, in God's name, never to give in to the temptation to discouragement—no matter how tremendous the opposition or how persistent the pressure. The battle which you are waging to protect human life is a battle for what is right. You are defending God's law—and so, God is on your side. If God be with us, what matters it who is against us? (cf. Rom. 8:31)

Let me bring my remarks to a close by making my own the stirring words of the Irish hierarchy, as found in the magnificent Pastoral Letter entitled "Human Life Is Sacred" (cf. *Doctrine and Life,* July 1975, pp. 530ff.);

"But we should not just say that the Church is 'against abortion.' We should say that the Church is *for* life. The Church says 'Yes' to life. The Church has been saying 'Yes' to unborn life, without any hesitation or reservation, for two thousand years. In recent years, since the abortion debate became a public issue in country after country, nearly every Catholic hierarchy in Europe, in America and everywhere the issue has been raised, has responded by once more clearly and strongly and unanimously repeating this great 'Yes' to unborn life.

"The Church says 'Yes,' not just to human existence, but to the quality and dignity of human life. The Christian demand is that all human life should be permitted and enabled to develop to the full dignity and quality of living which befit a human person and child of God. Nothing less than that is what is commanded by Christ's command to love our neighbor as we love our own self. The Christian 'Yes' to life includes a call for freedom, for adequate education, for proper living conditions, for a more just distribution of wealth and opportunity, for protection of the human environment, and for a more responsible use of the resources of nature. The Church is not simply 'against abortion'; she is *for* life and *for* man and *for* human dignity and *for* social justice."

And to those noble sentiments all of us say, "Amen."

Homily on Abortion

December 27, 1970

My dear brothers and sisters:

It is a happy occasion and a sad situation which gathers us here together this afternoon, so soon after Christmas Day, to commemorate the great Feast of the Holy Family and to recall the martyrdom of the Holy Innocents.

The birthday of Jesus established the Holy Family, giving us the model of the Christian home for all generations to come. Its head was Joseph, the strong protector and workingman, who watched over the fortunes of all three, guiding their ways and providing for their needs. His wife was Mary, the virgin and mother, whom God himself had selected as the one who should bear His Son and present Him to the world. And the Son of the family was Jesus, truly human and truly divine, who was born to redeem all men and to give them life everlasting. In these blessed three, we find inspiration for the concern of every father, the love of every mother, the filial obedience and happy promise of every child. Theirs was not an ordinary family, to be sure, but in these holy lives we find example for our own. We can admire their faith and trust in God, try to imitate their simplicity and style of life, make our own their acceptance of God's will, however mysterious it may seem to us.

Along with the Holy Family, we commemorate this afternoon the death of the Holy Innocents, that strange incident of human wickedness which follows so soon the birth of the Savior. King Herod had heard the news of the Messiah's coming, and fearing his power threatened, sought to destroy Him.

For this purpose, you will remember, he ordered the death of all Jewish boys in Bethlehem and neighboring areas who were two years of age or less. We do not know the extent of this cruel slaughter, but even one death would have been one too many. Little children were put to the sword, whose only crime was to be born in the day of Herod's anger, fear and insecurity. Who can say what died that day? The promise of a lifetime cannot be measured in advance. What of greatness, what of joy and happiness, what of holiness, perished that day by the sword's edge. All we know is that precious human life, God's own gift to man, was sacrificed to a tyrant's ambition, that little children paid the price of the anxiety of an avaricious man for his wealth and power.

As the Church each year reminds us of this dread event, we recognize how evil can take over the hearts of men and destroy almost all that is human in them. On occasion, some are not even reluctant to defy every divine precept for their own selfish aims; even life is considered cheap and expendable by those who put aside God and reject his teachings. The lesson cannot be lost upon us in our contemporary world where life has come under new assault in these last few years, both at its beginning and its end. The enemies of life in our time are not Herods, they are not tyrants willing to be bathed in blood; but, if I may be allowed to judge them, they are blind, as he was blind, to the value of human life, to the inviolable character of God's creation in man, to the precious personality of every being born or unborn, as one whom God loves and for whom Christ gave His life.

In our own country, we have seen various legislatures revising the traditional laws that have protected the life of the unborn and, by what they call "liberalization," they write new laws making abortion available and easy. Some of those supporting such legislation doubtless do so in good faith or out of ignorance of the consequences of their act. But what they do must be described for what it is—it is the destruction of human life at its source, and it is objectively evil. All the good reasons in the world—progress, pity, freedom, health—all of these together cannot justify or allow what we know to be wrong in itself.

This is not some new teaching, some new development in the understanding of Christian morals; on the contrary, it is as old as Revelation itself, confirmed in unmistakable language in the solemn declaration of God from Mt. Sinai—"Thou shalt not kill!" Through all the generations of men, from the curse of Cain to this hour, God has called us to the protection of life, and that summons we must heed. Christian history is witness to the ways in which the Church brought barbarian nations to an understanding of the Gospel, how they slowly put behind them their pagan ways, and were taught to put on Christ and live by his precepts. The Church's witness to Christ included always a respect for human life in every form, so that ancient ways destructive of life were rejected and the civilizing creed of the Christian Church prevailed, to the extent that it was accepted and lived.

So we can see that what is happening now is not, my dear brothers and sisters, a step forward, but a step backward. It is a new barbarism, which, under whatever name it may choose to call itself, is moving ruthlessly to upset the moral order established by God as the foundation of peace on earth. All the scientific advances of modern man, all the technology that is at his disposition, should serve life, not destroy it, should protect the unborn, not eliminate them. The new barbarism is a summons to death, the Christian faith is a call to life. This call must be shouted from the housetops, spoken in the market place, taught in the schools, and carried in the hearts of everyone who bears the name of Christian, or simply believes in God as the Lord of life and death.

Four Popes over the last forty years have indicated clearly and insistently that God is the Creator of human life; that He and He alone possesses dominion over human life; that innocent, unborn human life is sacred and inviolable; that the right of the unborn to live and to be born comes from God and not from parents, the state or society; that any direct and deliberate destruction of human life by abortion is an unspeakable crime and can never be justified, no matter what apparent good might be achieved thereby.

In the most recent of three pronouncements, the Bishops of the United States have solemnly stated the following:

"...Scientists tell us that, from the moment of conception, the child is a complex and rapidly-growing being, endowed with the characteristics of human life.... The function of law is to support and protect the rights of every person. The unborn child's civil rights have consistently been recognized by American law. Proposed liberalization of the present abortion laws ignores the most basic of these rights, the right to life itself.... Abortion is an unjust destruction of a human life and morally that is murder.... The law must establish every possible protection for a child before and after birth...direct abortion is always morally wrong" (Washington, D.C., November 18, 1970).

This is the authentic teaching of the Catholic Church. Any statement, which differs from the above, cannot be presented and should not be accepted as her authoritative teaching.

I know that some of my brothers and sisters will say that at least those children who will be born defective ought to be "freed" from life, since they will likely come to realize that not only are they no comfort to themselves but are rather a weighty burden on others. This is a weak attempt to avoid the stark reality that the direct and deliberate killing of the unborn is a heinous crime and a tired excuse for running away from sacrifices which must be part of every life.

The "exceptional" child is, we must remember, also God's gift, which, in His mysterious Providence has its part to play in the unfolding of His plan for all of us. How many families have treasured such a child, known its tender warmth and affection, watched over its simple needs, and made productive its unskilled ways! In the process they have learned what it means to sacrifice for others, to be patient and understanding, to give love as well as to receive it, to see God Himself in every product of His creative hand.

Here in this holy place, so beloved by our late Cardinal, one can speak with special poignancy of the "exceptional" child. One sees the child here not as a burden or an affliction, but for what he truly is—one of the truly innocent of this world. Here the children are accepted with love and taught to care for themselves and one another, and to make whatever contribution beyond this their abilities allow. Is it not true of us that we give to the extent that our talents permit, some more and some less? It is no different with them. The Lord asks of them only what they can give, and He blesses them, as He blesses all of us, in the measure of our striving.

With every passing day, new techniques are discovered that make the handicapped person more and more self-sufficient. Progress never ceases in the medical and educational research that opens new opportunities for our understanding of the causes that contribute to retardation. These must be continually encouraged and ways found to multiply their effectiveness. This is the positive and constructive approach to the problem of the physically and mentally handicapped. It is also the approach of love and compassion; it is the Lord's way and it should be ours.

My dear brothers and sisters, we cannot condemn Herod for the slaughter of the Holy Innocents and, at the same time, propose abortion as the solution to some of our pressing problems and the legalization of abortion as our legal policy. These are literally "dead end streets" that do not solve problems but only create larger ones. We cannot accept these, much less can we promote them. They will not fail to call down upon our nation and our world the judgment of the God of life and love. They are signs of the spiritual bankruptcy of our times and the moral decay of our society. Let us, then, defeat the new barbarism with the praise and practice of the ancient faith handed down to us by the saints. Among the first, Abraham stands out, whom we call our father in the faith.

My dearly beloved, I beg you to become personally concerned about God's rights over His unborn children and over their right to life and birth. I beseech you to see the legalization of abortion in its true light; it is the denial of God's rights over life and the denial of the unborn's right to be born.

As Christians we have an obligation in conscience to defend the rights of God and of human life which comes from God. Our voice must be heard loud and clear—and where it will be effective—lest our beloved country fall prey to the powers of darkness and corruption which will drag us down to moral ruin and eventual destruction.

May the living God protect us, may the Holy Innocents intercede for us, and may the Holy Family of Nazareth be the shining inspiration for the families of America and the world.

Defense of Unborn Human Life

By the Catholic Bishops of Massachusetts,
March 20, 1971

Dearly beloved in Christ:

The growing debate in the public media and in legislative halls concerning the morality of abortion impels us as the pastors of souls in this Commonwealth to present to all men of good will the basic principles and considerations which are necessary for an intelligent appreciation of this controversial and heart-rending issue.

We are not alone in our concern for the unborn. Others of different religious persuasions — Protestant, Jew and Orthodox — have expressed at both the local and national level their opposition to abortion. This opposition is based not only on religious principles but on human elements as well.

Even before Christendom, abortion was considered as the destruction of human life. And in the past two thousand years, no theological or scientific innovation has been presented which would impel the Church to alter its teaching. This time-honored opposition derives from the

Judaeo-Christian ethic which has been the fundamental touchstone of our moral culture and holds life to be a sacred gift from God. This ethic has been singularly responsible for inculcating society's respect for innocent unborn life.

The Old Testament teaches that "The Lord formed man out of the dust of the ground and breathed into his nostrils the breath of life, and man became a living being." (Genesis 2:7) Man's dignity stems from the possession of God's life and God's spirit. The love of God and His choice rest on each person from the very beginning of life. The prophet Jeremiah writes: "Before I formed you in the womb I knew you, before you came to birth I consecrated you."

Christian faith has always looked upon the human body with great reverence, believing that with the coming of Christ in the flesh human dignity was exceedingly enhanced. "Your body, you know, is the temple of the Holy Spirit." (1 Cor. 6:19) Those who devoutly pray in the words of the New Testament, "Blessed is the fruit of your womb," (Lk. 1:42) manifest their sensitivity to the sacredness of life even before birth. The Roman Catholic Bishops of the world at the Second Vatican Council witnessed to their conviction of the sacredness of life by declaring abortion to be an "unspeakable crime."

In the American legal system, man's dignity is seen as bestowed on him by God, who has endowed him with inalienable rights, chief among which is his right to life. The United Nations Declaration on Human Rights re-emphasizes this right.

While we are speaking directly to the Roman Catholic community in Massachusetts, we address ourselves to all our fellow citizens. We see a threat to the legal protection that the sacredness of human life now enjoys. The principle at stake is the sanctity of human life and concern for it is not sectarian.

Questions must be posed and answered before any action is taken to abrogate our abortion laws. Is the fetus living? Is the fetus human? Has the fetus the right to life and when does this right begin?

The pro-abortionists have remained strangely silent on these crucial questions. Certainly, any compelling scientific evidence which would support their contention that a fetus is not alive, is not human and has no right to life should be presented.

Embryology establishes scientifically that there is a living human being in the pregnant womb from the moment of conception. Geneticists confirm this view that there is no qualitative difference between the embryo at the moment of conception and the moment of quickening. As a consequence, direct and intentional abortion at any stage of pregnancy destroys human life.

The courts have acted consistently in giving full recognition to the rights of the unborn at all stages of pregnancy. They have declared the fetus to be a legally existing human being with inviolable rights, defendable in a court of law.

We are sensitive to the acute problems which face many women who are pregnant and reiterate what the Bishops of this country said in April of 1970:

"We declare our determination to seek solution to the problems that lead women to consider abortion. We pledge our efforts to do all that is possible to remove the social stigma that is visited on the woman who is pregnant out of wedlock as well as on her child. We also pledge the facilities and the efforts of our Church agencies to provide counselling and understanding to the woman who faces a difficult pregnancy. At the same time, we are encouraged by the scientific advance of recent decades that has already provided us with ways to support and maintain the life and health of the mother and the development of the child in the womb."

In summary, we are completely dedicated to the propositions that the fetus is a human being from the moment of its conception; that laws which recognize and apply this truth are humane and should be maintained; that an innocent life should be prized above lesser values; that life itself is precious and is to be safeguarded.

The law of this Commonwealth is the protector of the life of the most helpless of human beings, the unborn child. Let us keep it so.

Attacks Weaken Allegiance

*Pastoral Letter on Archbishop Lefebvre
and Sexuality Study, July 5, 1977*

Dearly beloved in Christ:

During the past few weeks two apparently dissimilar but essentially related incidents have disturbed the peace of the Catholic Church, adding to the confusion already existing among many of the faithful. In Europe an archbishop of the Church, who had expressed dissatisfaction with what he regarded as the dangerous directions of the Second Vatican Council, has now drawn the attention of the entire world to his attitude of dissension by conducting ceremonies of clerical ordination in defiance of the explicit prohibition of the Holy Father. In the United States, a group of Catholic theologians, commissioned by the Catholic Theological Society of America, has called into question the position of the Catholic Church on matters pertaining to human sexuality, for reasons which they have formulated on the basis of their collective examination of scientific evidence which they consider to be of preponderant validity. Both the archbishop and the commission of five theologians have been given wide publicity by the media of social communications.

In view of this, it is my obligation, my dear brothers and sisters in Christ, as archbishop of Boston, to point out, both for the Catholic faithful and for the entire community, the serious injury to the Catholic Church which has resulted from these irresponsible attacks on the Church's teaching authority which is a gift of service from God for the salvation of His People. Originating as they do within the Catholic community, and carrying the weight of influence generated by the Church's divinely instituted organization, these attacks have had the effect of weakening the allegiance in faith owed by Catholics to the Holy Father, and to the structure through which he chooses to lead, teach and govern the Church as its Supreme Shepherd.

The collegial unity which exists among bishops by divine institution is shattered when individual bishops declare their independence of the central and highest authority which God has provided as the visible and effective symbol of His own divine presence within the Christian community. And the unifying power of the truth, revealed by God for the direction of men's lives toward happiness and peace, is seriously impeded when individual theologians, who identify themselves as Catholics—and thus as accredited spokesmen for the Church—create the impression that they no longer accept the Church's officially presented guidelines for the moral regulation of an important area of human free activity.

In order for you to evaluate better the seriousness of these attacks on the teaching authority of the Church, I am forced to give you three lengthy quotations from the Council's Dogmatic Constitution on the Church in three different places of this brief Pastoral Letter. I do this because I know from experience that you seldom come in direct contact with the true teaching of the Church as taught by the Council. Here is the first quotation:

"This sacred synod, following in the steps of the First Vatican Council, teaches and declares with it that Jesus Christ, the eternal pastor, set up the Holy Church by entrusting the apostles with their mission as He Himself had been sent by the Father (cf. Jn. 20:21). He willed that their successors, namely, the bishops, should be the shepherds in His Church until the end of the world. In order that the episcopate itself, however, might be one and undivided, He put Peter at the head of the other apostles, and in him He set up a lasting and visible source and foundation of the unity both of faith and of communion. This teaching concerning the institution, the permanence, the nature and import of the sacred Primacy of the Roman Pontiff and his infallible teaching office, the sacred synod proposes anew to be firmly believed by all the faithful, and, proceeding undeviatingly with this same undertaking, it proposes to proclaim publicly and enunciate clearly the doctrine concerning bishops, successors of the apostles, who together with Peter's successor, the Vicar of Christ and the visible head of the whole Church, direct the house of the living God" *(Lumen gentium,* no. 18).

The Council set down very concisely the faith of the Church we are to believe concerning the Pope and bishops in the Church and their service of authority in teaching. Please listen to the following very carefully; it is the second quotation:

"Among the more important duties of bishops, that of preaching the Gospel has pride of place. For the bishops are heralds of the faith, who draw new disciples to Christ; they are authentic teachers, that is, teachers endowed with the authority of Christ, who preach the faith to the people assigned to them, the faith which is destined to inform their thinking and direct their conduct; and under the light of the Holy Spirit they make that faith shine forth, drawing from the storehouse of revelation new things and old (cf. Mt. 13:52); they make it bear fruit, and with watchfulness they ward off whatever errors threaten their flock (cf. 2 Tm. 4:14). Bishops who teach in communion with the Roman Pontiff are to be revered by all as witnesses of divine and Catholic truth; the faithful, for their part, are obliged to submit to their bishops' decision, made in the name of

Christ, in matters of faith and morals, and to adhere to it with a ready and respectful allegiance of mind. This loyal submission of the will and intellect must be given, in a special way, to the authentic teaching authority of the Roman Pontiff, even when he does not speak *ex cathedra,* in such wise, indeed, that his supreme teaching authority be acknowledged with respect, and sincere assent be given to decisions made by him, conformably with his manifest mind and intention, which is made known principally either by the character of the documents in question, or by the frequency with which a certain doctrine is proposed, or by the manner in which the doctrine is formulated" (*Lumen gentium,* no. 25).

With this teaching of the Council in mind and heart, let us continue our reflection. I can think of no period of history when the Church has been more open to legitimate exchanges of opinion, and more sympathetic toward honest differences of opinion than during the pontificate of our beloved and saintly Pope Paul VI. The view of contemporary social problems inspired by Vatican II has been evident in every aspect of the Church's formulation of policy, and in every pronouncement of the Holy Father as he endeavors patiently and firmly to bring the Church into more effective relationship with the modern world, and to level the barriers of injustice and hatred, of selfishness and greed which have separated the rich from the poor, the powerful from the helpless, worldly-wise from the supernaturally enlightened faithful, over the centuries of men's failure to discover their unity before God through their common human nature.

Dearly beloved in Christ, in a world which needs so desperately the "aggiornamento" or renewal of Vatican II, it is senseless—and I say this in deep sorrow for this tragedy we see—it is senseless for an individual bishop to demand that the directives of the Council be abandoned and to allege, as justification for his refusal of submission to the Holy See, his own conviction that the present directions of the Church are diabolically inspired! Lord, send him Your Holy Spirit of light for repentance, and courage to accept Your mercy in the Church.

It is likewise wrong, but for a different reason, for a group of professed Catholic theologians to suggest that the teachings of Vatican II have opened the way for a completely new formulation of the Church's position on problems relating to human sexuality. Let me assure you that no one who reads the documents of the Council carefully and without bias, can possibly gain such an impression. It is no argument against the teachings of the Council to assert that its true significance is to be sought in the developing thought of those who follow new directions of secular scholarship and scientific exploration. What Vatican II teaches is to be interpreted and applied not by individual theologians but by the magisterial authority of the Church which convoked the Council and teaches through the Council.

For the field of human sexuality this teaching has been summarized and reaffirmed in the December 1975 document issued by the Holy See entitled "Declaration on Certain Questions Concerning Sexual Ethics." I exhort you to study this "Declaration" in the light of the Catholic Faith for the proper formation of your conscience in these delicate matters. Together with it, study also the Pastoral Letter of the American Bishops concerning moral values entitled, "To Live in Christ Jesus," issued last November.[1]

Dearly beloved in Christ, there is no reason for confusion if we listen to those who are empowered by God to speak with the authority of Christ. Confusion spreads only when those who lack this authority speak as though they possessed it. In the Catholic Church the source of authority is the Pope and the bishops in union with him. Moreover, the right of each bishop to teach with authority is dependent on his fidelity to the teaching of the universal Church and on his collegial unity with the Holy Father.

Because of the vital importance of this matter, I must again quote extensively from the Second Vatican Council which teaches:

"Episcopal consecration confers, together with the office of sanctifying, the duty also of teaching and ruling, which, however, of its very nature can be exercised only in hierarchical communion with the head and members of the college" *(Lumen gentium,* no. 21).

"The college or body of bishops has for all that no authority unless united with the Roman Pontiff, Peter's successor, as its head, whose primatial authority, let it be added, over all, whether pastors or faithful, remains in its integrity. For the Roman Pontiff, by reason of his office as Vicar of Christ, namely, and as pastor of the entire Church, has full supreme and universal power over the whole Church, a power which he can exercise unhindered. The order of bishops is the successor to the college of the apostles in their role as teachers and pastors, and in it the apostolic college is perpetuated. Together with their head, the Supreme Pontiff, and never apart from him, they have supreme and full authority over the universal Church; but their power cannot be exercised without the agreement of the Roman Pontiff" *(Lumen gentium,* no. 22).

Such is the Faith of the Catholic Church concerning the service of authority given to it by Jesus Christ for the sake of the Kingdom of God.

Within the Church the position of individual theologians entitles them indeed to associate freely with one another in the pursuit of the theological enterprise and to work with one another for precise formulation and practical application of the truth as God reveals it and reason discovers it.

It is the responsibility of the teaching authority of the Church to listen to theologians and to judge whether their informed consensus is in harmony with the faith of the Church, and then to accept any fresh insights into the Faith for the advancement of the Kingdom of God. And it is the responsibility of theologians to work within the Church, as living members of the Church—and therefore as believers in the faith of the Church—and not to speak to the Church from the independent platforms of the secular academic world, as if they were non-believers. The Church suffers greatly when Catholic theologians, claiming the right to speak independently of ecclesiastical supervision— seeming to reject the service of authority given to the Church by Christ—continue to present themselves as molders of Catholic opinion and as authentic counsellors for Catholics in the formation of their judgments of conscience. When theological science thus takes on the forms of secularized scholarship, Catholic theologians who speak its language find themselves usurping the authority of the Church's hierarchy as they become publicly identified with secularized efforts to legalize sexual aberrations and to make immorality look respectable. May the Holy Spirit enlighten those who inflict such pain and confusion on the Church, fragmenting it against the will of Christ!

In conclusion, let me warn you all, my beloved brothers and sisters, against the disastrous consequences of the attitude of indifference toward the Church into which many Catholics seem to be falling today due in no small measure to the confusion created by those who should know better. The Church is God's Church, not just a human society to be governed by civil law and to be manipulated into the formulation of policies dictated by civil authorities. When the human structure which God has instituted for the governing of the Church is disregarded, the responsibility of man toward God which is fundamental to the sense of sin begins to disappear. We must not expect the Church to change the laws of God. However the world may seem to change, it is still God's world. However we grow in knowledge, or extend our conquest of the forces of nature, what we learn always reflects God's truth and goodness, and what we are called to do always demands conformity with God's will as it is embodied in our human condition and is made known to us by reason and the revelation of God.

As your Archbishop, it is my grave obligation to defend the integrity of the Church's Faith against both the erosion of its divinely instituted authority and the debilitating consequence of an irresponsibly liberalized immorality. In your confusion, look to the authentic teachings of the Church and your vision will become as clear as crystal. As you experience the perplexity of changing moral standards in the unchristian world to which the Lord sends us, follow the wholesome restraints of Christian morality as they are clearly and simply presented by the Church, and your self-discipline will bring you strength and peace. You can be certain that Jesus is with us until the end of time.

Listening to the voice of the Supreme Shepherd of the Church and of the bishops in union with him, you listen to the voice of Christ. May His peace be ever in your hearts.

---

1. Both these documents are available from any of the addresses at the end of this book.

Drugs and Our Children

April 9, 1971

My dear brothers and sisters in Christ:

Our celebration of these Easter days is, in fact, a participation in the great Christian festival of life and light. It is a time of joy and peace, love and togetherness, when we extol the powers of God's creation and the wonderful way He has re-created human nature through Christ's Resurrection.

Life, light, joy, peace, loving unity, renewed creation and resurrection: all of these flow from Christ, the real reason and source for hope in a bleak world suffering from an increasing hopelessness. We know that "hope springs eternal" in the human heart, and yet a pall of near despair seems to cover so much of our society today, especially large segments of the young. It is good and essential for us to ask pertinent and vital questions. It is urgent that we seek together the valid response to these if we are to grow and not decline as a human society.

One of the most critical questions we have to ask ourselves concerns a symptom of many of the ills in our society which is slowly becoming devoid of even the most basic human hope. We speak here of the widespread misuse of drugs, especially by young people. And we simply ask why?

Why?

Critical drug problems can be found in every school in our communities from college down into the elementary grades! The pressure of conformity is a heavy burden for many youngsters to carry, since conformity is in their minds the avenue of acceptance. Older adolescents become the models for their younger friends and acquaintances. School lounges and lavatories have turned into market places for drugs and laboratories for experimentation.

The crisis builds when commercialism exposes the young, sometimes the very young, to the philosophy that says medication can take away all pain, and the fact of pain becomes an intolerable reality. Modern man beats a path from cocktail party to medicine chest; from corner pub to street pusher. And why not? I am told that our society produces more medication than it could ever legitimately or reasonably use. Why have we forgotten that suffering and pain are redemptive, that God through Christ has made the cross the means of our liberation and fulfillment, both personal and social?

Anguish mounts painfully when our friends, neighbors, our own children, even we, misuse drugs. Though every human being is precious, the problem did not seem so important twelve or fifteen years ago when drug addicts represented a small number of people and perhaps only the ghetto type for which just a few had any sympathy. Now that adults use diet pills, tranquilizers and sleeping pills; that our children may be smoking pot in our attics or cellars; that our GI's are returning from Vietnam addicted to opium or dead, not from war but from overdoses of heroin; that even clergymen are falling into the ranks of drug abusers — perhaps now we can pause to ask why.

Why have we walled ourselves off from each other so long, my brothers and sisters? Why have we remained small and self-centered, failing to be compassionate toward one another, to communicate with one another, to encourage and respect each other's integrity and dignity? We must respond as Christ would have responded and does through many members in His Church. "Whatever you do for the least of these my brothers, you do to me."

The answers we seek are easily found. They, too, spring from the source of our hope, the wonderful mystery of the Easter season.

Sacredness of Life

As you know, I have spoken again and again of my deep concern for the protection of human life. It was God's most sacred creation and must always be considered as such. Drug addiction brings life down to the gutters of existence and degrades not just people, but life itself. So many of our bright and energetic youngsters, full of life so to speak, come to depend on drugs so much that they have to steal! Some even sell their young bodies in order to support their habit—many of them just to live! They are surely not to be condemned but loved and helped. Much of the condemnation we heap upon these children of our society comes back at us for never teaching them the real secrets of life and giving them a taste of the kind of love that makes it such a joy to be alive. Drugs can be a slow death or a quick suicide for them. In any case they snuff out life in those tender years, just when it should begin to grow and flower.

In the Gospel a man is attacked by robbers and left by the side of the road. A priest goes by and leaves him there. A levite does the same; but a Samaritan, who by tradition should have had nothing to do with him, stopped and took the time to care for this man. He took him to an inn and paid for his convalescence. We are asked to involve ourselves, to make up for the failure of human concern that leads to drug addiction — to people destruction! People are our responsibility!

Light of Christ

The liturgy of the Easter vigil is filled with the human and theological symbol of light, Christ resplendent, breaking out of the dark recesses of his tomb in a blinding manifestation of his power and glory.

Our light is Christ, but the symbol reminds us as well of the Spirit of illumination Who led the People of God and their prophets, guiding their minds, as the pillar of fire (the Holy Spirit); and the paschal candle (Christ) shed light and provided guidance for the progress of God's people.

In second Corinthians, St. Paul speaks of his extraordinary gift of visions and revelations "whether in the body I do not know, or out of the body I do not know" (2 Cor. 12:2). He was, one might say, turned on in the Spirit of Christ. Many young people try to experience some similar illumination of the mind through hallucinogenic drugs which "blow their minds." They sometimes call them "mind bending." Whether for mere thrills or a serious search for some profound mystical experience through drugs, there is great danger of severe damage to the mind in all of this. There are the possible effects of mental retardation, the dulling of conscience and there is a clouding out of the creative imagination that makes man man and not just brute. The idea that these hallucinogens stimulate creativity is, experts say, a mere illusion.

We have to pass on to our children the concept of learning as an often painful experience, but a valuable one if they wish to live in a world where knowledge is essential to success or happiness. To think one can bypass the hard but necessary discipline of the mind characteristic to the learning process is foolish. If it were so simple as taking a pill to get instant knowledge or wisdom this would be wonderful, but it doesn't work that way.

Resurrection, Renewal and Re-creation

The Christian community can take a lesson from the feast of the Resurrection, since the message of Jesus reveals the life and death cycle of change and growth. As an integrated person, Jesus stands bold in the face of change, bringing people face to face with the real issues in their lives. He meets them there and deals with them there. As Christ was immersed in life with His people and responded to them with the loving concern of the Father, so priest and people must exchange with one another their pains and joys. The clergy should lead with solutions that stem from the actual felt needs of their people. The total Christian community must share life and accept the challenge of Jesus to change by continual rebirth in Christ. The teaching of the Second Vatican Council is lucid on this point.

To change the world, to renew it in Christ, is itself a painful process. To do this honestly one must be willing to suffer change within oneself. Revolution is relatively easy. But the work of change that is sensitive to people, that is cautious to heal and not harm, to build and not destroy, is very difficult. Drugs provide an escape from the need to change things that are bad. They create the illusion that they never were there in the first place. And where there is a very real obligation to renew the whole of creation in Christ's image, drugs can falsely absolve a person from responsibility.

There are people who are hungry and need to be fed, imprisoned unjustly behind bars or the walls of fear and separation and these need to be freed. In the past fifty years one hundred million human beings have been killed by war, by automobiles and by drugs, to say nothing of the sapping of human life through emotional and spiritual starvation.

There seems to be a feeling among us that we cannot, or choose not, to tolerate much of the emotional pain we feel in the world. Men have discovered that they hold what may be considered an insignificant place in the universe—a little cog in a big wheel. This awareness along with the present alienation from social, economic and religious structures has made man feel helpless and depersonalized in the face of a complex society.

Some have chosen to live alone and independent. Not a few have turned to search out a way of placing themselves in a worthwhile relationship to the universe by collective living, and by searching out mystic religions. Others have concluded that human existence is totally absurd and have chosen slow suicide through drugs.

The ability to pull away from involvement in real life by changing artificially one's perceptions, by heightening only the pleasurable experiences, makes drug-taking an inviting prospect. Rather than cope with the feeling of failure as a husband or wife, a father or mother, a son or daughter—rather than cope with the pain of a poor job history, school record or social status—rather than try to overcome the hardship of not being able to relate to others because we remain truly unable or unwilling to listen, we accept the message that it is possible to avoid suffering in life through chemistry.

Adults tell youngsters by example that responsible use of pleasure is a definite good. This is fine. However, we go further and attempt to justify the pursuit of mellow feelings from alcohol at the bar, the country club or neighborhood pub by citing the need to relax. Young adults have learned the lesson well. They learn from our bad example as well as from the good they see us do.

Men have always sought and found pleasurable ways of relaxing from the tensions and anxieties of life. But at times, there is nothing to do but accept pain as one of the goods or realities in human life that foster our emotional growth and balance.

Community

In these days of global unity and ecumenism we still have divisiveness and fragmentation. The Church like other institutions is caught up in the divisions of society. There was a time when to believe was to have a vision of how to integrate one's life. This is and will always be true. However, recent history has shown religious institutions to be generally unable to cut across generational lines to touch the actual lives of many of its younger members. It is true that we can speak to an issue or a group of people in our culture, but do we make any real effort to understand other elements in it? This situation tends to divide rather than unite our society. One of the functions of religious bodies should be to help people integrate their lives in a responsible and satisfying way and to bring together people of all ages, cultures, political and social backgrounds.

Drugs tend to disintegrate personality and this is a crime when the world cries out for men who are whole, mature and capable of finding harmony and peace within themselves, to be able to act against the hostile environment of a divided world and bring the pieces together. The so-called drug culture of youth with all the fears it evokes in older people and the lack of understanding involved, only widens the gap that already exists between the generations.

As responsible members of communities, we must become a part of the solution. Isn't it true that we are all part of the problem? What can be done? With millions of people in greater Boston alone, there is a fantastic reservoir of human strength available to deal with the problems. Education about drugs and related factors in society is one thing. But more than this, we are urged to face the problems as they exist in our communities and in our family structures.

We have created community facilities and programs for drug abuse. We can reassess the ways in which these can be of greater use in dealing with drugs and the related issues. This goes further than physical buildings. It includes the cooperative effort of local agencies — counselling services for individuals, families or special groups. There is a need to integrate these in our response to the problem.

Our hospitals, both private and public, should be alerted to the number of beds needed for detoxification and treatment of addicts in their local communities. These, along with out-patient facilities are a valuable asset for community health. Hospitals can render a service to promote health, hopefully not by being selective but by meeting the need as it exists.

Our schools stand empty for large periods each day because we have not programmed their use for the needs of the total community. To use a ten million dollar school for seven hours a day while needy people in the community clamor for space to meet, to be together, to share, is a lack of response to reality. The claim that costs would prevent that kind of availability of a building could mean that we value money more than human lives.

Some of our buildings can be opened as halfway houses, as residences for people who do not have healthy family homes. This would allow them to learn about themselves and adjust to live happier and productive human lives. The need to get high may not be as acute if a person can be with others who care. And in this way they might come to respect themselves and not despair.

We could make accessible some of these facilities for the needs of street people, youngsters who are runaways or just have no place to go. With the increase in the number of wandering youth and their involvement in the drug culture, we are called to care for their hunger, their nakedness, their emptiness. Runaways represent some of society's hurting young people. Under the pretense of not wanting to encourage the runaway form of life, many adults and many institutions have resolved not to answer this special type of need. To acknowledge the presence and the needs of runaways is to risk involvement.

Next we address ourselves to the whole area of the government role in this issue and how the government reflects the will of the people. Unless concern is shared from the grass roots to the highest level of our leadership, the traffic in drugs will continue to increase as it has in the past few years. Police action after drugs have arrived is too little, too late.

Our people have the privilege and the duty to make known to legislators their concern about drugs and related matters. If they neglect to speak their minds to lawmakers they have no right to complain as, for example, when there are no controls set for the production of amphetamines, so-called pep pills, which are overproduced by several billion doses each year in the United States. People should also see to it, by expressing their will that laws regarding narcotics and dangerous drugs are sensible and not merely a harsh and inhumane way to punish people who are driven to drugs by their problems rather than by criminal character or intent.

Peace and Order

The subject of Peace is such a sensitive one these days. We can all agree that Peace is desired; no, not just desired but required if we expect to survive in this period of human history. But to define Peace is another thing entirely. Some seem to think that Peace, and also the kind of order called for by law, is made by force. For them it is simple enough: Crush or repress the forces that disturb the peace. As effective as this approach might be it

overlooks much of the underlying causes of
unrest that may very well be legitimate.
Adam's real control over nature and wild
beasts in the garden was due more to the
harmony that existed in his human nature
and between him and the rest of creation
than to his superior power to rule or en
force his will on the world.

Order is first of all personal. As cultural changes are taking place in our society
and new patterns of life evolve, we are all
called upon to look into ourselves, to question our own system of values. By seeking
to perceive a way of integrating our lives
in a human society, we will experience a
greater awareness of our own dignity as
persons. While this amalgam of human beings called society works out its own crisis
of identifying itself we will attempt to sal-
vage our own integrity as individuals.

When we have attained this security
in ourselves, convinced of our worth, we
can then begin to be open to others and to
foster their respect for themselves. St. Paul
writes:

"Love is always patient and kind; it is
never jealous; love is never boastful or
conceited; it is never rude or selfish; it
does not take offense, and is not resentful.
Love takes no pleasure in other people's

sins but delights in truth; it is always ready to excuse, to trust, to hope, and to endure whatever comes" (1 Cor. 13:4-6).

Order in community must be based on love. Attacking the drug problem in a concrete communal setting must go further than stopping the use of drugs. Asking for more police, increased arrests, a greater concentration on the reduction of drug availability as the only way of dealing with the problem, could be a monstrous escape route. This could be an easy way out and a way of transferring responsibility to someone else.

Besides, the causes of drug abuse sink so deeply into society that they cannot be rooted out merely by police control, repression of freedom to be on the streets, or the apprehension of pushers. More effective perhaps is our own openness and sensitivity and willingness to help, as well as the way we organize present community agencies and create new structures to deal with the social, psychological and emotional aspects of the total problem.

The family unit is undergoing its own time of crisis. Parents give over the responsibility of education to schools: not just mathematics, English and history, but sex-education, civic response and drug education too. The responsibility for religious education is turned over completely to the churches. Pressure for social discipline falls to police to establish curfews, limit drug use, and protect against vandalism. Rather than encourage our children to mature in the security of the family, we push them away to community institutions in the hope that others will pick up the parental role. It is not that the institutions are not trying to give what they can to provide what is missing. In fact they are, for the most part, successful. But no public institution, however hard it tries, can give a child the security and love that the family should offer him. And when this is missing a child easily drifts to drugs for whatever feeble support they can provide. The delinquency and erratic behavior of such a child is understandable but must be handled through love along with appropriate discipline by the community if this does not take place in the home.

And so we turn to law enforcement agencies and the courts for help. It would be naive to think that there are not imperfections in both. But I recognize that despite the inadequacies they themselves will acknowledge, they are dedicated to the task and are trying to learn from their mistakes.

There should be no need to say what I will say now, but in this day it has often been left unsaid, not by oversight but because of disproportionate criticism and lack of perspective. And so I make a point of commending the police for trying to bring about public order, even endangering their lives at times to do so. And I encourage them to continue. They are not their brothers' keeper as much as their brothers' brother. It is my hope that there will remain in them a deep regard for justice and the love that corrects but never hurts.

Joy

It is my task during these Easter days to bear witness to the true happiness which I find in Christ. I speak of the joy that comes from unselfish love, perhaps painful at times, but no loving sacrifice can diminish the underlying satisfaction of knowing that one receives love in return for love. Where there is no love, joy is not real, it is concocted to fill the void and is only a dim reflection of true satisfaction.

People who depend on drugs for happiness are only too aware that this is the case. We do not pity them. Rather we love them and want to give ourselves to them. We wish to help, but not as if we are superior to them in any way. We are servants as Christ wished to be a servant to those He loved. And in our service to these, our brothers and sisters, we hope to bring them at least some measure of the Easter joy that is now in our hearts.

On Penal
Reforms

December, 1971

Dearly beloved in Christ:

Nothing genuinely human is alien to the Christian heart (cf. Gaudium et Spes, 1). That is why such human things as crime, programs of human rehabilitation and penal institutions fall within the competence of the Shepherds of the flock of Christ. Commissioned to evaluate and judge all human activity under the moral law of our Holy Redeemer, a bishop cannot fail to teach in season and out of season, to rebuke and to correct, to encourage and to admonish, with love, understanding and compassion (cf. 2 Timothy 4:2-5). For this reason I request your enlightened help for all those brothers and sisters of ours confined to jails and houses of correction, as well as for those responsible for their operation. We need to encourage every effort toward the elimination of every deficiency and shortcoming in dealing with "the least" of Christ's brethren in prison (cf. Matt. 25:36).

As you know, in recent months not a few prisons of our Commonwealth, and indeed throughout the country, have been seething with unrest, confrontation and, in some instances, violence. In one at least the carnage has left us numb. Charges and counter-charges have been aired; grievances have been voiced; injustices have been alleged; inadequacies have been exposed and authority has been challenged. It would appear that in the harsh realization of our penal system's weaknesses and failures, there is developing a dangerous and pessimistic atmosphere of distrust, fear and discouragement, both inside and outside of jails. Our imprisoned brothers and sisters are angrily or hopelessly assuming that no one really cares about them or their needs; our correctional officers are wondering whether their dedication and efforts are really understood or appreciated; our prison officials are becoming disillusioned by the lack of recognition for their genuine concern and sincere efforts; the general public appears bewildered as people try to reconcile deep-rooted fears and misconceptions with their natural feelings of compassion and forgiveness; and the members of the legislature, somewhat confused by their role and responsibilities in the area of corrections, have reacted and responded to perhaps poorly informed and fear-filled misgivings of their constituents. There is evidence that mistakes have been made and that over-reaction to situations has caused inhuman treatment of prisoners and personnel alike. In some prisons, I know, the existing conditions do not adequately respect a minimal human condition, a situation which is not pleasing to the prison officials themselves, much less to those who are being humiliated by them.

I do not think that there is a simple solution to the challenge and need of immediate penal reform. Certainly, there will be no real progress, and very little change, in an atmosphere which is charged with mistrust, ignorance and some irresponsible accusations. I believe that basic to all efforts for penal reform is a realization of the worth and dignity of every human being, however obscured it may have become through circumstances, weakness or even deliberate malice. We are all made to the image and likeness of God, and Our Lord Jesus Christ has identified Himself with our brothers in prison. This calls at all times for humane and Christian treatment of all prisoners in line with the latest and valid findings of the behavioral sciences, and especially in the light of faith. While prisoners experience the fearful deprivation of their freedom, every effort must be made to instill or restore their sense of worth and dignity as persons; to provide the educational and vocational skills that they may lack; to counsel, encourage, guide and develop an attitude of responsibility that will enable them to function happily and constructively in a free community upon their release. Reciprocally, those in prison must be responsive to these efforts in their behalf; they must be honest enough to admit areas of need and guilt, to accept guidance and instruction, and be made hopeful by the wider community's attitude of forgiveness, acceptance and concern.

Correctional officers must daily realize their awesome, difficult and challenging role in the process of corrections. By their personal example, their idealism, their tried sincerity, their patient strength, their mature control, they are a vital force in the hopeful restoration of human beings. Prison officials have a profound and truly noble vocation together with a responsibility toward society, as they must constantly strive by leadership, policy, attitude and effort for the challenging, and at times discouraging, consequences of dealing with **human weakness, failure, and crime.**

A concerned public must face up to its responsibility of supporting meaningful legislative proposals in the field of corrections. Apathetic unconcern or timid misgivings can completely undermine the sincerest efforts at making needed changes. A competent and concerned legislature, guided by wise, thoughtful and progressive recommendations from professionals in the area of corrections and parole, advised by experts in human behaviour and treatment, and responsive to enlightened and responsible suggestions of the prisoners themselves, will effectively provide the changes in law that prison reform so desperately needs.

I wish to offer also a word of encouragement to those dedicated chaplains and ministers who bring God's saving mysteries of redemption to our brothers and sisters in prison. Their faith and ministry are particularly precious at this time of tremendous tension between the real and ideal order of things, between what is and what ought to be. Only God Himself knows how difficult it is for them to awaken in the hearts of those who suffer pain and at times unjust treatment, a personal belief in a living God Who sent His only Son into the prison of our flesh. That Son was born without sin for us in Bethlehem's cave.

His birth was heralded by angels singing: "Glory to God in the highest and peace on earth to men of good will" (Luke 2:14). Yet, He freely laid down His life upon a shameful cross knowing that through pain and death He would bring our mortal flesh with Him into the glory of His imperishable life. How especially dear to Christ is this message and the ministry provided to those who are imprisoned! It is for this reason that I pray particularly that they will continue to be at this time God's healers and peace-makers. God's "worthy servants" among divided men.

As we prepare anew this Christmas for the coming of the "Prince of Peace," we invite all men of "good will" to regard and respect every man as his brother. We pray that motivated by love they may bring about the peace and harmony which society seeks today with ever more deepening concern.

May this peace of Christ abide in your hearts during the Christmas Season and throughout the New Year.

APPENDIX

Faithful to That Heritage

Homily prepared by Humberto Cardinal Medeiros, Archbishop of Boston, for delivery on the 175th Anniversary of the Archdiocese of Boston, April 9, 1983.

"This is the day the Lord has made; let us rejoice and be glad." Words taken from the 118th Psalm (Ps. 118:24), and found also in the Alleluia Verse of today's Mass.

Your Excellency, the Apostolic Delegate, Your Excellency, Archbishop Borders of Baltimore, my brother Archbishops and Bishops, my brother priests, my brother deacons, beloved religious sisters and brothers, revered guests from other religious communities, distinguished members of State and City Government, dearly beloved in Christ:

As we gather this morning in this venerable Cathedral of the Holy Cross in the Archdiocese of Boston, we have indeed every reason to rejoice and be glad. This truly is the day the Lord has made, the day when we celebrate, through the solemn worship of God in the Holy Sacrifice of the Mass, the 175th Anniversary of the Founding of the Diocese of Boston. It was on April 8, 1808, that the Holy Father, Pope Pius VII, established this Diocese, including in it the entire area of New England.

We rejoice and we are glad—our hearts filled up and brimming over with the joy of the Risen Christ in this Easter Season. We have listened to the inspired word in today's Gospel passage (Mk. 16:9-15), summing up the appearances of our Divine Lord after His Resurrection from the dead. How truly appropriate on this Anniversary are the final words of the Gospel reading, wherein Jesus Christ, the Son of God, commissioned His Apostles: "Go into the whole world and proclaim the good news to all creation" (Mk. 16:15).

In this Eucharistic celebration, on this day that the Lord has made, we raise our minds and hearts to Him in profound gratitude for the countless graces and blessings that He has poured forth in such lavish abundance upon this Diocese and its people for 175 years. We thank God for the inspired leadership of the Bishops of this Diocese and for the apostolic zeal of its clergy and religious, and for the stalwart faith of its millions and millions of laity over the years. Thanks be to God for His goodness to us!

We pay well-deserved tribute to our forebears in the faith in the Diocese of Boston. Oftentimes against overwhelming odds and in the midst of oppression and bigotry and persecution—we cannot and dare not give the lie to history—they kept the faith, they lived the faith, they sacrificed for the faith, they suffered for the faith, they defended the faith, they spread the faith.

If, in spite of today's problems and challenges, the faith is alive and vibrant in the Archdiocese of Boston 175 years after its founding, that fact is due, under God, to the faithfulness of the millions of men and women and children who flocked to this sector of the Lord's vineyard from well-nigh every land in God's creation, afire with the inflexible determination to live, and if necessary to die, for their faith-conviction that they were God's children and sharers in His divine nature, members of His Church, and destined for an eternity of supernatural happiness in a life beyond the grave.

The Diocese of Boston has been witness to almost incredible growth and development. But in the course of the years it has lived not only in sunshine but also in shadow; it has experienced its joys and its sorrows; it has tasted successes and setbacks; it has seen its children prosper in peace and die in war; it has rejoiced with them in their good fortune, and wept with them in their pain and suffering and poverty and need and oppression and discrimination.

But always it has believed that in God's Divine Providence Good Friday's shame will be turned into Easter Sunday's glory. It has been on pilgrimage, encouraged by its faith in the Redemption of Christ, our Savior. And so today, 175 years after Boston's founding as a Diocese, we raise our voices aloud: This is the day the Lord has made. Let us rejoice and be glad, as we join the universal Church in observing the Holy Year of the Redemption of the human race by the Son of God made man.

A diocese is not simply a tract of territory. Rather, as the Second Vatican Council reminds us, it is that portion of God's people which is entrusted to a bishop to be shepherded by him under the guidance of the Holy Spirit. In the diocese is truly present and operative the one, holy, catholic and apostolic Church of Christ (cf. *Christus Dominus*, no. 11).

The Church teaches us that the diocese must be a community of faith, a community of grace, a community of love, a community of apostolate, and a hierarchical community (cf. *Directory on the Pastoral Ministry of Bishops*, no. 54).

The diocese must be a *community of faith*. Without cessation it must constantly teach and be taught the word of God. Young and old alike, the educated and the unlettered—each according to his own capacity must learn more and more, and with increasing intensity and depth, what God has revealed to the human race in order that His children may better know Him, and consequently love Him more ardently and serve Him more faithfully.

The diocese must be a *community of grace*. It is an instrumentality, by which the graces merited for the human race by Jesus Christ our Divine Redeemer are transmitted to souls especially through the Sacraments. First and foremost in importance, in the diocese is celebrated the Eucharistic Sacrifice, Calvary's Sacrifice made present on the altars of its Churches, and the Body and Blood of Jesus Christ given as food for its children at the table of the Lord.

The diocese must be a *community of love:* love of its members for God and for one another. This love is a response to God's love for us. No human being would exist "were he not created by God's love and constantly preserved by it. And he cannot live fully according to truth unless he freely acknowledges that love and devotes himself to his Creator" *(Gaudium et spes,* no. 19). Moreover, the members of a diocese must have love also for one another for the sake of God. The distinguishing mark of the early Christians was this: that they loved one another. Indeed our Divine Lord did not hesitate to identify Himself with His brothers and sisters as the object of this love (cf. Mt. 25:40). This brotherly and sisterly charity must be exercised "in both the spiritual and material order, flowing from the Eucharist as from its source" *(Directory on the Pastoral Ministry of Bishops,* no. 54). That is why the Second Vatican Council, teaching that the Eucharistic Sacrifice "is the fount and apex of the whole Christian life" *(Lumen gentium,* no. 11), warns us that "everyone must consider his every neighbor without exception as another self, taking into account first of all his life and the means necessary to living it with dignity, so as not to imitate the rich man who had no concern for the poor man Lazarus" (*Gaudium et spes*, no. 27).

The diocese must be a *community of apostolate*, in which each person is called to do his or her part in spreading the infinite treasures of Christ. Not only the Bishop and his priests and deacons and religious have a role to fulfill in building up the Body of Christ which is the Church. Lay persons also, precisely by reason of their Baptism, have a vocation to aid in the implementation of the Church's mission. As the Second Vatican Council declares: "The layman's apostolate derives from his Christian vocation, and the Church can never be without it" (*Apostolicam actuositatem*, no. 1).

The diocese must be a *hierarchical community* which, during its pilgrimage to the Lord, is entrusted for direction to those whom the Holy Spirit has appointed to govern the Church of God. It is this teaching of divine revelation which the Second Vatican Council propounds when it declares: "Christ gave the apostles and their successors the command and the power to teach all nations, to hallow men in the truth, and to feed them. Hence, through the Holy Spirit Who has been given to them, Bishops have been made true and authentic teachers of the faith, pontiffs, and shepherds" (*Christus Dominus*, no. 2).

In summary, then, the Church teaches us that the diocese is a community of faith, a community of grace, a community of love, a community of apostolate, and a hierarchical community (cf. *Directory on the Pastoral Ministry of Bishops*, no. 54).

Such has been, thank God, this Diocese of Boston for the past 175 years. Today we look back upon its history. And what a glorious history it has been, surpassing, I suppose, even the wildest dreams of those few hundred Catholics who lived in the new Diocese of Boston on April 8, 1808. On that day, in the territory which makes up now the Archdiocese of Boston, there were two Catholic priests and one Church. Today there are almost two million Catholics in the Archdiocese, served in 408 parishes. God has blessed us with more than 1,300 diocesan priests and over 950 religious priests, with 125 permanent deacons, with more than 4,600 sisters and 211 brothers.

If we look at the entire territory of New England (which was erected as the Diocese of Boston by Pope Pius VII in 1808), we find today two ecclesiastical provinces: Boston and Hartford. The total number of archdioceses and dioceses of the Latin Rite is eleven (in addition to the Melkite Eparchy of Newton and the Ukranian Diocese of Stamford)—serving well over five and one-half million Catholics. What a truly amazing and almost incredible exemplification of the parable of the mustard seed recounted by our Divine Lord.

On April 8, 1808, when the See of Boston was established, Father John Cheverus was named its first Bishop. Since 1796 he had been the assistant here of the saintly and zealous Father Francis Matignon. From the moment of his consecration in Baltimore in 1810, until his departure for France in 1823, this extraordinary ecclesiastical leader made an enormous impact on New England. One writer has thus described Bishop Cheverus: "His personality was irresistible. He carried Boston by storm. He could shine in the drawing rooms of the Brahmin caste...and he could also saw wood with his own hands for a poor widow.... An atmosphere of the most intellectual culture and at the same time of the sincerest piety and humility surrounded him. Without any doubt he was the best-loved man in the Boston of his day. He tried, without ostentation, to realize in his own life and character his ideal of the Nazarene" (William F. Kenny, *Centenary of the See of Boston*, pp. 191-192).

Under the leadership of Bishop Benedict J. Fenwick, who served the faithful of this Diocese from 1825 until 1846, the Diocese expanded by leaps and bounds—so much so that in 1843 Hartford was erected as a diocese, including all of Connecticut and Rhode Island. During his years as Bishop he established ecclesiastical institutions of all kinds, founded Holy Cross College in Worcester, held the First Synod of Boston, inaugurated a Catholic newspaper (which subsequently took the name *The Pilot*) and played an important role in the first five Provincial Councils of Baltimore.

Bishop John B. Fitzpatrick guided the Diocese of Boston in very trying times. The first native Bostonian to become the Bishop of his See, he served the people of God as Bishop until 1866, in a period marked by sordid bigotry and open persecution—much of it originating in the Know-Nothing movement. During his episcopacy, while Irish immigrants poured into Boston, so large did the Diocese become that two new dioceses were erected—Burlington in Vermont and Portland in Maine. An urbane, affable, scholarly, highly intellectual gentleman, he died at the age of 54.

In 1866, John J. Williams became Boston's fourth Bishop. During his years as Bishop, the Diocese of Boston continued to grow at a phenomenal rate—so much so that in 1870 Springfield was established as a new diocese. Five years later, Boston was constituted an Archdiocese, with all of the other dioceses of New England named as suffragan Sees. The four decades of Archbishop Williams' leadership witnessed astounding progress. Especially worthy of note is the fact that this Cathedral of the Holy Cross was dedicated in 1875, and St. John's Seminary was established in 1884. Archbishop Williams was a kindly, quiet, unruffled man, beloved by all his flock.

In 1906, Bishop William H. O'Connell, a native of Lowell and Bishop of Portland, became coadjutor of the Archdiocese of Boston, and a year later he took over the leadership of the Archdiocese on the death of Archbishop

Williams. In 1911, Pope St. Pius X named him a
Cardinal of the holy Roman Church. A very
vigorous and firm and forceful man, with singular qualities of leadership and exceptional administrative competence, for 37 years he was
one of the most prominent Churchmen in this
country.

Bishop Richard J. Cushing, a native of
South Boston, succeeded Cardinal O'Connell as
Archbishop in 1944. He sponsored an enormous
expansion program in the Archdiocese, creating
new parishes, colleges, schools, seminaries,
hospitals and institutions for social works of
various kinds—as well as bringing into the
Archdiocese numerous religious congregations
of men and women. He inaugurated a so-called
"lend-lease" program, allowing priests of our
Archdiocese to volunteer in large numbers for
apostolic work in other dioceses and as chaplains in the Armed Forces of our country. He
founded the Society of St. James for missionary
work in South America. He had a special
concern for the needy and the handicapped, and
he often condemned with great vigor any barriers among peoples based on race or color or
creed or ancestry or wealth.

In 1970, God called me, His unworthy
servant, to shepherd the flock in the Archdiocese of Boston. Acutely aware of the precious
heritage that has been bequeathed to all of us by
our ancestors in the faith in this Archdiocese, I
have been striving to be faithful to that heritage.

I have been striving to be faithful to the divine deposit of revelation that Jesus Christ left to His Church to be preserved and propagated through the Magisterium for the advancement of His Kingdom.

I have been striving to be faithful to the Vicar of Christ on earth, our Holy Father, the successor of St. Peter, the first Pope.

I have been striving to implement the teachings and the directives of the Second Vatican Council, so that, utilizing the bold new ways that the Popes have called for in order to make Jesus Christ better known and better loved throughout the world, the faith may become ever stronger and ever more vital in this Archdiocese, opening its doors wider and wider to the Redeemer.

I have tried to do all this, in the light of the same Council and under the inspiration of the Holy Spirit, Who guides the Church and remains with it until the end of time. In the light of this Holy Spirit, I have chosen also to strive to be a shepherd servant, not a ruler.

I have been striving in all my dealings with priests, deacons, religious, laity—men and women and children of all nationalities and creeds and colors and races and economic strata—to imitate and to reflect what I consider to be the gentleness and the understanding and the compassion and the forbearance of the Lord Jesus Christ, Whom I love and Whom I serve. May His name be blessed forever.

I have been striving to see in my neighbors—every man and woman and child with whom I have come in contact, but especially the destitute and the homeless and the shelterless and the forsaken and the lonely and the victims of injustice and the disadvantaged—I have been striving to see in all of these the Lord Jesus Christ Himself, Who told us 2,000 years ago: "As often as you did it for one of My least brothers, you did it for Me" (Mt. 25:40). I have been striving. I gladly and humbly leave the success and the fruits of my striving to the Lord, to Whom be praise and glory now and forever.

One hundred and seventy-five years have passed since the historic April day when the Holy Father, Pope Pius VII, erected the Diocese of Boston. Today we look to the past with thanksgiving. Today we look to the future with hope. Hope—not because progress can be made through our poor human efforts alone, but rather because we trust in the Lord. "Unless the Lord builds the house, those who build it labor in vain" (Ps. 127:1).

And so, on this happy day of thanksgiving and hope, we humbly offer the Eucharistic Sacrifice in gratitude to the God of goodness and the God of love. "This is the day the Lord has made. Let us rejoice and be glad."

INDEX

Daughters of St. Paul

MASSACHUSETTS
50 St. Paul's Ave., Jamaica Plain, Boston, MA 02130; **617-522-8911.**
172 Tremont Street, Boston, MA 02111; **617-426-5464; 617-426-4230.**

NEW YORK
78 Fort Place, Staten Island, NY 10301; **212-447-5071; 212-447-5086.**
59 East 43rd Street, New York, NY 10017; **212-986-7580.**
625 East 187th Street, Bronx, NY 10458; **212-584-0440.**
525 Main Street, Buffalo, NY 14203; **716-847-6044.**

NEW JERSEY
Hudson Mall—Route 440 and Communipaw Ave.,
Jersey City, NJ 07304; **201-433-7740.**

CONNECTICUT
202 Fairfield Ave., Bridgeport, CT 06604; **203-335-9913.**

OHIO
2105 Ontario Street (at Prospect Ave.), Cleveland, OH 44115;
216-621-9427.
25 E. Eighth Street, Cincinnati, OH 45202; **513-721-4838; 513-421-5733.**

PENNSYLVANIA
1719 Chestnut Street, Philadelphia, PA 19103; **215-568-2638.**

VIRGINIA
1025 King Street, Alexandria, VA 22314; **703-683-1741; 703-549-3806.**

FLORIDA
2700 Biscayne Blvd., Miami, FL 33137; **305-573-1618.**

LOUISIANA
4403 Veterans Memorial Blvd., Metairie, LA 70002; **504-887-7631;
504-887-0113.**
1800 South Acadian Thruway, P.O. Box 2028, Baton Rouge, LA 70821;
504-343-4057; 504-381-9485.

MISSOURI
1001 Pine Street (at North 10th), St. Louis, MO 63101; **314-621-0346;
314-231-1034.**

ILLINOIS
172 North Michigan Ave., Chicago, IL 60601; **312-346-4228; 312-346-3240.**

TEXAS
114 Main Plaza, San Antonio, TX 78205; **512-224-8101; 512-224-0938.**

CALIFORNIA
1570 Fifth Ave., San Diego, CA 92101; **619-232-1442.**
46 Geary Street, San Francisco, CA 94108; **415-781-5180.**

WASHINGTON
2301 Second Ave., Seattle, WA 98121; **206-623-1320.**

HAWAII
1143 Bishop Street, Honolulu, HI 96813; **808-521-2731.**

ALASKA
750 West 5th Ave., Anchorage, AK 99501; **907-272-8183.**

CANADA
3022 Dufferin Street, Toronto 395, Ontario, Canada.

GREAT BRITAIN
199 Kensington High Street, London W8 63A, England.
133 Corporation Street, Birmingham B4 6PH, England.
5A-7 Royal Exchange Square, Glasgow G1 3AH, Scotland.
82 Bold Street, Liverpool L1 4HR, England.

AUSTRALIA
58 Abbotsford Rd., Homebush, N.S.W. 2140, Australia.